Dad

Happy Birthday 2007.

Love David, Judy, Tom & Rachel

Isaac Foot

A Westcountry Boy – Apostle of England

ISAAC FOOT

Isaac Foot

A Westcountry Boy – Apostle of England

Presented by Michael Foot
and Alison Highet

POLITICO'S

First published in Great Britain 2006
by Politico's Publishing Ltd,
an imprint of
Methuen Publishing Ltd
11–12 Buckingham Gate
London
SW1E 6LB

10 9 8 7 6 5 4 3 2 1

A CIP catalogue record for this book is available from the British Library.

ISBN-10: 1-84275-181-6
ISBN-13: 978-1-84275-181-7

Designed and typeset by Louise Millar

Printed and bound in Great Britain by Cromwell Press, Trowbridge, Wiltshire

ISBN 1 84275 045 3

To the Foot family and especially the women,
with Eva Mackintosh at their head,
who speaks here as never before.

To Sally

To Jennifer, mother of Alison,
David, Christopher and Jasper

To Anne Foot, wife of John
and mother of Kate and Winslow

To Sarah Foot, daughter of Mac and Sylvia
and sister of Paul, Oliver and Benjamin

Contents

List of Illustrations

11

The Foot Family Tree

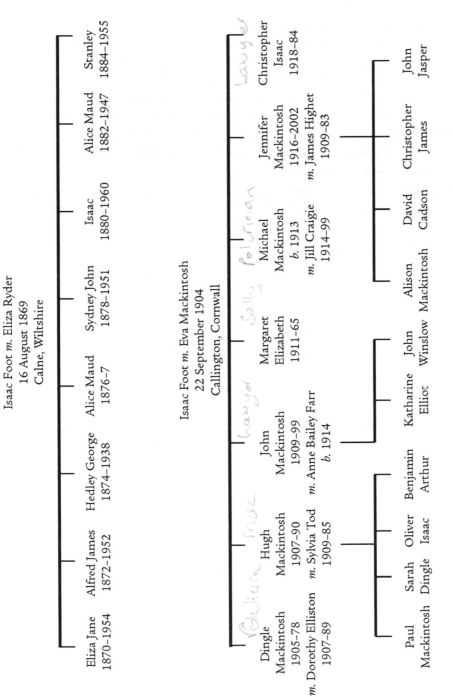

Isaac Foot *m.* Eliza Ryder
16 August 1869
Calne, Wiltshire

Eliza Jane
1870–1954

Alfred James
1872–1952

Hedley George
1874–1938

Alice Maud
1876–7

Sydney John
1878–1951

Isaac
1880–1960

Alice Maud
1882–1947

Stanley
1884–1955

Isaac Foot *m.* Eva Mackintosh
22 September 1904
Callington, Cornwall

Dingle
Mackintosh
1905–78
m. Dorothy Elliston
1907–89

Hugh
Mackintosh
1907–90
m. Sylvia Tod
1909–85

John
Mackintosh
1909–99
m. Anne Bailey Farr
b. 1914

Margaret
Elizabeth
1911–65

Michael
Mackintosh
b. 1913
m. Jill Craigie
1914–99

Jennifer
Mackintosh
1916–2002
m. James Highet
1909–83

Christopher
Isaac
1918–84

Paul
Mackintosh

Sarah
Dingle

Oliver
Isaac

Benjamin
Arthur

Katharine
Elliot

John
Winslow

Alison
Mackintosh

David
Cadson

Christopher
James

John
Jasper

Acknowledgements

Thank you to members of the Foot family: to Sarah Foot for her wonderful book *My Grandfather Isaac Foot*, published in 1980, with her personal memories of members of the Foot family and life at Pencrebar, some of which we have quoted here, and for photographs from her books *Views of Old Plymouth*, *Views of Old Cornwall* and *A Cornish Camera*; to Anne Foot for her memories, photographs and letters from which she allowed us to take quotations.

To Sean Magee and Brian Brivati who helped with Michael's previous book and recommended us to our present publishers, Politico's.

To our publishers and especially Alan Gordon Walker and Jonathan Wadman for their invaluable editorial advice and help.

In Plymouth: to Chris Robinson for his advice on the text and for the photographs and his pen and ink sketches of Plymouth which he allowed us to use; to Anne Morgan and the staff of the West Devon Record Office for being so helpful and allowing us easy access to the Foot family papers and other Plymouth records.

To the staff at Churchill College, Cambridge for allowing us access to Dingle Foot's papers.

To the volunteers at the Callington Museum for allowing us to research their records, in particular Anne and Arthur Eade and Sheila Lightbody.

To the Cromwell Association, in particular John Goldsmith, for allowing us access to the Cromwell Association records in the Huntingdon Local Record Office and the Cromwell Museum in Huntingdon.

To Pauline Quickfall of the Liskeard Liberal Democrat Office for their records and photographs, in particular of the 1922 by-election in Bodmin.

To the staff at the BBC Written Archives Centre and in particular Jeff Walden for his help in researching the scripts of the broadcasts made by Isaac Foot.

To the Department of Special Collections at the University of California, Santa Barbara for their description of the Isaac Foot library.

To Julie Hamilton for her photograph of Isaac Foot on the front cover of this book and to Tom Greeves for the photograph of Vitifer tin mine.

To Owain Morgan, without whose help this book could not have been written.

Preface

Right up to the actual day of publication the authors of this book found themselves in discussions about what the title should be. So we were all the more fascinated to see that my father's favourite, William Tyndale, was captivated by the same subject. Here is his first title:

The Newe Testament
Dylygently corrected and compared with the Greke
By
WILLYAM TINDALE:
And fynesshed in the yere of oure Lorde God
A.M.D. & XXXIIII.
In the moneth of Nouember

Now here is the exact quotation with which he ended his Preface to the Reader of his translation of 'The Newe Testament' in 1534:

Here endeth the new Testament dylygentlye ouersene and correct and printed
now agayne at Antwarp, by me wydow of Christophell of Endhouen.
In the yere of our Lorde. A.M.D. xxxiiii. in August.
Which tytle (reader) I have here put in because by this thou shalt knowe the
booke the better.
Vale

Foreword

by Michael Foot

Isaac Foot the reader; Isaac Foot the speaker; Isaac Foot the writer. All three, as we shall see, made a special contribution to the life of Plymouth and the Westcountry and a fresh appraisal of what the Westcountry gave the world. Isaac Foot's contribution to Westcountry life and Westcountry politics has never been properly presented before. Now his whole life and achievements are presented in a new way by two readers and writers who have freshly examined the whole subject – Michael Foot, one of his seven children, and Alison Highet, one of his ten grandchildren.

A chief reason why such a book has not been compiled before is now offered by the two new writers. The explanation has only become fully apparent as they have continued their investigations in the various literary archives left by Isaac Foot and the reason is a curious one. Isaac Foot was a great reader – all the evidence shows, one of the greatest ever. He was also a brilliant speaker both on the platform and in the pulpit in the age when public speaking was the chief means of political argument. He had learnt his way to speak chiefly in the Methodist chapels. Even when he was still in his early twenties, he was a well-known figure in the Methodist chapels of Devon and Cornwall. And all his achievements might have been proclaimed in his own writings, but here, as his new biographers constantly discover, he was especially modest. Time and again in his early twenties or even at a later age he would interrupt the book he might have in hand. He might claim that he had not done justice to his subject or that he felt a need to turn more urgently to other themes.

Reading these self-criticisms again today, most readers may conclude he was too severe in his judgements but still the pattern was often repeated. He would leave another project half-completed, protesting that he was not a natural writer, say like one of his favourites, his Macaulay or his Robert Louis Stevenson. Another explanation for his conduct may have been that he had discovered some new hero or heroine whom he wished to elevate to a higher place in his gallery. He must read everything about them before returning to his earlier favourites. With all of them, as he often reiterated, once they had captured his interest, he wanted to know everything about them, which meant a whole new addition to the library. Apart from my mother, Eva Mackintosh, and his children and grandchildren, the library was his truest love. The full records of that acquisition are given here in this book for the first time.

When I, Michael Foot, the co-author of this book, had once written about my father in my book *Debts of Honour*, I suggested that I might try and write a fresh book about him a little later. That volume, I am sorry to say, has been hopelessly delayed. But that was also the fate of some of my father's own books. After his death, I am glad to say, the next generation of the family was speaking for itself. In 1980 Sarah Foot produced *My Grandfather, Isaac Foot* and a splendid celebration it was. But still we all waited for more. So much of what my father had himself seen and written had never been published at all. This volume, which his son and granddaughter produce together, is drawn from the collection of material he left behind. Sometimes he speaks for himself – best of all in some letters and broadcasts recalling his own life. But three of his sons, Dingle, Hugh and John, write their own introduction to the whole story, which we reproduce most appropriately at the head of this volume.

I just give one example of my own late appreciation of my father's discoveries and his special ways of doing them. One of his last authors whose books he was collecting was Michel de Montaigne. I used to meet him for lunch at the Reform Club in the last years of his life and I can now recall how he mentioned he was relearning French in order to read Montaigne properly. My ignorance on that subject was complete. I had never read a word of Montaigne until after my father's death. At the end of the catalogue of his library made by the University of California, after they purchased his books, they remark how my father was starting a fresh library on this subject. What a fool I was not to have been able to discuss this subject with my father when I was with him. But all proper readers of this book will be able to make sure they commit no comparable folly. Isaac Foot the reader was the best reader of the lot – better even than Isaac Foot the writer, or Isaac Foot the speaker, although both of these deserve some honour too.

One other feature of this volume which especially wins my approval is the prominence it gives to the role played by my mother. Without her, not merely the Cornish connection but, even more, the ever-present Scottish connection would not have been established. I can hardly think of her at all without recalling how she would trace her ancestry back to William Wallace. It was not until several years later that I discovered that many other brave Scotsmen and women did the same. So she would recite the Robert Burns lines from 'Scots Wha Hae':

Scots, wha hae wi' Wallace bled,
Scots wham Bruce has aften led,
Welcome to your gory bed
Or to victorie!

Michael Foot
July 2006

Introduction
by John, Hugh and Dingle Foot

*Isaac Foot's three eldest sons, John, Hugh and Dingle,
remember their father*

JOHN FOOT: My father was born in Plymouth, Devon on 23 February 1880, the fifth child of Isaac and Eliza, née Ryder. His father was a carpenter and undertaker who, as a young man, had migrated from Horrabridge, Devon, the family home for at least three centuries, to Plymouth, building his own home at 10 Notte Street. Brought up a staunch Methodist, my father's political and religious beliefs were symbiotic and he first practised oratory in his local chapel. His formal schooling was limited by his family's pecuniary resources; he attended Plymouth Public School, paying twopence a week for the privilege, and then the Hoe Grammar School, leaving at the age of fourteen.

Not being of practical bent, he did not enter his father's carpentry business, instead leaving Plymouth for London to work in the Paymaster-General's department at the Admiralty, preparatory to the civil service examination. The lure of his native city proved too much, however, and he returned to train for five years as a solicitor, qualifying in 1902, and later forming the partnership with Edgar Bowden known as Foot and Bowden. The partnership provided my father with the ability, financial and otherwise, to enter into a political career, of which he was shortly to take advantage. Meanwhile, in 1904, he married a young Scots-Cornish woman, Eva Mackintosh, by whom, between 1905 and 1918, he had five sons and two daughters. She was, until her untimely death in 1946, his loving and beloved companion.

Aside from his nonconformity in religious matters, there was another spring to my father's political beliefs. From his earliest years he was a passionate reader. Later in his life, when his achievements came to merit an entry in *Who's Who*, he listed 'reading and book collecting' as his recreations. It was a description bordering on misrepresentation. My brother Michael, who, more than any of his progeny, shared our father's reading addiction, wrote of him, more accurately, that it was by reading that 'he taught himself almost everything he ever knew'. He read voraciously, but at an early stage one subject began to emerge as a dominating interest – the history of his native land, and, as Edmund Burke expressed it, 'the achievement of free government which is the main glory of the British nation ... this struggle for liberty throughout the world is supremely the effort and accomplishment of the British people.'

To that affirmation of the pre-eminence of the British people in the cause of freedom, my father would have added two riders – that the years of greatest glory had been those in the seventeenth century when an English Parliament had challenged and overthrown a tyrannical king, and that the supreme accomplishment had been achieved under the leadership of a handful of plain English 'esquires', all members of that Parliament, including John Eliot, John Pym, John Hampden, Oliver Cromwell, Henry Vane and John Selden.

Given these influences and associations, it was not surprising that Isaac Foot should have entered politics as a Liberal.[1]

HUGH FOOT: A few days before my father died at the end of 1960 he gave me a small volume of Edmund Burke's *Speeches on American Independence*. I knew the speeches from my school days when I had stolen many quotations from my father's commonplace books. I could quote several of the pages by heart. The book was my father's last gift to me and I value it as a sort of political testament. The famous Burke quotations which I knew so well as a boy have always been in my mind:

'Magnanimity in politics is not seldom the truest wisdom; and a great empire and little minds go ill together.'

'We view the establishment of English colonies on principles of liberty as that which is to render this kingdom venerable to future ages. In comparison of this, we regard all the victories and conquests of our warlike ancestors, as of our own times, as barbarous vulgar distinctions, in which many nations, whom we look down upon with little respect or value, have equalled if not excelled us. This is the peculiar and appropriated glory of England.'

'Slavery they can have everywhere. It is a weed that grows in every soil ... freedom they can have from none of you. This is the commodity of price of which you have the monopoly ... Deny them this participation of freedom and you break the sole bond which originally made and must still preserve the unity of empire.'

'Magnanimity in politics', 'the establishment of English colonies on principles of liberty', and 'the participation of freedom' – these are some of the principles I learnt from my father.[2]

DINGLE FOOT: My father was born at 10 Notte Street, Plymouth. That address was of the utmost importance. I once heard Lady Astor tell a public meeting that she would not have been born anywhere in the world except Virginia. In much the same way, I think that Father has always felt that he would not have been born anywhere in the world except Plymouth and that it had to be somewhere in the neighbourhood of Sutton Pool. We are

---

1. Adapted from John Foot, 'Isaac Foot', in Duncan Brack (ed.). *Dictionary of Liberal Biography*, Politico's, 1998.
2. Hugh Foot, *A Start in Freedom*, Hodder and Stoughton, 1964.

all of us conditioned, perhaps a good deal more than we realise, by the place in which we are born and brought up.

One of Father's principal characteristics, as his friends are well aware and his critics occasionally point out, is that he lives a great deal in the past and that the controversies of, say three hundred years ago, are no less real to him than those of today. And it is perfectly true that, even during the last war, he could get just as excited about the victories of Marston Moor and Naseby as about Alamein and Stalingrad. But, after all, that was perfectly natural. Personally I have never understood how any citizen of Plymouth could fail to have an acute historical sense. You may remember how John Burns, that most eminent of Londoners, used to describe the Thames to American visitors as 'liquid history'. Father is, of course, a kind of Westcountry John Burns and the 'liquid history', in his case, consists of the waters of Sutton Pool, the Hamoaze and Plymouth Sound. Whenever he goes into Plymouth I think he always has a clear picture before his eyes of the *Golden Hind* setting out on its journey round the world, the Elizabethan navy waiting at the mouth of the Tamar for the arrival of the Armada, of the Pilgrims in their leaky ship, about to cross the Atlantic and of the garrison of Plymouth sailing out after the three years' siege to rout the forces of the King and thereby determining the result of the Civil War.

My grandfather, known as 'Isaac Foot Senior' in Plymouth to distinguish him from his son, was a tremendous Methodist and in those days a great many of the services which are now provided by organisations – like technical schools, the WEA [Workers' Educational Association] or even social and athletic clubs – were furnished by organisations attached to the churches such as the Wesley Guild. So, at the age of about nineteen, Father delivered his first public address to the Wesley Guild at the Old Wesley Chapel in Ebrington Street. It was on a Wesley Guild excursion to Cambridge that he met my mother. She was a Miss Mackintosh and she then lived at Callington with her grandfather, whose name was William Dingle. So, each weekend after the Cambridge excursion, Father used to make the journey to Callington, wearing a top hat and frock-coat, which, in those days, were almost compulsory for a young man on such an errand.

My father earned his living as a solicitor. He appeared frequently in the courts. Both in the pulpit and on the political platform he exercised a considerable spell. He could make his village audiences laugh and weep. But looking back I think he missed his vocation. If he had been born in other circumstances he would have been a great actor comparable to Garrick or Irving. When he was first elected to Parliament in 1922 he sat through every parliamentary debate. Occasionally he took time off to go to the theatre. Whenever he returned home at the weekend, every parliamentary speech – by Lloyd George, Asquith or Churchill – would be fully described and every scene in the theatre would be re-enacted. We were therefore left with the impression that the House of Commons is the greatest theatre in the world and that the principal dramas of public life are enacted on its floors. This happens to be true.[3]

---

3. Dingle Foot, 'Western Men', 1951 broadcast.

PLYMOUTH in 1890

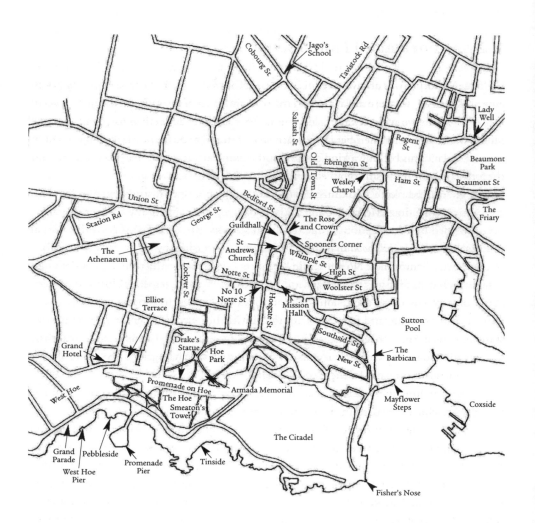

PART I

1880 – 1900
A Plymouth boyhood

1 I was born at 10 Notte Street

DINGLE: My father was always very proud of the fact that he came from working-class origins and, indeed, we were always reminded of it and, whenever we went away to school, before we went, we were always told we must remember where we came from and the phrase was: 'We must remember the pit from which we were dug and the rock from which we were hewn.' This became a kind of family slogan and whenever we had occasion to send telegrams, say on the result of an election or anything like that, we always ended up with the words 'pit and rock': 'Look unto the rock whence ye are hewn, and to the hole of the pit whence ye are digged' (Isaiah 51: 1).

Isaac Foot recalls his childhood in a 1951 broadcast
I was born in Plymouth at No. 10 Notte Street, in a house which my father had built two years before. Behind it was the workshop he had also built with its three storeys with timber and materials of all kind. The steam whistle blew with deadly promptitude at six o'clock every morning and from that hour until five in the evening it was a place of constant activity. In the centre of the large ground floor there was the steam saw-bench. That wonderful machine fascinated me as a child, especially as it was generally worked by my father, in whose company I delighted. All the workmen I knew intimately. I spent hours and hours watching them at their work and took a boy's keen interest in the scores of different tools which they used in their varied crafts.

Notte Street was not one of Plymouth's main streets but, as a birthplace, it was the one I should have chosen before all others. Like Southside Street, which led directly to the Barbican, it was the one street along which must have walked all the men whose names are most closely identified with the fame of Plymouth in past years: Humphrey Gilbert, Sir John Hawkins, Sir Francis Drake, Martin Frobisher, Sir Walter Raleigh, Admiral Robert Blake and, in later years, Captain Cook and Admiral Nelson and ever so many more. The main impression left upon my mind is that I lived in the midst of a multitude of people. Every house and indeed almost every room seemed full of people. The neighbouring streets had courts running at right angles and here, too, the place

Old houses in Notte Street, looking east towards the junction with Hoegate Street on the left. Numbers 9 and 10, the home and workplace of Isaac Foot Senior and his family, are on the corner.

seemed crowded. These courts had different names and in every court there seemed a separate and distinctive community. Sometimes there were fights between the streets, not mere scuffles and passing encounters, but battles. For some reason, which I never understood, a feud existed between Notte Street and High Street. High Street, which ran uphill and at right angles at the bottom, was not so important as Notte Street but when hostilities commenced those courts of theirs provided powerful auxiliaries. During one of those battles I saw the High Street army sweep Notte Street clear from the bottom to the top. The victors would then encamp in triumph, sometimes around an improvised fire fed with the weapons taken from the enemy. Meanwhile, the defeated Notte Streeters took refuge in their homes, nursing their wounds. That was literally true, for sometimes there was actual bloodshed. On these bigger occasions no policeman ever came in sight; nothing but a body of police could have coped with that formidable situation.

Notte Street had another special interest for me because my father had not only built his house and workshop there shortly before I was born, but there he also built a Mission Hall, completed when I was three years old. He bought the house and garden which had been occupied by William Cookworthy, the great chemist of Plymouth earthenware fame, and there, out of his own limited resources, he erected this fine commodious building with its handsome frontage. In this frontage my father was at pains to preserve some part of the famous Cookworthy house and, in particular, the pediment which had been above its central doorway. That remains to this day if any of you care to go and see it. Whilst the hall was being erected I somehow found my way to the building. I must have been about two years old. I could remember most vividly my father, then aged about forty, taking me up

The Mission Hall in Notte Street, built by Isaac Foot Senior in 1883 at the front of the site of William Cookworthy's former house, with the original carvings above the two side windows.

25

in his arms, clasping me close whilst he stepped from one timbered joist to another. It was on the first floor, about 20 feet above the ground. The height rather terrified me but I felt safe in my father's close grasp. My father carried on his evangelistic work in that hall for many years. There I received most of my early religious instruction.

*

The school I attended in those early days was Mr Charles Jago's. The formal title was the Plymouth Public School but it was always known as Jago's. It was in Cobourg Street about half a mile away. Four times a day, six days a week I did that walk to and from school, past St Andrew's Church into Old Town Street. That famous street was then pretty narrow but crammed full with interest. Every building was different, every shop window was exciting. I got to know every separate doorway. There was the inn, the Rose and Crown, generally with horses and coaches at the door, then up through Saltash Street. The main interest of Saltash Street was that it led halfway up on the left to the sugar refinery. Sometimes the great wagons would pass us laden with sacks of raw sugar.

Old Town Street, with the Rose and Crown on the right.

St Andrew's Church in the centre of Plymouth with the Guildhall, opened by the Prince of Wales in 1874, on the right and the Municipal Buildings on the left, taken from an etching about 1887.

Whenever that happened there was always the chance that one of our number would be daring enough to cut a hole in the bottom corner of a sack at the back big enough for a boy's hand. It was petty larceny, of course, but the driver in front had his horses to look after and each one of us filled his pockets with rough brown sugar as his rightful share of the spoils. I might add that I never had the pluck to make the hole in the sack myself.

Jago's School at that time numbered about a thousand boys. The classes ran from sixty to seventy, sometimes to a hundred. The fees were twopence a week and I was given this sum every Monday morning and always paid it over most grudgingly. I remember very little of what I was taught but I suppose I learned something. Emerson[4] says somewhere that 'we send boys to the schoolmaster but it is their schoolfellows who teach them'. Certainly I learned a great deal from my schoolmates, particularly those who did the journey to school from day to day. My special schoolmate was a boy whose name was Lovell Redmore Dunstan. I recall how beautiful my schoolmate's name seemed to be. Lovell and I constantly did the school journey together.

*

---

4. Ralph Waldo Emerson (1803–82), American author, poet and philosopher.

Somewhere about the year 1886 we had our Guy Fawkes. He was prepared for weeks beforehand and the work was done on the first floor of my father's workshop. His body consisted of a rough woolly mailbag. Two marbles served as glaring eyes. He was stuffed with squibs, Catherine wheels and rockets bought out of the combined financial resources of about a dozen Notte Street boys. The effigy rested upon a huge stake sharpened at the bottom. According to the ancient custom of Notte Street boys, it was to be burned on Plymouth Hoe. Then came the dreadful news of the new order or the fiat of the police forbidding the use of the Hoe for the burning of any Guy Fawkes. We held a council of war and it was decided that, police or no police, Guy Fawkes was to be burnt and burnt on Plymouth Hoe. We made one concession to law and order. We decided to burn it, not on the brow of the Hoe by Drake's statue, but on the edge of the quarries on the west end of the Hoe. We should then, we thought, attract less public attention. I, at the age of six, was the youngest of the party. My advice was not sought but, although frightened, I fully approved. Two or three of our number carried the Guy and then we all assembled in darkness on the edge of the quarries at about ten o'clock on that fateful night. Because of my age I was deputed to keep watch and to give the alarm at once on seeing any policemen. The Guy lighted gloriously and the blaze was in full vigour and it was at that point that I saw something approaching me. It was the clasp of a policeman's bell gleaming in the light of the fire. Fortunately I gave the alarm in time. The older malefactors, and amongst them were three of my brothers, determined that, whatever happened, Guy Fawkes was not to be

View of the Hoe from Plymouth Sound with Smeaton's Tower, the former lighthouse on the Eddystone reef re-erected and opened in 1884, on the left and the walls of the Royal Citadel, built in the 1660s, on the right.

The Promenade on Plymouth Hoe in the 1880s with the statue of Sir Francis Drake on the right and the houses of Elliot Terrace and the Esplanade in the distance.

captured. He was flung high in the air and by sheer good fortune came down dead straight on his sharp spike in a position almost inaccessible amongst the quarry rocks. The police were busy trying to make captures so Guy Fawkes burned down to the side and with the squibs he spat defiance to the last. The rockets roared, rebellion against our local tyrants. Two of our number were caught. They spent the night in the police station. I eluded capture and ran home like a hare. I went to bed very quietly to avoid parental inquiry. The merest chance saved me from being held up before the town the next morning as a dreadful example of juvenile delinquency. The quarries at West Hoe have long since disappeared. They were a part of the Hoe which has greatly changed.

*

Notte Street was very close to the Hoe and I was there nearly every day. It was, however, not the Hoe of today. There were no promenades, no asphalt, no roads to speak of, no restaurants, no smooth bowling green, no statues except one, but there was the rough grassland where we could fly our kites and play football with our coats for goalposts. There was a trench about three feet wide over which we loved to leap. Then, on the Hoe, there was the citadel, of whose history I knew nothing, but I understood from my elders that all Plymouth citizens had access there as a right. That right I constantly exercised. There were the turf ramparts, the embrasures, through which peered the mouths of the great cannon. There we played our boys' cricket and football on the pitch now occupied by the enormous naval memorial. At that time the Hoe was the people's promenade, especially on Sundays. It was, moreover, the trysting place of young lovers and the romantic playground for us youngsters. No monument was there, other than that of the Smeaton Tower and the stat-

Looking out to sea on Plymouth Hoe in the 1880s with the pier, opened in 1884, and Drake's Island and Mount Edgcumbe behind in the distance with West Hoe to the right.

ue of Sir Francis Drake, who then had the whole place to himself. The Drake statue was erected in 1884. The admission to Smeaton lighthouse cost one penny. I shall not forget my first ascent of those spiral stone steps soon after it was put up, also in 1884. I knew nothing of John Smeaton at the time. I knew nothing of the epic story of the light from the Eddystone Rock, but, at the top of the tower, there were the words inscribed in capitals at the very summit. I spelt them out for myself very slowly and the words were: 'Except the Lord build the house they labour in vain that build it.' The third memorial came later when I was eight years old – the Armada Memorial. I am one of those who think we might very well have stopped there. Man can make any number of statues and memorials but only God can make a Plymouth Hoe.

We grew up with an intimate knowledge of every part of the Hoe and foreshore. There was Pebbleside and Tinside and Shackey Pool. There was the foreshore, where they afterwards built Phoenix Wharf. There was Sutton Harbour, where we fished for crabs and launched our rafts. Sometimes we could get a boat and explore Hooe Lake and The Cattewater, and the more distant parts of the beloved estuary. Sutton Harbour for us was only two minutes away. More often than not that little harbour was full of ships – mostly fishing vessels – mainly of Plymouth, but ever so many with the familiar letters FY and PZ. There we learned about Fowey and Looe and Mevagissey and Mousehole and Penzance –

The Barbican Fish Quay in Sutton harbour in the 1880s.

those wonderful places that we had never seen. On occasions the Cornish fishing boats would come in over the Sunday, and then the fishermen would crowd the gallery of the chapel and make their presence known at once by their shouts of praise and volume of their song. Sometimes the great warships or liners would sweep across the waters of the sound – with the great sweep to keep inside Drake's Island on their way to and from the Hamoaze. But the smaller ships in Sutton Harbour interested us more. They were there so close we could see the men on the deck and sometimes talk to them. Every ship had her name on the bow. And there painted on the stern was the name and name of the port to which she belonged. Then the ship would pass out towards the great waters and world beyond, and strange thoughts would arise as we saw her leave. At that time I knew nothing of a poet called Robert Bridges but, just about then, he wrote a poem which says with rapture just what a boy thought standing on the Barbican fifty-five years ago:

Whither, O splendid ship, thy white sails crowding,
Leaning across the bosom of the urgent West,
That fearest nor sea rising, nor sky clouding,
Whither away, fair rover, and what thy quest?[5]

*

5. Robert Bridges, 'A Passer-by'.

But Plymouth meant more to me than all this. It meant the whole of Plymouth Sound, the whole estuary. It included Mount Edgcumbe on the right with its noble house and grounds, thrown open to us on the first Wednesday in every month, and then on the left there was Mountbatten, Turnchapel, Bovisand, the walk around Hooe Lake and, above all, Radford Woods with its mist of bluebells. It was the gate of Paradise. Then there was Mount Gould. That from Notte Street was a walk indeed. The houses stretched then to Friary and then began the beautiful path-fields, leading at last to the fairy lane, the little town at the end, the magic door, and the farm itself. Sometimes, but rarely, there was the bigger venture, the walk through Laira, past Crabtree along Bickleigh Vale, and even sometimes Shaugh Bridge and the Dewerstone. I think Shaugh Bridge and Dewerstone are still lovely places but I cannot recover the thrill of joy which the town-boy felt when he saw for the first time the beauty at the point where the two rivers meet at Shaugh Bridge or the majesty of the Dewerstone.

One day I walked further still to Plymbridge. That was a walk of at least five miles. On the left-hand side of the bridge was a path that gave access to the Plym River. For about two miles the river finds its way between high hills, towering woodlands and overhanging rocks. Every reach of that river has its own special and intimate appeal. Until then I had not known that such beauty existed. The Plym meant more to me than the lordly Tamar could ever become. Our early forebears first called this settlement Tamar Mouth. It was a wise instinct that decided on the new name 'Plymouth'. Nature made the whole of Plymouth Sound and Harbour one unity of wonder and beauty.

*

So far I have been recalling the first ten years of my life. When I reached that age my people moved into another part of the town.[6] At that time there was the excitement of moving into another and much larger house but, looking back, I can never be sufficiently thankful for the advantage of those first ten years at Notte Street. A larger house and a richer suburban neighbourhood had their attractions but the atmosphere was not the same. In Notte Street I seemed to know everybody and everybody knew me. Now each residence was self-contained and next-door neighbours seemed utter strangers. I felt sometimes almost like an alien, an intruder, and every now and again I would slip back to the old haunts.

Those first ten years meant for me a love for the kindly people around me. Into some of those homes I seemed always welcome and at their table I sat almost as a right. One of those doors led from a country lane into Mount Gould Farm. In my boyhood, Mount Gould meant for me paradise. At that time it was a farm occupied by a family who were close friends of my parents. The head of the family was Mr Hocking, Henry Dart Hocking. From

---

6. Lady Well House off Regent Street, built by Isaac's father for his growing family.

Notte Street there were two ways to Mount Gould Farm. One way was along the path-fields which lay beyond Ebrington Street. There was no Friary station at that time. The other, and the longer way, was up the Lipson Road and then half a mile or so down a country lane. The walk down that lane, or rather the saunter, never seemed long to me, partly because all the way there were hedgerows. I did that journey so frequently that Mount Gould became almost a second home. The farmhouse looked down across the fields across the wide estuary where the Plym River, for some unexplained reason, changes its name to the Laira. I got to know that farmhouse very well and more especially the kitchen and the farmyard and the farm buildings and the lofts and the shippens. I was often there when the cows were brought in for milking. On one memorable occasion I was allowed to milk one of the cows. Tremulously I took the pail and held it tightly between my knees at the right angle. I coaxed and caressed the cow's teats with my small fingers, waiting anxiously for the milk to come and then it came. I thought there was no music like that of the repeated beat as the pail became fuller and fuller and the cow's udder showed that my work was done. Before my pail was emptied into the great churn I was given a cupful of the new milk for myself and was commended for my skill. Straightway I determined to be a farmer.

*

The circle around Plymouth would, I suppose, have remained my circle throughout the whole of my boyhood had it not been for fortunate accidents depending upon family relationships and hospitality of relatives. One of those relatives lived at Horrabridge. Horrabridge had been my father's birthplace. There he had served his apprenticeship to his father, who was also a builder and carpenter. Horrabridge was, therefore, a name on everyone's lips. It was ten miles away. Three or four times a year the whole family went there on pilgrimage. My father would sometimes drive, sometimes my mother, and seven, eight, or nine of us would be crowded in the family trap or wagonette that was only intended for four. It meant starting early in the morning and getting back very late at night and we had to walk up all the hills and the journey took about three hours. The road became very familiar to us. The relative who lived at Horrabridge was my aunt, the widow of my father's brother Israel. The house in which she lived was halfway down the village and next to it was the workshop with a sign that then and for many years afterwards bore my father's name.[7] At the bottom of the village was the bridge over the Walkham River. On that bridge the villagers always met in conference. That was before the motor cars came. About a hundred yards above my aunt's house was a waterspout from which poured in never-ceasing flow the water which seemed to be the only supply for all the villagers around. For some reason I became the recognised water carrier. It was then I learned, much to my satisfaction, that

---

7. Isaac Foot & Sons.

if I used my iron hoop I could carry two buckets as easily as one. Just below our house there ran a stream. Where it rose and where it fl owed I never knew. It has now disappeared entirely but then it was to me a source of never-failing delight. On it the ducks of the village disported. On it the boys of the village launched their little ships. Each boat had a name. My vessel I named after one I had seen at home. That name was *Sir John of Plymouth*.

Close to my aunt's house was the London Inn. That interested me because I had so often heard from my father how, when he was a small boy, he would slip almost unnoticed into the skittle alley and watch the game. There, as long as he could stay, he would listen to the stories and conversation. And he told me again and again of the wit and humour of those people. Some of this conversation he repeated to me, always in the original vernacular. On one of these evenings at the London Inn, George had been sitting there hour after hour, leaning upon his stick. At that time there was a very great emigration to South Africa, where people worked in the mines for some time and generally came back with the miners' disease. It didn't kill them but it meant that they got whiter and whiter and often they'd be seen sitting at the side of a hedge recovering. But George was sitting there very white, watching the game. One night Bill came in. Bill was his friend and, as usual, asked after his health. 'Well, George, how be 'ee this evening?' 'Not so well, Bill, not so well. Bain't long for this world, I'm afraid.' 'Not long for this world, darn 'ee? You've been saying that for the last ten years to my certain knowledge. You won't go yet, George, you mark my words. 'Sides, when you do go, George, you'll go straight to heaven.' 'Well, what make you say that then, Bill?' 'Well, George, the Bible says that flesh and blood cannot inherit the Kingdom of Heaven and you're nothing but skin and bone.'

One of the roads at the centre of the village ran along the meadow towards the chapel I attended. I went, of course, to the Sunday school and was taught by a heavily bearded farm worker. His name was Mr Gulley. I was a little vain when I found I could read the Bible lesson more quickly than he could but he left an impression upon me when I realised that, after all, there was something in this man that made him sacrifice so much of his one day of rest in teaching a class of such thankless youngsters as we were. My particular friend in Horrabridge was a cousin of about the same age. He also was called Isaac Foot. He was one of four brothers. They were all village carpenters. They had been apprenticed to their father, as he in turn had been apprenticed to their grandfather and mine. These four brothers all went to South Africa, attracted as so many others were at that time by the high wages offered there. They only intended to work there for a year of two and then to return with their savings. My cousin, Isaac, did not return. He died there very soon afterwards. Only one of the four returned. That was before the Jameson Raid and the Boer War (1899–1902). That is what happened to these four brothers in one village family. Two of my brothers, also carpenters, went to work in South Africa about the same time.

*

High Street, Honiton on market day about 1900.

Another accident of family relationships took me to another place in Devonshire. This time it was further afield. It was not a village but a country town and that town was Honiton. At Honiton there lived another beloved aunt. She was one of my father's sisters, whose name upon marriage had been changed from Foot to Clark. To that marriage I was indebted for ten lively first cousins.

The High Street in Honiton is one of the noblest streets in the country. My aunt's house was at the bottom. On market days the broad highway was crowded with carts, wagons and stalls, and herds of cattle and flocks of sheep came in from the wide countryside. Halfway up High Street was New Street, which led to the railway station and then to a lofty parkland called Roundball. It was a place of almost constant resort especially of young lovers. They were wont to carve their initials on the trees there. Not to be outdone I carved my initials as deeply as any young Honitonian had done. There were four initials, two of my name and two of the name of a Westcountry girl who, like myself, was there on holiday. We were both under twelve at the time.

I got to know something of the beautiful east Devon countryside. One day I went on pilgrimage with a few Honiton boys to the hill a few miles on the east side of the town, where the summit is crowned by a cluster of trees. They still remain and are a commanding feature in that landscape as one crosses the Devon border. Three or four summer holidays were spent at Honiton.

*

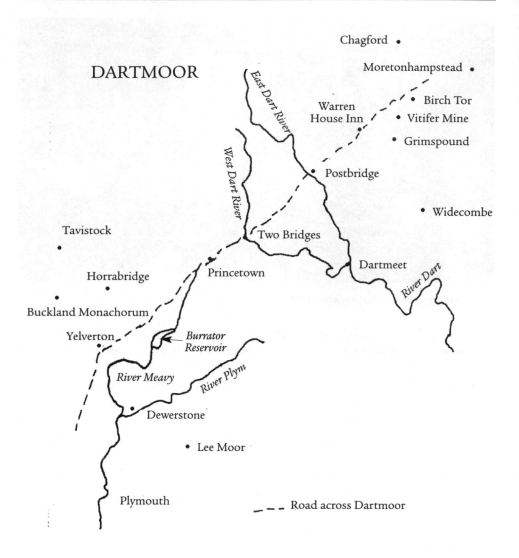

Horrabridge, Honiton and then a place more important still and here again, through the accident of friendship – Dartmoor. Two or three summer holidays were spent under the hospitable roof of friends of my father's who lived at Postbridge. Postbridge is six miles from Princetown in the very heart of the moor. Then, in one memorable summer, when Postbridge was crowded with visitors more well to do than I was, I was passed over to the keeping of a family who lived at the foot of Birch Tor, about two and a half miles from Postbridge in the valley just beyond the Warren House Inn. The name of the family was Jory. The father, Richard Jory, was the captain of Vitifer tin mine. The house in which they

Vitifer tin mine on Dartmoor, the dressing floor about 1905. The white bearded man in the centre is Captain Richard Jory, known as Captain Dick. He was responsible for the everyday working of the Vitifer and Gold Dagger mines and kept all the mine accounts.

lived has long since fallen into ruin. The mine has been abandoned but at that time the place was the scene of great activity and the crash of the heavy stamping machinery was heard throughout the valley from morning until night. Captain Jory had a profound knowledge of his craft. I took to him from the first. I think he took to me. I was constantly in his company. All that I know about tin mining I learned from him, how the tin was mined, separated and prepared in readiness for the great sacks which had somehow to be carted up the steep road to the highway and then despatched. The more I saw of Captain Richard Jory and his wife Anna the more I was impressed by their devout life and their independence of mind and their shrewd judgment of men and affairs.

But the interest of those holidays was not primarily in the Jory family, nor in the Vitifer tin mine, but in Dartmoor. I walked one day to Moretonhampstead, another day to Chagford, another day to Widecombe, but the attraction for me was not in these moorland towns, but in the moor itself. For the most part I did my walking alone and so, from day to day, I wandered over the vast unpeopled stretches of the moorland, sometimes not meeting a single soul from morning till night. Towards sunset I happened upon Grimspound.[8] There came upon me a sense of awe when I saw around me this unmistakable evidence of the life of my ancestors generations and generations ago. I returned to the

8. An ancient bronze settlement of stone hut circles on the moor.

Jory house parched and yet excited. I told them about the place I had found. Did they know of it? Yes, they knew. They had seen it. There was a lot of that sort of thing lying about on the hills around. I have read a great deal about Dartmoor since but I learnt something that day beyond anything I have since learned from the books.

After such adventures as these I would get home again. First there was the long walk from Postbridge to Princetown. Then there was the railway journey, first to Yelverton then to Millbay then home to Notte Street then to bed. But I would fall asleep with the thought of those hills twenty or thirty miles away. Dartmoor was the home of the friends I had made, but Dartmoor was also to me the rampart around Plymouth. Later on I was able to read many books on Dartmoor. I have some shelves in my library wholly given up to Dartmoor. When a youth, still under twenty, I began to read Eden Phillpotts's stories of the moor. From the first I have reckoned myself one of his disciples.

*

I have said so much about my holidays that some of you might be asking: 'Didn't this boy ever go to school at all?' Of course I did go to school like other boys, first to Jago's, then for a couple of terms to the board school at Mount Street and then later to the Hoe Grammar School for just over two years, where it was my good fortune to come under the influence of John Rounsevell and George Pearce Diamond. Then, again, like others, I picked up my education, what there was of it, as I went along. Bernard Shaw tells us somewhere that his education was interrupted by his schooling. That wasn't so with me, especially when I remember how much I owed to the Sunday school. At Jago's School in a class of sixty or seventy or more I saw the teacher at a distance. At the Sunday school I was one of eight or ten and every successive teacher became something like a personal friend, sometimes a friend for life. Attached to the Sunday school was the Band of Hope[9] and there, and not at school, I became acquainted with English poetry. One evening a youth, whom I never saw before or since, recited Macaulay's *Horatius* – not the whole of it, but enough to teach me more of the glory of words and the magic of poetry than all my teachers put together. The little poetry taught at Jago's I regarded as a task, even Wordsworth's 'Lucy Gray'.

*

Another day stands out in my memory. That was a holiday indeed. It was the Queen's birthday. On that day in every year I went on pilgrimage to the Brickfields. The Brickfields were then a vast grassy amphitheatre, just beyond the Ha-penny Gate. The

9. A children's temperance organisation founded in 1847 in Leeds.

38

soldiers and sailors marched past in grand parade. As each detachment passed, their band played their favourite march. I could sing them now. That for the soldiers was 'The British Grenadiers'; that for the Blue Jackets 'Nancy Loe' or 'Hearts of Oak'; that for the Royal Marines 'A Life on the Ocean Wave'. On some really great occasions the Highlanders were there, with their swinging kilt, their white gaiters and the daggers stuck inside their stockings. At the skirl of the bagpipes I felt I could cry out with emotion. Then, precisely at noon, there was the salute from a thousand rifles, not all at once, but from man to man in swift succession. The thin trail of smoke extended along the whole line. Then came the crash when all the bands together played 'God Save the Queen'. A lot of education was crowded into that one day. The great Queen, whom I had never seen, away in London was my Queen too. Her country was my country – the greatest country in the world, invincible, unconquerable, supreme. Then in 1887 there was Queen Victoria's Jubilee, which was celebrated by a pageant and procession on the Hoe fully a mile long, and by the firing of a huge bonfire, just below the Drake statue. This bonfire had been piled up to a tremendous height for weeks beforehand.

Jubilee Day on Plymouth Hoe, 22 June 1887, with the vast bonfire on the left.

The Armada Tercentenary Commemoration
Programme for the laying of the foundation stone of
the Armada Memorial on Plymouth Hoe in 1888 on
the 300th anniversary of the first sighting of the
Spanish Armada from the Hoe.

The Armada Tercentenary Commemoration
Programme showed the Armada Memorial, which is
now on the Hoe, as it would look when finished.

I well remember the unveiling of the Armada Memorial in 1888. Celebrating the 300th anniversary of that great victory, we were all assembled in our schools early that morning. Ours was our Sunday school. We were each given a medal and a bun and then packed on the temporary stand which had been erected in Osborne Place. We saw the procession come up Lockyer Street, the mayor – Mr Waring, as he then was – in his scarlet robe and HRH the Duke of Edinburgh, Queen Victoria's son, with scores and scores of town and country dignitaries and vast numbers of sailors and troops.

*

My knowledge of drama was limited to a single visit to the Grand Theatre in Union Street for the Christmas pantomime – that year it was *Cinderella* – I was about eight or nine. A schoolmate of mine had two complimentary tickets and offered to take me with him. After grave hesitation and some heart burning, I went on the Saturday afternoon. I dared not risk asking permission at home. I knew without asking that it was forbidden territory. But the temptation was very great and for about three hours I was thrilled to the depths of my being. That one enraptured experience of the drama had to suffice until I reached more mature years.

All the music I learned was at the Sunday school and Band of Hope. Quite early it was decided that I might learn the piano. Arrangements were made with a Miss Webber, who undertook the job at the fee of seven shillings and sixpence a quarter. For an hour once a week I went to her house in York Street and, within a year, I could play a few single pieces including many tunes from the hymn book. This proficiency led me into a biggish undertaking. Whilst I was staying at Postbridge on Dartmoor, I attended the little chapel there. One Sunday a calamity threatened. The lady who played the harmonium was unable to take the evening service. There was no one to play. Could I do it? After long discussion and much concerted pressure I agreed to play on the condition that I could practise for an hour or two as my experience of the harmonium was very limited – and that I could choose the tunes. The tunes I selected were those which allowed for a continuing bass note and with no more than one sharp or one flat. The hymns were from Sankey's.[10] I can remember three out of the four: 'I Am So Glad That My Father in Heaven Tells of His Love in the Book He Has Given', good, no frills about that tune; 'Sing Them Over Again to Me, Wonderful Words of Life'; and, as it was about harvest time, 'Bringing in the Sheaves'. After the service I was thanked by the preacher and others probably more for my pluck than my proficiency.

And now I must say something about the books of my boyhood. First of all, of course, there was the Bible. Every day from my earliest childhood until I left my parents' roof for a house of my own, I heard a passage of the Bible read. Generally it was a whole chapter. The Bible reading was as certain and regular as the sunrise. Sometimes it seemed tiresome, especially when my father went steadily, morning after morning, through the Epistle to the Romans or the Corinthians. But every day we heard the majestic language of the Authorised Version, and somehow, without any conscious effort on my part, a standard of English prose was set up in my mind, and by that standard everything else I read had to be judged. After the Bible came Bunyan's *Pilgrim's Progress*. Our copy – a large folio – had pictures on every other page, and those I soon knew by heart. Then I learned of Plymouth Public Library and I borrowed and read all the books I could get of R. M. Ballantyne, G. A. Henty, George Manville Fenn and W. H. O. Kingston. Kingston was a special favourite about that time. Other writers came along later. I got to know of Conan Doyle, beginning with *The Sign of Four*. Quiller-Couch became known to me, first through *Dead Man's Rock*. Then came the sheer delight of Stevenson's *Treasure Island*, which I read in serial form in Chums. Two other books made a special appeal to me at that time, Charles Reade's *Cloister and the Hearth* and Charles Kingsley's *Alton Locke*.

*

---

10. *Sacred Songs and Solos*, compiled by Ira Sankey (1840–1908), an American gospel singer and writer of hymns, originally published in 1873.

Perhaps I might here say something upon that familiar topic – the cost of living. In my early days the golden sovereign was something worth thinking about. On three occasions I had a sovereign of my own, once as a parting present from my father's brother John, when, after a long visit, he was returning to his home in Australia. Another red-letter day was when I picked up a sovereign in the street. I thought it was a halfpenny shining in the light of a street lamp. Then, with amazement, I saw that it had on the back St George and the Dragon. I ran home all the way, uphill. On another really great occasion my father sent me with a small Gladstone bag full of money, mostly golden sovereigns, to pay a bill he owed for timber. It was due to the firm of R. and R. Bayly at Coxside on the far side of Sutton Pool. The money was turned out on the counter, and checked with the bill. It was correct to the penny, and over one hundred pounds. The cashier looked at me, about as high as the counter, and I looked at him. 'What is your name, my boy?' 'Isaac Foot!' I replied. That was the name on the bill. He left me for a moment or two and then I was summoned into an inner room. Two gentlemen were there, seated at a table. 'These won't be R. and R. Bayly,' I thought. Again they asked my name and again I replied: 'Isaac Foot.' Then R. and R. Bayly said something kind to me and handed me back one of the sovereigns for myself. That firm ever afterwards had a high place in my regard.

Another recollection of the golden sovereign is that every Saturday morning my father passed that coin over to my mother who was expected, with that money at her disposal, to provide all that was needed in the way of housekeeping for the whole week. There were nine of us, without counting frequent visitors. The fare was Spartan, but we never went short. Oatmeal was the staple food for the breakfast table. Sometimes it was burnt, but it was on the plate, and we were expected to clear our plates. The milk was scald milk. Eggs were kept for special occasions like birthdays.

Potted pilchards were another staple food in our household. They were kept in a huge brown jar with vinegar in which bay leaves floated. You could eat those pilchards bones and all. Tinned salmon was an occasional delicacy. Those tins, like many other receptacles on our table, bore a message signed by a lady named Elizabeth Lazenby. The handwriting of that gracious lady was all over the place. I wondered what sort of person she really was – a sort of Florence Nightingale, perhaps.

On Sundays things were always different. The principle was that that day should be different. We wore different clothes. We even washed differently. We had our meals on chairs in the front room, instead of on the long bench in the kitchen. On Sunday afternoon there was cream for tea. I learnt a good deal in those days about the cost of living. Eggs were a penny each, counting thirteen to the dozen. There was one stall at the market where lovely tripe could be bought cheaper than anywhere else. For some reason it was always sold by the stick. Sweets were fourpence a pound and Norman's ice cream was a halfpenny a glass. Two other items in the cost of living I have special reason to remember. At the bottom of

Isaac Foot Senior (1843–1927) with his wife Eliza Ryder (1842–1922)

Notte Street the corner shop was a chemist. He was not only the chemist, but the pharmaceutical chemist – whatever that meant – and, as such, treated the minor ailments of the whole community. Amongst his activities was dentistry. Now and again when trouble arose I was sent down to him. The offending tooth was carefully pointed out. He would then take me into the neighbouring store-room, put me on a little cane-bottomed chair, tell me to hold the chair handle tight when he pulled, and then send me home with a few kind words. I paid him his fee – sixpence. That was, I thought, if anything, on the high side.

*

I have been making constant reference to my father. I would like now to say something more about his business activities, not through filial adulation or anything of that sort, but simply because his affairs were better known to me than those of anyone else. My father was the second youngest of ten surviving children. Leaving school at the age of

43

twelve, he was apprenticed to his father, James Foot, who was a carpenter and builder at Horrabridge. There was little machinery in those days and the work of a village carpenter included everything from felling timber to putting on the roof and the last slate coat of paint on the walls. Upon the death of my grandfather – whom I never saw – my father came to Plymouth to find employment as a journeyman carpenter. He had no capital whatever, and had to depend solely upon his earnings for his daily bread. After a few years in Plymouth, he set up in business for himself and built his own dwelling house and his workshop. In that workshop he made everything that a carpenter could make, but his pride was in his building. He surveyed the land available on the outskirts of Plymouth, selected the piece of land most suitable, negotiated the purchase, raising, somehow, the money necessary for his many enterprises. Having acquired the land he would clear the site, demolish the existing buildings and then build the houses. There were no sub-contractors. He and his workmen would build the house from top to bottom. The men who worked for him seemed almost like members of the family, some staying on until extreme old age. There were labourers to clear the site, masons to build the walls, carpenters and joiners for the woodwork, slaters for the roof, lime burners, glaziers, plumbers, polishers and carters. Short of felling the timber and quarrying the stone and making the bricks, he and his men carried through the whole thing. He built some hundreds of houses, taking pride in his workmanship, and, to the last, could handle the tools of his trade as well as any of his workmen. For nearly a century these houses of his have provided home and shelter for some thousands of Plymouth citizens.

The houses he built were mainly for the working class, but he had some larger schemes. I have already mentioned the Mission Hall he built in Notte Street. Not long after that was completed my father met, for the first time, General William Booth, of the Salvation Army. This was late one evening at the house of a friend. My father was introduced to the general as the man who had recently built a Mission Hall. 'Oh,' said the general, 'that's what I want. Why don't you build a hall for me?' 'Very good, General,' said my father, 'I'll build a hall for you if you want one; and, what is more, will show you where to build it.' General Booth had to leave Plymouth the next day, but, before he left, he met my father very early by appointment and he was shown the place where, if the land could be acquired, the hall could be built. The site was in Martin Street, just off Union Street, near the Octagon. 'That's the place for your hall,' said my father. General Booth at once agreed and he said: 'You get the land and build the hall and I will see that you're paid for it.' They shook hands. There was no other contract. Not a word in writing passed between them. My father bought the land and built the hall. Towards the end the general's money ran short. Thereupon my father lent the general the money still needed, raising it by mortgaging two of his houses. That was how the Congress Hall was built. The hall stood there for over half a century as the headquarters of the Salvation Army in Plymouth.

The Salvation Army
Congress Hall, Plymouth,
built for General Booth
by Isaac Foot Senior.

Isaac Senior recorded his meeting with General Booth in January 1884 in his diary:

At Albert Hall in evening heard General Booth, took supper at Mr Davey's with him. Praise the Lord. All well. The General at the Supper table asked me why I did not build them a Hall. Martin Street proposed. Oh dear Lord I am in thy Hands for anything as thou dost impress for thy Glory. O keep me humble enough to be used by thee for anything. Dear Father I shall as thou knowest well take it from thee as a favour and a special honour to do anything for thee.

*

These recollections cover no more than the years 1880 to 1895. Then, at the age of fifteen, I went to London to earn my living as a civil servant. I had twelve months or so there, but the call of the West was very strong and at last I found my way back.

Isaac Foot returned to Plymouth and in 1897 began five years of study and practice of the law as an articled clerk in the offices of solicitors Skardon and Phillips.

PLYMOUTH AND CALLINGTON

Tavistock

DEVON

Bodmin
Moor

Kit Hill

Horrabridge

CORNWALL

Callington

St Cleer

Pencrebar

Yelverton

River Lynher

River Tamar

River Tavy

Liskeard

Menheniot

Trewidland

Tideford

Saltash

Hessenford

River Plym

Plymouth

Looe East & West

Downderry

Torpoint

Plymstock

Mt.
Edgcumbe

*Plymouth
Sound*

Rame Head

PART II

A Callington courtship

2 1901 'I am longing intensely for Saturday. Are we going on Kit Hill?'

MICHAEL: I once wrote a piece about my father based on Wordsworth's 'Happy Warrior'. I thought he was the truest exponent of the idea that could be imagined. Despite the seemingly impossible competition from his other heroes and heroines – John Milton and Shakespeare himself were already there – William Wordsworth was the one who helped guard my father's proper peace as he picked his way for the thousandth time along the river Lynher, just below our Callington home. Wordsworth also has the advantage that he had already given the best description of my mother, my father's of course, but mine too:

> A perfect woman, nobly planned
> To warm, to comfort and command
> And yet a spirit still and bright
> With something of angelic light.'[11]

Kit Hill with the old mine chimney stack, standing 1,000 feet above Callington with views of the Tamar valley, Dartmoor and Bodmin Moor.

---

11. William Wordsworth, 'She Was a Phantom of Delight'.

Eva with her first child, Dingle Mackintosh, born in 1905.

Isaac Foot in 1901.

Time and again, naturally enough, my father would recite these precious lines, but thereafter, in my own piece about him, she hardly gets a look-in. My main reason for returning to the subject is to remedy this monstrous injustice. 'The Mother of Seven', she would proudly call herself in her public statements or private remonstrances. But, first, the previously untold story of how it happened. My father would often remind us how one of his favourite authors, Thomas Carlyle, always liked to have before him the best portrait of the hero about whom he was writing. For my father the picture he cherished above all is one of the first taken of her after her marriage holding in her arms the maybe one-year-old Dingle. This is what she looked like at the time of their Callington courtship. For him, it was love at first sight. For her it was something, maybe, not so different in the end. All the letters were written by my father from his family home in Plymouth. All were preserved by Mother. A selection of them is published here for the first time with a special thanks due to the Methodist chapels which both of them loved and honoured.

It was on 4 April 1901 that Isaac Foot met Eva Mackintosh at a Methodist Wesleyan Guild out-ing in Cambridge. Isaac was now working as an articled clerk in the office of a local solicitor's practice, in his fifth year of study of the law before taking his final solicitor's examinations in 1902. Known as Isaac Foot Junior to distinguish him from his father, he lived with his parents, Isaac Senior and Eliza, his brothers Sydney, Hedley and Stanley and sister Alice at Lady Well, off Regent Street, the new house built for his family by Isaac Foot Senior. His older sister Janie lived nearby with her husband, James Nash. At the age of twenty-one, he was a Methodist local preacher planned to preach, often twice on a Sunday in the Plymouth Methodist Ebenezer Circuit, which included not only the Plymouth churches but also a wide area to the north and east of Plymouth. He also played a prominent part in the recently formed Guild of Wesley Church in Ebrington Street, being elected general secretary in 1898. The Wesleyan Guilds attached to the Methodist chapels organised a programme of activities for their members with classes, social meet-ings, debating and literary meetings, and outings. The guild secretary was responsible for arrang-ing their programme.

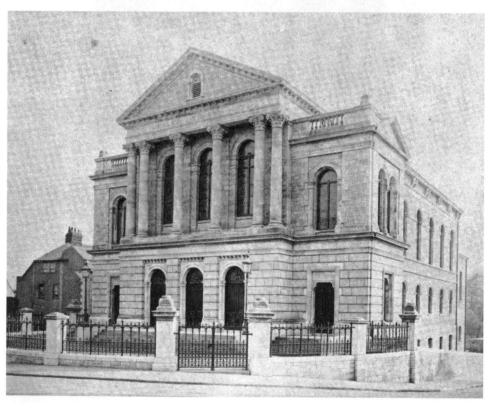

Wesley Methodist Chapel in Ebrington Street, Plymouth, opened in 1879 with seating for 1,150 and school rooms below for 600.

Father and Son: the two Isaacs outside Lady Well House in 1902

Eva Mackintosh was the daughter of Dr Angus Mackintosh from Blair Atholl in Perthshire and Sarah Dingle, the only daughter of William Dingle of Callington, a prominent businessman and member of the Wesleyan Methodist West End Chapel in Callington. Angus had met Sarah Dingle when he was working as a doctor in Callington. He and Sarah had married in 1873 and moved to Chesterfield in Derbyshire, where he was to take up the post of Medical Officer of Health. There their three children, Ida, Eva and Hugh, were born and brought up. After the death of her older sister, Ida, and her parents, Eva came to live with and keep house for her grandfather in Lower House, Church Street, Callington. Eva too was secretary of her local Wesleyan Guild.

Immediately after his return from Cambridge, Isaac began his courtship of Eva in letters written daily from his office or home whenever he had a spare moment. There were at that time at least three postal deliveries every day of the week.

View of Callington circa 1900 looking down Church Street, with a view of Kit Hill in the distance and Lower House, the Dingle family home, halfway down on the right.

West End Methodist Chapel in Callington in 1901.

1901 12 April Friday

Dear Miss Mackintosh

Perhaps you will be surprised to hear from me but I couldn't resist the temptation to write. If you are coming into Plymouth on Monday, I wish you could arrange so that we could spend half-an-hour together. We could slip into a café in the town. You will forgive, I hope, this audacious request but my only excuse is that there are many things which can be better spoken than written. I am afraid you will consider this letter rather presumptuous but I will offer no excuses.

Believe me, Yours, Isaac Foot Junior

Isaac Foot's first letter addressed to Miss Eva Mackintosh on 12 April 1901 on Wesley Guild notepaper.

Following their first meeting in Plymouth on the following Monday:

1901 16 April Tuesday

My Dear Miss Mackintosh

I think this heading is a very long one. I shall risk using a shorter one next time I write. I saw Janie last night and Father this morning and gave them the gist of our conversation and especially in relation to your Grandfather. They do not think that this obstacle is too great to be overcome. They point out that I shall not be in a position to marry until at least three years hence and mentioned many other things which take away the force of your objections altogether. You cannot tell what a relief it was to me when I found that your objection was not a personal one. You say again that you don't know me and vice versa. But we've been known to each other by repute and we've spent more time in each other's company than many who have been acquainted for a twelve-month. Another objection is that I may change my mind. You said yesterday that this must end, but I don't think you really meant it. On the one hand, we have many interests in common, kindred sympathies and, speaking for myself, love, and I think this combination is too great to make your objections have any weight. I am greatly thankful that we made the understanding so favourable as we did. For twelve months we are to be something more than friends and then you will give me your answer definitely. I suppose you do not intend letting your Grandfather get an inkling of the news – don't you think he will get to know of it? He must expect it to come some day but I suppose you will not allow me to speak until 15 April 1902. I am beginning to appreciate the story of Jacob and Rachel.[12] I think Job should be taken down from his pedestal and Jacob put in his place. I shall anxiously expect your promised letter, don't make it out that you will give me discomfort. Let our special friendship be recognised. I shall endeavour to prove myself worthy of you and I believe God's blessing will rest upon us.

Believe me, Yours ever, Ikey

1901 17 April Wednesday 10.50 p.m.

I have just returned from the Guild Social and find your letter awaiting me. I went upstairs and knelt down to read it, and you may be sure, I rose 'sadder and wiser'. Let me first thank you for the honest way in which your letter has been written. It breathes a spirit of sincerity which makes me admire you all the more. Of course the letter was anything but pleasant to read, but that can't be helped, it must be borne. I quite agree with you when you say that an Engagement is inadvisable under present circumstances – it would be unjust to you. But I think our special friendship should be acknowledged – between ourselves – and that we should see each other as often as possible. The words I like least in your letter are those where you say, 'Unless my feelings change towards you very much'. I thought that you could have brought up no objection that would have at all availed, but I never expected this one. You speak about 'unknowingly doing me wrong' – there is no need to write in that strain; the fault is due entirely to my presumption and the construction which in my zeal I put on many chance phrases and actions. You say that – 'It is possible I may change.' It is no use my inveighing against this conjecture. Of course it is only reasonable to consider the possibility, but I am sure that the lapse of the twelve months will convince you otherwise. I don't think I've had the chance of writing or speaking it plainly as yet – I love you. And the circumstances being such as they are, I love you too much even to wish you had written a different letter. As to the twelve months, supposing your mind changes in my favour before its expiration, you must tell me of it. It is now two weeks, and scarcely that, since I first met you. I introduced myself and you thought – 'Here's the young man who messed up the floor by sharpening his pencil.' What a great deal has happened since. A new world has opened to me, and I hardly know what has happened to you. I don't

---

12. Jacob had to wait seven years to marry Rachel.

know whether your liking for me is strong or feeble. A year seems a terrible time to wait, especially when there is no definiteness to be relied on at the end, but I am deeply thankful for the hope and encouragement which your letter does contain.

Good-bye.

Believe me, Yours ever, Ikey

Isaac Foot had agreed to speak and sing at Eva's next Guild social meeting in Callington the following Thursday.

1901 19 April Office Friday am

Janie tells me I was looking miserable yesterday but your letter of today has put a wonderful smile on my face. Whether that is so or not, I feel greatly different, I can assure you. Mr Wherry's lecture at Battisborough yester-night was very good indeed. The people we stayed with are large farmers and they did make us feel comfortable. After breakfast we rode to the station and the weather was lovely – 'glorious' as you put it. If I had only had your letter then I should have felt as if I were in heaven. The lark was singing, the view was magnificent, the sky was streaked with fleecy clouds and I seemed to bubble over with thankfulness, and couldn't help thinking: 'O Lord! How wonderful are thy works. In wisdom hast thou made them all. The Earth is full of thy riches.'[13] It is on occasions like these that one appreciates the privilege and joy of living.

Friday pm

I will bring down *The Trumpet Major*[14] on Thursday. I should like you to read it. I've fished out my Longfellow and am going to read 'Hiawatha'. We shall then see if we agree as to its being the finest poem in the English language. Have you read those three of Milton's I spoke of? 'Lycidas,' 'L'Allegro', ' Il Penseroso'?[15] On Sunday I have to preach at Noss.[16] It is a pretty little fishing village where the Methodist people are few but hearty. I am looking forward to the day. I'm glad you prefer 'Isaac' to 'Ikey'. I do myself but of course I'm more used to the latter.

1901 21 April Sunday night

I have just returned from Noss and thought I should like to start answering your letter before going to bed. Father has a great joke over your letters. When the one came on

---

13. Psalm 104:24.
14. A novel written by Thomas Hardy in 1880.
15. 'Lycidas', 'L'Allegro' and 'Il Penseroso' are three of the best-known pastoral poems by John Milton (1608–74), written in 1638, 1645 and 1633 respectively.
16. Noss Mayo, part of the Plymouth Ebenezer Methodist circuit along the coast to the east of Plymouth.

Wednesday night he secured it before my arrival home and took it upstairs, and when I went up for it, he said he thought I could sleep all the better if I waited until the morning and so on. And so this morning he pocketed your missive and told me to wait till tomorrow. I should be able to preach with a freer mind. The Program you send is, I think, alright. How long do you want me to speak? I will send on my songs. Perhaps the 'Longshoreman' and 'Sailor's Grave' will be acceptable. I have read several pages of 'Hypatia'[17] and so far have been greatly interested. I've often wished we could read it together. Somehow, whenever I have a happy experience now, I want to share it with you. Perhaps I'm reading a striking poem, or story or an interesting article or I'm looking at some beautiful scenery and it's a sort of regret that you are not present to participate in the appreciation. It takes the edge off the pleasure. I've had a fine time at Noss. You say you would have liked to have been with me. I wish you had been. I expect I could have found a suitable text. Perhaps Proverbs 13: 12 or Romans 15: 4 – 'That we thro' patience might have hope', might have afforded topics for profitable conversation.

1901 22 April Monday

I had to go up to see Mr Horne, our Minister, this morning. I have never told you, I think, but he is anxious that I should go into the Ministry, but, as I told him, there is no likelihood of that, none whatever. I think that in 'the law' I am in the position best fitted for me. I am getting up our Summer Program for the Guild. If there was only a railway station at Callington, I should like to arrange an outing there. I hope we shall have the chance of a good chat together when I come down.

1901 23 April Tuesday night

You think this letter writing is a form of self-indulgence. I'm afraid your conscience becomes so tender we shall have to get you a golden halo, name you Saint Eva and send you off to a nunnery. I shall have to exercise a wonderful self-restraint on Thursday, if I obey your wishes as to keeping the thing very quiet before all your neighbours. You don't know how I'm looking forward to Thursday – I have never felt such eagerness before, that I remember. My existence seems to have changed on to entirely new lines. Now, as to that point in your letter which to me is the principal point, as to your doubts as to my future feelings. When you feel ready to make a decision, pray don't hesitate. I feel sure we have both made this a subject of prayer, and, if, after such prayer, you quench your feelings and suppress your promptings, it is certainly a great mistake – a mistake fraught with unfairness to you and misfortune to me. My love for you is not a transient impulse, I am confident. You must believe this. I shall wait until you feel towards me as I feel towards you. But don't ward the feeling off when it does come. I am convinced that to do so would be wrong.

---

17. A novel written by Charles Kingsley in 1853.

On returning from his visit from Callington

1901 26 April Friday afternoon

I must say how much I enjoyed the stay with you. It came quite up to my expectations and they were very great. I can hardly understand my good fortune in securing your regard. My cup is full now but when you decide it will run over. I wonder what Mr Dingle thinks of me? Might I suggest that, although you may not yet feel inclined to alter the heading of your letters, you might alter the ending. I think 'Eva' will be quite sufficient for purposes of identification.

1901 27 April Saturday afternoon

You don't know how much I looked forward to your letter. My anticipations were great but your letter put me in a perfect ecstasy and I've been brimming over with joy ever since. My thoughts are all at Callington and I am sure my heart is. I try to settle down at office to study Snell's *Principles of Equity* and I find myself reading paragraph after paragraph mechanically, whilst I'm thinking of you. The only way to relieve this strain, or to calm this excitement, is for you to decide. You will say 'Decide what?' Well I suppose you would put aside entirely the idea of an engagement – let me then become a recognised – is the word 'Sweetheart' too old fashioned? I am convinced that it was no chance work that brought us together. I wish we could read together – I mean contemporaneously – but that is too long a word to use in a love-letter. Supposing we read 'The Holy Grail' from Tennyson during the next week.[18] I am so excited and happy. Some little time ago I came across a translation of one of Euripides' plays and a phrase that stuck in my memory and which has been recalled by the experiences of the past week is:

'Love is a mixture of the sweetest joys
And torments most severe'

When are you going to drop the cloak and all this clandestinity (this word is patented)? That will be the time when I have to speak to your grandfather. I am glad you are liking Alton Locke.[19] When I was reading Hypatia I was almost every moment, saying to myself, 'How did Eva like this paragraph?' I shall go to the morning service at Wesley tomorrow with a happy heart and a cheerful countenance. I never had so much to be thankful for as I have today. Your great objection is I believe now become very small. Give the matter the essential finish, and with the help of One mightier than ourselves, I will be true to your trust and will prove myself worthy of you.

---

18. 'Holy Grail' was part of Lord Tennyson's epic poem *Idylls of the King* (1885), based on Arthurian legend.
19. A novel written by Charles Kingsley in 1849.

1901 1 May Wednesday am

I am glad you have told your grandfather; I shall also be glad when I have gone through the ordeal of speaking to him. I am looking forward to Friday. I will be at St. Andrew's Cross, opposite the bottom of Old Town Street at 1.30. I shall have three hours and a half in your company; have you all to myself. I am looking forward to it. I think you might be ready to admit the relationship of 'Sweethearts'. There ought to be no objection to that. You end your letters 'with love' and I think you mean what you write. I've been reading parts of 'The Holy Grail'. I rather like these words – I've changed a pronoun or two:

'I wrought into your heart
A way by love that wakened love within
To answer that which came.'

Do you think the quotation applicable? If anyone had told me a few weeks since that I should ever write letters such as I have written lately, I should have laughed at the idea as impossible. It reminds me of the remark of the Lawry's: 'We cannot imagine Eva being in love.' To think that I should have accomplished the miracle.

1901 3 May Friday Evening

What I have now to wish for is that your love should reach that stage that will make you assent to an engagement. I think that, if you wished for it as well, it would come very speedily, don't you? But I want all your love, Eva mine and for that prize will gladly wait; but there is no virtue in waiting longer than necessary is there? How is *Alton Locke* getting on? Have you finished it yet? Or are you so busy that you have no time for reading (this is sarcasm). If I come early next Saturday perhaps we could go to Kit Hill; in pursuance of the agreement entered into at Cambridge. What shall we read together next week? Will *The Courtship of Miles Standish*[20] be suitable? I've never read it through yet, although I've often pecked at it. I must rush off to Class now, and recognising that – 'Every good and every perfect gift is from above'[21] – my Experience should be one of almost inexpressible thankfulness. What I wait for and what I pray for now is that you might soon grow to love me even as I love you.

From 1897 until 1899 Isaac Foot kept a journal detailing activities in his Wesley Methodist Chapel Guild. This contained press cuttings, copies of the guild magazine reports, programmes, various posters and other items. Isaac was the correspondent responsible for reporting the guild's various activities to the area Wesley guild magazine. In the summer of 1898 he reported on the first year of the Guild: 'There is every reason to be satisfied with the results of the experiment ... this first session must be regarded as a feeler or as a "plucking of the grass to see where sits the wind".'

20. A narrative poem (1858) by Henry Wadsworth Longfellow.
21. James 1:17.

YEALMPTON
WESLEYAN CHAPEL.

On Wednesday next, March 8th,
A
TEMPERANCE MEETING

WILL BE HELD IN THE ABOVE CHAPEL.

THE CHAIR WILL BE TAKEN AT 7-30 P.M., BY
Mr. ISAAC FOOT.

THE MEETING WILL BE ADDRESSED BY
Sergt. H. R. HOLCOMBE, R.A.
Mr. H. HAYNES,
Mr. I. FOOT, jun.

A HEARTY WELCOME GIVEN TO ALL.

Collections in aid of Chapel Funds.

JOHN SMITH, PRINTER, PLYMOUTH.

Isaac Foot Junior is to chair a Wesleyan Chapel temperance meeting at Yealmpton in the Plymouth Ebenezer Methodist Circuit.

1901 4 May Saturday morning

I am going to Lee Moor next Monday. Am taking the chair at a Temperance Meeting. I wish you could come with me. I think you would see village Methodism there at its best. We shall get the Chapel packed with working men and their families – fine specimens of manhood many of them are too. The Super. calls it 'Mount Lebanon' and certainly the breezes there are very celestial. I went to Class last night. The leader spoke of 'Purity', and in my testimony I followed up his remarks with a sermonette on:

'His strength was as the strength of ten
Because his heart was pure.'[22]

These words were the keynote of the meeting and we had an inspiring time. I wish I was an author, I think I could write some 'Methodist Idylls'. I owe nearly everything to 'Methodism'. I suppose, if I hadn't been a Methodist, I should never have met you darling! I had reason to love my Church before but what cause I have now. I think that during our united lives and with our united influences, we may do much to help the Church which has done so much for both of us. I am glad you are a Methodist, Eva, dear. Did you have a good Class meeting last night?

---

22. From Tennyson's 'Sir Galahad'.

Saturday afternoon

I've just been looking over my diary and I see that it is exactly a month ago that I saw you first. We went to Cambridge on April 4th. Who would have thought, when I introduced myself that morning, that such momentous issues were to hang on that meeting?

Sunday afternoon

Now for Chapter Two. As to next Saturday – you ask what I'm going to preach about. I don't know myself yet. How would an Exposition of 'Solomon's Song' suit? I hope you won't be disappointed; I must try and forget all about you when I'm preaching. Else I may break down. You don't imagine how much your love means to me. I think of it when I fall asleep and I wake with the memory of it in my mind. Again and again the knowledge that you love me comes to me with such force that I almost jump for joy. I spoke to Father and Janie about our Engagement and told them that the twelve months regulation had fallen through and that the event might come about at any time. Eva! You must agree. I'm sure of your constancy and love whether we are engaged or not but it will make all the difference as to our attitude towards others. I've got to parry with every individual I converse with. Give me permission that when I come down I might have something definite to ask of your Grandfather.

Sunday evening

I've just come back from the evening service and want to finish this letter for post. The day has gone off splendidly. This evening's service has been immense. The Chapel was packed, scores being unable to get inside the doors. I should have liked you to have heard our singing. To hear 900 children and a strong choir singing some vigorous tunes is inspiring to say the least. My throat is almost raw. I have read the first two phases of *Miles Standish* and have enjoyed them greatly. I like the way in which John Alden couldn't get rid of the name of Priscilla – I felt that Longfellow was recording my experience when I read that. My life is becoming Eva-centric. Don't dismiss this as rubbish. Dinsdale Young is preaching at Ebenezer on Sunday week.[23] Wouldn't you like to hear him?

1901 7 May Office Tuesday morning

I went to Lee Moor last evening and we had a capital time. You must come up there one day with me. The choir is almost wholly composed of finely built men with lusty voices and they did pitch in to 'Sound The Battle-Cry'.[24] I'm starting singing lessons again this morning. I like them very much. I think I will bring down one or two songs on Saturday. Shall I?

---

23. Dinsdale Young (1861–1938) was a leading Methodist preacher based at the Methodist Central Hall, London.
24. Words and music by William F Sherwin (1869).

Tuesday afternoon

You certainly have had to bear much sorrow but I believe that it has all tended to beautify your character. As a family we have been peculiarly free from bereavement, and my troubles, although they seem great at times, have been trivial compared with yours. I want to make your life happy and cheerful and if our sorrows are shared they will be so much the lighter. As to your decision on Saturday, between ourselves, I look upon the Engagement as a symbol. In my own heart I am determined to love you as long as you will receive that love, and I am desirous of the Engagement mostly because it will give me a 'locus standi' which otherwise will be wanting. You know that I love you now but I think that love will become stronger and holier as time goes by and I get to know you more. Pray over the matter and you will be guided aright; and don't let my ardour force you to do anything that seems wrong.

Tuesday evening

I've been reading, during the last few days, a few chapters from Carlyle's *French Revolution*.[25] I'm very fond of Carlyle. He expresses my own feelings and thoughts better than any other writer I know. I've a great love for Democracy. 'Blue-blood' and 'Aristocracy' are words I abhor, and when Carlyle says: 'Wouldst thou rather be the peasant who knew that there is a God in Heaven and in Man, or the Duke's Son who only knew there were two and thirty quarters on the family coach,' I feel inclined to cry, 'Go it Thomas.' Oh! I forgot, you have an intense veneration of 'the ancient' haven't you? Then must I desist. However the first forty pages of *The French Revolution* are very fine and very thought provoking. I'm trying to get a sermon up on 'the Kingship of Jesus', but can't make much progress. The subject has attracted me considerably but I can't mould my thoughts on the matter into sermonic symmetry. Can you give me any ideas on the subject? You say you are always wondering what I saw in you to fall in love with. Well! I think that question is almost paradoxical. When a man 'falls' in love he falls. He doesn't choose, select, reject and compare, as Priscilla put it, but he falls because he can't help himself. I think what attracted me was your winsomeness, and, when I spoke to you, it seemed strange to find a girl that was natural.

Tuesday night

I have just come back from autograph collecting and have got about 18/- – which isn't bad considering that everybody wanted me to stay to supper.[26] When the work of the day is over, when something has been attempted, something done, I think of this great joy that has so recently come into my life and that so completely possesses me and, as I kneel beside my bedside, I thank God that he has brought our two lives together. Our joy is increased

25. *The History of the French Revolution* by Thomas Carlyle (1795–1881), published in 1837.
26. Enrolling new members, obtaining their subscriptions to join the Guild.

tenfold when we recognise that our love for each other is not the result of an accident, but a token of God's providence and benediction.

1901 9 May Thursday The Office pm

I'm quite delighted to find that we differ on the question of 'The Aristocracy and blue-blood.' It's quite a change to find that we hold opposite views on one matter at least. But I really didn't think that your Veneration of the Ancient would lead you so far on the path of the illogical. When I read your reference to 'The growing want of respect for those whom God has placed above them' as a sign of the degeneracy of the race, I chuckled mightily. And when you clinched the argument by saying that such a tendency is unbiblical, I chuckled yet the more. Why should I reverence the man who can trace his family back to the Conqueror? My family is as old as his, and probably has been far more useful. But I won't argue the matter here. I will leave that sweetmeat untouched until Saturday. How I am longing for Saturday, it will soon be here now. I am doing half-an-hour's organ practice again, now, every day. During the last 5 or 6 minutes I drop fugues, and exercises and go in for some rousing hymn tunes. I like to pull out every stop, open the swell, couple the manuals and play, say – 'The Foe Behind'. It's congenial to my destructive tastes. I wish I could play properly, the fact is I am too much of a dabbler – a dilettante, I need more stick-ability to succeed. I love fingering the keys of a piano, but I haven't the power to keep at the necessary exercises week after week.

Lady Well

When you say you are struck with 'blank consternation' at my reading forty pages of Carlyle I perceive signs of sarcasm. I think you read a good deal more than I do. I used to read – that is 3 or 4 years ago – a very great deal but since I've been a Guild Secretary and a local preacher, my opportunities for retirement have become very few. When I was in the Civil Service I first received my thirst for reading. I would spend all my pocket money at the bookstall and I think I valued my little library of say 30 or 40 books as much as I value my bigger collection today. I used to walk across the parks to the office in the morning and read as I went and in this way I waded through Green's History[27] and Macaulay's Essays. I would often stop in a secluded part and hold forth to the trees who applauded me with nodding heads and rustling leaves. Ah! Those were innocent days! But I wouldn't go back to them for anything. It was in one sense a waste of time, my going into the Civil Service, but the venture had its compensations. I was in London for 18 months, I learnt to appreciate my home, I learnt the value of money, I came into contact with some of the most subtle forms of scepticism and infidelity, and I learnt to rely on myself far more than I should have done if I had stayed at home.

---

27. John Richard Green (1837–83), *A Short History of the English People* (1874).

If you will give me an opportunity I will speak to your Grandfather early on Saturday afternoon – or perhaps I had better wait until we come back from Kit Hill. I shall be uncomfortable until it's over, and of course, it may happen that I shall be more uncomfortable after. You ask what we shall read together next week. Supposing we try Tennyson's 'In Memoriam' – do you think it too long?[28] I've never been able to understand it yet. Or if you like we will read 'Marmion'[29] or something of Drummond. I've given you all my love, unreservedly and complete and, as you have said, this is the greatest gift and the highest honour I am able to give. I am eager to know your decision. Let 'mercy season justice', don't let prudence have it all her own way. I will be with you early Saturday afternoon. I am literally counting the hours that separate us.

The entry in Isaac Foot's diary for Saturday 11 May

Callington 11.5 train. Splendid ride down by coach. Mr D. met me. Dinner: rode to Kit Hill and walked. Eva said 'Yes'. Glorious time on hilltop. Tea: walk to Frogwell. Spoke to Mr D. Result favourable. This day a red letter day in my history. 'Praise God from whom all blessings flow.'

1901 14 May Tuesday am

How are you after the weekend dear? I did enjoy the visit. I derived as much enjoyment from the ride back as was possible under the circumstances. Mr Rickard was obligingly funny. When he was putting his mailbag into the coach he remarked with a huge smile: 'That's where all the love goes, in here.' He said it quite loud enough for your grandfather to hear, and he quite appreciated the humour of the thrust. Mr Rickard told me that the whole town is interested – nay almost excited – over the matter. Mr Venning asked him if it had come to an engagement yet. Rickard very generously said to me: 'I think the old gentleman is quite agreeable, you know.' I suppose he thought this assuring remark would set at rest many burning fears and tormenting anxieties. I told Father and Mother and Janie, and indeed all the rest, of what we had decided upon. Mother was very humorous over the matter as were my brothers. Janie was surprised and pleased. Father said: 'Well! If you've both made up your minds, alright'. I am sure he was glad to hear the result, although he didn't say very much. I went up to Spear's last night.[30] He was very hearty in his congratulations. Miss Mabel Trehair who was present said: 'But I thought it was all strictly private.' 'Yes,' said Spear, 'so it is, strictly private. In fact there are only six hundred people who know anything whatever about it.' I thought the joke a very good one. I will continue this evening.

---

28. Published in 1850 in memory of his friend Arthur Hallam.
29. 'Marmion', written in 1808 by Sir Walter Scott.
30. Lawrence Spear was also preparing to take his law exams in order to become a solicitor and remained a friend of Isaac Foot's in Plymouth all his life.

Saltash Station and the Royal Albert Railway Bridge over the Tamar in 1900, designed by Isambard Kingdom Brunel and opened in 1859. This was one of the ways Isaac Foot would travel to from Plymouth into Cornwall to see Eva at Callington.

Tuesday evening

I have just returned from the Guild Committee Meeting of the Parliamentary Debating Society. I found a notice awaiting me acquainting me with the fact that I have secured the second place in honours in the Local Preachers' Connexional Examination. Considering that my Intermediate law examinations largely interfered and that the questions were hashed up, I am rather gratified with the result, although of course I should have liked the first place again, because I know it would have pleased you.

1901 16 May The Office Thursday afternoon

I am surprised that you should be so set against ladies taking part in political life. Don't you think Lady Henry Somerset,[31] and a few others like her, would grace and stir the House of Commons? Fie on you Eva! You, you, above all people, you the prospective President of the Callington and District Women's Liberal Association. Well! I'm surprised. I finished 'In Memoriam' this morning. It is fine. I don't understand several parts of it, but I've gathered its meaning on the whole pretty well. Try and finish it this week, dear, then we will reread it in about a month's time. I am glad you are enjoying *Alton Locke*. Why don't you admire Alton? I thought his character on the whole a very fine one. Kingsley makes him very real, doesn't he? I always feel as if I have met him, and that he was a sort of personal friend.

---

31. Lady Henry Somerset (1851–1921), née Isabella Somers Cocks, an English philanthropist and temperance leader.

LOCAL PREACHERS' EXAMINATION, 1900.

EXAMINERS—REVS. JOHN S. BANKS AND GEORGE G. FINDLAY, B.A.

LIST OF SUCCESSFUL CANDIDATES.

Honours Division (Order of Merit).

Foot, Isaac, Plymouth (Ebenezer)

Newsome, F., Sheffield (Brunswick)

Pescott, F., Guernsey

Bates, T. W., Manchester (Droylsden)

Dowsett, George, London (Mostyn-road)

Howard, W. F., North Shields

Leman, E. S., Bristol (King-st.)

Randell, J. H., Plymouth (Ebenezer)

Francis, B. J., Southend and Leigh

Oliver, J. E., Hartlepool and W. Hartlepool

Power, John, Derby (King-street)

Senior, Chas. V., Fareham

Ware, W. F., Exeter

Brookes, W. B., Guisborough and Redcar

Maxfield, W., Doncaster (Oxford-place)

Matthews, Edwin, Chertsey

Summerfield, A. J., Northwich

Parkinson, J. W., B.A., London (Tottenham)

Child, G. B., Batley

Marshall, W., Hull (Great Thornton-street)

Saunders, W., Guernsey

Isaac Foot comes first with honours in the Methodist Local Preachers Connexional Examination in 1900.

1901 20 May Monday morning

I heard Dinsdale Young preach both times yesterday. In the morning he preached on 'The hireling fleeth because he is an hireling'. Character determines conduct. In the evening we had a sermon on 'Radical Religion', the text being the words of Job – 'The root of the matter is found in me'. I wish you had been there dear. He is a fine elocutionist, a clear expositor and eloquent. He draws some wonderful lessons out of a single word. For instance, last night he took the word 'Redeemer' – 'I know that my Redeemer liveth' and he showed that the original word illustrated an old Mosaic institution. It meant a man's nearest relation – his next-of-kin – his 'Goel' – whose duty it was to pay his debts, ransom him from captivity, avenge his death, vindicate his character and reputation. Job fastened on to God the duties and responsibility of the 'Goel'. He used some magnificent language and many a word of stately carriage. I've read about 135 pages of Stopford Brooke,[32] since Saturday. He is wonderfully interesting and he does illuminate the meaning of the *Idylls*. Shall we commence reading them this week? I think we could finish them in a fortnight. I read Augustine Birrell's *Obiter Dictum* on Carlyle, last night.[33] It was refreshing.

Father is greatly taken up with you I think. He said he thought you were 'very sensible'! Sid and Stan haven't said much, and that is decidedly favourable. However much they liked you, they would never say so much to me. It isn't their style. I am glad that everything has been so favourable to my courtship. The barriers have been removed with ease, and our wooing seems to have the favour both of God and our friends. Don't you remember on that Monday evening, just before we entered Goodbody's, saying: 'This must all end now'

---

32. Stopford Brooke (1832–1916), author of several commentaries on English literature.

33. Augustine Birrell (1850–1933), author and politician, wrote *Obiter Dicta* (1884), a volume of essays.

and my answer: 'It must not'? That was on April 15th, on May 11th we became practically engaged!! We do live in stirring times! But, joking aside, I feel unutterably thankful. I have had very numerous congratulations in reference to the L.P. Exam: but it is amusing the way in which people express surprise at my not getting first. The people at Wesley have put me on a sort of pedestal and I am certain that I shall do something one day that will cause the flimsiest structure to give way and I shall come down ignominiously. 'Oh what a fall will be there, my countrymen.'

Monday afternoon

I shall be extremely glad when I have finished my articles for many reasons. Father, of course, made a fairly considerable outlay to make me a lawyer and during the five years of apprenticeship I don't earn a farthing. Consequently I have to come on to Father for everything. My expenses are fairly heavy. I learn singing and playing, I buy many books, I've to contribute to this and to that, I've to subscribe to several societies to which I belong and consequently I'm often 'hard up'. Whenever I ask Father for something 'extra', he gives me what I want willingly and almost gladly but you can understand that I don't like asking him for this because it might make my brothers envious. Therefore I shall be glad to be out of time and earn money that will give me independence.

Monday 10.45 pm

I have just returned from Dinsdale Young's lecture on 'Spurgeon' and want to add a few lines before I despatch this epistle.[34] Young was magnificent tonight – magnificent. It is no use my trying to describe him – especially in a letter. I've been reading some more of *Obiter Dicta* today. I will bring the two volumes down with me on Sunday week. I'm sure you will enjoy the majority of the essays. I have half-an-hour's organ practice every day still and I enjoy the little chink of music in the prosaic-ness of daily life but my life isn't prosaic now, I often think of the vacancy of my life up to a few weeks since. What a difference you have made. I have won – what must be the greatest victory of my life. I have won your love. I am thankful, darling, to God and to you.

1901 24 May Friday 9.30 pm

I came back from the station and, having had tea, settled down to an evening's reading. I took an armchair out on the veranda and calmly, meditatively, read Augustine Birrell's *Essays on Pope and Emerson* and then read a long chapter on 'Principles of the Common Law'. I intend sticking into Law now fairly strong and doing my best to get Honours in my final because I know you will like it. I do like these summer evenings. One is not worried by a deal of Church work and evenings are fairly free. And I always go to sleep with a happy

34. Charles Haddon Spurgeon (1834–92), leading Baptist preacher at the Metropolitan Tabernacle in London.

conscience, when I've done something worth doing. As I sat on the veranda tonight looking out on the sea, I thought how much I had to be thankful for. Well clothed, well housed,
well familied, with your love assured and the inclination to thank God for it all. The only
dash of bitterness is the misery of so many around.

'Never morning wore to evening
But some heart did break'[35]

I'm rather surprised at your not liking 'Gareth' much. I think it is exhilarating, and the
teaching is very fine. Perhaps you would appreciate it more if you had Stopford Brooke's
second volume. I will bring it down on Saturday. Just think of it! Becoming engaged! I've
often thought of these things and guessed the future, but little did I think that my die
would so soon be cast. There is certainly a good deal of romance in our courtship, don't
you think so?

Saturday afternoon
I finished 'Geraint and Enid' this morning. There are some fine passages in the poem
– I like the way in which Tennyson squeezes so much into a line:

'And watched the sun blaze on the turning scythe.'
'And now the wine made summer in his veins.'
'A noise as of a broad brook o'er a shingly bed brawling.'

I expect it will take us another fortnight to finish the *Idylls* won't it? Of course we've
read the 'Holy Grail'. We shall be quite Tennysonians before we've finished. I am at
Horrabridge tomorrow morning and am rather looking forward to it. I expect the congregation will largely consist of distant relatives. In the morning I shall preach on 'Spying out
the Promised Land'.[36] And I think I shall venture to take 'The Kingship of Christ' in the
evening. You can never tell what a subject is like until you have tried it. I'm going to get my
sermons ready for tomorrow now.

1901 28 May Tuesday The Office 1.45 pm
I went to Horrabridge on Sunday and had a good day – especially in the evening. I
prayed for freedom of utterance and got it. I had a large number of visitors from Plymouth
at both services. Yesterday we had a fine time on the Guild Outing. My mind was harassed
on the Sunday and Monday morning by the prospects of rain. If it rains it means we lose
our numbers at tea, I have to make it up accordingly. However we went out and had glorious weather. I went out with a smaller group by the twenty-to-nine train and had dinner

---

35. Tennyson, 'In Memoriam'.
36. Numbers 13.

picnic style. We climbed the Dewerstone in the afternoon. There were about 70 of us altogether. You would have enjoyed it sweetheart. The Dewerstone is a splendid hill, far prettier than Kit Hill – but with no historic associations – and the little grassy walks, sylvan glades and sequestered nooks by the riverside are simply entrancing.

4.30 pm

So you have got through *The Trumpet Major*. Neither do I like it as well as most of Hardy's novels but there is an originality and vividness of perception and description about him that make all his novels intensely interesting to me. There are only a few days between now and Saturday.

Tuesday evening 8.30 pm

Mr Herbert asked me this evening if I intended going in for the L.P. exam of next year. I said 'No' because my law work would command all my attention. But he, not knowing the reason, hinted that with new responsibilities some irons would have to be taken out of the fire. I soon disillusioned him however by telling him that you were a Sunday School teacher, a Class leader and a Guild Secretary and that therefore your influence would be likely to make me a more earnest worker in the Church than ever. Darling, before next Tuesday this time we shall be engaged. 'My cup runneth over.'[37] I don't envy anybody, not the wealthiest, cleverest man on earth – that is I wouldn't change positions.

1901 29 May Wednesday 10 pm

When I spoke in my letter about hardly any right to be happy – of course I was writing merely of a passing thought which came to me whilst I was feeling so joyful myself. Of course I think happiness is not only a privilege, but almost a duty, but still one feels too often a disinclination 'to weep with them that weep'. I am greatly edified by your views on the marriage question. You have expressed my latent thoughts. I quite agree with you that most marriages are failures. I've met very few married couples who have realized the ideal of their courtship. Darling, we must be an exception, we must. I believe, if we are always frank with each other and exercise the common sense with which I feel you are gifted in no ordinary measure and of which I think I have a fair share, we shall do this. I don't think business ambitions will becloud my love ideal. I would infinitely rather realise the supreme happiness of wedded love than be a famous lawyer with a joyless hearth. It's just striking eleven, and I'm as sleepy as possible. I am longing intensely for Saturday to come. Are we going on Kit Hill? I don't think it will be too hot to go up there in the afternoon, will it dear? Darling, you are everything to me.

---

37. Psalms 23:5.

On Saturday 1 June 1901, Eva and Isaac walked from Callington up to Kit Hill above the town and she agreed that their engagement should be made public. Isaac continued to write letters giving full details of his life day by day. He travelled to Callington to see her whenever possible.

3 1902 Isaac Foot's London letters to Eva

Between June and November 1902 Isaac was in London on an intensive revision course for his final law exams to be taken in November. He stayed in Wandsworth with his elder sister, Janie, and her husband, Jim Nash. Here, when he had time, he took every opportunity to hear the sermons of the leading Free Church preachers – Baptists and Congregationalists, as well as the leading Wesleyan Methodists. He attended concerts and the theatre. Later he recalled this time, when he attended the Promenade Concerts in London: 'When reading for my Final, my weekly relief and entertainment was at the Queen's Hall at the Saturday night concerts, conducted by Henry Wood; this experience was unforgettable.'

He continued to write regularly to Eva in Callington. The following is a selection of his letters.

1902 7 June Saturday

The dirty, beastly, blasted, sickening, damnable drizzle has at last shewed signs of cessation and I have made up my mind to go about for an hour or so. I was so glad, dearie, to get your letter this morning. I went out last night for a little while. It was pouring yesterday during the whole walk and the Common was practically deserted. I scorned to take an umbrella and found the soaking rain was quite congenial to my feelings. The Classes begin on Monday at 10. I see Forbes-Robertson is giving six *Hamlet* matinees at the Lyric.[38] I must go if I can. Well, dearie, I will stop now and after another half an hour's 'Bankruptcy' will go out to see the golden streets! Au Revoir.

Sunday 8.55 pm

This morning I went with Janie and heard J. B. Cowl. He gave a splendid address to the children on the words 'Nevertheless Afterwards' from Hebrews XII. And a good sermon on 'Christ's Compassion on the Multitude'. I had a walk on the Common this afternoon. I went to hear E. F. Benson B.A. at Broomwood Church – Clapham Circuit. He preached on the man who wanted to say farewell to his friends before following Christ – putting hand to the plough. It was a splendid sermon: the Chapel was crowded and there were several conversions. The singing was swingified and the tunes were such that I could pitch into. In spite of these good sermons, I have felt it, dearie, being away from you. I don't like to let my mind dwell on it or I should get the hump in an advanced stage but it does take the savour out of the day.

---

38. Sir Johnston Forbes-Robertson (1853–1937), leading English actor and manager.

1902 13 June Friday

I've been to Class this morning and don't go again until Monday. I have to be at Chancery Lane by 10. I am aroused at 7 and read the paper in bed besides revising my Class work, in the same position. I have breakfast at 8.15 and leave the house at 20 to 9, having to catch a train at Clapham Junction at 9.5. Class finishes about ¹/₄ to 12 and I catch the 12.15 or 12.32 from Waterloo home again, getting back about 1.10. I read all the afternoon and evening – if possible on the Common. I went to this political meeting at Battersea Town Hall last night and by going early had a capital seat, third row from front. Subject – Education Bill and Corn Tax. Speakers: Lloyd George, John Burns, and others.[39] It was a good meeting. L.G. is a very fine speaker who has a conscience. The Classes are exceedingly enjoyable: both Gibson and Weldon are nice fellows and splendid tutors. They are very funny at times and are able to put the most important facts in skittish language which is very attractive. I must to my books now, dearie, Snell's *Equity*!!

1902 16 June Monday 6.50 pm

I am going out on the Common to put in a few hours study, but must start my letter to you first. In the evening Piper and I went to Balham Congregational Church and heard Rev. Griffiths-Jones B.A. It was a beautiful service and a masterly sermon on Jeremiah V.1. The subject was true manhood and his three main lessons were: Be true to yourself – with remarks on individuality; Be true to others; Be true to God. We greatly enjoyed it and I shall go to hear him again when I have an opportunity. I went to Class this morning and we had some difficult chapters in *Equity* dealt with. On Thursday I am intending to go to the great City Temple Service – Preacher, Dr R. F. Horton. I do feel it, darling, being away from you: it's a good thing I have my mind occupied.

1902 27 June Friday 8.30 pm

Well! To begin. The theatre we went to on Saturday was the Duke of York's, the play being *The Gay Lord Quex*.[40] The comedy was very clever and John Hare acted splendidly. You would have enjoyed it, had you been there, dearie. We've had three Classes this week – Monday, Tuesday, Wednesday.

1902 8 July Tuesday 7 pm

I have just a few minutes I can spare for my letter to you. I went up listening to the band in Hyde Park on Saturday evening and Sunday afternoon. I heard Sylvester Horne, of

39. John Burns (1858-1943) was a prominent socialist London politician. The Education Bill introduced by Arthur Balfour in 1902 was to set up school boards to control all schools. It was fiercely opposed by Nonconformists as it meant they had to contribute to the funding of Church of England schools through the rates and there were areas where there were no alternative schools for their children to attend. 'Corn Tax' refers to the issue of free trade.
40. A comedy written in 1900 by Arthur Wing Pinero (1855–1934). Sir John Hare (1844–1921) created the title role.

Kensington, in morning – he is a Congregationalist, aged about 33 – and a beautiful preacher. His text was: 'Ye believe in God: believe also in Me.'[41] It was a powerfully argued sermon. He has a musical tenor voice and can swell out into a mighty shout.

1902 12 July Saturday 12.55

I've been keeping very respectable hours this week and have been in every evening before 10 – except when I went to see *Charley's Aunt*.[42] On Wednesday I went up to the City in the afternoon – at least about 5 o'clock – and bought three of Phillips Oppenheim's novels which bear the respectable titles of – *Mysterious Mr Sabin, A Monk of Cruta, A Daughter of the Marionis*.[43] I have already devoured the two latter, and have had difficulty in restraining myself from commencing the first. They are very, very interesting. If you like I will send them on. I couldn't help laughing yesterday. We were having tea in the garden when Jim bitterly regretted that we had no cream wherewith to enhance the attractiveness of the apple tart, and Janie remarked that she was rather surprised that I had had no Cornish cream sent up. Of course, as you know, I don't mention this incident with any ulterior motives; in fact I shouldn't have mentioned it, but I know that you are acquainted with my entire absence of guile.

I had another letter from Father yesterday. He seemed to have felt it about my smoking, more than I should have expected. He said if I had failed in my exam he shouldn't have felt it half so much. I haven't smoked since Monday and suppose I shan't for some time. It's jolly hard, tho': it shews how a man – open-minded and reasonable in other respects – may nurse a prejudice until it grips him more strongly than does the habit which he denounces in others. I'm going to the Promenade Concert at the Queen's Hall tonight and, if I can manage it, on Thursday next, I'm going to Covent Garden to see the opera *Maritana*[44] – Madame Fanny Moody's party. I shan't be able to go, however, unless Father sends me my sub. – in the heat of the smoking controversy he's forgotten all about my allowance. Oh! How I long to be earning my own money!

1902 18 July Friday 3 pm

I went to hear Forbes-Robertson on Tuesday. I intended to sit in the gallery as is my wont but after having taken my place in the queue for 20 minutes, I found that I was in the pit crowd instead. It was too late to change, so I had to plonk down 2/6, a calamity which put me in a bad humour for the play. I say, though, wasn't it fine? I couldn't catch what was said very easily but the stage effect was very magnificent. Ophelia wasn't up to the mark, she was alright, but not stately and enticing enough for a prince – she acted very

41. John 14:1.
42. A comedy by Brandon Thomas (1850 1914).
43. Edward Phillips Oppenheim (1866–1946) was a novelist and short story writer.
44. An opera by the Irish composer William Vincent Wallace (1812–65).

prettily however, especially in her madness. What a mind that fellow Shakespeare had! I must go and see *The Merry Wives of Windsor* at His Majesty's. Beerbohm Tree as Falstaff is very fine they say.

11.25 pm

Just a few lines before going to bed. This evening I have been to a meeting of the Irish Land League held in the Battersea Town Hall.[45] John Dillon was advertised to speak, but failed to turn up. It was a fine meeting however. P. J. Power, M.P. for Mayo, Alderman Joyce, M.P. for Limerick and Willie Redmond were the speakers. I greatly enjoyed the fun and was glad to have the opportunity of listening to these men. They are glorious patriots, and are entirely misunderstood by the English people. I intended preparing some sermons whilst I was up here, but it seems as if the Gospel is entirely buried by the Law. However November is drawing near, and whilst I abhor its approach because of the ordeal it brings with it, yet I welcome its coming, because it means getting back to you, dearie, it means earning my own bread and it means getting nearer the day when we shall start off to Switzerland and Italy as man and wife!!

1902 23 July Wednesday

I have just a few minutes to spare before dinner, having just come home from Class as tired as a dog. On Sunday I heard Dr Clifford at night. He is a magnificent preacher and I think the most eloquent man I've ever heard. When living at Bayswater, I used to hear him very often. I had a letter from Father yesterday enclosing a sovereign. It was very welcome I can assure you, as I had been reduced to the magnificent sum of thirteen pence. I am getting to feel that having been born a man, I am going to die a lawyer. I never read anything but law now, except the newspaper: and the reading of Tennyson or a novel seems a ridiculous waste of time and energy. I feel the want of a piano very much and haven't sung a song for I don't know how long.

1902 26 July Saturday

I see by this morning's paper that England is whacking Australia and the news has made me feel quite joyful. I shan't go to Her Majesty's today after all, as I have some class notes to enter; but I mean to go to Hyde Park tonight and listen to the band.

1902 2 August Saturday

It isn't a bad morning and I'm taking books on the Common directly. Watteau!! Beet returned to Richmond!! A glorious triumph for broadmindedness, tolerance and fair play!

---

45. The Irish National Land League was formed in 1879 to help Irish tenant farmers own the land they worked on.

It's almost as good as Leeds isn't it?[46] I think Rosebery's speech on Thursday was a howler, to put down the victory as one for the Liberal League is puerile and foolish.[47] I'm afraid, unless he begins to do something, he will lose his opportunity and he will lose the sympathy of the people and will degenerate into a mere 'picturesque figure.' I bought two sixpenny novels sometime ago – *Sappho* by Alphonse Daudet and *The Massarenes* by Ouida.[48] *The M.* is alright but Sappho is hardly a proper book for prim young lady Sunday school teachers to read. Howe ver I will send them on if you like. I'm going to finish wo rk today at 7 and then am going to Hyde Park where the Coldstream Guards are responsible for the music.

1902 9 August Saturday 12 o'clock

I was reading hard till teatime yesterday and then went up to the City and saw *The Merry Wives of Windsor* at His Majesty's. The doors opened at 8, performance at 8.30, I took up my stand in the gallery queue at 7.15 but didn't get a seat after all. The house was packed in every part, in fact it has been so all along, and last night was the last performance. I got very tired standing so long and could hear and see very indifferently. Consequently I didn't enjoy it to the full. However I'm glad I went. Tree was very good as Falstaff and Miss Ellen Terry and Miss Kendall were fine as Mistress Page and Ford. Tree made a speech after the play which was received with great enthusiasm.

I get on capitally with Janie and of course Jim's alright. But he's rather inclined to think that he's right and that isn't so certain about other people. I don't say anything against the Pentecostal League,[49] but I'm inclined to think that it tends to produce in some natures a sort of religious pride and exclusiveness. Holiness becomes a sort of a mania, and anything outside the exclusively religious circle e.g. politics, music, art, civic legislation, literature is let severely alone. I feel as if I want to preach on the words 'God – who has given us richly, all things to enjoy'.[50] Jim went for me, ve ry strongly about smoking a couple nights since, and spoke about sacrifice and the narrow path. However I told him that there was just as much danger – and perhaps more – in making the path narrower than God intended as in making it wider. I twitted him upon his resolve to have no pictures in his house, except religious scenes. In fact we had a warm discussion but, of course, we are on the best of terms. It seems to me that the P.L. owes too much towards producing amiable and well-meaning monomaniacs. I suppose the Coronating is now in full swing.[51] I've been at my Conveyancing all the morning and shall be all the afternoon but I hope to go up to town this evening to see the illuminations – that is if Jim will let me!

46. Reference to a Liberal victory in a by-election in Leeds and a Labour gain in Richmond.
47. Lord Rosebery (1847–1929), a former Prime Minister (1874–6) and leader of the Liberal Party, was now opposed to some Liberal policies. He was president of the Liberal League, founded in 1902.
48. Alphonse Daudet (1840–97) was a French novelist. He wrote *Sappho* in 1884. Ouida is the pseudonym of the Anglo-French novelist Maria Louise Ramé (1839–1908). She wrote *The Massarenes* in 1897.
49. The Pentecostal League of Prayer, an evangelist movement founded in 1891 to which Jim and Janie Nash belonged.
50. 1 Timothy 6:17.
51. A reference to the celebrations for the coronation of King Edward VII.

1902 12 August Tuesday 11 pm

I had a good time on Saturday night; I put aside my Conveyancing before tea and after tea went up to the City. There were dense crowds in the streets but the folk were very good humoured and I put aside all restraint and had a rare old beano! I sang 'Rule Britannia' with the crowds till I was hoarse. I was covered with confetti by charming ladies who were doubtless struck by my attractions and my blue miner's suit. We went up to Whitehall to the accompaniment of a song which ended like this:

'Oh I say!
A little bit here, a little bit there
The Union Jack is Everywhere
We haven't got all S. Africa yet
But, we're getting it by degrees.'

I reached home dead tired about 11.15 – which, I consider, was excellent time. I expect you think I'm a pretty fine specimen of a young lawyer and local preacher withal – but I've one extenuating plea to make – I left the girls severely alone!

I bought *Tatterly*[52] by Tom Gallon this morning but haven't started it yet. I've felt keen on novel reading lately; I've wished more than once that I had brought my Tennyson or Browning. I'm afraid the poetic and aesthetic side of my nature is being seriously neglected.

Wednesday 6 pm

I intended finishing my letter before this but this morning I made up my mind to see the Test Match between England and Australia at the Oval. I took my Student's Conveyancing with me and have been there all day. The match was fearfully exciting and exceedingly interesting. England won by the narrow margin of a wicket. I am hoarse with shouting. I have enjoyed the day, but I question whether it has done me much good as the excitement has given me a headache.

1902 20 August Wednesday 12.10

On Sunday I heard two Congregational ministers, one at Wandsworth and the other at Balham. Rev. Treffry of Southsea in the morning preached a very beautiful sermon on 'He calleth his sheep by name and leadeth them out'. The evening preacher was fair on 'He giveth his beloved sleep'. Coming home across Clapham Common at night I found an atheistic meeting assembled. I listened to their rotten ignorant arguments for a while and then threw down the glove. Watteau! From about 8.45 to 10.15 I withstood some of them and brought a large part of the crowd round to agreeing with me. I had them on point

---

52. Tom Gallon (1866–1914) was an English writer. *Tatterley*, his first novel, was published in 1897.

after point, the more reasonable part of the crowd were delighted and pressed me to come round again. I felt in good form, kept my temper, gracefully evaded points I couldn't explain, forced home almost with vehemence the points on which I had them and spoke of Darwin, Hurley, Kelvin and others as if I knew their writings from end to end. One young fellow – a well-dressed and seemingly well-educated fellow– walked all the way home with me and urged me to go up again next Sunday. It was a delightful tussle, did me no harm, might have done some great good and certainly brought discomfort to the enemy.

1902 27 August Wednesday

I went to the Queen's Hall Concert last Saturday. The orchestra there is a very celebrated one – it numbers nearly 100 – concerts are given every night for 11 weeks. The music was very, very fine, the Overtures to *Tannhäuser* and *Carmen* were enough to make one squirm. Tickets for the Promenade are 1/- each, and, as the affair lasts from 8 till 11, it becomes very tiring to stand all the time. On Sunday morning Jim spoke about the Concert and said that to be able to spend a whole evening at such a place argued a very poor standard of Christian Experience. We had a delightful argument. I asked Jim the conundrum 'When is a man only half a man? – When he's a member of the Pentecostal League'. If I ever join the League or become a devotee of their crabbed, niggardly teachings, let my right hand forget its cunning

AT THE OVAL IN 1902

TO THE EDITOR OF THE TIMES
Sir,—In your leading article of yesterday you refer to the "loyal supporters of past glory." As one of those may I recall another day at the Oval on August 13, 1902, when many of us saw the last innings in the fifth Test match with Australia ? Australia, batting first, had scored 324 and 121. England, having scored 183 in the first innings, needed 263 to win. MacLaren made two (no 400-odd that day, alas!), Palairet was out for six, Tyldesley made nothing, Hayward seven, and Braund two. The gloom at the Oval was only slightly removed by Jackson's 49.
It was then that Gilbert Jessop came to the wicket. His was not so much an innings as a hurricane. He hit 104 runs and he did it in 75 minutes. We youngsters held our breath and old men wept for joy. After Jessop's departure Lockwood made two and Lilley 16. But Hirst was still there, and there he remained until he was joined by the last man in, Rhodes. Hirst was not out for 58, Rhodes was not out for six. Their singles could be counted by our heart-beats. With the last single from Rhodes England won by one wicket. Let all praise be given to Hutton and his merry men, but, Sir, *Vixere fortes ante Agamemnona multi.*
Your obedient servant, ISAAC FOOT.
Pencrebar, Callington, Cornwall, Aug. 21.

Isaac Foot's letter to the editor of the Times in 1952, describing the test match between England and Australia which he had watched and described to Eva on 12 August 1902.

and my tongue cleave to the roof of my mouth. I say dear, the latter would be a calamity, wouldn't it? Of course, Jim and I are on the best of terms but on these matters we are hopelessly irreconcilable. On Sunday I went to the Balham Congregational Church in the morning and I heard Watkinson at the City Temple in the evening. I'm reading one of W. Pett Ridge's books now – *A Son of the State*.[53] It is rather cleverly written and shews a good knowledge of London life but seems rather dull after Phillips Oppenheim's blood-curdlers.[54]

1902 30 August Saturday 12.15

On Thursday evening I went to Covent Garden and heard *Maritana.* I think it was the finest thing I've heard in my life. Madame Fanny Moody has a voice as sweet, clear and pleasing as a lark's. The tenor, John Coates, however, was even more attractive to me, his voice was perfect. He sang 'Let Me like a Soldier Fall' so magnificently, that I wanted to lie down and curl my legs round my neck. The chorus was splendidly trained, the scenery was gorgeous, and the dresses very pretty. To look at a gypsy party of about a hundred dressed in glowing Spanish costumes, in a romantic Spanish market square and hear them sing like angels was indescribable – there was one great drawback to the whole performance – your absence. All the time, dearie, I was wishing that you could have been there enjoying it too – 'In Happy Moments Day by Day,' 'Scenes That Are Brightest', 'There Is a Flower That Bloometh', 'Hear Me, Gentle Maritana' were some of the solos that brought down the house.

I'm glad you agree with me about Jim's views. Of course, Jim does not know what you think of these things. I'm glad you're so reasonable, dearie. I had another argument with him yesterday. I had been reading a little of Milton; and I extolled to him the beauties of 'L'Allegro' and 'Il Penseroso'. He said he hadn't time to study and appreciate the Scriptures thoroughly; and that, consequently he had no time to waste on Milton. Just fancy, shutting out Milton, Tennyson, Browning, Longfellow. Jim is certainly one of the sincerest men I ever met; but, all the same, I wouldn't be like him for anything. I'm quite certain that, if he knew I went to the Opera on Thursday, or that you went to see *Hamlet* at Sheffield, he would think it was necessary that we should go to the penitent form. A man may become so absorbed a religionist, that he may degenerate into a monomaniac.

1902 21 September Sunday 9.30 pm

We went to the Wesleyan Church this morning and heard Rev. J. Critchinson on 'The Miracle at Cana'.[55] He was fairly good although he has a strange style of delivery. This afternoon we walked to Wimbledon Common about four miles away and this evening we went to hear Griffith Jones at Balham Congregational Church. He preached a magnificent sermon on 'The Dignity of Jesus'. You would have enjoyed it dearie, had you been there. I did

53. William Pett Ridge (1860-1930) wrote *A Son of the State* in 1899.
54. E. Phillips Oppenheim (1886-1946), a popular short story and thriller writer.
55. John 2: 1-11. The miracle of Jesus turning water into wine.

wish you could have been. I was struck with a text last night – 'Bow down thine Ear and hear the words of the wise'.[56] Will you give me your thoughts on it dearie?

1902 25 September Thursday 9 pm

Jim and I do argue in spite of all Mother's and Janie's efforts to stop us. We had yesterday a great discussion on Pentecostal bonnets![57] I referred to the model woman described in the last chapter of Proverbs who clothed herself in silk and purple – a becoming and attractive dress. It was a duty with all women to dress as attractively as their position allowed. All this is good practice for me as I am learning to split hairs with remarkable precision. I don't know exactly what day I shall come home. Most probably on November 8th Saturday. The exam days are the 3rd and 4th, 6th and 7th. I shall spend the 8th, 9th and 10th at Callington and the following weekend you will spend at Plymouth, won't you, dearie? I thought on my text – 'Bow down thine Ear and hear the words of the wise' – the first clause betokens attentiveness and humility – getting off one's pedestal so to speak. Then again 'Bow down thine Ear and hear'. The importance of hearing the best: we hear so much that's unimportant and secondary and worthless: our faculties should be employed for the highest purposes: hear more to speak less. Do you see what I mean? I'm counting the days now dearie. My study often gives me a horrible hump now: I've got to stick at it all my time and it gets so monotonous.

1902 30 September Tuesday

We had a fine discussion at the tea table tonight. Mr Thomas declared it as his opinion that General Booth is a greater man than was John Wesley. However, before we finished, he was prostrate. I don't think you had better put me down dearie on your next winter's Program; as soon as I have time I'm going to get up a lecture on Gladstone and John Hampden,[58] but I don't think I shall have it in shape until next session. I intend to do some all-round reading when I'm through – my appetite is very keen for it. Two of the first books I intend to get through are Motley's *Rise of the Dutch Republic* and the recently published life of the late Lord Chief Justice – *Russell of Killowen*. I want to talk with you about my reading program. I'm afraid, if my general reading fails, I shall not prove much of a preacher.

I'm thinking now on a good subject for a sermon – 'Felix'.[59] I should deal incidentally with 'Tertullus the orator' – his character rather fascinates one as a study. Then again, contrast the defence of Paul with Tertullus' oratory. The one tackled the ear and pleased the intellectual palate, the other gripped the conscience and stirred the convictions:

---

56. Proverbs 22:17.
57. A reference to the bonnets worn by women who belonged to the Penetcostal League of Prayer, a fundamental evangelical movement founded within the Methodist Church in 1891, to which Jim and Janie Nash belonged.
58. John Hampden (1594–1643), a cousin of Oliver Cromwell, played a leading role in the English Civil War.
59. Felix was one of the Roman governors of Judea. The apostle Paul was brought before him for trial. Tertullus was employed to accuse Paul before Felix.

Tertullus was an orator, Paul was a man of eloquence. Paul 'reasoned': his sermon to Felix was personal: he spoke of righteousness i.e. justice – to a corrupt governor and of temperance – to a man living in open idolatry to an unjust judge of a judgment to come. 'Felix was terrified' – the majesty of conscience: compare Elijah the man of integrity fronting the people unanimously dumb in the sense of their guilt and faithfulness. 'Felix's opportunity' – one of the three New Testament characters who almost did a great thing: Pilate–Agrippa– Felix. I think I shall be able to make a good sermon out of these and other thoughts with those you will suggest.

1902 4 October Saturday Morning 11 am

Tomorrow Alf Gilbert is coming to tea and we are going to track off to hear the immortal Clifford whose subject, I see, is to be 'Passive resistance: Is it just and wise?'[60] It is Citizen Sunday tomorrow and the worthy Doctor will be in his element and will mop the floor of Westbourne Park Chapel with Balfour, Cecil and Co. Well, dearie, goodbye: another five Saturdays and I shall be with you again. I hardly dare to anticipate.

1902 6 October Monday 7.30 pm

I had a letter from Father on Saturday evening. He's had a long talk with Skardon and Phillips and the latter is suggesting that I should join the firm. I don't know of course what the conditions would be but they have to be very favourable and liberal as I am fond of my own freedom. A partnership of course has great advantages especially to a young fellow starting but there are decidedly two sides to the question. If it is referred to again I shall decline the offer. I'm sure it won't be satisfactory and whilst a junior partnership has its present advantages, it limits a man's scope, success and individuality. I would be satisfied with a much smaller salary if I had the sense of being my own master. What do you think, dearie: for after all you are the person to be considered. I must to Equity. Goodnight dearie.

Tuesday afternoon 2.15

I am very sorry to read your views of the passive resistance resolve on the part of the Free Churches. I am afraid that you are not very staunch in your Free Church principles. 'Absurd, mean and contemptible' are strong words to use but, if they are to be used at all, they should be applied to the reputed descendants of Puritans and Dissenters who are prepared to pay to support the schools of a grasping, greedy, arrogant and largely corrupted church in which are taught the children of the nation. If your words are justifiable then Bunyan, Hampden, Fox and the Seven Bishops and Luther were all 'mean and contemptible'. I am afraid, dearie, your descent from William Wallace does not show itself in

---

60. Dr John Clifford (1826-1923), a leading Baptist preacher, led the 'passive resistance' movement to the 1902 Education Act, by refusing to pay the part of the rates allocated to education.

your present attitude. I am quite certain that, if I become a ratepayer before this Bill is over-thrown, I shall not pay it and shall be glad to get the privilege of refusing to do so. I quite agree with you that some great Educational measure is necessary, but the present Bill is a remedy worse than the Evil itself. However, don't let us dwell on this point of contention. Your reference to the Education Bill has quite depressed me today. Well! I have tons of reading to do before I go to bed tonight – or rather tomorrow morning. Write soon, dearie, but please don't say anything more about the Education Bill, there's a good girl. We went to Westbourne Park Chapel in the evening and heard Clifford. He was immense.

1902 16 October Thursday 4 pm

What do you think of the Irish members last night? It's simply disgusting to see the way in which they are being treated; if Fenian Societies were established again all over the country I would join them like a shot. We refuse these men self-government and then, when they are practically compelled to come over here, we expect them to treat our Assembly with reverence and respect! If you wrongfully throw a man into gaol you can't blame him for scratching paint off the door!!

1902 21 October Tuesday 2.30 p.m.

I have had 3 or 4 letters from Father since last I wrote you. He has secured my offices, not those I spoke to you of, but better ones – immediately opposite Spooner's Corner, two doors from the bottom of Old Town Street. Four decent rooms in the front first floor, over Collier's Wine Offices, £60 a year. More money than I intended but still worth it. The posi-tion, in my opinion, could hardly be beaten in the town. Father is giving me a suit so I have spent 50/- of your money in getting an overcoat. With the two garments I ought to look resplendent, didn't I?

1902 25 October Saturday 10 p.m.

I'm joyful to think I have only one such week more to go through. These past couple days I've been suffering from the chronic hump. Wherever I go I see LAW. My thoughts are all of LAW. I can understand the Ancient Mariner who went mad to see 'Water, Water Everywhere!!' It isn't so much the work I am putting in, but the sickening sameness and awful monotony. If I were sitting for a degree – B.A. for instance, there would be several and diverse subjects to study – taxing different parts of the brain but I'm fastened down to one topic – LAW, LAW, LAW. For the time being I'm a monomaniac. I hope when you see me next I shall be clothed in my right mind. The Devonport result knocked me silly. It's too awful to contemplate. Even the *Times* and the *St. James Gazette* speak harshly of Lockie because of his corrupt tactics – all through the contest Lockie has appeared to the people the 'bread and butter' politician and has referred to the Education Bill as a 'red

Spooner's Corner in 1902, a popular meeting place in Plymouth, at the at the junction of Old Town Street and Bedford Street.

herring' drawn across the trail.[61] I'm going to Bayswater tomorrow. On Sundays I must go somewhere and with those where I and with whom I can be so occupied to forget, if possible, the horrible demon LAW who dogs my steps, laughs horribly in my ear and even disturbs my slumber. I haven't been to bed before one any night this week: I think that is a noble record.

1902 4 November Tuesday 9.30 pm

Well! The Exam is over and the result is very disappointing. The questions were on outside points, unusual and unlikely and such as did not test a candidate's real knowledge. I hope I have passed but there is a great, very great possibility that I haven't. All the fellows I have spoken to are simply disgusted.

1902 13 November Thursday 11 a.m.

I haven't had much time to myself since last I wrote and it isn't more than a few hours before I shall see you, so it will not be necessary for me to write a long letter, will it? I am greatly enjoying these few days of sight seeing. Now for the record of my doings. On Friday night, after the Exam, Pearce and I went into a restaurant and had a good feed and then

---

61. John Lockie won a by-election in Devonport on 22 October 1902.

Isaac and Eva's wedding at West End Methodist Chapel, Callington on 22 September 1904. Her bridesmaids were the two daughters of Isaac's eldest brother, Alfred. Isaac's best man, to the right, is his friend Lawrence Spear.

went and saw *A Chinese Honeymoon* – a sort of comic opera after the style of the Geisha that has had a remarkable run – it was indescribably funny and we did enjoy it.[62] I came back and went to the last Concert at Queen's Hall with Williams. There was no room in the Promenade so we had to sit in the 3/- seats – it was a magnificent concert – Williams was transfixed with ecstasy. I went to Law Courts again on Tuesday and spent the afternoon and evening in the House of Commons. It was a full dress debate. I heard Lloyd George, Trevelyan, Chamberlain, Asquith and many others. Tomorrow I shall come down by the G.W.R. – I expect I had better come down by the 5 to 7 train on Saturday. It will be a glorious Saturday. Now, dearie, will you let me stay down with you until the following Friday I wonder. If so, I will have the result sent on to Callington – it comes out on that Friday. If I fail I'm coming right back to London. I can't stay down there to face all my friends. Last night Williams and I went to the big Queen's Hall Concert *Messiah* and had a good time.

---

62. *A Chinese Honeymoon*, by George Dance and with music by Howard Talbot, ran at the Strand Theatre for more than 1,000 performances between 1901 and 1904.

Isaac Foot passed his final law exams and was admitted to the Roll of Solicitors in December 1902. He returned to Plymouth and set up his own practice as Isaac Foot, Solicitor and Notary Public at Old Town Chambers, Old Town Street with financial assistance from his father. In 1908 he joined with Edgar Bowden to form Foot and Bowden. Over the following years he built up a large and successful practice to provide the financial resources to set up their first home. In the absence of any close family, Eva had to make arrangements for the care of her elderly grandfather. It was not until September 1904 that they were able to marry in Callington's West End Methodist Chapel.

4 The Foot family at home: -
1 Lipson Terrace, Ramsland and Pencrebar.

Isaac and Eva were living at 1 Lipson Terrace, Plymouth, when their first son, Dingle Mackintosh – named after his grandfathers – was born in 1905. Here four more of their seven children were born: Hugh Mackintosh, known as 'Mac' in the family, in 1907; John Mackintosh in 1909; Margaret Elizabeth, known as Sally, in 1911; and Michael Mackintosh in 1913.

1 Lipson Terrace, the first family home of Isaac and Eva Foot, opposite Freedom Fields in Plymouth, the scene of the Sabbath Day Battle in the Civil War.

The Foot family in the garden of 1 Lipson Terrace with Harry Lauder, the Scottish singer and entertainer, sitting to the left of Isaac. The younger Foot children are (left to right) Christopher, Jennifer, Michael and Sally.

Dingle, John and Mac, the three eldest sons of Isaac and Eva Foot.

During and after the First World War the family lived at Ramsland, near St Cleer in Cornwall, on the edge of Bodmin Moor. The two youngest Foot children were born here – their second daughter, Jennifer Mackintosh, in 1916 and their youngest son, Christopher Isaac, in 1918.

Isaac continued to build up his solicitor's practice, travelling by train to Plymouth every day from near-by Liskeard. He had been turned down for war service due to his bad eyesight. He spent some of his time defending conscientious objectors before military tribunals. He was not a pacifist but these objectors had a legal right to be represented. He had already begun his political career in local politics when he was elected to a seat on Plymouth City Council in 1907, serving on the city council for twenty years and as deputy mayor in 1920/1.

The Foot children remember these childhood homes

HUGH: When we were small, in 1914, very early in the war, we all went to live near the village of St Cleer, high on the edge of the Cornish moor – this became my favourite place in the whole world. We were a self-sufficient family and we needed few outside friends. We were united in our devotion to our parents – and in a sneaking respect for each other. There I developed an affection for gypsies. When I was about ten years old I used to escape to the gypsy encampments. There in their tents I learnt how to make clothes pegs and broom handles. My father would stride out early to walk down over the moor and along the narrow lanes to Liskeard, declaiming poetry as he walked, there to catch his train to Plymouth where he had a growing solicitor's practice. He had already entered Westcountry politics and had been narrowly defeated in the Totnes division in January 1910 and in Bodmin in December, the second general election of that year.

The law and politics would have been enough for most men. But he preached in the Cornish chapels on Sundays and had already started collecting one of the greatest private libraries in England. And when he came back late in the evenings from Plymouth he had time to play cricket with us in the back field and to read to us under the big lamp in the crowded main room of our thickly populated home. He was teaching himself French and read to us *Les Misérables*, translating as he went. I have a picture of us under the lamp – there wasn't electric light in those days. Later on I earned a shilling an hour teaching him my schoolboy Greek so that he could read the New Testament in the original. It was difficult to know what progress he was making, for, once he had got a new phrase or a word of the text, he knew the rest of the chapter by heart. And when he was not reading to us he did a prodigious amount of reading of his own – poetry, history and biography. He could concentrate on his reading with all the pandemonium of the family going on around him and would look up occasionally to join in any argument amongst his children which interested him. He took a tremendous interest and unreasonable pride in the activities of his

Ramsland House, St Cleer, on the edge of Bodmin Moor, where the Foot family lived during the First World War.

Isaac and Eva's seven children: left to right *John, Michael, Christopher, Dingle, Sally, Mac and Jennifer.*

85

offspring. One of the accomplishments of my father was that he succeeded in some way or other in paying for the education of all seven of his children – all five of the boys went to boarding schools and then to university, four to Oxford and myself to Cambridge. All paid for. We never got any scholarships, except I think Michael got a minor exhibition at Wadham. He managed in some way or other, out of money he earned as a solicitor, to pay for our education, which was a considerable achievement. Of all the many privileges of my life the greatest was the privilege of being brought up in this good Methodist home.

JOHN: We used to have family prayers every morning after breakfast. There were two rooms in the two family houses we lived in – the family house at 1 Lipson Terrace – and one would be held in the dining room there. I think we used to have one or two servants in those days, and they would come in and then I think there was a reading and then we would kneel and pray with all of us in the room, and that was the same procedure when we moved to Ramsland and then to Pencrebar right up until 1939. Both my father and my mother were very strict Methodists and we were brought up in a very strict regime, if that's the right word. There were no heavily involved compulsions brought upon us but it was the naturally expected thing. We would go to chapel in the morning and in the evening on a Sunday and it was naturally expected that you would go to some sort of Sunday school in the afternoon. We went to the Wesley Chapel in Ebrington Street in Plymouth, which was later destroyed by fire. When we were living during the First World War out at St Cleer near Liskeard we used to usually walk about three miles over to Crow's Nest to a little tiny country chapel deep in the countryside there. Or we would attend the nearer chapel closer to home – they were both of course very simple country chapels but I think both my father and mother preferred them to the large urban chapel.

MICHAEL: Two places stick out in my memories of childhood, two places where we lived before and during the First World War – 1 Lipson Terrace just opposite and looking over the famous Freedom Fields in Plymouth and, as treasured by us children, Ramsland, St Cleer, where the Cornish moorland came right up to the door of our house. All my own recollections of these times and places are tied up with my sister Sally, just a year older than me, but occasionally inciting me to revolt, even against our magnificent mother. She it was who led me on explorations of the Cornish moors. Her love of books was as strong as her love of animals so, from the earliest age, I thought my father was establishing an especially loving relationship with my sister. It stayed bright and burning till his dying day. He kept his office going all through the war and sometimes invited criticism by the way in which he would offer defence for the conscientious objectors. He was never a conscientious objector himself. He had been disqualified by his poor eyesight from joining the forces. His solicitor's firm certainly profited in the war but he somehow combined it with his own political and literary development. He could recite Shakespeare and Milton with equal ease and did it on the journey between St Cleer and Liskeard hundreds of times.

DINGLE: We had all kinds of livestock. Above all there was the donkey. It was one of those donkeys which can never, by any precaution, be kept inside a paddock or a field. No matter how carefully gates were latched or keys were turned or gaps repaired, sure enough the donkey would find its way out onto the moor. This caused a good deal of trouble with local authorities and eventually, so serious did the matter appear to have become that Father received a letter from that august body the county council, complaining that the donkey was constantly at large. He replied that he himself was at a loss to prevent its escape but that he had better read their letter to the donkey and hoped that it would have the desired effect.

Isaac Foot himself later told the whole story and it was recounted in the Cornish Times in 1931:

Mr Foot's 'Coming-of-Age' supper on Saturday was a cheery affair, and as I anticipated, he indulged in some reminiscences of his 21 years' campaigning in the Bodmin division. I hardly expected, however, when I happened to mention the famous donkey of St. Cleer in last week's recollections that I should be so successful in 'drawing' him out. He is, of course, a reader of the *Cornish Times* and when he saw my brief allusion to that wayward and historic quadruped, evidently could not resist telling the full story of its escapades and adventures. For ten minutes the company was kept shaking with merriment. Mr Foot recalled how he bought the animal for 30s. while walking between Looe and Polperro and met it at Menheniot station with a pony and jingle, thinking all he had to do was to drive the pony in front and lead the donkey on behind. It had other ideas, would not budge and held up oncoming traffic. Eventually the cavalcade got as far as Liskeard where Mr Foot gave two boys a shilling each to take it on and it was eventually brought to St. Cleer 'very much like the Wooden Horse was brought to Troy'. He told how it ate neighbours' cabbages, on his difficulty in keeping it off the Moors, how he had a lawyer's letter for 'causing' the donkey to graze on other people's rights, how he had read the letter to the donkey without effect, of paying small boys 6d. a time whenever they brought it back, of political supporters pleading with him to get rid of it, but nobody wanted it, and finally he jumped at the offer of a Plymouth man to buy if for 10s. The last we heard of the donkey was at Torpoint. 'When it saw the ferry it would not get on, and four men were paid a shilling each to carry it. When it reached the Devonport side of the Tamar it would not get off the ferry, and another four men were paid another shilling each to lift it off.' It was certainly the story of the evening.[63]

---

63. *Cornish Times*, 27 November 1931.

In 1927 the family moved to Pencrebar, a large house set in extensive grounds near Callington.

HUGH: Most of my grown-up life I have been away in Arabia and Africa and America but what a thrill it always was to come home – to St Cleer or to Callington and later to Saltash. My affection for my Cornish homes has not been diminished by my absences – it has been intensified. And Callington has meant so much to me especially because it was my mother's home. It was her triumphant achievement that she brought the family first from Plymouth over the Tamar and then from St Cleer over the Lynher back to her own Callington.

Pencrebar was remembered vividly by the ten grandchildren, who loved to visit there when they were young. In her book My Grandfather Isaac Foot *Sarah Dingle Foot, daughter of Mac and Sylvia, remembers this family home.*

It had been one of my grandmother's earliest wishes that she might one day live in Pencrebar near Callington. In 1927 the family moved to the white Victorian house with its three peaked facades, wide-sashed windows, large rooms and out-houses and wide sweeping lawns and shrubberies. Pencrebar was the centre created by my grandparents from which their varied family of seven children could go out into the world, but know they could always return and feel welcome. It was a magic house with all the ingredients, it seemed to me, for a happy home. It became a symbol to many of the local people of Liberalism, Methodism and, of course, literature.

Ruth Stephens, who started work there as a parlour maid at fourteen years of age, remembers how the day began there for her with a knock on the door at 6 a.m. and Mrs Foot would leave them a pot of tea. At 6.30 they were downstairs, laying the breakfast and preparing it. 'At eight o'clock sharp the gong went for breakfast and everyone was expected to be there on time.' Straight after breakfast the whole household gathered for morning prayers in the dining room. Then Mr Foot would leave for his solicitors' office in Plymouth.

> Every morning Mrs Foot and I waited by the window for you could be sure that Mr Foot would have forgotten something. Half way down the drive he would toot and shout what he needed. Mrs Foot would get it and I would go hurrying down the drive to him. We were all expected to go to chapel on Sundays. Mr and Mrs Foot always sat in the back pew. I can see Mr Foot sitting there now, with his Bible open, following the service. Sometimes I heard him preach and it was always a great experience. On Sunday mornings Mr Foot would play on the piano – his father's favourite, 'Beulah Land'. Many dignitaries came to stay at Pencrebar in those days.

Pencrebar, described as 'a handsome modern mansion built in 1849, occupying a very commanding position situated midway between Callington and Newbridge on the Lynher river.'

Often they were speaking for Mr Foot at election time. I remember Sir Donald Maclean, Lord Samuel, Lord Grey, Norman Birkett, who came to defend Annie Hearne in the poisoning case. Mr Foot used to get them to plant trees in remembrance of their visit. Of course no drink was ever served in the house. People knew that this was Mr Foot's way and just accepted it.'[64]

---

64. Sarah Foot, *My Grandfather Isaac Foot* (1980).

PART III

Isaac Foot the reader

MICHAEL: My father was the greatest reader who ever read. Apart from our mother, books were his real love. He taught me how to read and love them too; not, alas, on his own comprehensive, catholic scale but at least in such a manner that every other activity – politics especially – has become associated with books and, in particular, with books about books. When he was a young man in London, since every minute was precious, he acquired the trick of reading and declaiming as he walked. The great passages from Macaulay's 'Essay on Hampden' he could recite by heart. Soon the little yellow volumes of W. T. Stead's Penny Poets added to his repertoire – Milton, Shelley, Keats, Coleridge and most important of all an abridged version of Carlyle's *Letters and Speeches of Cromwell*.[65] He rolled secular words round his tongue as readily as the hymns he learnt at Sunday school, trained himself to wake ever earlier in the mornings to snatch more time for reading, lavished a prodigious proportion of his fourteen shillings a week allowance on the second-hand bookshops in the Charing Cross Road. On his return to Plymouth and thereafter, new authors were his milestones.

Isaac Foot describes how his love of reading and book collecting developed from an early age

It was in the Band of Hope we children were taught to recite. That to me was a fine concern. One evening I heard a young man recite. He was a visitor. His recitation was Macaulay's ballad 'Horatius'.[66]

>'Lars Porsena of Clusium
>By the Nine Gods he swore
>That the great house of Tarquin
>Should suffer wrong no more...'

I sat ravished by the entertainment – the thrill of the story, the agony of the fight, the crashing fall of Astur, the Lord of Luna, and above all the glory of the words. 'By the Nine Gods he swore' – I held my breath whilst Horatius was in the Tiber – would he yet be saved,

---

65. W. T. Stead (1849–1912), a journalist and philanthropist, set up a publishing company to make cheap reprints of poetry anthologies known as the Penny Poets.
66. Thomas Babington Macaulay, *Lays of Ancient Rome* (1842).

and whilst the axes were plied on the bridge – would they get it down in time to save the city? Everything ended alright, the bridge down and Horatius safe. Who the young man was I do not know, but blessings upon his head! The story itself gripped, but what I felt was the glory of the words. I walked home that night on air. A fire was kindled within me which has never ceased to burn. My love of poetry was, I think, born that evening in the old school room at Wesley.

As a youth I needed guidance. Indeed, I needed guidance so much that, looking back, I wonder how I managed to scramble through it all. Leaving school at fifteen to try to earn my own living, I was, I suppose, like most boys of that age, less than half educated. I was, however, a voracious reader. In my boyhood I hadn't a very wide choice of books. There was, of course, Bunyan's *Pilgrim's Progress, Robinson Crusoe,* Grimm's *Fairy Tales* and *Swiss Family Robinson*. These I knew nearly by heart. Then there was every morning the reading of the Bible at family prayers. Apart from this, and Wesley's hymns, there was very little bookmanship in our household. I had therefore to find my own way. I knew, of course, of Shakespeare and Milton, but each of these always seemed to be spoken of as if he were a system or an institution rather than a man. Apart from those two dominating names, I had to make my own assessment. I read not so much from choice but because some few books happened to be within my reach. I read Mrs Henry Wood's *East Lynne*[67] and Charlotte Brontë's *Jane Eyre*, and had to decide for myself which was the greater book. Scott's *Lady of the Lake* appealed to me, I am afraid, more than Coleridge's *Ancient Mariner*. I read Mrs Browning's *Aurora Leigh*, but knew nothing of Robert Browning's *Ring and the Book*. I knew Tennyson's 'Brock' and his 'Enoch Ardon' and 'Dora' almost by heart, but I can't recall ever hearing of 'In Memoriam'. Apart from 'Lucy Gray', which I had to learn at school when I was about six, I knew nothing of Wordsworth, and I should certainly have reckoned Longfellow's 'Hiawatha' and 'The Courtship of Miles Standish' above *The Lyrical Ballads*. Probably because the book was available, I read the whole of James Russell Lowell's poetry from end to end, before I ever knew that there was such a poem as Wordsworth's *Prelude*. I am thinking of the five or six years before I was twenty. Of course, things sorted themselves out later on. But it wasn't until I got hold of Palgrave's *Golden Treasury*[68] that I was able to check my own assessments. Fortunately W. T. Stead's Penny Poets were published about that time and they did for me pretty much what Chapman's 'Homer' did for young John Keats. Perhaps it was just as well that I had no more guidance. There are some things we have to find out for ourselves. It is a good thing, after what may be discursive, wide and perhaps desultory reading, to decide what is our own special interest, our own special territory.

---

67. Mrs Henry Wood (1814–87) was an English novelist. *East Lynne*, her most popular work, was published in 1861.
68. Francis Palgrave, *Golden Treasury of the Best Songs and Lyrical Poems in the English Language*. This highly successful anthology was first published in 1861 and, after many revisions, is still in print today.

My interest in buying books began when I was about nine years of age. In a household where money was not very plentiful, and where my mother was given a sovereign every Saturday morning to provide for all the needs of nine of us, there came an unexpected benefaction. My father, to mark some family red-letter day, once gave to each of us the sum of five pounds. It seemed a staggering sum to possess. Five Golden Sovereigns! The question arose as to what was to be done with it. The proper thing, of course, was to invest the money and to keep it safe; and I was taken up by my father to the local savings bank, introduced to the actuary – the name sounded very impressive to me – and I came away with a little dark-grey square-shaped deposit book recording the fact that I was entitled to the sum of Five Pounds, with interest at the rate of 6d for every pound for every year that it remained there. Unfortunately, it did not remain there very long. A week or two later, I passed a bookshop in a street in my native town. Both the shop and the street have long since disappeared. In the window was a pile of books – a tier of books – not side by side, but built up like a tower in the very centre of the shop window. There were, I think, forty of them – 'The Story of the Nations'. There was a card commending the series as a bargain not to be missed, and the price was five pounds. Five Pounds! At home there was the bank book recording the sum of five pounds – there in the shop were the books with the card – Five Pounds! The struggle went on for about a week. From day to day I went up to the shop window, half-fearing and half-hoping the books would be gone. Then the inevitable happened. There was the second visit to the savings bank, and the money was withdrawn. I was afraid to meet the eyes of the actuary – a word or two of warning or reproach from him might have made all the difference. The books were brought home. There was no open rebuke, but I suspected questioning glances. That was the first of my temptations – the first of very many. I have those books still. They are kept on a shelf by themselves, reminding me of my first temptation and my first fall.

My collection grew slowly. There were, alas, no more five-pound windfalls. I was in my later teens when I made another purchase of that same amount. This time it was Gardiner's *History of England*.[69] It was Cotheran's shop – then in the Strand, near the approach to Waterloo Bridge. Eighteen volumes – ten on James I and Charles, four on the Civil War, and four on the Commonwealth and Protectorate. How I got the money I cannot remember. But I recall that there was something of the same temptation, the same delay, the same final surrender. These were my big ventures, but, in between, other books had come along, very slowly, and generally singly.

I spent a year and a half of my life as a boy clerk in the Civil Service. The nation had the full advantage of my services as a pay clerk in the Paymaster General's Department at the Admiralty. My salary was fourteen shillings a week, with a steep rise at the end of twelve months to fifteen shillings. Receiving a subvention of a pound a month from home, I had twenty shillings to cover everything. Things often got a bit sticky towards the end of the

---

69. Samuel Rawson Gardiner (1829–1902) wrote the history of the Puritan revolution in several volumes.

month, and there wasn't much margin for books, but still I got them. I found I could save fourpence a day in bus fare by walking the four miles from my Bayswater lodgings to Spring Gardens. Fourpence a day came to two shillings a week, and two shillings was almost a princely sum if you had plenty of time to spend in Holywell Street and cared to go systematically through the threepenny boxes. Then there were also the sixpenny paper-backed standard works. These books could be slipped into the pocket and could be read as you walked. I learned to read while walking and also learned to measure distances by my reading.

I lodged for a time at Battersea where I shared the sitting room with a man who was twice my age and I was a little in awe of him. He would read for hours sitting on the other side of the fireplace. One evening he spoke to me about the book he was reading, and quoted from it. I asked what it was called, and he replied: 'A Pair of Blue Eyes.' 'Who wrote it?' I asked. And he said: 'A man called Thomas Hardy.' The name meant nothing to me. It was to mean a good deal to me later on. Because of my fellow-lodger's enthusiasm, I began to read the books of Thomas Hardy. Within a year or two, after my return home, I had come to Tess of the d'Urbervilles and I remember being so shaken with emotion as I came to the end of the story that I had to lay the book down for a while before I could face those last lines:

> Upon the cornice of the tower a tall staff was fixed ... a few minutes after the hour had struck something moved slowly up the staff, and it steadied itself upon the breeze. It was a black flag. Justice was done, and the President of the Immortals, in Aeschylean phrase, had ended his sport with Tess.

And then the closing words about the two who watched Angel Clare and Tessie's sister, Liza Lu: 'As soon as they had strength they arose, joined hands again and went on.' And even then I saw some parallel between their departure and the closing lines of Paradise Lost: 'They, hand in hand, with wandering steps slow, Through Eden took their solitary way.'

Later in life I had to walk four miles every morning and evening between my Cornish home and the station and sometimes in the early morning I had to be pretty quick about it. There was no time for a book but, having memorised about a hundred sonnets – my own anthology of what I thought pure gold – I found I could do thirty of them in an hour. Later, when I was Secretary of Mines, I found that, on my luncheon walk through St James's Park to and from the Reform Club, by dividing the poem into two, I could comfortably begin and complete the reading of fifty-five stanzas of Adonais.[70]

From those days I have always had a preference for the book that will slip easily into the pocket, and generally I have never been without one. I read with interest, and in after years, of the body of Shelley being identified because there was a Sophocles in one pocket and a Keats in the other. On my return to Plymouth after those eighteen months in London, I brought with me a hundred books or so, including the Penny Poets of W. T.

---

70. Shelley's elegy for the death of Keats (1821).

Stead. The enterprise of that man put within the reach of boys like myself the richest resources of English and American literature. For two or three shillings I had Shakespeare, Milton, Keats, Shelley, Wordsworth, Coleridge, Matthew Arnold, Walt Whitman, James Russell Lowell, and the rest. I have kept many of them. They were anthologies, admirably chosen. Most of them were new to me, and, with me, Stead's seed fell on virgin soil. Many of us rejoiced a month or two ago on the 100th anniversary of the birth of that man who in those days we regarded as a public benefactor.

I needed guides, of course. One such guide was Robert Blatchford and his weekly paper the *Clarion*, which I read eagerly from week to week.[71] What Blatchford taught me of socialism passed away, but he wrote fine English and commended noble English reading to others, and book after book I bought, solely on his recommendation. I learned from him about a writer named James Anthony Froude and his *Short Studies of Great Subjects*. I got those four volumes in 1897 and this, of course, led later to Froude's *History of England* in the twelve volumes.[72] That history I read slowly for the sheer joy of it. The masterly narration, the clear, lucent English, the story of the English Reformation, the early records of the English Bible, the work of William Tyndale, and then the drama of the long Elizabethan conflict with Spain, the glowing story of Sir Francis Drake and his voyage around the world, and then the Armada. Froude was a Devonshire man, and the story he had to tell was largely of the Westcountry. I know what has been said of his limitations but in my collection Froude will always keep his place. Then Froude led to Motley's *Rise of the Dutch Republic*,[73] and anything on William the Silent I could lay my hands on. That is how my collection grew. There was no design, no planning. When I got interested in Tyndale or Sir Francis Drake or William the Silent or some such man, I wanted all the books about him. Sometimes it meant getting a dozen or so, sometimes a score, sometimes a hundred, and on one or two themes, perhaps many hundreds.

I have five sons and two daughters. They have all received much longer, fuller and wider education than I ever had. They have been brought up in a home full of books. I don't know that I ever gave these children of mine much guidance or direction in their reading, but if I did it had singularly little result. As the children grew up one after the other, I read to them a good deal, but the staple fare, year after year, was Stevenson's *Treasure Island* and great chunks from Victor Hugo's *Les Misérables*. My children have since grown up and they are all readers, some more widely read than others, but all book lovers. But no one of them in literary preference has followed in my footsteps. The books that meant much – almost everything – to me for the most part remain untouched, and indeed, on occasion, those children of mine scoff at my so-called library, where, among the thirty thousand books or so, they cannot find what they want on, say, William Blake or Cobbett, or the poets who

71. Blatchford (1851–1943) established this socialist weekly in 1890.
72. Froude (1818–94) wrote his *History of England* between 1856 and 1870.
73. *Rise of the Dutch Republic 1574–1584* by John Motley (1874–77), published in 1855.

have been writing in the last twenty years or so. Now, if any guidance of mine has availed so little with my own flesh and blood, it seems unlikely that I can give much effective advice to those like yourselves whom I have never met. None the less, here is my advice for what it is worth – advice which to me as a youth would have been invaluable.

First of all, read all you can. Make time for it somehow. I have never met man or woman really eminent in politics, in conversation or in parliamentary or forensic eloquence, who was not a wide reader. Read the big book. Go right through your Gibbon, your Clarendon, your Burke, your Froude or the other writer that appeals to you. Remember that the classics which have survived the vicissitudes of centuries, and the critical judgement of many generations, have at least a 'prima facie' claim upon your attention. You will get your own books, of course. You will have to borrow some, but a borrowed book can never become what a good book should be – an abiding friend. Find out for yourself what is your own special interest, what appeals to you most, and what subject gives you the most pleasure in study and then concentrate. It might be a special period of history, say, the revival of learning in Europe, or the early history of the North American continent, or it might be a great personality like Tyndale, or Erasmus or Lincoln or Cromwell or Wordsworth. Whatever your theme, let it be your special interest. For the time, consult the authorities, all the authorities as far as you can get hold of them. Make up your mind that upon your special subject you will, as far as possible, get to know all that there is to be known. Use the authorities but don't let them dictate to you or dominate. The time will come when you will be able to judge those authorities and to put them in their proper place.

As this reading of yours might run on for many years let them be a worthy one, a 'life-long friendship'. When the personality you are studying has really become your friend, you will probably want to know all about him. You will get his authentic picture, the books that he published, and you will probably want to read every line that he wrote. Get his letters to read. Given the man's letters, you can make your own biography. If you can, get some piece of his actual handwriting; it will be worth your study. Sometimes one actual letter in his authentic writing will tell you more of the man than reams of his literary criticisms. In the course of my reading, I have, as far as possible, committed to my memory the great passages of poetry and some prose that most appealed to me. This has meant no little effort, harder as I got older, but I did this because I found I could not judge sufficiently when I only had the printed page and that I needed the judgement of the ear as well.

The greatest wealth in life is friendship. In the course of time many friends are lost and many friendships broken. There comes a time, if a man lives long enough, when almost from month to month, the friends of his boyhood, his schooldays and his youth pass away, but there are some friends whom we need never lose and who can remain with us until the end and there are some friendships which need never be broken. More than most men, Wordsworth realised the meaning of this living and continuing companionship. That is why he once wrote:

> There is
> One great society alone on earth
> The noble living and the noble dead.[74]

(1946 broadcast)

JOHN: My father was giving public lectures from quite early on in his life – I don't remember anything of it until after the First World War – at that time he used to go round to chapels and literary societies lecturing. These public lectures, before the coming of the cinema in small country places, were very considerably attended. You would get most of the male population of a small village attending a public lecture of that kind and he used to lecture upon a variety of subjects – mostly Shakespeare. He was a great authority upon Shakespeare – particularly the tragedies. I can remember him lecturing on *Macbeth* and *Othello* and *King Lear*. And he used to lecture upon other subjects. Conrad was one of his interests. This always seemed to me a strange one for him because Conrad is an obscure and difficult writer in my opinion, rather sort of philosophic. It surprised me that my father was so taken with him but my father was one of the first people who recognised what a considerable writer Conrad was and he would speak quite simply although he had a profound knowledge of the scholarship of Shakespeare and Conrad. But he could tell the story of one or two of the books of Conrad in a sort of abbreviated form and he was introducing the audience to the subject completely afresh, certainly in the case of Conrad.

The following are excerpts from Isaac Foot's notes for lectures given over many years on some of his favourite literary heroes, particularly if he could find some Westcountry connection.

5 William and Dorothy Wordsworth

Anticipating the celebration of the centenary of William Wordsworth's death in 1950, Isaac Foot wrote this letter to the editor of the Times in November 1949:

Sir, While one reads gratefully the letter you publish announcing the preparations for the commemoration of the Wordsworth Centenary next April at Grasmere, may a Westcountry man respectfully suggest that, on this occasion, the claims of other places should not be overlooked? Racedown in Dorset, the Quantocks and Alfoxden and Nether Stowey in Somerset, are names associated with the 'Maytime and the Cheerful Dawn' of

---

74. *The Prelude* (1850).

Dorothy Wordsworth (1771–1855).

William Wordsworth (1770–1850).

Wordsworth's genius. These Westcountry names will recall the healing ministry of Dorothy Wordsworth and the yet unclouded friendship with Coleridge, when they were 'three people with only one soul'. That was the time not only of the *Lyrical Ballads* but also of the early associations with Charles Lamb, Southey, Hazlitt, Cottle, Thomas Poole and the rest of that shining company. That was the time, too, of the walk through the Wye valley, when, on the banks of that 'delightful stream', the brother and sister 'stood together'. Perhaps it was an admonition not only to Dorothy but also to us with which Wordsworth brought to a close his noblest poem:

> Nor wilt thou then forget,
> That after many wanderings, many years
> Of absence, these steep woods and lofty cliffs,
> And this green pastoral landscape, were to me
> More dear, both for themselves and for thy sake.'[75]

I am, Sir, your obedient servant, Isaac Foot

In a broadcast he was invited to make on this Wordsworth centenary, Isaac Foot recalled more fully the time Wordsworth spent in the Westcountry when he was a young man:

---

75. 'Lines Composed a Few Miles above Tintern Abbey' (1798).

One hundred years ago, at noon, on the twenty-third day of April 1850, William Wordsworth died. It is fitting, and indeed, inevitable, that the day should be marked, first of all, at Grasmere, in the very heart of his 'dear native regions'. But happily for us, Wordsworth was something more than a Northcountryman. Wordsworth was a wanderer. All his life he was a wanderer – up to the very last – but in his early days wandering, he said, was his passion; and in his youth he would have been regarded almost as a vagrant. He wandered, however, to some purpose. His wanderings took him to France just at the time of the French Revolution, and if he hadn't wandered there we might never have heard of him at all. Certainly we shouldn't have had his greatest poetry. When he was a young man of twenty-three, almost penniless, he walked alone into south Wales and along the valley of the Wye and on to Salisbury Plain – it was a much wilder place than now – and wandered alone over that solitary place for three days and three nights. That was an experience he never forgot. Some years later he wandered into Scotland – this time not alone, but with his sister Dorothy. Had he never crossed the border, we might never have heard of 'The Solitary Reaper' – we might never have beheld 'yon solitary Highland lass reaping and singing by herself', and we might never have read the magic lines:

> A voice so thrilling ne'er was heard
> In spring-time from the cuckoo bird,
> Breaking the silence of the seas
> Among the furthest Hebrides'.

Wordsworth lived in our Westcountry for three years. He had been here before. As I said just now, he had already wandered over Salisbury Plain and along the Wye valley. But now the vagrant was to settle down – at least for a time. And it so happened that he settled down with us. It all seemed chance work. He didn't come to live amongst us by design. A series of little trifles led to the decision. With no ties whatever, with no profession, with no recognised occupation, with very little money, barely enough for the most frugal living, and with only one friend in the world whom he needed to consider, he might have chosen to settle anywhere on the face of England. But led, as I said, by strange circumstances, he came to the Westcountry. Not the least consideration was that he could have a roof over his head, that there was a house open to him, furnished and unoccupied, and that he could live there rent free. The house was called Racedown. It was a farm-house in Dorset –·almost in Devon – a little brook dividing the two frontiers was only a field or two away. The English Channel was seven miles off; the house lay midway between Lyme Regis in Dorset and Crewkerne in Somerset, the nearest market town. That is where he came to settle in September 1795. He walked there from Bristol, a walk of about fifty miles – a three-days loitering journey, as he called it – and the story of that walk is told in the opening lines of one of the very greatest poems of our literature – the poem which was not published until after his death – the poem to which his wife gave the title *The Prelude*.

Wordsworth did not come to the Westcountry alone. There was his sister, Dorothy. She was two years younger than William. The story of William Wordsworth and his sister, Dorothy, is of course a cherished possession. There is nothing quite like it to be read anywhere. Racedown was Dorothy's first real home; and to live, day by day, with her beloved brother was the fulfilment of her deepest longing. She knew all about his distress, all about his moral crisis, and she gave herself to the one business of her life: to care for him, to provide for his daily needs, to nurse him back to health and to happiness, and to revive the sense of the high mission to which she was sure he was called. Looking back upon these early days, she once wrote: 'I think Racedown is the place dearest to my recollections upon the whole face of the island.' It was the immeasurable service and gracious ministry of this woman that her brother acknowledged in the lines so often quoted:

> She gave me eyes, she gave me ears,
> And humble cares, and delicate fears;
> A heart, the fountain of sweet tears,
> And love, and thought, and joy'.[76]

William and Dorothy lived together at Racedown from September 1795 until July 1797 – nearly two years. They had few visitors. But they had one guest who, in after years, looked back upon Racedown with almost the same joy as Dorothy. That guest was Mary Hutchinson. William had known her before. They had both been together at the Dame's School at Penrith. He had met her since when she had joined William and Dorothy on a glorious holiday at Penrith. There is every reason to believe that she had been William's first love – 'The maid to whom were breathed my first fond vows'. Later she was to become his wife. So much has been written about Dorothy that we are inclined to forget Mary, but she was to become the real mainstay of that family. Everything that one reads of Mary tends to heighten the conception of her character. Some day her story will be worthily told, and it will then be seen why she was almost worshipped by those who knew her best. Mary made a long stay at Racedown – during the winter of 1796 and the spring of 1797, and it may well be that the early love was revived and renewed in the countryside of Dorset and of Devon.

So far we have seen William and Dorothy in their Westcountry home with Mary Hutchinson. There was to be yet another. He bore a great name – Samuel Taylor Coleridge. We cannot be quite sure when and where Wordsworth and Coleridge first met. Almost certainly it was at Bristol and in the autumn of 1795. Bristol owes to Coleridge her share in the glory that is associated with the name of Wordsworth. At about the Christmas of 1796 Coleridge made his home at Nether Stowey, a small village near Bridgwater. That was soon after his marriage. At that time, the Wordsworths had been living at Racedown for about

---

76. From 'Memorials of a Tour of Scotland' (1803).

fifteen months. One day, about six months after his settlement at Nether Stowey, Coleridge paid his first visit to the Wordsworths' home. It meant a walk of thirty miles or so. Nearly fifty years later, Wordsworth recalled how he came. 'He did not keep to the high road but leaped over a gate and bounded down a pathless field by which he cut off an angle.' That was when Dorothy saw him for the first time. He leapt into the lives of both of them. He was at that time twenty-five years old, two years younger than Wordsworth and just younger than Dorothy. He came again soon after, this time with a horse and cart to take William and Dorothy for a fortnight's holiday at his home at Nether Stowey. That was to be a memorable fortnight. Now, whilst the Wordsworths were with Coleridge on this fortnight's holiday, it was learned that in the neighbourhood a house was available. This time it was a mansion, but, seemingly by a miracle, it was to be had at a trifling rental which was within the Wordsworths' narrow means. It was only about four miles away from Nether Stowey. It meant being near to Coleridge. Instantly the decision was made, and by the fourteenth of July of that year – 1797 – William and Mary were settled in their new home. The name of their new home was Alfoxden. The Wordsworths were to live there nearly a year, from July 1797 until midsummer of 1798. The days, and the weeks, and the months of that year were to be recorded in letters of gold.

The story of this year is given to us in literature that is imperishable. There are first of all the many letters that were written during the year. Then there are the recollections of Joseph Cottle, the young Bristol publisher, a man to whom Bristol owes a great deal.[77] Then there is the essay of Mr Hazlitt, who was then nineteen years old, who came down on a visit to Coleridge.[78] He stayed for about three weeks in the early summer of 1798, and his essay, written years later, is Hazlitt at his very best – which is saying a good deal. Then there was the journal of Dorothy – the 'Alfoxden Journal', as it is called – every line of it alive with interest and beauty. Then there is above all the poetry of Coleridge, written at that time, and the poetry of Wordsworth. How much these two men meant to each other we can only guess. Our scholars and critics have discussed and debated the question: which owed the other the more? We need not attempt to answer that question but we can be thankful for the rich harvest reaped from that friendship when, as Coleridge said, 'we are three people but only one soul'. Wordsworth was then a young man. He was to live many years. He had yet to write some of his noblest poetry but, if he had died before he ever went to live at Grasmere at the age of thirty, his poetry written at Racedown and at Alfoxden would have given him a place amongst the immortals.

We may think not only of the poetry finished there, but of that begun and inspired under our western skies. Some of the noblest passages in the poem *The Excursion*,

77. Joseph Cottle (1770–1853), publisher and author.
78. William Hazlitt (1778–1830), radical literary critic. His essay 'Mr Wordsworth' in the *Spirit of the Age* was published in 1825.

published years later, were written in the Westcountry.[79] The scene of the first book in *The Excursion* is a common in Somerset, and when, in that same book, Wordsworth wishes to describe the idyllic life of lovers newly married he didn't choose the Northcountry for his picture of the Garden of Eden but the county of Devon. The Quantocks are not high mountains but great rivers took their rise there, and our western counties – Somerset, Dorset and Devon – can proudly claim their share in the frame of Wordsworth's achievement. This wonderful year at Alfoxden was to be remembered by Wordsworth, not only for its poetic achievement, but for its story of happiness. It was for Wordsworth the hour of recovery when he learned that, instead of striving, he had only to receive. It was the time of unbroken friendship, and unclouded skies. Estrangements were to come, misunderstandings, partial reconciliation, the long sickness of Dorothy, the moral failure of Coleridge – separation and, at last, the separation of death, but those Alfoxden days were spent when they were all three in their golden prime and when, not only Coleridge, but all three, were in the strength and plumage of their youth. Wordsworth would have applied to those days the words he used elsewhere: 'Bliss was it in that dawn to be alive, but to be young was very Heaven.'[80]

The most wonderful event in that year was the walk to Lynton and back. Late one afternoon, in November 1797, William, Dorothy and Coleridge started out. The distance to Lynton was thirty-five miles and they went along by the northern coast through Watchet and Porlock. They returned by the road through Dulverton. The walk was to last some days, and, as they had no money, they proposed to pay for the holiday by composing a poem which they hoped to sell for five pounds. They found that the joint poem was not likely to succeed, and they decided that they would compose separately. It was from that walk that the book was written and published a year later by their friend Joseph Cottle, under the title of *The Lyrical Ballads*.[81] That book has come to be regarded as one of the great books of the world. The book opened with a poem by Coleridge and closed with a poem by Wordsworth. The Coleridge poem is well known to most of us. It bore the title of *The Rime of the Ancient Mariner*, in seven parts. It was begun on the November evening as they walked through the darkness on the road between Alfoxden and Watchet, but was not finished until the following March.

> It is an ancient Mariner,
> And he stoppeth one of three.
> 'By thy long grey beard and glittering eye
> Now wherefore stopp'st thou me?'

---

79. Published in 1814.
80. 'The French Revolution' (1805).
81. Written in 1798.

We all know that poem, and many of us remember the first shudder when we came to the lines:

'God save thee, ancient Mariner!
From the fiends that plague thee thus! –
Why look'st thou so?' – With my cross-bow
I shot the ALBATROSS.

It was with that poem that the book opened. It closed with another and it is that poem that I now wish to say something in bringing my talk to a close. After leaving Alfoxden, William and Dorothy went to stay with Coleridge for a few days – at Nether Stowey. Then they walked to Bristol and stayed at the house of Joseph Cottle. That was in July and one day William and Dorothy went for a walking tour along the Wye valley. They were away for about four days. Wordsworth, on the last day, began to compose the poem and he finished it just as he was entering Bristol that evening. Not a line of it was written down until they reached Bristol. The title of the poem was 'Lines Written a Few Miles above Tintern Abbey on Revisiting the Banks of the Wye during a Tour, July 13, 1798'.

You may remember that I spoke earlier on about his solitary wanderings back in the year 1793, when he had gone along the Wye valley. Well, he was here again but this time not alone. The poem was a favourite one of Wordsworth. It was one of the few poems that he wrote there and then. Generally, he wrote only after long reflection. It contains some lines so familiar that they have become household words throughout the English-speaking world. There are hundreds of thousands of people who will never see the Wye River but yet will walk along its valley with William and Dorothy. It is, above all, a Westcountry poem, the crown and glory of Wordsworth's association with us. I read it first about fifty years ago. Then its beauty took my breath away and it means much more to me now than it did then:

Five years have past; five summers with the length
Of five long winters! And again I hear
These waters, rolling from their mountain springs
With a soft inland murmur...

Isaac Foot reads the poem 'Tintern Abbey'

6 Thomas Hardy:
'How I came to read him thirty years ago'

This paper is in no sense a criticism of the work of Thomas Hardy. For the work of criticism I have no capacity. Just as a man who, having been through a pleasant country, comes back refreshed and quickened by his experience and is happy in telling his friends of the things he saw and the people he met, so I, having gone into the realms of gold with Thomas Hardy, give to you the hurried notes of a busy man telling of the joys I have had and the pleasures awaiting those who will come within the range of his influence. My references here will be mainly confined to the Wessex novels. The others are his lesser achievements and have little or nothing to say of the peasantry. What Scott has done for the Borderland of Scotland Hardy has done for the Wessex country. We associate Quiller-Couch with Troy Town and the Delectable Duchy, Eden Phillpotts with Dartmoor, and

Thomas Hardy (1840–1928).

Hardy with Dorset and the parts of Somerset, Wiltshire, Berkshire, Devon and Hampshire which Hardy called Wessex. This district is one of the most beautiful in England.

In his great and enduring books Hardy has almost confined himself to one class of person. He has little to say of towns folk and very few of his men and women move in polite society or in the walks of life where we are supposed to look for refinement and culture. His characters are 'racy of the soil', for the most part men and women who gain their livelihood in some association with Mother Earth. They are rustics, some farmers, yeomen, millers, carriers or tranters, village tradesmen and then the others: shepherds, thatchers, drovers, woodlanders, dairymaids and farm-hands labouring on the soil. And what creations they are! Michael Henchard, Bathsheba Everdene, Bob Lourdnay and his brother John, Dick Dewy, Tess, Sue Bridehead, Anne Garland, Gabriel Oak, Clym Yeobright, Giles Winterbourne and Marty South, Diggory Venn, Fanny Robin. These, to the Hardy lover, are not so much the creations of a novelist. They are human beings. They live and we know them, know their fare more intimately than the people we meet. They are flesh and blood. Each man stands upon his own feet and each woman lives her own life. What the novelist does for us widens the circle of our friends and enlarges the world in which we live. Hardy's men and women live in their own right. To the casual observer these country folk may seem all of a piece and commonplace. He gives them their rightful dignity. We get to know them, to love them and find them delightful company –

and this because Hardy himself loves them and because their comp a ny was delightful to him. Not only are they living characters, warm and attractive but, as I have said, they are country people, rustics, racy of the soil. Hardy has a knowledge of country ways, sheep, bees, cows. I have read many novels where the chapters are, at certain intervals, interspersed with some rhapsodical description of nature. The development of the plot is suspended to allow of some description of the scenery. In Hardy's Wessex novels the life of the people is intertwined with the inanimate world around them. The rain and sunshine, the moors and the rivers, the sky and the stars become part of the story and the expression of the country folk. Nature is not with him a background for the story he tells, but almost a sentient thing entering into the lives and destinies of the men and women with whom he lives with intimate association. Egdon Heath is almost one of the characters in *The Return of the Native*. It plays its part in the dreadful tragedy. In the opening passages of that fine book Egdon Heath, with all its sights and sounds so vividly and inescapably imagined, presses over the story, a vast careless oppression.

7 'My enthusiasm for Joseph Conrad'

Joseph Conrad's first book was *Almayer's Folly*, published in 1895. The story of that book is amazing. He began writing it in obedience to a queer impulse. He says:

> It was not the outcome of a need – the famous need of self-expression which artists find in their search for motives. The necessity which impelled me was a hidden obscure necessity, a completely masked and unaccountable phenomenon. It was begun in idleness – a holiday task and was a much-delayed book. It was never dismissed from my mind even when the hope of ever finishing it was very faint. Till I began to write that novel, I had written nothing but letters, and not very many of these. The conception of a planned book was entirely outside my mental range when I sat down to write.

Joseph Conrad (1857–1924).

He wrote at odd moments; 'it grew', he says, 'line by line rather than page by page.' Wherever he went about the world, the manuscript went with him. After twice losing the manuscript, he carried it about like a talisman or a treasure and it was somehow saved by a special dispensation of Providence. In his book *A Personal Record* he relates his first meeting with the man named Almayer. He saw him first one early morning from the bridge of a steamer moored to a rickety little wharf forty miles up a river in Borneo. This meeting was a great event in Conrad's life and in the world of letters. He says: 'If I had not got to know Almayer pretty well it is almost certain there would never have been a line of mine in print.' Readers of *A Personal Record* will remember how often the name Almayer recurs throughout that book – just as the name Kurtz comes again and again in the pages of that powerful story *Heart of Darkness*. The first reader of *Almayer's Folly* was not in a publisher's office. He was a passenger on the S.S. *Torrens* of whom Conrad writes with tender gratitude because 'he has had the patience to read several of the many pages with the very shadows of Eternity gathering already in the hollows of his kind, steadfast eyes'. In 1894 it was sent to Fisher Unwin and, after a few months, it was accepted. Had it not been accepted Conrad would never have written again but the reader was Edward Garnett,[82] to whom a monument might fittingly be erected.

The story of his second novel, *The Outcast of the Islands*, published two years later, is, in its way, almost as interesting. He was in doubt whether he would ever write another line for print. He says:

> Neither in my mind nor in my heart had I then given up the sea. In truth I was clinging to it desperately, all the more desperately because, against my will, I could not help feeling that there was something changed in my relation to it. *Almayers Folly* had been finished and done with. The mood itself was gone but it had left the memory of an experience that, both in thought and emotion, was unconnected with the sea and I suppose that part of my moral being which is rooted in consistency was badly shaken. I gave myself up to indolence.

And so the books have gone on. Altogether he has written twenty-two books. The work which reaches the high-water mark and which will one day be recognised as one of the few great novels in the English language is *Nostromo*, published in 1904. It deals with the disturbed life of a South American republic and, whilst its characters are drawn with convincing realism, the whole story glows with the splendour of high romance.

It will, I assume, be fairly evident that I am something of a Conrad enthusiast. 'Are you Conrad mad?' a friend asked me the other day. Well, I suppose I am. I have a friend who was also Conrad mad. Whenever we met, if only for a few minutes in the street, we generally managed to discuss something of Conrad. It may be asked why Conrad has had to wait so long for his popularity – or for such measure of popularity as he has today. Well, his style does not appeal to some people and they will not give themselves the chance to get to

82. Edward Garnett (1868–1936), English author.

like it. His form too is unusual and to some people irritating. One critic says that 'his long stories, at times, come out as awkwardly as an elephant being steered backwards through a gate'. Yes, they do. His parentheses sometimes run into a dozen pages or more and it is not uncommon to find that we are farther on with the story at the end of, say, the third chapter, than we are at the end of the tenth. Still these to me are spots in the sun.

A Personal Record is an autobiography without beginning or end but is a wonderful book nonetheless and, somehow, with all its hither-and-thither-ness, it achieves its purpose of revealing the personality of the man far more than many of the autobiographies that give the regular story from birth to old age. Many readers miss Conrad because they want a novel which can be read with half the mind. We often listen to sermons with half the mind and some aren't worth anything more and we like our novels in the same way. But half our minds will not do for Conrad.

> Come with me [says Conrad] and I will take you to Costaguana.[83] We will live together for a time in Sulaco and we shall meet many people: Charles Gould, Emily Gould his wife, Dr Monygham, old Viola and his two daughters Linda and Gisella, Avellanos, his daughter Antonia, Captain Mitchell, Sotillo and Martin Decoud, Montero and Barrios and Nostromo, the Capataz of the Cargadores now on his silver-grey horse with his silver buttons, now at night in the lighter loaded with silver, holding his breath as the steamer crowded with Sotillo's troops draws near in the darkness, now the rich captain of later years hugging the treasure of the hidden silver to himself. I will show you the great silver mine of San Tome and we will see what the silver does for them all, how it eats up the mind and heart of Charles Gould and robs his wife of her happiness and saps the faithfulness of Nostromo and drives Sotillo stark mad and prompts revolution and bloodshed and draws all men and things into its embrace.

All this Conrad will show us if we go with him. I have never been to South America and don't suppose I ever shall but I know Costaguana. There is no such country, but I could draw a map of it and there are few towns I know so well as Sulaco and, if it comes to that, many of the people I meet and have to do with are not so well known to me as those whom I have met there.

---

83. The imagined, mystical setting for *Nostromo*.

8 Robert Louis Stevenson on the 50th anniversary of his death in 1944

Robert Louis Stevenson died in December 1894. The fiftieth anniversary of his death will doubtless call for several reminders of his work and personality, but Westcountry folk will, I think, be glad to recall their special association with this famous Scot who, although a son of Edinburgh, has written his name on so many places throughout the wide world.

Robert Louis Stevenson (1850–94).

Stevenson was a good deal of a traveller even from his boyhood. His first visit to the Westcountry was in the spring of 1864, when he was fourteen years of age. He then came to Torquay with his mother and the visit was repeated in the following year. Twelve years later Stevenson paid his third visit to the Westcountry when he came with his father and mother on a holiday in Cornwall. His father having returned to Scotland, he stayed on with his mother and went with her to the Isles of Scilly. We have some of his impressions in the letter written from Penzance in August 1877, to his friend Mrs Sitwell: 'Cornwall is not much to my taste, being as bleak as the bleakest parts of Scotland and nothing like so pointed and characteristic. It has a flavour of its own though, which I may try to catch ... in the proposed article.' The 'proposed article' was a reference to an essay he intended to write on 'The Two St Michael's Mounts'. It is something of a tragedy that, whatever progress may have been made with this essay, nothing has come down to us. Edmund Spenser, Michael Drayton and John Milton were in their turn moved to write of St Michael's Mount. Inspired by their articles, what treasured pages might have been given us by Stevenson!

The next visit to the Westcountry came in 1885, when Stevenson, now married, began his residence at Bournemouth. In August of that year he started out on an intended visit to Dartmoor. He had with him his wife and stepson, Lloyd Osbourne, and three friends. The journey was broken at Dorchester, where they stayed a few days at the Kings Arms Hotel, and there he called on Thomas Hardy. This was the only occasion when these two men met. Unfortunately the visit to Dartmoor was never made, as, at Exeter, Stevenson, who had been for some years a sick man, fell seriously ill. There he stayed for some weeks and on his return to Bournemouth in October he wrote to a friend: 'I have been nearly six months ... in a strange condition of collapse.' That appears to have been Stevenson's last visit to the Westcountry. While he was at Exeter Stevenson stayed at the New London Hotel. The visitor's book contains the entry made by R.L.S. with the words: 'I cannot go without sending my obligations to everyone in the house; if it is your fate to fall sick at an inn, pray Heaven it be at the New London! Robert Louis Stevenson.' Many years later, in 1912, a memorial window in stained glass by Wilfred Drake was placed by his mother and his brother, Maurice Drake, the novelist, in the room Stevenson had occupied during his illness. The window is illuminated with a Latin inscription with a tribute to his life and achievement.

One further memorial to Stevenson's Westcountry associations is, of course, to be found in the opening chapters of *Treasure Island*. Everyone will recall that the earlier scenes of that immortal story centre in a village on the Devonshire coast. Stevenson gave a handsome return for any Westcountry hospitality when he selected Devonshire soil for his Admiral Benbow and made Jim Hawkins, a Devonshire boy, the hero of that glorious adventure.

It is comforting to remember that, while Stevenson could make nothing of the Cornish, there was one Cornishman at least who understood Stevenson very well. He was one of the younger writers of that time and his name was Arthur Quiller-Couch. Writing from Vailiana, his home in Samoa, in October 1891, Stevenson asked for *Noughts and Crosses* by 'Q'. One would like to know what he thought of the book when he read it. We know what 'Q' thought of R.L.S. and we are glad to remember that 'Q' wrote the most memorable lament on the news of his death and was the disciple chosen to write the concluding chapters of *St Ives*. In those sixty-five pages we have Stevenson's happiest and most enduring association with the Westcountry and in writing them 'Q' must have rejoiced that he was thus enabled to touch the hilt of his master's work.[84]

Like most people, I suppose, I first came across Stevenson in *Treasure Island*. That was back in the year 1894 or thereabouts, I bought every week a boys' paper called Chums. They had a serial entitled *Treasure Island*. That was the first I knew of Robert Louis Stevenson. I didn't trouble much about him but – *Treasure Island*! I know that map of Stevenson's imagination better than any authentic map I had studied at school. I read then for the first time about Jim Hawkins, who came from the Westcountry, about Black Dog, and Captain John Silver. Unhappily the story was a serial, and I had to wait a whole week before I could learn what had happened to the *Hispaniola*, and Jim's fight with Mr Israel Hands, the coxswain. I bought the paper on the way to school and looked first at the pictures and then read the whole weekly part. Looking back, I seem to have been reading Stevenson off and on ever since. His work has been honoured in the fine successive collections of his works. There are the Edinburgh, the Swanston, the Tusitala, the Skerryvore, and the Pentland editions. Mine is the Pentland. It is worth while to take down the volumes one by one – there are twenty of them – and to turn the pages slowly, catching sight again of the arresting phrase, the gleaming sentence, and the long paragraph which – twenty, thirty, forty years ago – we marked for its beauty and cadence.

---

84. Stevenson (1850–94) died with this novel, begun in 1893, unfinished. Quiller-Couch finished and published it in 1897.

Have we ever thought what a gap would be left if we had to tear out of the literature of our generation all that Stevenson gave us? His life seemed to hang on a very slender thread. Had that slender thread snapped, as well it might have done, when he was twenty-four as it did when he was forty-four, we should have known nothing of Robert Louis Stevenson and nothing of the scores of men and women who people his books. All the work contained in these twenty volumes was done within the short space of less than twenty years. Throughout nearly the whole of that time Stevenson lived the life of a winged bird. He was a sick man and his life could hardly be reckoned at a pin's fee. Deprived of the use of his right hand, he learned to write with his left. When unable to write at all he fell back upon dictation, and, on occasion, when unable even to speak, he resorted to the alphabet of the deaf and dumb. To most men these disabilities would have been virtually a sentence of death, and the achievement of Stevenson, despite what his friend Henley called these 'bludgeonings of fate', has rightly come to be regarded as a triumph of the human spirit. The Pentland edition, with the four volumes of the *Letters*, might very well stand as a monument of fortitude, endurance and moral heroism. Out of the weakness came forth strength, and this man dying daily – in Pauline phrase – wrote with gaiety, gallantry and residence of his favourite themes – of the river, the open road, the stars, the heavens, the dawn and sunrise, and the shining morning face. In a generation which gave us the mournful resignation of *Omar Khayyam* and the pessimism of Thomas Hardy with his president of the Immortals, Stevenson wrote his brave affirmations of his belief in the ultimate decency of things. He was, throughout, on the side of the angels, and it is safe to say that no man of letters in the past century has added more to the sum total of human happiness. So let there be grace before Robert Louis Stevenson, and while we give thanks for *Treasure Island* and *Kidnapped*, and rejoice in the essays and letters, let us not forget the poems. Apart from the *Child's Garden of Verses*, which I suppose has delighted every boy or girl who has read anything at all, there are the other verses which gleam with significance and beauty. There are at least twenty-five of Stevenson's poems – I must forbear quoting even their titles – that should live and sing in our memory.

The question has been put a hundred times: will Stevenson live? Well, he has lived so far; and my conjecture is that in the year of grace 1995 *Treasure Island* will still be read; John Silver will still be one of the best-known characters in fiction; *Dr Jekyll and Mr Hyde* will still enthral. *A Child's Garden of Verses* will still be in every child's nursery; and 'Requiem' will still be reckoned one of the few great short poems in the English tongue.

9 Sir Arthur Quiller-Couch: Isaac Foot's tribute to his old friend

Sir Arthur Quiller-Couch (1863–1944), known as 'Q', on the eve of his eightieth birthday on 21 November 1943 in the study of his house, The Haven, overlooking Fowey harbour.

We always think of Arthur Quiller-Couch of course as a Cornishman, but really he had a Devonshire mother and he was half Devonshire and educated in Devonshire. I had a great love for Quiller-Couch, but he got his inspiration, strangely enough, not in Cornwall but in Devon. When he was a schoolboy he went to Budleigh Woods, near Newton Abbot, and he says he was met that afternoon by a vision. He was alone: 'It was nothing more than sunlight, slanting down a broad glade between two woodlands that drowsed in the summer heat, but it held me at gaze while the mere beauty of it flooded into my veins and the mysterious bliss of it shook my young body.'

It would probably be impossible for anyone outside the Westcountry fully to understand our sense of personal loss when we learnt that 'Q' had, at his death, left his autobiography unfinished. *Memories and Opinions*, with its hundred precious pages, included no more than the record of his boyhood and youth, and ended with the publication of his first novel, *Dead Man's Rock*, in 1887. 'Q' was then only twenty-four years old. It is true we had the memorable chapter on his Cornish grandfather, Jonathan Couch – a giant in his way – and on his father, the Bodmin doctor, whose carriage was generally stacked full with books, and on his schooling and courtship and marriage. But what would we not have given for the full story?

Most happily, 'Q' was a prophet honoured in his own country, in his own house and by his own kin. His kin was, indeed, the whole Westcountry and certainly not less Devon than

Cornwall. Cornish on his father's side and born in the Duchy, his mother – 'the most beautiful thing in the world' – came from the ve ry heart of Devon, and was herself of long Devonshire lineage. His upbringing was actually more in Devon than in Cornwall. It was at the head of Bradley Woods that the young Newton Abbot schoolboy had the 'vision', when 'the mere beauty of it flooded into my veins and the mysterious bliss of it shook my young body'.

'Q' might, indeed, well have found his later home in Devonshire and have done for Devon what he afterwards did for Cornwall. But there was Fowey. Fowey, too, at first sight, had taken captive his young heart. Beyond all this, it was the place of his courtship and marriage. Cornwall and Fowey hardly realise how much they owe to the gracious lady who still lives at The Haven. Fowey became famous as Troy Town; The Haven became probably the one Cornish home best known throughout the land, and, in the course of years, 'Q' became, not only the mayor of Troy, but the leading citizen of our two western counties, and the most famous Cornishman of his generation. Gradually, by his spoken and written word – line upon line, precept upon precept – and by his unstinted public service, he gained for himself a devotion and regard which, with some of us, was only 'on this side idolatry'. In his essay on the death of Stevenson 'Q' wrote: 'Surely another age will wonder over this curiosity of letters – that for five years the needle of literary endeavour in Great Britain has quivered towards a little island in the South Pacific, as to its magnetic pole.' A good many needles of literary and other endeavour quivered towards that modest house and garden overlooking the estuary of the Fowey. The house itself was a symbol of the three things that counted so much in 'Q's life – the town, the river, and the sea.

One day, I trust, we shall have the fuller biography, the fuller story of this man whose kingship grew with the years. A great bookman, he was greater than all his books. Learned and unlearned came under the sway of one who kept in mature years and old age the high standards of his youth, and who never lost faith in goodness and in his fellow-countrymen. They marked his bearing and longed to share his proud sorrow when he lost his only son. To use his own words spoken of a friend, in like bereavement: 'But though the roof had fallen, the pillar stood upright.' 'Q's own autobiography, and the book that will yet be written, will tell us the story of the man who was our friend; of his deep sense of duty, his scorn and passion when deeply moved, his whimsicality and fun, his deep respect for his Methodist ancestry and his tolerant regard for his Nonconformist neighbours; his radicalism and Liberal faith, his love for the children of the poorest homes, and his constant championship of the dispossessed and the disinherited. The whole story, when told, might conclude with the suggested epitaph with which, some thirty years ago, 'Q' ended the biography of his friend, Arthur John Butler: 'He loved his fellows, his books, and the flowers of the field. Here lies a scholar and a Christian gentleman.'[85]

---

85. 'Man of Troy', review of Frederick Brittain, *Arthur Quiller-Couch: a Biographical Study of Q* (Cambridge University Press, 1947). Isaac Foot's 'Troy' was Fowey.

10 Eden Phillpotts: a tribute to a Westcountryman

Isaac and Kitty Foot toast Eden Phillpotts (1862–1960) at his home in Broadclyst on his ninety-first birthday with water taken from the river Dart at Postbridge on their journey over Dartmoor from Cornwall.

I have read very many of Eden Phillpotts's books. Not all of them by any means. Two hundred and fifty books – that is said to be the number – are a formidable proposition for any common reader. One of my weaknesses is that I am a book collector. I have the added weakness in my desire to acquire first editions. I have, I suppose, about a hundred of Eden Phillpotts's books filling five or six shelves. They are kept side by side with all the first editions of Sir Arthur Quiller-Couch. In this house of mine, which seems to be filled with books from cellar to attic, Eden Phillpotts and 'Q' demand a whole landing to themselves. It is well known that books can give a special atmosphere to different parts of any house. Every book lover can discern the difference as he passes where Robert Louis Stevenson, Thomas Hardy, Joseph Conrad or Arnold Bennett may hold sway. And there are the books of Eden Phillpotts and sometimes, as I pass, I glance from title to title. As things are, I cannot hope to read all these books again but it is good to greet the faces of old friends. One of the oldest of these friends is a soiled volume of sixty-three pages published at a shilling and with the title *My Adventure in the Flying Scotsman*. It bears the inscription in the familiar handwriting, 'Eden Phillpotts wrote this, his first story printed in covers, in 1888 and autographed in 1946.' The place of honour on the Eden Phillpotts landing is given not even to the stately Widecombe edition of later years but to this unpromising frontrunner.

I can recall reading many of Eden Phillpotts's books when they first appeared. The book I began with was *Children of the Mist*, published in 1898 and dedicated to R. D. Blackmore of *Lorna Doone* fame. I was then a youth of eighteen and Eden Phillpotts was nearly twenty years my senior. It was to be the first of the Dartmoor Cycle. In that cycle there were twenty volumes, written during a period of twenty years and concluding with *Children of Men*. They were republished in the handsome Widecombe edition in 1927 and the first of that series, *Widecombe Fair*, carried a notable introduction by Arnold Bennett. That introduction was not only the noble salutation of one master-craftsman to another, but the outcome of a rich literary friendship. Returning to *Children of the Mist*, published in 1898, it might be well to remember that, although the first of the Dartmoor Cycle, it was not the first book that Eden Phillpotts wrote on the Dartmoor theme. Seven years earlier he had written *Folly and Fresh Air*, the frolicsome story of a holiday at 'Tavybridge'. That book contains many pages devoted to the glory of Dartmoor. It concludes with a valedictory ode, bidding farewell to Dartmoor:

> Farewell to thy manifold glories and graces,
> Thou heart of sweet Devon so wild and free.

Happily for us the farewell was not final. Then again, in 1896 Eden Phillpotts published a series of short stories under the title *Down Dartmoor Way*. That is a lovely title for a book, and it might almost be the title for Eden Phillpott's whole life – 'Down Dartmoor Way'.

Looking back again to my first reading of *Children of the Mist* I can recall why the book made such a deep impression on me. It was not so much its literary artistry or its delineation of character. Upon these I was hardly qualified to judge. What held me was that I found myself reading a story of my own homeland. As I have previously said, it was my good fortune, when a boy, to spend holiday after holiday on Dartmoor in and around Postbridge, at the very heart of the moor. One of these days I recall vividly when I had to return home. This time I was not alone. I was with my brother. He was about ten years old and I was about eight. We walked all the way from Birch Tor to Princetown. The eight or nine miles would not have mattered so much, but it was a day of rain – Dartmoor rain, moreover. We had our small knapsack, an umbrella, and a large square biscuit tin full of whortleberries, 'whorts' they call them, which was to be a present to our mother. Before long the umbrella was torn to ribbons. The rain was ceaseless and pitiless and, when at last we reached Princetown station, we were soaked to the skin. Still, Dartmoor was not always like that and I generally returned to my home in Plymouth, where we lived in a crowded street, and at night I dreamed of these hills not so very far away and longed for the day when I could see them again. It was against this background and with those recollections that I first read *Children in the Mist*. Here was a writer recalling the memories of my boyhood and describing things I could not say for myself.

At first I naturally assumed that this new writer was a Devonian but it was much later that I learned that Eden Phillpotts was not a Devon man by birth, but, as he himself says, an 'alien'. Born in India and being brought to England when he was still very young, his widowed mother established her new home in Dawlish. What Dawlish meant to the boy we can read of in some glowing pages in *A West Country Pilgrimage*, but, of course, Dawlish meant Devon. A good deal depended on his mother's choice of abode. Had she, with all Britain to choose from, made her home elsewhere, presumably there would have been no Dartmoor Cycle and this symposium would never have been written. Fortunately for us, Mrs Phillpotts chose Devon as her place of residence and, more wisely still, she chose Plymouth as the place for her son's education. Plymouth was, of course, not far from Dartmoor and thus began the lifelong friendship between this wholly desirable 'alien' and our beloved Westcountry.

But Dartmoor is not his only territory. A year before *Children of the Mist* there appeared *Lying Prophets*, which is a story of Cornwall. Eden Phillpotts, at that time, went to Cornwall designing a story of the Scilly Islands. An illness, however, prevented him from going farther than Penzance and, during his enforced stay there, he wrote the novel based on the country-side around Land's End and this book he has himself described as his 'first serious effort'. How keen has been his interest in Cornwall is also shown in his novel *Old Delabole*, published in 1915 and dedicated to Thomas Hardy. Three of the most striking chapters in *A West CountryPilgrimage*, published in 1920, are devoted to Cornwall, and his chapter on 'A Cornish Cross' reveals the warmth of his affection for the neighbouring county. Fortunately, as we think, the lure of Devon asserted itself and there, after a brief exile in London, he found his home, first at Torquay and then at Broadclyst, near Exeter. He has lived long enough amongst us to know our countryside as perhaps no one else has done. Over that countryside where, as a boy, he loved to roam alone he has led tens of thousands of readers in this and other lands. There are multitudes of people on both sides of the Atlantic, most of whom will never set foot on Dartmoor, but who will know and love the place because Eden Phillpotts has told them so much about it. He has told them not only of the great spaces and the high hills, and the rugged tors, but of the rivers – the Dart, the Teign, the Tavy, the Okement, the Walkham, the young Tamar and the tiny Dartmoor streams.

For these folk, many of whom will never visit our shores, he will have preserved so much of our Westcountry speech and especially our country dialect. As a boy I learnt something of that dialect from my country neighbours and relations. Somehow, the music of the streams, the smell of the earth and the sparkle of the peat fire had passed into their voices. Eden Phillpotts happily lived long enough amongst us to learn something of this language and a hundred years hence his books will be there to tell those who care to learn what manner of people we were and how we spoke to one another. They will read of Clem Hicks reciting his love-song to Chris Blanchard, 'the handsomest girl in Chagford', 'with that grand, rolling sea-beat of an accent that Elizabeth once loved to hear on the lips of Raleigh and Drake'. Not the least debt we owe to Eden Phillpotts is that so many of these old records and so much of this folklore will have been preserved 'against the tooth of time and razure of oblivion'.[86]

---

86. Isaac Foot's contribution to Waveney Girvan (ed.), *Eden Phillpotts: An Assessment and a Tribute*, Hutchinson, 1953.

Over the years Isaac Foot and Eden Phillpotts regularly sent each other birthday greetings:

Phillpotts to Foot, 1954: Very Many Happy Returns of this auspicious anniversary. May Cornwall enjoy sunshine appropriate to the occasion ... I live indoors and spend my working hours at my desk. There my present work is the novel which grows slowly but steadily. Incidentally the scene of the story is Postbridge and the title 'Love In a Mist'. The angle of love is rather a misty memory in any case but I am doing my aged best to revive the emotion and indicate its complexities and surprises in Mid-Moor. Your books are all duly signed and I hope that spring may see you here to recover them.

Your old friend Eden Phillpotts.

Phillpotts to Foot, 4 November 1954: Very cordial thanks for your letter which helps one to confront my entry into another year. It is a very great privilege to enjoy your good will and I am proud of doing so. Last birthday is vividly in memory this morning, when Mrs Foot and yourself toasted me in the sparkling waters of the East Dart after your morning dash over the Moor. Who but you would have done such a thing and given me so much pleasure. I shall always regard that event as marking a very red-letter day.

Phillpotts to Foot, 24 February 1957: One line to wish you very many happy returns of remarkable birthdays – for, with you, there came into the world one who has made it better than he found it.

11 Oliver Cromwell: 'I was not always a Cromwellian'

Back in or about the year 1894, I took part in the opening debate of the Hoe Grammar School in Plymouth. The proposition selected by Mr Dymond, the headmaster of honoured memory, was: 'The execution of Charles I was not justifiable.' We were invited to append our names. I had some cogitation and a night's hard reading from an encyclopaedia from my father's bookshelves, and the next morning I remember signing my name 'I. Foot' on the list of intending speakers, and in favour of the motion. That was my maiden speech at the age of fourteen, made, as I now think, on the wrong side.

Oliver Cromwell (1599–1658).

115

A year later I was in London, a boy clerk in the Civil Service. Living at the same lodgings at Wandsworth was another civil servant and amongst his books was John Richard Green's *Short History of the English People*. The hero of my young manhood was Dr John Clifford. He is my hero still. He once broke off in one of his speeches and said, turning to some youths in his audience: 'Have you read your Green's *History*, you young men? If not, sell your boots and get it.' That was enough for me. A word from Dr Clifford was for me almost gospel. I didn't sell my boots but I got my Green's *History* alright. My fellow-lodger saw that I coveted that book and one day sold it to me for eight shillings and sixpence. That was a lot of money in those days. It was more than half my weekly salary. It was paid in instalments. I have the book before me now bearing his name and mine. It is a little ragged and would fetch very little on the outside shelves in Charing Cross Road, but for me it seems worth its weight in gold. That book helped to make me a Cromwellian. I had some queer ideas about Charles I in those days and hadn't quite made up my mind about Oliver Cromwell. Upon those things John Richard Green put me right and put me right once and for all.

Not long after, I read for the first time Macaulay's 'Essay on John Hampden'. I was then living at Bayswater and it was my custom to walk four miles each way from my lodgings to Spring Gardens. I liked to read as I walked. I learned the shortest cut from the first gate in Kensington Gardens, across Hyde Park or Green Park. For long stretches there was no sight of human habitation. One half of the essay I could read on my way to work and the other half on my way back. If I felt like declaiming, I was free to do so and Macaulay's 'Essay on Hampden' I could almost recite by heart. That essay is virtually Macaulay's history of Charles I and the Civil War. Its great phrases are still fresh in my memory. 'The nation looked round for a defender. Calmly and unostentatiously the plain Buckinghamshire Esquire placed himself at the head of his countrymen and right before the face and across the path of tyranny.'

A little later, in the year 1899, the three hundredth anniversary of Cromwell's birth gave rise to a lot of writing. One Sunday when I was preaching there I was the guest of a gracious lady at Ivybridge. Upon her table was a copy of the *London Quarterly Review* for July 1899. The magazine contained an article by Sylvester Horne – I had often heard him preach in London. That article of his I read, and then I read it again. From that time I was a Cromwellian. Being a Cromwellian I began to read all the books I could lay my hands on. They were, of course, for the most part borrowed books. The Plymouth Library was naturally my main source of supply. I got to know almost every page of Gardiner, Firth, Morley and the other biographers, but my main desire was to know what Cromwell himself had to say. I wanted to hear Oliver's own voice, to hear what he himself had said and to read what he had written himself. And that of course brought me to Thomas Carlyle. I was introduced to Carlyle by W. T. Stead, the benefactor of that generation when he was publishing his series of the Penny Poets. All my first reading of Milton, Shelley, Keats, Coleridge and the rest was from those little yellow penny volumes. I have about thirty of them still. But one of his books was larger than the rest. It was his abridgement of Carlyle's *Letters and Speeches of Cromwell*.[87] In his introduction to that slim book of 160 pages he said that when he was a boy in his teens he borrowed Carlyle's book from the library and, because he could not afford 3s. 6d. to buy a copy, he wrote out for himself all the passages that seemed memorable and noteworthy. He describes Carlyle's book as being 'compiled by the literary master of one century as a tribute to the greatest of our race'. Of course I read Carlyle. As soon as his book was published he made two presentations. The first was to his mother in Annandale in Scotland, who, we are told, lapped up Cromwell's words, skipping all her son's comments and so-called elucidations. That book is, I suppose, somewhere in the world. If so, I would like to learn of its whereabouts. The other presentation was to his wife. That copy I have in my hand as I am talking to you with Carlyle's bookplate. On the first page, in Carlyle's handwriting, is the inscription 'To Jane W. Carlyle Her Own T.C. Chelsea 12th November 1845'. That was a noble gift from a man to his wife, and it was a yet nobler gift to the English-speaking world.

A few years ago Professor W. C. Abbott of Harvard University died at Cambridge, Massachusetts. Before his death he completed his four volumes, *The Writings and Speeches of Oliver Cromwell*.[88] That massive edition, comprising in all some thousands of pages, is now the authoritative record of Cromwell's spoken and written word. That, too, was a noble gift to the world. When I was last in America about thirteen years ago, I was welcomed at his house at Cambridge. That monumental work was only made by the generosity and resources of Harvard University. Oliver Cromwell's first love was England. His second love was New England. That love was munificently recognised in the great work completed only a few years ago. Professor Abbott's four massive volumes are almost unprocurable in this country. As a result, a generation has grown up in this country to most of whom Cromwell is virtually unknown. Carlyle, I understand, is in these days almost unread. It would seem therefore, that Cromwell is no longer allowed to speak for himself. That, I believe, to be a great loss to the nation. That is why well-meaning people are so often being misled. I have come to see that the only safeguard against this is the reference to Cromwell's own words. There is no real substitute for the actual words of Cromwell. My emphasis today is not so much upon the speeches of Cromwell but on the letters. The speeches can come later, and we can never be sure that the words as reported were precisely those that were spoken. But the letters we can be sure of. They are there. About 400 of his letters have come down to us. They were written in different places: some at home, some on the field of battle – some on Cromwell's long journeys, and some in the very midst of actual military operations. Some

---

87. Published in 1845.
88. Published between 1937 and 1947.

are intimate and, like those written to his wife and family, were never intended for the public eye. Some were written to Mr Speaker at the Parliament, some to his officers and generals, including his great generals at sea, like Blake. Some were written to foreign potentates and ambassadors. They extend over about thirty years – thirty of the most eventful years of our history, and are indeed a chronicle of the times.

Read these letters for yourself, and, if you will read them with an open mind, you will find the story of a man of great humility and simplicity. You will be struck with the fact that on every page there is shown a profound knowledge of his Bible. No ruler in history – not even his hero Gustavus Adolphus of Sweden – has so intimate a knowledge of the Scriptures. You will find that he never takes praise for himself but is lavish in his praise of others. Sometimes he wrestles with the theologians of his time. Sometimes there is quiet banter, sometimes grim irony. Every now and then he strikes out a phrase which has passed into our English literature. The greatest soldier of his time, he writes with a hatred of war and a fierce condemnation of those who would be peace breakers. His almost every letter reveals the love of his country. Someone has said that, when he writes of England, it is always with the language of a lover. His letters to foreign powers were often for the relief of the oppressed. Sometimes a letter of his would stay the upraised sword of the oppressor. That is why the hunted and the persecuted in other lands prayed for him in their cellars and their forbidden assemblies. I sometimes say that, if I have a man's letters, I will make my own biography. Do you remember how Tennyson, in his *In Memoriam*, speaks of the hunger of his heart for the letters of Arthur Hallam – the noble letters of the dead?

> So word by word and line by line,
> The dead man touch'd me from the past
> And all at once it seem'd at last
> The living soul was flash'd on mine.[89]

---

89. Tennyson wrote *In Memoriam A.H.H.* in memory of his friend Arthur Hallam. It was published in 1850.

12 Isaac Foot's commonplace books

As a youth I was impressed by what Plutarch said about Julius Caesar, that he kept a commonplace book in which he wrote down every memorable saying he heard or great passage that occurred in his reading. In this one respect, at least, I determined to emulate Caesar. As a result, I now have a series of commonplace books and anthologies of all my old favourite writers ... I do not believe in quotation for the sake of quotations. They should come from a man's reading. If anything I have read nails home what I want to say, I feel at liberty to use it. In particular, I think an appropriate line of poetry gives colour and vividness to any man's discourse. The quotation, however, to be fully effective, must be from a man's own reading and not something stuck in a speech like a piece of ornament. Take Matthew 13, verse 52: 'Every scribe which is instructed unto the Kingdom of Heaven is like unto a man that is an householder, which bringeth forth out of his treasure things new and old.'

MICHAEL: As he read, my father made constant notes in his little red notebooks. No doubt other writers or readers have produced books with the same name or title. But, since my father seemed to start on this enterprise early in life and never ceased adding to their number, he covered wider fields than anyone else had done before. There were several hundreds of his own commonplace books, which comprise the essence or the main things that he selected from his reading. As he returned to these subjects again and again, his whole collection in this field was unique. Indeed he produced towards the end an index of all these volumes which itself filled a whole note book.

My father would make anthologies of poetry. For him Wordsworth's phrase, 'Poetry is the breath and finer spirit of all knowledge' was true. He had the best anthology of sonnets ever collected, all these written out in his own hand, which must have taken him hours, but by doing this, he could memorise them better and could always draw on this tremendous stock of literary knowledge which was quite incomparable, in my opinion. A particular subject which attracted him at first was an anthology on rivers.

Isaac Foot recalled his first interest in the rivers when he was a child in Horrabridge, his father's birthplace, where the river Walkham flows under the bridge.

There at Horrabridge was the street leading to the bridge; the bridge seems a very small bridge today but then I thought it was a most wonderful structure. And the bridge at that time was the sort of centre for the conversation of the village. They have the town halls, the village halls today but at that time the bridge was the place where the people made converse. But I got interested in the bridges, and particularly in the river; and I would go down and look at the river and wonder where it came from and where it was going. I didn't know at that time that it joined the Tavy later on, and then went into the Tamar and then it went to wash the foreshore with other water of my own beloved Plymouth. Well, ever since, I've been interested in the river. And so much so that I've written down anything that appeals to me because of its beauty – I've written down in my commonplace books all that has been written by our Westcountry poets upon the river. That's why I've rejoiced in the writing of Sir John Squire, who wrote a magnificent poem upon the river, but in the end he came back not to the great rivers of the world but to the small rivers, and his poetry upon that I think is very beautiful.[90] Have you heard it? I remember how it concludes here, where he says:

> No, even were they Ganges and Amazon
> In all their great might and majesty,
> League upon league of wonders,
> I would lose them all, and more,
> For a light chiming of small bells,
> A twisting flash in the granite,
> The tiny thread of a pixie waterfall
> That lives by Vixen Tor.

And then he went on to speak about the rivers at Tavistock and elsewhere:

> For many a hillside streamlet
> There falls with a broken twinkle,
> Falling and dying, falling and dying,
> In little cascades and pools,
> Where the world is furze and heather
> And flashing plovers and fixed larks,
> And an empty sky, whitish blue,
> That small world rules.
>
> There, there where the high waste bog-lands
> And the drooping slopes and the spreading valleys,
> The orchards and the cattle-sprinkled pastures
> Those travelling musics fill,
> There is my lost Abana,
> And there is my nameless Parphar[91]
> That mixed with my heart when I was a boy,
> And time stood still.

90. Sir John Squire (1882–1958), poet, writer and historian. His *Collected Poems* were edited by John Betjeman and published in 1959.
91. Abana and Parphar were two rivers in Damascus.

That's how Squires writes about the river and I've been interested in all the rivers of the world when I've been abroad. And so, wherever I've gone, I've tried to see the river – these big rivers. But I've come back like Squires does to the small rivers. I think the most of the little streams that I know, particularly the little stream below Buck's Tor, two and a half miles beyond Postbridge, where I had to stay in the company of a mine captain and his family. That taught me a great deal when I was a boy, because there it was, I was not only on the moor, but I was on the moor alone. And the only time to see Dartmoor is to see it when you are alone – to see it particularly when you are a boy, when you are very young. To see it if you can against the sunrise. And therefore that little stream that runs in that valley that used to work those tin mines, that is the poetry that appeals to me.

I like to think that Coleridge when he was a boy went out and spent one night in the woods right in the depth of summer. And during that night he heard that music and he traced the music and traced it to a tiny stream, and it sang all night, and he remembered it afterwards when he wrote a poem – not about the woods of Devonshire, but about the distant seas and the Ancient Mariner when he went on with beautiful language and some of the simplest and the shortest words of English speech:

It ceased [he said]; yet still the sails made on
A pleasant noise till noon,
A noise like of a hidden brook
In the leafy month of June,
That to the sleeping woods all night
Singeth a quiet tune.

SARAH: Once when my grandfather and Lady Astor were travelling up to London together by train she asked if she could see what he was reading. It was one of his many common-place books, in which he wrote his favourite passages of literature, and this one was devoted to one of his favourite authors – Milton. When the train arrived in London Nancy Astor asked if she might borrow it for a few days. Reluctantly Isaac lent her the book. When a week had passed he telephoned Nancy Astor's secretary and asked her to arrange for the return of his treasured book. But after repeated enquiries it was still not returned. Isaac was distraught. If the book had been lost or mislaid it could mean the end of a lasting friendship. Eventually Lady Astor not only returned the book but presented him with several leather-bound gilt-edged copies which she had had printed especially for him. The inscription on the front in gold letters read: 'To I. F. from N. A. On the first page is printed: 'John Milton: Selections from His Works and Tributes to His Genius. Arranged by Isaac Foot and presented to him by Nancy Astor 1935.' He was overcome and often told this story in later years.

13 Michael Verran of Callington and Thomas Carlyle

MICHAEL: Isaac Foot, the great reader and book lover, was somehow not so eager to write books himself. He would say that writing to him 'was most irksome'. He was always too busy reading to waste time writing; he needed to move on to the next great interest. Maybe also he was contrasting his talents too harshly with his favourites. One exception to this practice was the book he did actually complete in 1946, even while he was still working as Lord Mayor of Plymouth. He had long intended to write a book, the materials for which he had especially collected, on Michael Verran and his devotion to the Methodist cause, so he fulfilled this work himself. He had special guidance from the same Thomas Carlyle who had also been for him the chief defender of Oliver Cromwell. He did this book to honour Verran for his Methodism. His distaste for the actual process of writing makes it all the more remarkable that, amidst all the other distractions of the post-1945 world, he found the time to write this book on Michael Verran. His preface, reprinted here, explains the special circumstances that persuaded him to make time for this book.

Isaac Foot's preface
If any apology is needed for this little book I can only say that, for quite a long time, I have felt an obligation to gather together the materials for this story of Michael Verran. I first came across his name when reading Carlyle's *Life of Sterling* over forty years ago. Later I became the fortunate possessor of the *Journal of Caroline Fox*, with its glowing pages devoted to the story of Thomas Carlyle's intervention on Verran's behalf. Everything about the man Verran interested me. He was a Methodist and moreover a Bible Christian. From my boyhood I have had a great respect for the Bible Christian Church which has done such beneficial work, particularly in our two Western counties. At school I had the great advantage of being taught by two fine Bible Christian masters, George Pearse Dymond and John Rounsefell. I am very much in their debt. Then again, Verran belonged to Callington, a place which has been my home for twenty years and which I first came to know over forty years ago. Callington stands next to Plymouth in my affections. Furthermore, Verran was a Cornish miner and my work at the Mines Department gave me a special interest in the men engaged in that industry. Then, early in 1944, a seemingly trifling event drew my attention again to the Verran story. Almost by accident I became the possessor of a small file of papers which were being sold by the Sterling family. I bought the papers because they related to correspondence between Carlyle and Caroline Fox about a Cromwell medal which, strangely enough, had also come into my possession many years before. But the file of correspondence I found included something else. There was the actual Memorandum drawn up by Carlyle in December 1842 for the purpose of assisting Verran, and on the

'Petition' were the names of those who had come to his help. Thereupon I determined to write something upon this man whose story seemed to be constantly recurring in my mind.

Michael Verran of Callington and Thomas Carlyle *was published in 1946 in London by the Epworth Press. Nancy Astor, in her letter of thanks to Isaac Foot for sending her a copy, described it thus:*

> A little gem: so neat, so tidy, so unexpected, so apparently artless. You are so much at home in the great treasure house of English literature, have illumined a dark corner and, in so doing, have created another treasure. The great humanists would have loved your little essay. Carlyle will no doubt return dusty thanks to you from beyond the shades.

PART IV

Isaac Foot the electioneer

MICHAEL: My father made himself a formidable figure on the platforms of the Westcountry in the first two decades of the twentieth century. We should remind ourselves that this was, more than any other age before or since, most surely the age of the platform. Gladstone had shown the way in his great Midlothian campaigns. Lloyd George had carried the idea from his own native land of Wales across the whole country. Emmeline Pankhurst was proving that the women could master the art and command her audiences no less than the men. Isaac Foot, in the Westcountry, had learnt his platform style especially from the Methodist Church as one of its local preachers, from the Sunday schools and from the Wesleyan Guilds. He never ceased to pay tribute to those who had taught him his trade but he performed the whole role with a special Westcountry accent. He honoured his own Plymouth above eve ry other place but he had learned too in all the chapels in the neighbouring districts of Devon and Cornwall. He actually fought his first parliamentary election in 1910 and was only narrowly defeated by a few dozen votes. If he had won that Totnes election he would have already sta rted making his ma rk in the Parliament that he honoured so greatly. He would doubtless have played his own individual part in arguments going on in the Liberal Party bet ween the Asquithians and the followers of Lloyd George. He originally owed allegiance to both of them and recognised how each had made their own contribution to the Liberalism they inherited from Gladstone, who remained my father's number one political hero. It was sad that his own appearance in Parliament was delayed but when it happened he made up for lost time.

14 1910–18 Early election campaigns

Isaac Foot first stood for Parliament as the Liberal candidate for Totnes in the general election of January 1910, the first of two in that year. He achieved the best result for the Liberals there for twenty years. David Lloyd George had been one of the young Isaac Foot's political heroes.

I first heard Lloyd George speak at the Battersea Town Hall on John Burns's platform. That was in the year 1896. I was then a boy of sixteen and Lloyd George was a member of Parliament aged about thirty-three. His name meant nothing to me but I remember the flash of his eye and his burning eloquence and my young blood tingled in my veins as he spoke of the quarrymen of Penryn: 'Lord Penryn owns a mountain. At a word he can lock up that mountain, put the keys in his pocket and send hundreds of my fellow-countrymen over the face of their native land to beg their bread.' Then, as always, he spoke in metaphor, and gave to his listeners a picture. I saw the picture alright and as I went back to my lodgings in Wandsworth I saw Lord Penryn with the keys, I saw him put the keys in his pocket and I saw the workless Welsh people streaming over the countryside.

In January 1910, Lloyd George addressed a great meeting at the Drill Hall, Plymouth. As one of the local candidates I had to take a small part. I was thirty years of age, he was forty-seven. He was then at his full height and 10,000 people – some of whom had tramped from the neighbouring countryside through the night – were there to give him a welcome a king might have envied. There were no loudspeakers in those days. But from the very first sentence he had the vast throng in his grasp. Men were moved to ecstasy as he spoke of the coming triumph and in some passages of deeper emotion the great company swayed like a field of corn moved by the breeze.

Isaac Foot's own part in this meeting was noted.

Liberals still recall that, though Mr Lloyd George had a great reception from the 10,000 Westcountry Liberals who filled the huge Drill Hall, Mr Foot had a greater, because the courage of the young Liberal who was going to lead a forlorn hope in the Totnes Division in which the strongest Unionist in the West, Colonel Mildmay, had been entrenched since 1885, had captured popular imagination. Mr Foot stood by Mr Lloyd George and delivered a fighting speech that was cheered to the echo.[92]

Isaac Foot's long association with the Bodmin division of south-east Cornwall began when he was adopted as their Liberal candidate to fight in the second general election of 1910 in December. He was again defeated but only by forty votes. His adoption for this division was later recalled in a posthumous tribute.

In retrospect it is curious that they should have selected Isaac Foot from all the scores of potential candidates of far greater fame who would dearly have loved the chance of such a political plum. The strength of the Conservative Party was reason enough for selecting an experienced and mature fighter, and, whatever his qualities, this could not be said of the young Plymouth lawyer. Those who were present at his first adoption meeting before the First World War were immediately aware that, even though he would not be able to make the then customary contribution to the expenses of a campaign, and although his only claim to political distinction was a single fight at Totnes where, however good the result, he nevertheless lost, they had chosen a man who possessed the essential qualities of leadership. A shrewd choice not untypical of the Cornishman who combines with his charm and kindliness a hard-headed realism.[93]

92. *Westminster Gazette*, 13 November 1919.
93. 'To the Memory of Isaac Foot', special issue, *Spotlight on Cornwall*, 1961.

The general election of 1918
After the War Herbert Asquith's Liberal followers – known as the 'Wee Frees' – could not forgive Lloyd George for what was seen as 'a gross betrayal' in 1916 when he forced Asquith to give way and took over from him as Prime Minister and leader of the coalition government. Michael describes the bitter feelings felt by his parents.

I was brought up in a home where the name of David Lloyd George was, above all others, the most accursed. The charge was that he had broken the once so powerful Liberal Party; that he had thrown open the gates to triumphant, gloating Toryism; that the deed had been done in pursuit of raw, personal ambition; a heavy indictment for sure and one not easily refuted or forgotten. Later there was some change of feeling. My father's suspicions and my mother's scorn never subsided altogether, but somehow or other the Lloyd George sunshine - such a burning oracle as it is now difficult to conceive casting its rays across our political planet - penetrated the darkest corners, even in our far-away, Westcountry, one-time Asquithian, retreat.

Isaac Foot himself looked back to his worship of Lloyd George in the days of 1910.

That great moment was never to return. Things happened later giving rise to doubt, hesitation and pain. The leader was lost, at any rate, for the time and, although he returned, there was never 'glad, confident morning' again. In the course of events strange things happened. Three times I fought against political opponents who held as their chief weapon the letter of commendation from Lloyd George. Mine is the melancholy distinction of being the only man in the country who had to fight three times against the Lloyd George 'coupon'. Relationships became strained but there were reconciliations later and, whatever happened, I could never forget the earlier Lloyd George of Battersea Town Hall and of the Plymouth Drill Hall. Having once seen the high hills with the sunlight on their summits, I knew they were there, whatever were the mists and fogs which might otherwise rise to obscure my vision. It may be, as some say, there were two Lloyd Georges. That may be said of a good many of us.

JOHN: In normal circumstances, my father might have hoped to win Bodmin in the general election of 1918, but political events during the First World War dramatically altered the course of his career. As a noted supporter of Asquith following the formation of the coalition government under Lloyd George in 1916, my father was not in receipt of the notorious 'coupon' granted to supporters of the coalition at the 1918 election and lost Bodmin by over 3,000 votes.

Isaac Foot's election address of 1918 set out his opposition to Lloyd George's coalition government and resistance to pledging support for the coalition.

I have the honour to stand as Liberal candidate at the forthcoming general election. This election has been forced upon us with unjustifiable haste, and I associate myself with the general protest against this hurried appeal to the country with altogether inadequate time allowed for consideration of the momentous issues. In my opinion there is no reasonable excuse for this autocratic decision to hold an election in which large numbers of soldiers and sailors will be debarred from taking part. An election held under these conditions will deprive the new Parliament of the full and unquestioned authority necessary to meet the difficulties of the period of peace, settlement and social reconstruction. The peace, made possible by the unexampled valour and sacrifice of the men in our army and navy and mercantile marine, has been won at so great a cost that its full harvest should now be reaped. The first business, both of statesmen and people, must be to establish a democratic partnership and a League of Nations united in the purpose to make an end of war. No other task can compare with this in importance, and, I believe, the longing of the common people throughout all the freedom-loving nations is for the realisation of this long-cherished ideal, thus making the world safe for democracy. We rejoice in the overthrow of despotism and autocracy, and we must make certain that the lives and fortunes of millions of peace-loving folk in all the nations shall never in future depend upon the will and whim of a few men sheltered behind a secret diplomacy. I am opposed to bureaucracy, and would press for the abolition of the irritating, costly and often clumsy control imposed upon us in so many directions during the last four years. Now that a war for freedom has been waged throughout the world we must be the more determined to safeguard and widen our liberties at home. Briefly stated, I support a policy including: the maintenance of free trade; home rule for Ireland; a radical measure of land reform; housing of the people upon an adequate scale; licensing reform, including local option.

I respectfully decline to take the pledge the coalition government seeks to impose. Any such pledge would deprive your representative of that proper independence without which membership of the House of Commons would be a barren honour. The next few years will be a time of uncertainty and surprising developments, and, if the people's representatives are tied and bound by definite pledges to support the executive, the best traditions of Parliament are broken and the future is put in jeopardy. The privilege of representing you would be worth little if I could not do so as a free man. I welcome the spirit of unity, which has marked our public life during these tremendous times, and I believe that unity can best be realised by the honest and fearless expression of that diversity of opinion which is the source of reform and the salt of life. All reforms having for their purpose the destruction of poverty and securing for every citizen the chance to live a full and useful life will have my fervent support, and this support I promise irrespective of the source from which the proposals for reform may come.

As an earnest advocate of adult suffrage I welcome the cooperation of women in the working out of a new social order, and the building up of a new international life based, not on jealousy and fear, but on peace and common sense. If the policy I have advocated commends itself to you I shall welcome your support, and, if I am chosen as the representative of the constituency, I shall be proud to discharge the duties of that great office.

I am, ladies and gentlemen, yours faithfully, Isaac Foot.

15 1919 The Plymouth Sutton division by-election

JOHN: My father's fourth electoral contest was in a by-election against Nancy Astor in Plymouth Sutton in 1919, when he was prevailed upon to uphold the Liberal cause in what was from the beginning a hopeless venture. The electors were still in a state of feverish support for Lloyd George's coalition which had characterised the 1918 election; in a three-cornered contest my father was at the bottom of the poll, only narrowly saving his deposit. Any grief he suffered was more than compensated for by discovering in Lady Astor a life-long friend. I had a very bitter experience during that same by-election because I was so unfortunate at that time to be going to school in Plymouth and at the school I went to – I think there were about a hundred boys altogether – I was the only Liberal and the other ninety-nine were Tory and I remember the way in which I crept to school trying to keep out of the way.

MICHAEL: This election campaign in my father's own native Plymouth achieved world-wide recognition. It was the first election in which a woman was elected under the new rules for membership of Parliament. Lady Astor, wife of Waldorf Astor, the previous MP for the Sutton division of Plymouth, naturally dominated all the reports of that notable event. Previously my father had been a strong opponent of all Tories who had dared to win seats in his beloved Plymouth and Lord Astor had been the most prominent of these. This was my earliest recollection of my father's campaigns. I remember going round in a carriage with

Nancy Astor at the time of her election in 1919 as the first woman to take her seat in Parliament.

my sister, Sally; I may say there wasn't much enthusiasm shown for the Liberal candidate on that occasion. I remember going through a street where there was a Labour poster in every window saying 'Vote for Gay' and a sign up saying 'All Gay for Sutton'. The song we children sang was:

> Who's that knocking at the door?
> Who's that knocking at the door?
> If it's Astor and his wife, we'll stab 'em with a knife
> And they won't be Tories any more.

This was the first song I was encouraged to sing by my father, who was always a furious opponent of Tories, and by my mother, who was an even stronger one. But Lady Astor won that election, not only because of her husband and ancestry, but because she was as good an electioneer as some of us will ever see. She had her own way of using the platform and no holds were barred in the way she dealt with hecklers. She was the truest expositor of the women's case and from the start she proved herself a wonderful new speaker on behalf of the people of Plymouth.

Once again Isaac Foot was faced with an election opponent who, although not a Liberal, had received the public support of the Prime Minister, Lloyd George. This was Isaac Foot's challenge to the leader of the coalition government, delivered in public and in the press:

Dear Mr Lloyd George,

May I be allowed to draw your attention to the letter which you have written to Lady Astor, the Coalition Unionist candidate at the present by-election here, in which you say: 'I am very glad to hear that you have been nominated to contest Plymouth as a Coalition Unionist ... I hope the electors of Sutton Division will return you to Parliament by a large majority ... I cordially recommend your candidature to the electors of Plymouth and trust that they will return you at the head of the poll.' May I remind you of your utterances to a meeting of Liberals addressed by you just a year ago at Downing Street when you used these words: 'From the old leaders of Liberalism I learnt my faith. Even if I had the desire, I am too old now to change. I cannot leave Liberalism. I would quit this place tomorrow if I could not obtain the support of Liberals. I must have Liberal support. Now is the great opportunity for Liberalism.' You cannot surely be unaware that I am standing here as Liberal candidate preaching the Liberalism you have always preached and which you have publicly declared you 'cannot leave'. For many years I have championed your policy and stood up for you when you were assailed with obloquy and bitterness by those who are your present associates. You will surely recognise the crying need for real genuine Liberalism in our legislation and government at the present time. Yet, when an opportunity arises to return a representative of Liberalism to the House of Commons for this constituency, you urge the electors to vote for the Unionist candidate. May I respectfully ask whether you still adhere to your utterance of 12 November last and whether you still regard yourself as a member of the Liberal Party? This is the second election in which you have sought to prevent my return to Parliament. The result of this election is quite a secondary matter. Win or lose, I have a great joy in my advocacy of undying principles which greater men than ourselves have suffered for in past generations. We younger Liberals want to know where you stand with us. We have work to do and cannot wait. If you are with us, let us push on together. If you are not with us, we will read Browning's 'Lost Leader' once again and give ourselves with more devotion to the cause, which is happily greater than one man and more enduring than a single generation.

Yours truly, Isaac Foot.
(12 November 1919)

That letter drew an immediate public response from Lloyd George: 'Mr Isaac Foot has "drawn the badger" as Lord Randolph put it in a famous phrase. The Prime Minister has emerged from the crowd of aristocratic and plutocratic mercenaries who surround him to explain his position towards the Liberal cause.'

Dear Mr Foot,

I observe from the newspapers that you are said to have written me a letter in regard to my Liberal principles and that you have published it in the press without extending me the courtesy of allowing me to read it first and to send a reply. Before the last election I came to the deliberate judgment that it was essential, if the country was to pass safely through the difficult period after a five years' war, that the unity and cooperation of parties and a national government should be continued. I felt sure that the policy of renewing party strife, before the unrest and disturbance consequent on the war had settled down in the world and when, above everything, national unity in restoring the wastage of war was necessary, would be entirely contrary alike to Liberal principles and to national interests. Hence the continuance of the National Government. I am glad to think that both our allies, France and Italy, came to the same decision and that the policy was endorsed in this country by a majority of Liberals at the election itself.

You, yourself, evidently held a different opinion, and stood for the policy of the renewal of party strife. You have no more justification for holding me unfaithful to the Liberal party because I believed that national interests could best be served by continuance of the National Government than I would have the right to deem you a traitor because you believed that the immediate renewal of party strife was more important than national unity. As to the character of the government's legislation, I think that the great pro-gramme of progressive and democratic legislation which the present administration has not merely promised but carried through, which includes, amongst other measures, the Franchise Act, the Education Act, and the minimum wage for the agricultural labourer, will bear favourable comparison with the record of any government, however Liberal its constitution.

Reply communicated through newspapers. D. Lloyd George.
(13 November 1919)

Isaac Foot wrote in reply:
I thank you for your letter. No discourtesy was intended in reading to the electors of Sutton the letter I had already dispatched to you. You have not replied to the questions I respectfully put to you ... I was reading recently Mr Hammond's book on Charles James Fox and there he says: 'A true statesman uses the sober moods of the people to guard against the hour of delirium.' You deliberately used the hour of delirium to obtain your docile majority and in so doing struck down many of your truest friends. The suggestion that I am renewing party strife is, as you must know, misleading and I am quite content to take the advice of our greatest political philosopher, who said: 'No man could act with effect who did not act in concert; no man could act in concert who did not act with confi-dence; no man could act with confidence who were not bound by common opinions, com-mon affection and common interests.' That is the opinion of Burke and when you have time to read again his 'Thoughts on the Present Discontent' you will find there this prophetic passage:

> For my part I shall be compelled to conclude the principle of Parliament to be total-ly corrupted and, therefore, its end entirely defeated when I see ... a rule of indis-criminate support to all Ministers; because this destroys the very end of Parliament as a control and is a general previous sanction to misgovernment.

You demanded indiscriminate support last December and obtained a majority pledged to that policy. In doing so, you helped to destroy the very end of Parliament and strength-ened, unwittingly perhaps, the advocates of direct action which find their main argument in the weakness of Parliament today. This letter is written in the midst of a strenuous con-test in which I am seeking to secure the thoroughgoing and enlightened application to present-day problems of the old Liberal principles – peace, retrenchment and reform. You will no doubt remember quoting these old watchwords a few days ago amid the derisive amusement of your old friends.

Yours truly, Isaac Foot.

MICHAEL: My father fought the coalition government after the war more fiercely than anyone else. He argued with Lloyd George over the latter's perceived betrayal of the true Liberal principles and party so much so that he won enthusiastic support from 'Q' – Sir Arthur Quiller-Couch – which he treasured all his life.

'Q''s Message to Mr Foot

I am sure it is permissible for an old friend in south-east Cornwall to wish you well in the battle you are fighting – always with the sincerity of mind and the old chivalry of conduct – in the Sutton division of Plymouth. These appear to me to be times when it is almost as shameful to be frivolous as morosely to prefer the interest of any one class in face of the common danger to the State, almost as wanton to caper on the crust of ve ry serious fires as it is to stoke those fires with fuel of ill will. Our common danger is economic; and eve ry serious man knows it to be at this moment an appallingly serious danger. What this country wants now is men in Parliament able to cross-examine upon the country's finances and – for another thing – pertinacious in digging for truth through the sinister silence that visits our commitments in Russia. I am sure that, if the electors of the Sutton division keep this most immediate need of their country before their minds, you are the candidate most worthy as their representative to face it and bring the best help to the Inquest of the Nation in this most critical hour. But, if it is possible, I am sure that they will do themselves honour in selecting a man who, however provoked, ever fights clean and by gentle courage dignifies the cause of the whole people which fires his heart.

With all good wishes, Arthur Quiller-Couch.
(14 November 1919)

Nomination Day

It so happened that Nancy Astor and Isaac Foot arrived at the same moment at the town clerk's office with their nomination papers and their cheques for the deposit, which a candidate forfeits if he polls less than one eighth of the votes. As Isaac Foot handed over his cheque to the town clerk, Nancy Astor loudly exclaimed: 'You're the father of seven children! I don't think it right in your position to throw your money away like that! You really oughtn't to risk forfeiting your deposit and impoverishing your wife and children. Far better withdraw straight away.'[94]

The scenes on 28 November 1919, the day of the announcement of the result

This Sutton by-election in 1919 was table talk far beyond the bounds of the west. Plymouth knew Lady Astor's way with the sharp impromptu. They did not realise how electrical she could be until they heard hecklers, who had considered her a simple target,

---

94. Christopher Sykes, Nancy: *The Life of Lady Astor* (Collins, 1972).

Nancy Astor speaking after the declaration of the result of the poll in the Sutton Plymouth by-election in 1919. Isaac Foot is on the far right and the Labour candidate, William Gay, second left, with Nancy's husband, Waldorf Astor, to Gay's right.

shrivelling before the forked lightning of her retorts. As a boy up from the Lizard, I was in town on the cold November Friday when the votes were counted. Passengers in a tramcar rocking down Old Town Street heard a shout of cheering ahead. 'She's in,' said the conductor appreciatively. He was right. She was. A roaring multitude packed the Guildhall Square, the space between the Municipal Buildings and Guildhall.[95]

MICHAEL: My father loved Lady Astor ever afterwards and there was never so much as a streak of hatred in the mixture. He was stunned to see some of his own favourite causes – temperance, anti-Popery, Plymouth's greatness as a Protestant city – defended in such style. He was even prepared to forgive her – a dispensation allowed in no other case – for being a Tory. In the next general election campaign, my mother was so scandalised by masculine opponents of hers, particularly the brewers, that she attended a meeting to support Nancy Astor in Plymouth. The local newspaper provided the headline.

Mrs Foot speaks her mind: principles before party policies

Mrs Foot, the wife of Mr Isaac Foot, explained why she had decided to support a Conservative candidate in the contest at Sutton. Mrs Foot said she was not there to make a speech but only to give an explanation. 'Now, I am a Liberal,' Mrs Foot proceeded. ' I was brought up a Liberal and have always been a Liberal, because I think that Liberal principles

---

95. J. C. Trewin, *Up from the Lizard* (Carroll & Nicholson, 1948).

are the only principles that are going to save the country. But there are times when one must put principles before policy. That is why I am here tonight because I don't consider that this is a party question at all and because I think that Lady Astor stands for principles and not for politics. I am not here to support Lady Astor solely because she is a woman. As you know, my husband fought Lady Astor on party politics, but, if only for the magnificent wo rk Lady Astor has done for the women and children, not only of Plymouth, but of the whole country, and considering the base attacks which have been made on Lady Astor, we cannot do other than support her. It has ta ken us a good deal of time to come to this decision and when I was asked if I would speak on behalf of Lady Astor, at first I thought I could not do it. Then when I heard that some of Lady Astor's party were not going to support her, I decided that I could not do ot he rwise and I have come up from Cornwall on purpose this evening to attend this meeting. The question we are everywhere being asked is: "Are you supporting Lady Astor?" and my husband always replies: "What would you do yourself?" and the reply has always been "I will support her" and my husband tells them he would do the same. I am sure that the people of Plymouth will not let Lady Astor down."[96]

Nancy Astor wrote this private letter of thanks to Eva for her support on this temperance issue.

Dear Eva, I want to send you a line personally to tell you how deeply I admire and thank you for the stand you took on the moral issue in this election. I realise the sacrifice and perhaps unpleasantness which it may have meant for you, but I know that your courage has won, not only my gratitude, but the gratitude of all right-thinking men and women in Plymouth. I can never forget your splendid stand that night ... I hear the 'trade' are determined to get me out.

Nancy

After the death of Lady Astor in 1964 John Foot wrote this tribute on behalf of the Foot family.

The walls of one of the rooms in my father's home at Pencrebar were covered with a collection of photographs. Many record and illustrate the memorable events of his life, many more are of his children and their various activities but there are a few portraits of those of his contemporaries whom he held closest in his affections. Among this select few there is a photograph of a woman of extraordinary beauty. The portrait was presented to him by the sitter with an affectionate inscription more than 40 years ago and has excited the interest and fascination of countless visitors. It is a picture of Nancy Astor soon after she became the member for Sutton in 1919 and the first woman to enter the House of

---

96. *Western Independent*, 10 November 1922.

Commons. My father had been one of her opponents in that historic by-election and they remained in political opposition, except on the temperance issue, all their lives but their affection and respect for each other was quite untouched by their differing political persuasions. Their friendship was at first sight an odd one. My father was born in Plymouth, the son of an artisan. Nancy Astor was the daughter of an old Virginian family who had married the son of an English peer and into a family of legendary wealth. It was, so far as I know, a mere chance that brought the Astors to Plymouth in the first place but they were for ever afterwards passionately devoted to the City and well-being of its people and it was this love of Plymouth which formed one of the many bonds between her and my father. Nancy Astor was beyond question, one of the great women of her age.[97]

16 1922 'Our Isaac' – by-election victory in Bodmin

MICHAEL: My father and my mother were horrified at the developments of politics in London at this time where the coalition government of the day was moving in what they thought were most dangerous waters. Lloyd George was held responsible for the lurch of the government towards Tory policies which favoured the return of Tory candidates. The Liberals in Parliament, led by Herbert Asquith, were moving more and more in opposition to the coalition policies of the government, especially in Ireland, where they seemed to be returning to the kind of Tory measures which Gladstone had opposed so many years before. My father now fought and won a famous by-election victory in February 1922. In this brilliant campaign he knew all the weaknesses in the Lloyd George armour and hit where it hurt – where Lloyd George, once the champion of great Liberal and Nonconformist causes, knew that he was vulnerable. My father unloosed his invective against the Black-and-Tan terrorism in Ireland, against the barren and vindictive terms of the Versailles peace treaty, against the smell of corruption, which seemed to characterise the preferred coalition method of doing business; altogether, against the surrender in almost every field to this raucous, bovine, flag-wagging majority in the House of Commons brought into being at the 1918 'Hang the Kaiser' election. His victory in Bodmin was one of the most deadly blows against the Lloyd George coalition. It was a sensational by-election victory by a 'Liberal Wee Free Asquithian'. Hence the cartoon 'Bodminton'.

Dingle remembers this campaign: I have, of course, the most vivid recollection of the days when Father represented the Bodmin division, especially the early days, when I used to go with him to meetings and socials in the Cornish villages. It may be my imagination, but I have a

---

97. John Foot, obituary, *Western Independent*, May 1964.

very strong impression that people in all parties enjoyed their politics a great deal more than they do now. At all events, when we went to Looe or Cardinham or Trewidland or any of the other hundred or so places in the Bodmin division there was always a rollicking atmosphere about Liberal meetings of those days. Father was not only expected to speak. He was also, as a general rule, expected to sing and the proceedings were not regarded as completed until he had rendered the 'Farmer's Boy'. He has always had a taste for music of a kind and, even today, he has what his family regards as the deplorable habit of waking up the household by playing hymn tunes on the piano at seven o'clock in the morning.

Nowadays the heckler has almost ceased to exist. In those days he was a very formidable figure and you had to think about the questions you were going to be asked at meetings, the way in which they were going to be put and what you were going to say, and of course you had a certain amount of physical violence. I always remember the first time that father was elected. We went from Liskeard to Bodmin and he was being carried shoulder high and I saw a Tory pick him off with a tomato on the back of his neck at about 30 yards' range. I always thought it was a remarkably good shot. Well, of course, he fought a very tough constituency most of the time and he did arouse more animosity against himself than some other candidates. The Tories in the Westcountry would fight harder against my father than anyone else. Moreover he didn't fight safe seats. The Westcountry was the place he loved and here there weren't safe Liberal seats. At the age of sixteen I attended the

Isaac Foot canvassing at Tideford in the Bodmin by-election of 1922, watched by his wife, Eva, and the seventeen-year-old Dingle on the right.

Liberal meeting at Queen's Hall on 25 January 1922 and heard the immensely impressive speeches of Asquith and Grey. It really seemed as if the Liberals were coming back. This impression was confirmed when, in the following month, my father won a sensational victory at the Bodmin by-election and entered the House of Commons for the first time.

Once again, Isaac Foot's Coalition Unionist opponent, Major General Sir Frederick Poole, had the official backing of the Prime Minister. Isaac Foot's adoption speech at Liskeard set out his position.

There has been throughout the country, during the past few weeks, a manifestation of the revival of Liberalism. If it is true that there is no alternative government, the country is on its way to intellectual bankruptcy. Sir Frederick Poole suggests that the present coalition government represents the best brains of the country. If that is true, we might reverently say 'God save England!' Is there anything more ridiculous than the claim of this government of 'indispensables' – these Greenwoods, Monds, Macnamaras and Kellaways who 'drest in a little brief authority, play such fantastic tricks before high heaven as makes the angels weep'? John Milton used to speak of England as 'that noble and puissant nation' and, even if Mr Lloyd George were taken to heaven tomorrow, only two things would happen – the coalition would die and England would survive.

What is Liberalism? Liberalism does not consist of a programme of reforms like an auctioneer's catalogue, nor a mere statement of policy. Liberalism is a spirit and an attitude of mind. It is a faith that holds on to be a part of a man's resolve to see that his country is well governed. It is a temper that regards liberty as the vital spring of energy of the state itself. It is the attitude of mind that makes injustice an intolerable thing and regards wrong to any one citizen as an injury to the whole community. It demands for all our people an equality of opportunity and a fair share of the good things of life. It recognises that we have been variously and diversely endowed but that each citizen has his own individual contribution to make to our common citizenship. It honours the sanctity of human difference and has learnt from John Stuart Mill that whatever crushes individuality is despotism, by whatever name it may be called. It strives for a state of society where every man's work and worth will be measured not by his wealth but by his service and it looks for a future where the several nations shall be at peace and shall have learnt that their nationality can best be realised in the common service of mankind. That is Liberalism and a Liberal devises liberal things and by liberal things shall he stand.

In conclusion I hope that the fight we shall wage in this constituency will achieve such a result that the political historian may be able to write in later years: 'The fires of liberty and Liberalism after the war died low. Some said the fire was out and only embers remained. But the fire burned again and the flames first leaped up in the Bodmin division of Cornwall.'[98]

---

98. *Western Independent*, 5 February 1922.

This campaign was fully reported by the local press.

'Support for Isaac Foot from "Q"'

On Nomination Day, 16 February 1922, Sir Arthur Quiller-Couch signed Isaac Foot's papers as his principal proposer – 'A Commonwealth such as ours will always need two things far more important than brains – the first character, and the second public confidence. This opportunist government never had the one and by consequence have fatally lost the other.'[99]

'Labour bombshell in Bodmin'

The Executive Committee of the Labour Party of the Bodmin Division issued a strong indictment of the government's record including 'its wanton waste of the country's resources' and recommended that the Labour electors voted for Foot. 'The overthrow of the present coalition government is the supreme political necessity.'

'The later days of the campaign'

'Fo ot This Time' is the slogan of the Liberal wo rkers. They find it echoed everywhere in the division with increasing confidence and in growing volume. Mr Fo ot himself is wo rth any ten machines. He seems to have discovered the two secrets that have baffled philosophers of all time – Pe rp etual Youth and Perpetual Motion. His energy never flags, his flow of ideas never slackens and his enthusiasm never wavers. He does more wo rk, makes more speeches and makes them better than anybody else. He contrives, if he cannot emulate the classical b i rd of Hibernian legend and be in two places at once, to be at seven places in one evening, to make seven different speeches and to be practising in the courts next day as fresh as if he had never addressed a political meeting in his life. This is the kind of candidate who keeps up the spirits of his supporters. Not that they are in any danger of going down.

The constituency was not very fully polled at the last election. The figures will probably be much larger next Friday. With fine weather the women will no doubt go to vote in far bigger battalions than when they first enjoyed the privilege. This should be to the advantage of Mr Foot, who is well known to be an ardent supporter of women's causes and an apostle of the things political that most matter to them – temperance, criminal law reform, and the commercial and industrial policies that have the strongest effect on the household budget. The gathering of farmers at Callington market when Mr Foot spoke there was remarkable ... the Cornish farmers are largely imbued with Liberalism. Old-time Liberal workers aver that never in the history of the division has there been such wholehearted enthusiasm for any Liberal candidate as is being manifested for Mr Foot. Mr Foot himself observed yesterday that meetings he addresses are 'just like revival meetings – not

---

99. Letter from 'Q'.

A young well-wisher at Landrake presents Isaac Foot with a lucky horseshoe.

ordinary services at all – and we are getting plenty of penitents every day. We are going to win by fair argument and honest persuasion.' The Liberal favours, yellow and blue, are making a brave show in every town and village and the candidate himself is wearing a wish-bone decorated with the colours, which was presented to him at a Liskeard meeting.[100]

'The flying tour'
By this means Isaac Foot visited about a score of villages on the morning, addressed a women's meeting in the afternoon and spoke at several places in the evening. In all there are eighty places to be visited. Many villages were said to have requested a personal visit – Mr Isaac Foot is wooing the electorate with all the fervour and confidence of a thorough optimist. His campaign is being carried on with the utmost vigour. One story was told: 'Hi!' Mr Foot's motor was splashing through the mud and drizzle in one of the outlying parts of the constituency when out of the darkness this peremptory challenge rang out. The car pulled up and a broad-shouldered countryman came running up. 'You be Mister Foot, bain't you?' he asked. 'Yes I am,' said the candidate. 'Well, I only wants to tell 'ee that you be sure 'wain

---

100. 'Election Notes', *Western Independent*, 19 February 1922.

this time. Us be workin' 'art and us ban't gwain to leave no stone unturned.' This was the cheery message and, as the car splashed on its way, a tardy 'Good luck' was not drowned in the whir of the engines. It left one with a great sense of its sincerity.

From the start of the campaign it was obvious to an outsider that the tide was running with Mr Foot. The Bodmin division, spread over so many miles and with many isolated hamlets, was not an easy one for a candidate to cover but Mr Foot's campaign was arranged with the precision of a military operation. Every morning at 10 o'clock we left Liskeard in an open tourer-car for what was described as a 'flying tour' which led us into every village and hamlet before polling day. Usually we had a break for lunch in the home of some Liberal supporter and if, as often happened, there was a piano in the house, we invariably got down to a little sing-song – Mr Foot's speciality being 'The Farmer's Boy'. After lunch the journey was continued until three o'clock, at which time every day there was a meeting somewhere for women voters. Generally we returned to Liskeard for tea and then off again into the darkness of the night to as many as four and sometimes five meetings in different villages ... Mr Foot's great henchman during that campaign was Ernest Brown, who in later years became a Liberal MP ... another famous Liberal member who did a lot of speaking was the late Sir Francis Acland. It was Ernest Brown who composed the little doggerel to an old army marching tune which played no small part in the campaign. It began: 'If you want to find our Isaac we know where he is' and ended with the words 'right at the top of the poll'. That lively little tune echoed through the constituency during the campaign and I can recall it being sung with gusto outside.[101]

Another song sung at this election, to the tune of Trelawney, *is given below.*

We'll hold aloft our banner high
Like Bannerman of yore;
With Asquith, Grey – true men are they
We'll storm their castle doors.
The Coalition would not help
The Cornish miners poor;
Come vote against them 'one and all'
And make them think the more.
And shall our Isaac win?
Say, shall brave Isaac win?
Yes, high above the Tory din,
Let's bear good Isaac in !

101. Walter Taylor, 'When Isaac Foot first went to Parliament', *Western Independent*, 18 December 1960.

An enthusiastic greeting at Trewidland.

'*Enthusiastic reception on flying tour*'

Confidence in Mr Foot's camp is growing every hour. Particularly in the villages there is enthusiasm without parallel in the history of the constituency. There is not the slightest doubt that Mr Foot is gaining ground rapidly and many who were formerly his opponents are coming to his support in order to show their disapproval of the Government's mis-management. Mr Foot did splendid work yesterday when he made a flying tour of about a score of villages lying between Liskeard, Downderry and Torpoint. Posters had been issued to announce that he would arrive in each village at a certain time and at every halt he found enthusiastic supporters awaiting him. At Trewidland, where there are only about a score of cottages, the enthusiasm was wonderful for so small a place. Immediately Mr Foot's car drew up, the energetic local Liberal 'leader' set up a shout which brought out the rest of the inhabitants. 'Come on, Gran, come out and see the candidate,' he yelled and 'Gran', an elderly lady of nearly 90, came along with surprising agility to wish the candidate luck. At Hessenford the candidate had a conversation with the postman, the mason and the miller. Then at Downderry Mr Foot had as cheerful a reception as he had had all day, a crowd of men and women awaiting him and greeting him with the ringing of a hand bell. 'We are winning all along the line,' the candidate told them. A man in the crowd declared that Mr Foot would leave Liskeard next Saturday with an ejectment order for the Government in his pocket. 'Yes,' retorted the candidate, 'and there'll be no alternative accommodation! The women are on our side and the men are rolling along as they have never rolled along before. We have fought a losing battle for a long time but now the tide has turned.'[102]

'Mr Foot's triumphal tour rollicking enthusiasm'

The pace quickens in the Bodmin fight. Anticipating a close result, both sides are making strenuous efforts to secure every available vote and the electors are having no more peace than the hard-worked candidates, who are addressing about twenty meetings a day. 'I have seen nothing like it for years,' said Mr Foot. 'This is pre-war electioneering.' We were making a flying tour of some of the outlying areas. The only difficulty was to get along quickly enough. Constantly the car was held up by little groups of men and women who had collected by the roadside to cheer the candidate and wish him success. When a village was reached, there was no need for Lt Brown's dinner bell. People were there waiting all along the road. The enthusiasm of the women was remarkable. It was quite unnecessary to call at their cottages. Hurriedly abandoning their housework and not waiting to take off their aprons or roll down their sleeves, they rushed out on the approach of the car to shake hands with the candidate and assure him of their support. The most impressive incident of the tour was at the top of the hill in the little parish of Duloe, between Liskeard and the sea. We found some fifty women and children clustering round a plain stone obelisk that stands on the crest of the hill to keep fresh the memory of the men of the parish who died in the war that was to end war. I don't know whether they had deliberately chosen to wait there out of sight of any house and of their own little hamlet but it seemed they had chosen well. The significance of the little group round the windswept memorial was not lost on Mr Foot. His whole outlook is based on acceptance of the silent challenge of the dead. He spoke movingly of the world for which they died; then amidst cheers, the car went on, and the little group of women and children broke up and the memorial was left to its solitude on the hill. There seems to be no doubt that the people of the Westcountry are again politically awake. At one stopping-place Mr Foot asked, 'What is the name of this village?' 'It's Herodsfoot,' replied a woman and then added with a smile, 'But it's going to be Isaac Foot's on Friday.' Mr Foot's name has been one of the assets of the election.[103]

'The Liberal campaign: special interview with Isaac Foot'

Asked to sum up his prospects he replied cautiously: 'I have gone through too many fights – parliamentary and municipal – to indulge in prophecies but, if the result depends on the public meetings, there could be no reasonable doubt. My general policy is pretty clear to the electors with whom I have been in touch more or less for the last twelve years. It is my business in this election to insist upon the main issue – whether or not the Bodmin elec-

102. *Western Morning News*, 21 February 1922.
103. *Daily News*, 23 February 1922.

tors will give a vote of confidence to this government. The significance of the election in other parts of the country will be interpreted almost entirely in the light of this one issue ... throughout this campaign I have made peace the master word and I have explained the causes of the Versailles treaty. The other subjects I have emphasised have been retrenchment, unemployment, the veto in the House of Lords, licensing reform, free trade and proportional representation.[104]

On 24 February 1922, after a lengthy count at Liskeard, the result was announced. Isaac Foot's campaign had turned the majority of 3,585 against him in 1918 into a majority in his favour of 3,141.

'The scenes at the declaration of the poll outside the Liskeard Guildhall'

The crowd outside was swelling and from time to time cries of 'Up Foot' mingled with the counter-cheers of the Conservative supporters. By 3 o'clock the streets were choked with an animated throng. From every surrounding district people had streamed in to hear the result of a momentous by-election. It was the custom for the winner and defeated candidate to speak from the balcony of Webb's Hotel in the Square. No sooner had Mr Foot emerged from the Guildhall than he was seized by his supporters, now wild with joy, and carried shoulder high up the street. A huge crowd had gathered. Mr Foot's appearance on the veranda was the signal for a tremendous outburst of cheering and the singing of 'He's a Jolly Good Fellow' and it was some time before he could make himself heard. After paying tribute to his opponent:

> This magnificent victory will ring throughout the country. It shows that a genuine revival of true Liberalism is at hand. Three and a half years ago we were a broken and scattered party but they had now set the flame of Liberalism burning again. Now we have defeated the coalition. Our victory has given us a seat not only for today but for the next election and afterwards. We have won because people are bitter and angry at the broken promises, the waste and extravagance and because the people of the constituency think that the Cornish miners have been treated with great meanness by the government. The country is sick and hungering for Liberalism and to the little band in the House of Commons who have borne the heat and burden of the day for the last three years, that victory will be a message of hope and encouragement.

The now-famous election song was sung. Mr Foot was then seized by his supporters and borne shoulder high across the Square surrounded by the cheering supporters and afterwards spoke from the window of the Liskeard Liberal Club in the Parade, which had been his HQ during his campaign.[105]

---

104. *Western Gazette*, 23 February 1922.
105. *Western Morning News*, 27 February 1922.

'The Hour of Our Isaac': Isaac is chaired through the crowd after his victory in the Bodmin by-election in 1922.

'My election', Mr Foot said afterwards, 'is the reward of twelve years' hard work mainly in the villages, apart from political propaganda altogether. I am at home among these village people and have learnt to love and admire them. My keenest workers are frequently my brother Methodists. The village chapel is the rural citadel of democracy.'[106]

Report from a special correspondent of the Observer

Mr Foot has won a resounding victory in Leonard Courtney's old constituency. The scenes on Saturday afternoon beggared description. They were Cornish of the Cornish; the enthusiasm of Nonconformist farmers, of earnest local preachers, of dark-eyed women and fiery Celtic youth had something religious about it. No fervour could be seen elsewhere outside Wales. Mr Foot's campaign has been a crusade and he has been the dominant figure bearing the fiery cross. Distinguished people have been down to help him – Sir John Simon, Mr Masterman et tout ça; but what mattered was Mr Foot. He was always the most eloquent speaker, the wittiest, the most ardent. His victory is a victory for what his friend Sir Arthur Quiller-Couch called 'political character' and a recovery by east Cornwall of its faith in Liberalism.

Mr Isaac Foot is forty, but he does not look it. He is a slim, boyish figure – high brow, clean-shaven, gentle eyes regarding the world through spectacles. This is his fifth contest.

---

106. *Cornish Times*, 3 March 1922.

Four successive defeats within a radius of fifty miles and two of them in this very division seemed to leave him fresher, more hopeful, more vigorous each time. He was predestined for Parliament, and, with opportunity, will make a fine House of Commons man. Mr Foot is an uncompromising Radical and Progressive. He has left no doubt about where he stands. He is for economy in administration, but not for indiscriminating 'axes'. He stands for the fullest educational development, for the fullest measures of public health reform, and for an adequate Navy. His victory is part of the general movement to the left which is to be noted in the west of England as elsewhere. The election will have important reactions in Devon and

'Bodminton'

Cornwall, which are now over-represented by Conservative members of the coalition. There are now only three Independent Liberal members in the western peninsula – Mr Acland, Mr Lambert and Mr Foot. Their numbers will certainly be doubled and perhaps trebled when the appeal to the country comes.[107]

'If you want to find "Our Isaac"'

On the Monday following the declaration of the poll, Isaac and Eva Foot made a 'Triumphal Tour', involving fourteen meetings and over one hundred miles of motor travelling. Everywhere he went he was received with the utmost enthusiasm. One veteran worker at Callington told us that never in his memory had he witnessed such enthusiasm as he had seen that night. The approximate time of the new member's arrival had been communicated by telegraph to the various places at which it was intended to make a brief halt but very early it was found that the times could not be kept, so loath were Mr Foot's supporters at the earlier places visited to allow him to leave. It was a veritable triumphal tour, commencing at Polperro with a shoulder-high ride in a flower-bedecked chair, and finishing at Callington shortly after 11 o'clock with a torchlight procession. Mr Foot was visibly touched by the cordiality of his reception everywhere. Everywhere there had to be sung the election refrain:

---

107. *Observer*, 4 March 1922.

If you want to find our Isaac
We know where he is –
Right at the top of the poll.

'Our opponents beat us by 41 in 1910,' said Mr Foot. 'This time we took the 41 and put 31 in front of it, making it 3,141. Let it be 5,161 next time.'[108]

'Our Isaac'

Isaac Foot, a Wesleyan standing as an Independent Liberal, triumphed at Bodmin over a Coalition Unionist and thereby launched what was surely the last of the great Nonconformist parliamentary careers ... The Bodmin result fuelled the Conservative revolt against Lloyd George, gave a much-needed fillip to the Asquithians and induced Free Churchmen to keep their distance from the coalition, whose break-up seemed imminent. After 1922 Lloyd George, although still very influential, did not recover real power or leadership. Who could possibly rival him for Nonconformist adulation? Simon, Runciman and Maclean did not have the same attraction. Instead it was Isaac Foot, a newcomer on the parliamentary scene, who quickly emerged as Lloyd George's counterpart among the Asquithians ... His standing among Westcountrymen, to whom he was known as 'Our Isaac', was comparable to Lloyd George's among Welshmen.[109]

---

108. *Cornish Times*, 3 March 1922.
109. Stephen Koss, *Nonconformity in Modern British Politics* (Batsford, 1975).

PART V

Member of Parliament for Bodmin

17 1922–4 Isaac Foot's first session in the Commons

Isaac Foot was forty-two years of age when he took his seat in the Commons for the first time in 1922. He remained the Liberal member for Bodmin until 1924, winning the two general elections of 1922 and 1923, but lost his seat in the general election of 1924.

MICHAEL: My father's victory in Bodmin in February 1922 had been a political sensation of the first order. As the cartoonists showed, he might have been seen as the political figure who dealt the last blow to the Lloyd George coalition and was the great hope for the revival of Liberalism in Cornwall. Now my father quickly applied his mind to a whole range of different topics. After his maiden speech, his fellow-Asquithian Liberal, Donald Maclean, wrote a personal note of congratulation: 'Thank you very much. It was excellent. It was as good as I wished it to be. There is no higher praise I could give, as I wished for the very best.' My father said of it: 'I managed to do very well under the circumstances. I was very nervous about it. The House is a hard place to speak in. But everybody was very kind.'

In the Commons Isaac Foot continued to speak out against Lloyd George's coalition government. In a speech to Plymouth Liberals, he gave his first impressions of the House:

If you had been sitting on the benches in the House of Commons as I have for the past two or three days you would not have thought there was any unity in this government. In fact, there is bitter rivalry and a great many personal animosities. This talk of unity is so much eyewash. The government is doomed and the members of the coalition there are walking about with the mark of death upon them. Our victory in the Bodmin division has signalised a very great Liberal revival in the west of England. 'The people who walked in darkness had seen a great light.' In 1918, I came home a disappointed man, but still knowing the cause I advocated was a great cause and a right cause; and, in this last election, I simply preached what I preached in 1918. Then the Liberal Party was a broken army; but now there is a great change. As long as my energy allows me I intend to devote it to that cause which I consider the only cause that is going to save this country. There is no hope for this broken and distracted world except in the service of Liberalism. I am not concerned as to who leads me; all I am concerned with are the principles of Liberalism. I ask you to be comrades in arms, to help in getting our people back to the Liberal faith. That is a faith which is worth all our endeavour.[110]

In October 1922 Lloyd George's coalition government finally collapsed when the Conservative Party withdrew its support. Isaac Foot retained his seat in the following general election, which brought in a Conservative government.

MICHAEL: One of the earliest motions my father put down for discussion was for a debate on the women's right to vote. He was as much committed as his neighbour, Lady Astor, that women, excluded from voting until thirty years of age in the Act of 1918, should have the vote on the same basis as men from the age of twenty-one and that there should be more women MPs. Several of his interventions in this parliament and the following ones in 1923 and 1924 showed his immediate interest in the continuing arguments about women's suffrage. Individual members of the House of Commons can reveal their special interests in the choice of an introduction of a Bill under the ten-minute rule. He availed himself of this opportunity to introduce a Bill in 1923 designed to make the vote available to women on the same terms as men. He was already an expert on that subject, having received his instruction from John Stuart Mill, the first and most consistent of the spokesmen for women's rights.

Isaac Foot introduced his Bill with this speech:

Nothing was more noticeable in the last election than the keen interest taken by the women electors. I think, generally speaking, the women were just as keen upon their political responsibilities as were the men. It is suggested that women do not want this Bill. The answer is the organised demand of many associations throughout the country. It is certain, when you have growing up in the same household a boy and a girl, and the boy is able to exercise his vote when he reaches twenty-one and the girl not until she reaches thirty, that you have real ground for resentment and indignation. The assumption I suppose is that it takes nine years longer for the woman's mind to mature than the man's. It is the same sort of resentment and indignation that I used to feel when I was one of a family of six exercising the vote and my mother could not exercise it, although she had more sense than the rest of us put together ... Nothing is more certain than that the reform must come. I only urge that it may be given as a concession and not be extorted in later years.[111]

---

110. *Cornish Guardian*, 5 March 1922.
111. Hansard, 25 April 1923.

Isaac Foot was unable to obtain a second reading for his Bill. In a debate on the same matter in 1924 he continued with his argument:

What about the hardest-working part of the community? I refer particularly to the young mother, under thirty years of age, who has upon her all the cares of her home. No class of the community works longer, harder or for less acknowledgement than this. They have no trade union to protect their interests and there are thousands and tens of thousands of women in that position who have not even the protection of the vote today. That vote should be secured to them by this Bill and that is why we give it a warm welcome ... How farcical it is to talk of the Prime Minister collecting the voices of the country when, on the morning of polling day, the doors of the polling booths have been deliberately shut in the face of nearly five million people who are just as qualified to express their opinions as any other portion of the community. It is a loss also to the House of Commons. It was our greatest political philosopher who said: 'The virtue, spirit and essence of a House of Commons consists in its being an express image of the feelings of the nation.'[112] We cannot get the express image of the feelings of the nation as long as we deprive nearly five million women of the vote. We are left with this anomaly, that a woman under thirty years of age can stand as a candidate and may be returned to Parliament and yet she is not qualified to cast her own vote as an elector. I think all it is necessary to do is to refer to the famous essay written over sixty years ago by John Stuart Mill in which he said: 'This difference of sex is so entirely irrelevant to political rights as difference in height or in the colour of the hair.'[113] We do not ask for this concession as a favour. It is the granting of a right. This reform is inevitable. Is it not wise that reform should come now and be peacefully conceded than later in anger and turmoil? I should like to give a quotation from a passage written by Burke to the Two Gentlemen of Bristol: 'If there is any one eminent criterion which, above all the rest, distinguishes a wise Government from an administration weak and improvident, it is this – Well to know the best time and manner of yielding what it is impossible to keep.' It is impossible to withhold this reform. Let us give it now.[114]

It was not until 1928, however, that women over twenty-one years old were enfranchised.

The flowing tide: the Liberal defeat in 1924
Isaac Foot lost his seat in the general election of 1924 by 615 votes. On the occasion of this defeat, Dingle sent his father this telegram from Oxford:

'Congratulations Glorious Failure Flowing Tide Nearly Dammed'.

---

112. Edmund Burke (1729–97), statesman and philosopher.
113. 'On the Subjection of Women' (1869).
114. Hansard, March 1924.

JOHN: My father lost his seat in the general election of 1924, which was a disaster for the Liberal Party with the loss of 118 of their 158 seats in the Commons. In the south-west, the twenty-three Liberal seats were reduced to two. Despite fighting eight elections and winning three, he had sat in Parliament for only two years. Nevertheless, he had established a national reputation as a debater and an orator. As one of his constituents wrote:

> It is not you personally who has been rejected, but the party to which you belong. We are all feeling as if we have lost a personal friend. The only consolation is that all Cornwall is the same: there's a turn in the tide against good Liberals, just now, but it won't last, if we stand firm and don't make any pacts with either of the other parties.

Out of Parliament my father was able to concentrate on his work and family affairs, without any relaxation in his work on the party's behalf.

Isaac Foot gave his own summary of his record in his first years in the Commons:

Mr Foot made his maiden speech in the House on 17 March 1922, and from that time took an increasing part in parliamentary debates. He was frequently chosen by his party to be their spokesman in debates of considerable national importance. In 1923 he was appointed by the House as a member of the select committee on the proposed betting duty and his minority report against the practicability and desirability of the proposal, although narrowly defeated in the committee itself, attracted the attention of those interested in his social question. He served as a member of the small committee of Lords and Commons charged with the responsibility for the consolidation of the laws of the land. On the nomination of the Speaker, Mr Whitley, he served as a member of the Ecclesiastical Committee, consisting of representative of both Houses. In 1924 the Speaker nominated Mr Foot to be a chairman of the House and, as occasion required, he was called upon to preside over the debates. In the parliaments of 1923 and 1924, Mr Foot acted as secretary of the Temperance Committee, comprising a large number of members. As secretary of this committee it was his duty to watch the work of the House, in so far as it touched all questions of licensing and temperance reform. Both at the elections of 1923 and 1924, the name of Mr Foot was included in the Short White List of Members, containing the names of the members specially recommended to the electors by the organization concerned with the claims and interest of women and children.[115]

---

115. Election address to the Bodmin constituency in 1929.

18 1929–35 Isaac Foot returns to the Commons

Isaac Foot did not return to the Commons until he regained his seat in the general election of 1929, which brought in the second Labour government under Ramsay MacDonald.

MICHAEL: After the Liberal election defeats of the early 1920s, an attempt was made, chiefly on Lloyd George's initiative, to repair some of the old party wounds. My father was one of those Asquithian nominees who went on a mission to his house at Churt, for this high purpose. After a weekend of negotiation, the compact was signed and on the Monday morning Lloyd George bade farewell to his guests with the cheerful appeal: 'Let our slogan be "Measures not Men".' 'Edmund Burke', replied my father, 'had something to say about that. I think you'll find it on page 530 of that beautiful Beaconsfield edition of Burke I saw on your shelves.' On his return home he looked up his own edition, slightly anxiously, and read: 'The cant of "Not Men but Measures": the sort of charm by which many people get loose from every honourable engagement.' Neither my father nor Lloyd George ever referred afresh to the tender topic of Edmund Burke. My father never took the risk of examining further whether Lloyd George's renewed geniality was due to tact or laziness or just the joyous resolve to face the future, which was one of his most notable qualities. Nothing for a while impaired the new association.

In this election Isaac Foot for the first time received a personal letter of support from the Liberal leader, David Lloyd George:

Dear Isaac Foot,

I send you my best wishes for a great Victory on May 30th ... The dominant issues before the electorate are Unemployment, Peace and Disarmament. Your invaluable work and experience in the House of Commons must make the people of the Bodmin Division feel every confidence in you as their representative and we look forward to your return in the next Parliament, where your gifts and courage will be one of the Liberal Party's greatest assets.

Sincerely yours, David Lloyd George.

JOHN: Campaigning strenuously in favour of the policies contained within the Liberal Yellow Book,[116] my father could claim some credit for the Liberal victories in all five Cornish seats, including his own, in 1929. The Liberals swept the board in Cornwall but

---

116. The 'Yellow Book' was the nickname given to a report by the Liberal Industrial Inquiry entitled *Britain's Industrial Future*, published in 1928. This formed the basis for Lloyd George's Liberal Party campaign 'We Can Conquer Unemployment' in the 1929 election.

Lest we forget.

Bodmin Division
Parliamentary Election
May 30th, 1929.

Foot (L)	16002
Harrison (U)	15088
Reed (S)	3437
L Maj.	914

ONCE AGAIN M.P.

'Once Again MP': Isaac Foot wins back his seat in the general election of 1929.

the national result confirmed the Liberal's relegation to the electoral wilderness. The Liberal Party attracted an extra two million votes in this election, but only fifty-nine Liberal MPs were returned to the Commons.

MICHAEL: In the 1929–31 parliament, in which the Liberal Party held the balance between the new Labour government and the Tories, so long as the Liberals themselves held together, my father was now one of Lloyd George's most devoted assistants. It was a House of Commons in which other Liberals, John Simon, Walter Runciman and Leslie Hore-Belisha,[117] turned rightwards into the arms of the Tories; my father and his friends, aiding and abetting Lloyd George's radicalism, moved leftward and would perhaps have sustained the MacDonald Labour government, if it had had the will to sustain itself.

In August 1931, faced with the worsening economic and unemployment crisis, the leaders of the three parties agreed to form a National Government with Ramsay MacDonald remaining as Prime Minister. In the general election of 1931, which was an appeal to the country for support, the Conservative Party won a large majority. After winning a by-election in Dundee in 1931, Isaac Foot's eldest son, Dingle, now joined his father in the Commons.

117. Simon was Liberal MP for Spen Valley in Yorkshire, Runciman for St Ives in Cornwall and Hore-Belisha for Plymouth Devonport.

Isaac and Eva celebrate Dingle's Dundee by-election victory in 1931 at Pencrebar with other members of their family: from left Christopher, Sally, Dingle, Michael and Jennifer.

1931–2 Isaac Foot, Minister for Mines

JOHN: In the negotiations before the 1931 election, my father, like Herbert Samuel – now the Liberal leader in the Commons due to the illness of Lloyd George – had agreed to join MacDonald's National Government only for the purpose of carrying through the economies necessary to meet the immediate financial crisis. It was clearly laid down that on all other matters there should be 'an agreement to differ' – that is, the Liberal members of the government should be free to express their opposition to certain measures. On this limited basis my father accepted the office of Minister of Mines. In the feverish political atmosphere prior to the election of 1931, Leslie Hore-Belisha, with the concurrence of John Simon, circulated a document among his parliamentary Liberal colleagues which invited them to pledge their unqualified support for the National Government in any measures it might take after its election. Over the next eight years those who signed it, now known as the Liberal Nationals, fulfilled their undertaking to the letter, never dissenting over the emasculation of the League of Nations, the betrayals of Abyssinia and the Spanish Republic, or over Munich or appeasement. My father rejected the invitation with scorn, reminding Hore-Belisha and Simon that subservient submission of individual MPs to the executive was what the Civil War had been about.

DINGLE: In this National Government in 1931–2 the Liberals, who were in temporary coalition with MacDonald's Labour followers and the Conservatives, were in a position of utmost difficulty. The Conservatives, led by Stanley Baldwin and Neville Chamberlain, believed that the only remedy for the nation's ills was to impose tariffs. Now Neville Chamberlain, the Chancellor of the Exchequer, was determined to introduce an Import Duties Bill to impose protective tariffs for members of the British Empire. This was anathema to the Liberals led by Herbert Samuel. To Liberals, free trade was the ark of the covenant. Every Liberal had been brought up to regard the repeal of the Corn Laws as one of the great milestones of British history.[118] In 1906 they had achieved a record electoral landslide mainly on the issue of free trade versus protection. The folly of tariffs had been a major theme of Liberal speeches for many generations. But now the protectionist enemy was at the gate.

'Resign! Resign!'

In February 1932 Isaac Foot was one of the Liberal ministers who spoke out from the National Government front bench against the Import Duties Bill. On this occasion Michael, who had previously written to his father – 'I hope you are feeling thoroughly uncomfortable in your present position' – sent his father this telegram: 'No jiggery-pokery.'

Dingle described the atmosphere in the House on 25 February 1932 on the third reading of the Import Duties Bill:

Time was limited. A single day had been allotted for the completion of the report stage and the third reading. It had been arranged that there should be only three speeches. My father was to speak from the front bench for the dissident Liberals. The report stage dragged on through the afternoon and evening. The Liberal members suspected that the Conservatives were deliberately playing out time in order, if possible, to avoid any but a formal third reading. In the event, an hour was left. Isaac Foot was told he must confine his speech to six minutes. In this brief space he had to express the free trade convictions of a lifetime. That he succeeded in doing so was shown by the response he obtained. When he sat down the Conservative backbenchers rose as one man, shouting, 'Resign! Resign!' Chamberlain described the speech as 'the last despairing cry of one who knows that he has seen the end of free trade'.

1932 Isaac Foot resigns his post

JOHN: My father's only experience in office was short lived. When Neville Chamberlain, as Chancellor of the Exchequer, sought to implement the protectionist Ottawa agreements he was one of eleven ministers to resign his post with their leader, Herbert Samuel. My

---

118. The Corn Laws, first imposed in 1804 to keep the price of corn and bread artificially high to protect the interests of the landowners, were repealed in 1846.

father was deeply interested in his work in the Mines Department and to give up that post after only a year and walk out into the political wilderness without much prospect of getting back to that level again was a very considerable decision to take. It would have been much easier to have said: 'Well, I think that duty requires that I stay at my post,' but he had no hesitation about that whatever.

MICHAEL: Outside the Commons a few days later my father spoke more plainly on his resignation at the Queen's Hall Free Trade Demonstration. He took this opportunity to express his long-standing faith as a free-trader, but also took revenge on those who had previously tried to shout him down in the Commons.

ISAAC FOOT: Why are we out of the government? Our agreement was to get the ship off the rocks and not to take her into the protectionist port. Our arrangement was to serve under the White Ensign and not under the skull and crossbones of protection. They have got their protectionist goods now over the political customs frontier; but they were smuggled, and they only got them across because they took off the Tory label and put on the National label ... We fought them; Sir Henry Campbell-Bannerman fought them; Mr Asquith fought them; and we beat them, as we always have beaten protection if we have been given a fair fight and a free and open encounter.

The national emergency was exploited for party advantage, and the huge Conservative majority used that opportunity because they thought they had precious little chance of getting any other, and the result was that, within a month or two of the last election, Mr Neville Chamberlain went up to Birmingham and said, 'Free trade is as dead as mutton.' If it is dead, how was it killed? When a man is on his trial he is allowed to put himself upon his country. Free trade was never given that chance. Free trade was killed by political lynch law, and when the third reading of the Imports Bill came along and I was allowed, by the grace of the Tory backbenchers, to speak for six minutes in that great controversy, Mr Neville Chamberlain turned to me after I had finished and after they had shouted 'Resign' and he said: 'We have had tonight the passionate and despairing cry of a man who is convinced that he has seen the last of free trade.' It was not despairing, but it was passionate, and it was passionate because of the way in which free trade fell; it did not fall in open battle. This Caesar did not fall in the long campaigns of Gaul and Spain; this Caesar did not go down on the stricken fields of Thapsus and Pharsalia. This Caesar fell by the stroke of the dagger of Casca Chamberlain and the sword-thrust of Cassius Simon and Brutus Runciman.

Free trade to us is what Richard Cobden called it, 'the international law of the Almighty'. Free trade to us means international cooperation and interdependence. Free trade we believe to be the only wholesome way of living in the world. Free trade can only be explained in the language of peace. Protection can only be explained in the language of war. Protection develops the psychology of militarism and can only adequately express itself in the terminology of war, and the result is that tariffs become industrial armaments and trade is spoken of as the invasion of markets, and the political customer becomes the fiscal enemy. Free trade is to us much more than a fiscal expedient: it is our outlook, it is our philosophy. Our free trade thrives on international good will. Free trade is the strongest factor in the appeasement of international rivalry. That is why free trade is our life-blood. The world is in trouble today, and the great thing is that, in getting out of our trouble, we get out the right way, and, if we are in the Slough of Despond, I suggest to you that, unlike Pliable, we should not get out with our faces towards the City of Destruction, but we should get out with our faces towards the Celestial City. We ought not to get out towards economic isolation, national self-sufficiency, or imperial self-sufficiency.

We have to make, as we can, our contribution of Liberalism at this time at home, in India, in the Empire and in the world; and I close with some words that were said a long time ago, and they are these: 'God has brought us where we are in order that we may consider the good we have to do in the world as well as at home.' Where was that said? – in Parliament. When was it said? – nearly three hundred years ago. And who said it? – Oliver Cromwell. Let the government put those words in the next King's Speech, let them determine their proposals by that standard, and let that be the ideal and the responsibility of their efforts, and we shall be eager to help them and to restore the ideal that Wordsworth spoke a hundred years ago:

> Be each in this land again
> A bulwark for the cause of man.[119][120]

Isaac Foot was now one of only thirty-three remaining Liberal 'Samuelite' MPs. Later he recalled these years:

We had six strenuous and tumultuous years under the leadership of Herbert Samuel. Our party held a precarious and invidious position. We were the subject for daily attack. We were called 'Samuelites'. We accepted the epithet as a distinction. We Liberals had a rough time during those years and many of us went down on the same stricken field. I recall the time when we had decided that we must resign from the National Government. For some weeks there had been much discussion and communication, and at last the day came when all the resignations were signed and despatched. It so happened that on that day I was alone with Herbert Samuel on his last day at the Home Office. The time came for him to leave. He gathered up a few private papers, said goodbye to his secretaries, walked along the corridor seemingly unending, down the broad stairway, acknowledged the salute of the messengers assembled in the hall, and then down the steps and along Whitehall. I reflect-

119. Wordsworth's sonnet 'England', written in 1802.
120. 'The Faith of Isaac Foot', *Free Trade*, 1950.

Isaac Foot speaking to his constituents outside the House of Commons.

ed that that morning he had been the Secretary of State, holding one of the greatest offices in the land. Now on the pavement of Whitehall, he was again a private member of Parliament and next morning a storm of criticism would break upon his head. He made no comment upon this. There were no histrionics and there was nothing in his conversation to suggest that this day was different from any other.[121]

Isaac Foot's Commons speeches

MICHAEL: My father was now a leading Liberal speaker on the many issues which arose in this parliament. The following excerpts from his speeches in the Commons can only be a small selection of the many contributions he made to the debates in these years.

1929: The Poor Prisoner's Defence Bill. The need for the provision of legal aid was the subject of Isaac Foot's first speech back in the Commons.

I was interested to hear what the Right Hon. Gentleman said about the nervousness of speakers in this House. After an absence from the House for some years, I feel something

121. 1950 broadcast tribute on Samuel's eightieth birthday.

157

of that nervousness in getting up to address the House again. I represent a constituency that was once represented by Edward Gibbon, the historian of Rome. He became a member for Liskeard and was a member of this House for three years but he never dared to make a speech. I think he said that he was just engaged in writing his history on destroying an army of barbarians when Mr Eliot asked him to stand as the candidate for Liskeard. The Home Secretary commented on the support given to this Bill by lawyers. As a matter of fact, most of the law reforms of this country have been brought about by lawyers in this House. One need only refer to the story of a man like Sir Samuel Romilly[122] and his association with those reforms and to the fact that one of the greatest documents of freedom in the history of the world, the Declaration of Independence, was mainly signed by lawyers; and it was Edmund Burke who said that revolution was brought about mainly by lawyers, who, by reason of their training, were able to sniff tyranny in every tainted breeze.[123]

1930: Crisis in Malta

MICHAEL: In 1930 a crisis arose over elections in Malta, a member of the British Empire, where the Vatican sought to bring pressure to bear on the Catholic Maltese electors to vote for the Roman Catholic candidates. This raised questions of civil and religious liberty of a much larger nature. My father played a leading part in making sure that the principles he saw were challenged here were properly discussed in the House of Commons and throughout the country. This controversy aroused very bitter feelings and my father was strongly attacked for his Free Church stand in the leading Roman Catholic paper.

Isaac Foot gave this interview on that subject in the Methodist Times *of 21 August 1930:*

If the claims of the Vatican and the Roman ecclesiastics are accepted, constitutional government, as British people understand it, ceases to exist, and the ultimate and effective control of Maltese affairs passes over to the Roman Catholic Church. The line dividing civil and religious authority has never been easy to draw since Our Lord told His questioners to render to Caesar the things which are Caesar's and to God the things which are God's. The claims of Rome have vexed statesmen in this country through many troublous generations and, in seeking to understand this problem now in our own day, we shall need to take many books down from our shelves including, I hope, the writings of John Milton, who said: 'Popery is a double thing to deal with and claims a two-fold power, ecclesiastical and political, both usurped, and the one supporting the other.'

---

122. Romilly (1757–1818), legal reformer.
123. Hansard, 8 November 1929.

1931: The Sunday Performance Regulation Bill, to allow the opening of places of entertainment on a Sunday.

We are face to face with grave issues here. We are not dealing with something that concerns only chapels or churches, we are dealing with something which is recognised to be a common possession of the people of this country ... We have to judge this matter by the needs of our own time. Our case does not rest on any claim to interfere with the habits of other people. We are not entitled to impose our wishes upon the community. Bur my desire is to resist any efforts to exploit this day of rest and recreation. I take my stand upon what a master teacher said many years ago: 'One man esteemeth one day above another: another esteemeth every day alike. Let every man be fully persuaded in his own mind.'[124] It was Dr Johnson who said: 'I would have Sunday kept, not with rigid severity and gloom but with a gravity and simplicity of behaviour.' My happiest days were when the members of my family came together on the Sabbath.

The case of those opposed to this Bill does not rest upon any lack of sympathy with the poor ... I was sorry to hear from some of my Labour friends the suggestion that you have to provide facilities for entertainment in order to make the present social conditions tolerable. I remember an argument used in another place by a Noble Lord who said that he wished to maintain the existing conditions in relation to the supply of intoxicating liquor because liquor was the shortest way out of Manchester and he said that, if the facilities for obtaining liquor were taken away, there would be an uprising against social evils. Our business is to remedy evil social conditions and not to make them tolerable by dope and I have founded my view largely upon the opinion of the poorest people. Many of the opinions I have obtained from the fisher-folk who attach great importance to Sunday and in my constituency fishermen will not take out their boats on Sunday.

I want the House to distinguish between the personal observance, of which so much has been said, and the institution of Sunday. The distinguishing feature of the English Sunday is the difference between that day and the other days of the week. This distinction is of the utmost importance and this has been made possible, very largely, by restrictions. If the restrictions had not been there, many of us today would not be enjoying the privileges of Sunday that we now have. Not only do you want one day in seven, but, what really constitutes the advantage of Sunday is that you get your rest in common with the rest of the community. The relations between man and man and business and business make it essential that the cessation of all kinds of labour, except that which is absolutely necessary, should be on the same day. If the Sunday is a communal day of rest and recreation, then you have to establish safeguards for all in the interests of all. I judge the Bill by what it will do for this institution. Will the proposals preserve the institution or weaken it?

124. Romans 14:5.

The real enemy of the Sunday is the exploiter and commercialism. The exploiter looks upon the Sunday just as the general looked upon London and said: 'What a city to sack!' So the exploiter says about Sunday: 'What a day to exploit!' He knows very well that, if he can get that day, he will be getting the day when the best takings are possible and, if this Bill passes, I believe it will strengthen the forces of exploitation and enlarge the area of their activities ... I do not think this Bill is the right way of dealing with the situation. We are trustees in this matter for a very precious thing that is committed to our trust. Against the Sundays are arrayed many enemies, many hungry interests and many who have no interest in the Sunday but are out for exploitation. I want to resist those exploiters. I want to fight those mercenary interests. I believe I can do this best by voting against the second reading. If I voted for this second reading I should think I was one who had helped 'to break down the dykes and let in the waters over the land'.[125]

Licensing Laws: Isaac Foot was now the leader of the temperance group of MPs. In his first session in the Commons he had been one of the promoters of Nancy Astor's Intoxicating Liquor Bill to make it illegal to sell alcohol to those under the age of eighteen.

MICHAEL: As a boy my father saw the effects or the causes of addiction to alcohol in the crowded, violent back streets of Plymouth. Once he saw a particular carpenter friend of his reeling into the street, fighting drunk, and when his mother came out to protest, striking her a cruel blow across the face. So Isaac Foot, aged nine, signed the pledge. In 1933 he unmasked Sir Edgar Sanders, director of the Brewers' Society, for his speech to the brewers initiating a campaign to make the 'younger customer the mainstay of the public house' and proposing that sportsmen should be recruited to advertise their wares.

Isaac Foot's speech in reply was printed as 'Blood Money?', an open letter to Sir Edgar Sanders, the director of the Brewers' Society:

Sir Edgar,

Your recent speech reveals a conspiracy, an underground conspiracy, and an underground conspiracy which is a danger to the public. What is your design? You say:

> Unless we can attract the younger generation to take the place of the older men, there is no doubt we shall have to face a steadily falling consumption of beer. That is what may happen unless we do something to attract and secure the younger customer, who, in turn, will become the mainstay of the public house. Unless steps are taken to say to him that England's beer is the best and the healthiest beverage he

---

125. Hansard, 20 April 1931.

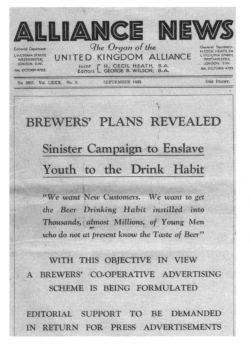

ALLIANCE NEWS

The Organ of the
UNITED KINGDOM ALLIANCE

Editorial Department
4, VICTORIA STREET
WESTMINSTER,
LONDON, S.W.
Tele. VICTORIA 4765.

Joint [H. CECIL HEATH, B.A.
Editors L. GEORGE B. WILSON, B.A.

General Secretary,
H.CECIL HEATH, B.A.
4, VICTORIA STREET
WESTMINSTER,
LONDON, S.W.
Tele. VICTORIA 4765

No. 3917. Vol. LXXX. No. 9.   SEPTEMBER 1933.   ONE PENNY.

BREWERS' PLANS REVEALED

Sinister Campaign to Enslave
Youth to the Drink Habit

"We want New Customers. We want to get
the Beer Drinking Habit instilled into
Thousands, almost Millions, of Young Men
who do not at present know the Taste of Beer"

WITH THIS OBJECTIVE IN VIEW
A BREWERS' CO-OPERATIVE ADVERTISING
SCHEME IS BEING FORMULATED

EDITORIAL SUPPORT TO BE DEMANDED
IN RETURN FOR PRESS ADVERTISEMENTS

'The Brewers' Plans Revealed'.

can consume, and to bring before him all the good will and contentment that the public house imparts in England, and to carry on this good will, we shall certainly see the Trade on a declining basis. We want to get the beer drinking habit instilled into thousands, almost millions of young men who do not at present know the taste of beer.

This, then, is your beneficent design. How is to be accomplished? Mainly, apparently, by advertising:

> The main lines would be press advertising, bill-posting, advertising on public vehicles, possibly by illuminated signs, distribution of literature, lectures and articles by prominent persons, and press propaganda by means of editorial and news items ... In that way it is wonderful how you can educate public opinion, generally without making it too obvious that there is a publicity campaign behind it all. There are plenty of footballers, plenty of cricketers, plenty of prize fighters, and so on, who would like to appear in the press saying that their strength is derived from beer – at any rate, we should consider this in connexion with our scheme.

Footballers, cricketers, prize fighters, and so on. Why did you stop there? Strangely enough you did not mention motorists. What about chauffeurs? What about lorry drivers? Why not give us poster pictures of the chauffeur or a bus driver at the wheel, saying 'I drive on beer', and 'I am the mainstay of the public house'? Would any one of your brewers trust this gentleman with his lorry or his Rolls-Royce? You give us clearly to understand that the press is to be bribed: 'If we begin advertising in the press, we shall see that the continuation of our advertising is contingent upon the fact that we get editorial support as well in the same papers.' Why not go a step further? Would it not be as well to take over the newspapers altogether?

I wonder what will be the comment of the press upon this insolent proposal? Already I have seen two references which suggest that the press might not be as amenable as you led the brewers to believe:

If the Press allows the public to believe that it can be coerced as the brewers cynically threaten, it will have defrauded every honest advertiser, who asks for nothing but the privilege to state his case in its columns.

The legitimate advertiser does not buy merely space; he buys reader-respect. The integrity of a newspaper is an invisible factor in the calculation of rates.

To me, as one of the ordinary public, it is reassuring to read these protests against your proposals. Herr Hitler has his special way of dealing with the press in Germany but his methods, though marked by force and violence, are avowed and open. Your method, if it succeeded, would have the same result in the suppression of independent opinion, but would be far more dangerous, as it would be done in secret.

Is not this blood money?

I have in my professional life as a lawyer, and in the relations with my fellows, seen something of the results of the drinking habit. In my public life I have seen many good men go wrong because of the habit that you wish to instil into thousands and millions. I know of the risk and danger, and so must you. In advocating your scheme to the brewers you told them that there is money in it. Are you sure it is not blood money? Your scheme is concerned with profit. Here is a passage on profit: 'But who so shall cause one of these little ones ... to stumble it is profitable for him that a great millstone should be hanged about his neck and that he should be sunk in the depth of the sea.'[126]

Yours faithfully, Isaac Foot.

Isaac Foot's leadership of the temperance group in the Commons made him one of the main targets for attack by what he called the 'vested interests of the drink trade'. Giving evidence to The Royal Commission on Licensing in 1933, he described this pressure in his election campaigns:

Most of the members, like myself, are frail creatures and, if the member is convinced that there is a strong public opinion, he is more than mortal if he ignores it. In my 1924 campaign the pressure was so heavy that the Post Office arrangements were disorganised and actually a new room had to be requisitioned for the purpose of dealing with the post cards and petitions on this matter ... It is against the best interests of democracy and of public life that a vested interest, which, by nature, is frequently in conflict with the national interests, should by virtue of its wealth and power be able to influence the fate of a political party in a general election.

---

126. Matthew 18:6.

In 1935 the brewers expressed their delight at Isaac Foot's election defeat:

The defeat of Isaac Foot has left the Temperance party without a leader in the House of Commons. Of that party, such as it is, he was the brains. He was the chief obstacle in the way of anything in the way of legislation being done for making the licensing laws more human and more suited to the needs of the present day. The loss of him to the teetotallers is irreparable. Perhaps it is not quite so serious to the House as a whole but he will certainly be missed and now, perhaps, we shall be able to get on.[127]

1934: 'The growing menace of the gambling evil.' Isaac Foot gave this interview on the Betting and Lotteries Bill of 1934, which proposed limitations on organised betting.

It may be true that the betting habits of the community are too deeply rooted to be easily eradicated but surely something could be done to check the incitements and inducements to gambling which seem to be multiplying in every direction. The danger and the extent of the betting habit are little realised by the ordinary individual. I had the opportunity of learning something of these when, in 1923, I sat on the select committee which had to consider the advisability of introducing a duty on betting. The evil, which then was widespread, has since that time become vastly greater ... I suppose there is no one habit that is responsible for so many ruined homes as the gambling craze. It is, as any magistrate or judge will agree, a prolific source of crime. Beyond all these considerations, every student of the betting evil agrees that its most disastrous effect is in the deterioration of character. Once a man becomes a victim of this habit his usefulness as a citizen has gone. The habit brings about a sort of atrophy of the mind. The habitual gambler becomes of no use to his family, his trade union, his political party, his employer, or to the state. He degenerates into a burden on the community. This is just what the gambling habit does, and its effects are beyond the computations of economists or statisticians. They tell us nothing of the broken lives and ruined homes, of the waste of good citizenship. The report of the Royal Commission in 1933 came deliberately to the conclusion that there were 'serious social consequences' following the widespread growth of the evil. 'A disquieting feature of the position today is that there is a deliberate exploitation of the propensities of the people for purposes of personal gain.'

Every community, anxious for its self-preservation, must fight those individuals and organisations that exist only to provoke and entice citizens, particularly young citizens, into anti-social channels. These organisations make a dead set on youth. Just as the brewers have published their scheme of turning the young people of the country into beer drinkers, so the huge gambling interests are out to exploit the youth of the race to their

---

127. *Morning Advertiser*, 16 November 1935.

own advantage. Of course, anyone who stands up against this exploitation or exposes its cynicism and self-interest is at once condemned as a fanatic, or put on one side as a man with a bee in his bonnet. It is only necessary to point out that gambling and betting have always marked the times when nations have become degenerate, and that there is an insistent and imperative call, therefore, for men and women of good will and high principle to stop the rot. The organisers of the dog track totes and others have raised the cry about the liberty of the subject. A man can be a true disciple of liberty, and yet a fierce opponent of those interests which only want a spurious freedom which will allow them to exploit their fellows, and put no limitation on their endeavour so long as there is a chance of drawing a dividend from their destruction.[128]

1934 Road Safety debate: on publication of the road accident statistics for 1926 to 1933 – 50,837 killed and 1,421,083 injured – Isaac Foot urged the government to take action.

Whatever differences there may be in this House, there ought to be utter discontent with conditions which make possible these figures. My experience is that nothing is done in this country until there is an outburst of public indignation. I do not think this is a case for language which has to be nicely balanced. I do not think that anything which happened in the Great War or has happened in the history of this country has been worse than these figures. The *Times* recently told of an inquiry that arose in one accident which showed that three little children had been killed on one day. These children have just as much right as any children in our homes to safety and protection which was the main responsibility of the government. Every one of us knows of village streets where the cottages are built right on the road. We hear of children running into the streets. What do we expect children to do? What must be the plight of those villages, the terror in the lives of the mothers, because they cannot but consider themselves fortunate that they have any house to live in at all? These children have first claim on the consideration of this House and of the Ministry of Transport. There was once a prophet who drew a picture of the ideal city: 'There shall yet old men and old women dwell in the streets of Jerusalem and every man with his staff in his hand for very age, and the streets of the city shall be full of boys and girls playing in the streets thereof.'[129] That was not the ideal city of the motorist. We understand that in the Holy City the streets will be of pure gold. That will not suit the motorist – ribbed concrete will be asked for, probably, as a change in those conditions.

I suggest that it is the first mark of a higher civilisation that the people have a care for their older people and for the children. Is there any social student or statistician who can calculate the aggregate of human sorrow and misery caused by this? I do not believe there

128. Isaac Foot papers.
129. Zechariah 8:4.

is one sovereign remedy but there are a great many things that could be done. Our real danger is our indifference to these casualty figures. The question of speed is a most essential factor in our discussion. There is no doubt whatever that, if speed were halved, fewer people would be killed... If there is a demand in a village for the lessening of speed why should not people have that protection? Why should not a speed limit be readily given? I feel very deeply on this matter because I think it concerns liberty. All the grandiloquent talk about Habeas Corpus and Magna Charta and the Petition of Right is nothing unless we can have the primary protection for our people, protection of life and limb. That is what liberty is for. It is because liberty in its first and essential elements is being threatened under these conditions, which no one ought to tolerate, that I ask the Minister to take a very strong line. I ask the Minister to have regard to the rising indignation of the people of this country. I ask him to see that after their great history they shall not be 'chivvied' off their own highways and made to run before the machine like a lot of rabbits. They deserve something better than that and I hope the Minister will fulfil his responsibility to them.[130]

Isaac Foot was one of the first to voice his concern about the effect of alcohol on motorists. In 1924 with other MPs he had called for an inquiry into the relation between road safety and alcohol.

Henry Ford was quite right when he said that mankind would have to make up its mind to give up alcohol or the motor car. How much liquor can a man consume and drive down a hill or a crowded street? The only safe answer to that question is none. There is no safeguard for the motor driver except total abstinence. And, if liquor unfits a man for control of a car, how much more does it unfit a man for control of a machine far more delicate and intricate – himself?[131]

From 1944 to 1950 as president of the Pedestrians' Association, whose slogan was 'Safe Roads for All!', Isaac Foot continued to work to publicise the need for safer roads. For him this was a moral issue:

The association is one without any sectional interest and has for its purpose the rights of the people to their common inheritance in the King's Highway. We seek to quicken the conscience of the people of Britain about the great injury and wrong done to so many on the roads from day to day. This is a moral issue. Every man or woman killed upon the King's Highway is made in the image of God and against the constant record of the loss of a child's life might be written the words of Our Lord on 'one of those little ones'.[132]

130. Hansard, 7 February 1934.
131. *New Chronicle of Christian Education*, 22 May 1930.
132. Notes in Isaac Foot papers, 1946.

1933: The Franchise. As a member of a minority party in the Commons, Isaac Foot argued the case for a fairer system of representation.

Today we are pleading for the many people, the minorities, who are denied the right of representation in this House... Surely they have the same right to representation as those who are fortunate enough to vote for the majority. Under our present system of voting they are shut out from consideration... I would like to tell Members why I feel so strongly on this subject. I ask them to give me credit for not being concerned merely with the fortunes of my own party. There are some things that it is very difficult to define. It is very difficult to define liberty or to define democracy, but, whatever definition of democracy there may be, there are two fundamental things we are entitled to look for in a democratic system. First of all under the system, if it is democratic, the will of the majority for the time being, as it is expressed at the polls, shall prevail.

The other fundamental thing is that substantial minorities shall have a representation that corresponds approximately with their influence and power. Judged by that test our system stands condemned and, to the extent that it falls short of that, it ought to be improved, if it is within our power.

I ask Hon. Members to consider what has been the long struggle for the representative institutions in this country. The fight for the franchise, for reform, extended over the latter part of the eighteenth century and went right on to the big measure of 1832. Members opposite can take pride in the work they did for the extension of the franchise in some of the later years. The franchise has been the dominating issue for, I suppose, a hundred years... Yet in spite of all that effort, in spite of all the laws we have set up during successive years to get fair representation of the people's will, when we make the supreme effort and we converge upon the elections, we have no assurance after an election that there is any approximate correspondence between the votes cast and the constitution of the House. I believe that we have got to maintain representative institutions in this country and that the responsibility rests upon this country more than upon any country in the world. When William Wordsworth said, over a century ago, speaking of this country, that it was a bulwark for the cause of men, it was just after the Napoleonic struggle. It is very much more true today. Now that we see representative institutions going down all along the line and Kings going down and dictators locking up the doors of Parliament and putting the keys in their pocket, there are very few countries left where representative institutions are maintained and it is not going one word beyond the bare truth to say that if they went down in this country, they would go down everywhere. Therefore there is the responsibility upon us.[133]

---

133. Hansard, 6 December 1933.

1934: Liberty and the 'Blackshirts' at Olympia. Following reports of violent behaviour at a recent meeting at Olympia of Sir Oswald Mosley's British Union of Fascists, known as the 'Blackshirts', Isaac Foot called for and opened a debate on this subject in the Commons.

As we have read in our newspapers during the last week, certain events have occurred, at what is now called the Olympia meeting, which have very much stirred the public mind. I would like right away to refer to what took place. It is very evident from these reports that this is something new in the way of public meetings. Apparently the arrangements on this occasion included bands, 'sonorous metal blowing martial sounds', uniforms, flags, salutes, a 'gang shout-leader' and it seems almost as if one had there all the incantations which one associates with an African witch doctor.

Interview with Isaac Foot in the Methodist Times
Mr Foot referred to his three grounds for apprehension which he spoke of in the debate in the House – that what had happened at Olympia was no isolated occurrence, but a symptom of a return to violent ways of thinking; that public apprehension had grown by familiarity of experiences abroad on the Continent; and the third was the claim of this sinister movement to concurrent power with the state through the possession of a private army and a semi-military force claiming alternative powers with the police. Quoting Edmund Burke, in his *French Revolution*, Mr Foot said:

'The preservation of law and order in this country must be left to the police, who can be brought to account, and to the executive, which stands impartially for the whole community. No party faction can be allowed to claim concurrent power with the government and its instrument, the police.' The issue now is not the supremacy of fascism over communism or communism over fascism, but the danger of the liberty of the whole community being lost in the strife of these two contending factions. It is neither rhetoric nor exaggeration to say liberty is in danger and that, if liberty were to go down in this country, it would inevitably go down throughout the whole world. A hundred years ago Wordsworth said: 'Dearly must we prize thee, We who find in thee a bulwark for the cause of man.' Those words of the poet are more significant today than when Wordsworth wrote them at the time of the struggle with Napoleon. I asked the House to remember that many tributaries had helped to form what Wordsworth had called 'the flood of English freedom'. I told the House that, as I was coming to speak that day, I had passed all the great reminders of the struggle for freedom, which, after all, is the greatest achievement of our race. I passed the place where Charles I stepped out of his room at Whitehall on his last journey; along Whitehall, where John Hampden's freeholders marched in their thousands to protect their champion. I passed the pit outside Westminster

Abbey where the bodies of Robert Blake and John Pym were flung after the Restoration, and through Westminster Hall, on the roof of which the head of Oliver Cromwell was exposed to the derision of the mob. And through St Stephen's Hall, between the statues not only of Pitt and Fox, but of Clarendon and Hampden. All these are the reminders that the inheritance of liberty we have secured is a very wonderful one, to which men of different character and outlook and of conflicting philosophies all contributed. It will be the most lamentable tragedy in history if, in a generation which, in so many ways, is the most wonderful in the history of the world, when scientific knowledge has been applied to life and industry on a scale never before known, we should lose our hold on intangible and spiritual things in comparison with which all our material advantages are far outweighed.[134]

1930–5: The Government of India Bill; 'The Member for the Depressed Classes'. The 'Untouchables' were the Hindus outside the Indian caste system working in occupations regarded as ignominious, polluting and unclean in Indian society led by Dr Ambedkar

MICHAEL: Something like four years of my father's parliamentary life became dominated by India. When in 1930 the Labour government, led by Ramsay MacDonald, appointed a Round Table Conference to deal with India's demand for self-government, my father was appointed one of the four Liberal spokesmen on that and the two further Round Table Conferences. He had never been to India, although he would have loved to have done so. He acquired a whole new library in the attic of his home on Indian matters and made himself a master of the subject, starting with Edmund Burke's and Lord Macaulay's original instructions.

Isaac Foot, as the chairman of a Liberal dinner held at the House of Commons on 20 January 1931, chose the quotations on the menu. His favourite was that of Edmund Burke speaking in the House of Commons on the East India Bill, 1 December 1783: 'Depend upon it, this business cannot be indifferent to our fame. It will turn out a matter of great disgrace or great glory to the whole British nation. We are on a conspicuous stage and the world marks our demeanour.'

MICHAEL: My father saw how great were the issues at stake for the human race as a whole in these debates on the Government of India Bill. One of those who had no such understanding of the significance of the argument on the Tory benches was Winston Churchill. My father took a special relish in fighting Churchill's reactionary views on the subject. His exchanges with my father became the sharpest in the whole story. Sadly, the Winston

134. *Methodist Times*, June 1934.

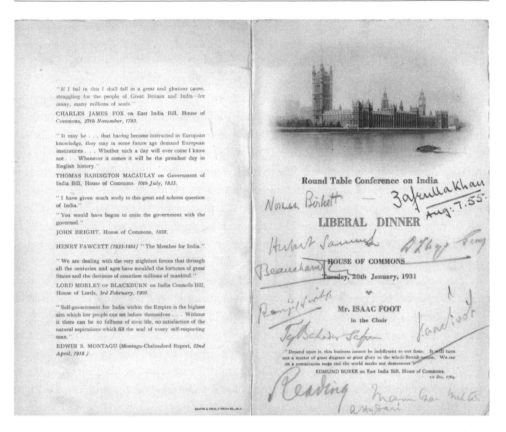

The programme for the Liberal Dinner in the Commons after the First Round Table Conference on India in 1931, signed on the front by those attending. Isaac Foot supplied some of his favourite quotations for this.

Churchill of that parliament shared no such vision for the future and showed no understanding of the great issues for the world at large involved in the India controversy. For my father it did not go far enough. His contribution kept open the door for the approach to full Indian independence which would dominate the years to come. Over these years my father made many lasting friends in India, headed by Dr Ambedkar, the leader of the 'Untouchables', who never ceased to acknowledge my father's services. I had an especial interest in the matter myself, since I can recall coming to London during the Round Table Conference, when I was just about to go to Oxford to sit for a scholarship examination. My father discussed with me one evening what was to come out in the next few days as a main recommendation of the conference and, when I sat down in the examination room next morning, I was surprised to have as the first item an essay subject something like: 'What recommendations do you think are likely to be put by the Royal Commission on India?' I recall that I was given an exhibition for Oxford.

The India Round Table Conference: Isaac Foot gave his views on the publication of the report of the First Round Table Conference on India, published in 1931. This was the speech which earned him the title of 'The Member for the Depressed Classes':

I think we can already judge that this matter is, above all other matters that come before the House, one of supreme importance. In my opinion, all our domestic disputes are in comparison no more than dust in the balance. The difference between a friendly India and an alienated India is a difference so great that there is no statesman in the country who can appreciate and no economist who can compute what that difference means ... The Indian believes that his country should not be subordinate. He believes that his people are the equal of any race in the world, and that he is not one of the subject people, and a conquered race. He has a high lineage. He comes from a proud descent. He claims that he should have a right to hold his head high among the nations of the world. He compares his civilisation with ours, not always to our advantage. He sees in our Western civilisation much that he does not want in India – materialism, alcoholism, industrialism, the sick hurry and aggression and the desperate scramble of an acquisitive society. He believes that, in our Western civilisation, there are some elements that he would adopt, but he wants to adopt them as a free man, and not because he is obliged to do so as a member of a subject race. It is not a claim merely for status, but also for liberty. The Indian has learned from our literature something of our love of liberty. Freedom knows no frontiers.

We have given to the Indian people a literature full of this love of liberty, and when we are told that Gandhi-ism and all that it stands for is to be crushed, I would like the Right Hon. Member for Epping (Mr Churchill) to tell us what we are to do with English literature. What books are we to shut out? When he has excluded all the literature of liberty he will have practically excluded all the great literature that we have got. All the really great sonnets of Wordsworth were written when he was a Liberal. His later sonnets, written when he was a Tory, were in defence of capital punishment. In excluding the literature of liberty, the Right Hon. Gentleman would need to forbid the New Testament. The New Testament contains more dynamite than all the rest of the world's literature put together...

I should like to deal with one further subject which, in my opinion, is of commanding importance. I refer to the question of the depressed classes, who are known by the unfortunate name of the 'Untouchables'. I have been at some pains to follow their case. The Hon. Members need to realise to some extent the exceedingly bitter sufferings of these people. With all the desire that I have to support the proposals for self-government, I say that, if we take no precautions and if we establish no safeguards for the protection of these defenceless people, it may be that their blood will cry out against us. We have placed upon us the great responsibility of securing protection for these people. If Hon. Members will read the report, they will see that the children of these classes have often been kept out of the public school. They will read of wells that cannot be touched by the depressed classes, of wells going dry and the mothers unable to get any water to slake the thirst of their children, because they belong to the Untouchables. If I had any advice to give to the future governors of India it would be this: Let your main concern be for these people. There are forty to sixty millions of them. They may be defenceless now, but one day they will be strong. As there is justice upon this earth, there are neither dams nor dykes that can keep back for ever the accumulated wrongs and sufferings of these people. The real test of the progress of India twenty years hence will be: 'What have you done for these people?' Dominion status means nothing unless we meet the just claims of these people. India cannot expect to go into the Promised Land and to leave forty to sixty millions of her people behind in the Wilderness.

Our task is great. To bring India within the Commonwealth is the biggest thing that we have ever yet attempted ... We have had a long association with India. When we come through Westminster Hall, we see the place where Warren Hastings, India's first governor general, stood upon his trial. When we come to St Stephen's Hall, we see the picture of the Englishman who in the times of James I visited the court of the Mogul Emperor desiring permission to trade. We see there the statues of Burke, Fox, Bright and others. We are indeed compassed about with a great cloud of witnesses. There has been put upon us a responsibility greater than we have had before.[135]

In 1935 Isaac Foot made his final speech in the long debate on the third reading of the Government of India Bill to give India a limited measure of self-government:

We ought to congratulate ourselves that this big change in India is to come about as a result of discussion and persuasion and not as a result of violence and force ... The very fact that we sought to settle these differences round the table, and that the matter was one for persuasion and argument rather than of arms and force shows, at any rate, that this world is making some progress. Those of us who support the Bill have no illusions as to the future. We have no belief that there will be an easy progress for this measure in India ... One of the most notable political utterances ever made was by General Smuts last year. He said: 'A new portent of a first order is appearing in Asia. Sleeping Asia is awakening, is stirring, from one end to the other. Two-thirds of the human race is on the move, and no one knows whither.' That was said by an Empire statesman who commended in general terms the proposals now before the House.

We are dealing with the relations between East and West and with questions of race. We shall not be troubled twenty years hence with some of the political problems which have occupied our attentions during most of our lifetime but mainly with the impact of one race upon another and it may be that we have something in this Bill upon which may hinge the

---

135. Hansard, 26 January 1931.

peace of the world. The most distinctive feature of our history has been the association of India and this country. It has been one of the most significant things and it marks our most distinctive task in this generation. I hope and believe that, out of this controversy and these discussions, out of the efforts that have been made by this house, something greater will emerge than can be done by this country or by India ... At these times I am not an imperialist. I have no sympathy with the Empire as it is sometimes proclaimed, but with something a great deal broader. I am sure that our hopes do not depend upon the sections and clauses in the Bill but on the measure of good will and understanding existing between the two countries. Those are the things which Burke spoke of as the ties of empire and John Milton as being the bonds and ligaments of the Commonwealth. It is in that sense that, greatly daring, and following the example recently set in another place, I quote the words of one, who in some senses, might be regarded as the greatest of all Englishmen: 'Oh Thou, who of Thy free grace ... did'st build up this Britannic Empire to such a glorious and enviable height, with all her Daughter Islands about her, Stay us in that felicity.'[136] [137]

Sir Shafaat Ahmad Khan, a colleague on the Round Table Conference, and leader of the Moslem community in India wrote this letter thanking Isaac Foot for his work on India:

Dear Mr Isaac Foot,

I knew, of course, that you had sacrificed considerably when you resigned from the government and we all had, and have, the greatest respect for your loyalty to your party. You have risked a lot for our sake, and done service to India in general, and the depressed classes in particular, which will be gratefully remembered by us. You are carrying on the traditions of Wilberforce and Clarkson, and upholding the traditional Nonconformist policy of supporting the under-dog. You have departed from that policy, in as far as you have taken under your protecting wings, not merely the depressed classes, but also the Moslems of India ... Your work on India must, no doubt, have cost a great deal and your constituents must have voiced their resentment against your preoccupation with a problem with which they are not directly concerned. But Edmund Burke suffered much more, and gave the last eight years of his noble life to a cause which brought upon him ridicule, obloquy and death.

---

136. Oliver Cromwell.
137. Hansard, 5 June 1935.

Silver Jubilee in Bodmin

1935 was the twenty-fifth year of Isaac Foot's association with the Bodmin division of south-east Cornwall. Sir Herbert Samuel, the Liberal leader, came and spoke at a Liberal Party rally at the Foot family home, Pencrebar, in July, when he paid this tribute to Isaac:

In Cornwall Isaac Foot has a wide popularity and a position of distinguished leadership. In Parliament he enjoys, not only the affection of his Liberal colleagues, but the respect of the whole House who honour his unswerving devotion to Liberalism and his untiring activity in the services of the state. His work on the India Bill alone, year after year of committees, conferences and discussions in Parliament, should entitle him to the gratitude of the nation. He is one of the few in the present time in this modern world who carries on the great traditions of parliamentary eloquence. He speaks with dignity and yet with humour, he speaks with sincerity, eloquence and power. Not only does he occupy a great position in the Westcountry and in Parliament, but he is a national figure where all meet together who are concerned with three great causes – those of the Free Churches, temperance and Liberalism. He is one of those always on the alert to defend the interests of those causes. He represents those strong thoughtful religious elements in the nation which have made England great at home and a power for good in the councils of the whole world.

The Liberal Garden party at Pencrebar in July 1935 – Isaac and Eva Foot with their guests: left to right *James Venning of Callington; Dingle and his wife Dorothy; Isaac and Eva; Herbert Samuel, leader of the Liberal Party in the Commons; and Sir Francis Acland, the Liberal MP for the neighbouring constituency of North Cornwall.*

Isaac Foot replied:

Twenty-five years is a big slice out of a man's life and I think, sometimes, of the temerity I had when I came down in December 1910, as the result of a very urgent call, to enter upon a fight in a new constituency. I was a Liberal then and I am a Liberal still. We have had rough weather and bright weather. I think the election to which I look back with most pride is not the by-election we won in February 1922 but the fight we put up in 1918 when we were beaten by 3,500. We never lowered our flag at that time. If there are speeches I have made in the division during the last twenty-five years that I would desire to see reprinted and republished most of all it is those I spoke in the election of 1918 ... We insisted that there was no chance of reconciliation in Europe or peace throughout the world unless the war and all that war stood for could be broken down, not only in institutions but in the minds of men. Those are the days upon which I look back with the greatest pride. It is upon the loyalty of what John Milton called 'the common people' that I depended. The great principle of the division is in the words of St. Paul: 'Let every man be fully persuaded in his own mind.'[138] I have learned during twenty-five years that it is part of a man's religion to see that his country is well governed and that a man who surrenders that principle does so at great risk to himself. This is the lesson we have learned in south-east Cornwall in times of success and diversity but more often in times of adversity. As to the future, no one can speak, but I look back over these years with very profound gratitude. Of all the prizes that have come to me in life – and I have had a few prizes – the thing I appreciate most of all is that I have been the spokesman upon great interests of the people among whom I have lived.[139]

---

138. Romans 14:5.
139. *Cornish Times*, 19 July 1935.

PART VI

The Methodist message

Isaac Foot, vice-president of the Methodist Conference 1937–8.

MICHAEL: As their early letters have already shown, my mother and father believed that the Wesleyan Methodist Church was the truest exponent of the Christian faith and ideas. Each of them had been taught in their Wesleyan Sunday schools and came to understand, even more deeply in the years together after their marriage, that the interventions of the Almighty could be delivered in direct and unmistakeable terms. They both remained convinced of this throughout their lives.

19 Isaac Foot the Methodist

In 1937, when Isaac Foot was installed as the vice-president of the Methodist Conference, he gave this description of his Methodist upbringing and faith:

In taking this office, there is in my mind only one element of pride, and that is that, in this great succession, I have been able to inscribe my father's name. When, nearly eighty years ago, he went with a company of village youths to mock the Methodist preacher and to disturb the Methodist service, the few words he heard, spoken by that unlettered evangelist, struck home to his heart. He was apprehended by the Spirit, went back home along the village street, which was for him the road to Damascus, and there and then commenced the business which has led directly to his son writing his name this day on this historic roll. My mother gave her heart to God. She had a beautiful voice, and it was her singing in the choir of the Methodist chapel at Plymouth that first attracted my father's attention. They both loved singing, especially the singing in the House of God, and the hymns of Charles Wesley were familiar in their mouths as household words! To the last my mother led the singing in chapel, because, becoming rather deaf in her older years, she generally led off the first note before the choir. She had, in earlier years, a hard time trying to train her five sons and two daughters and her discipline was severe, but in her later days she became all gentleness, all fragrance, and all grace. [J. M.] Barrie said: 'The God to whom little boys say their prayers has a face very like their mother's.' I expect most of us here have found that to be true.

I had the rare privilege in my youth of seeing what could be done in a home where ordinary folk, the common people, could reach enriched personality when they had the Bible, the hymns of the Wesleys, and the grace of God. My father was a Methodist preacher for over sixty years. His working library was the Bible, the *Methodist Hymn Book*, Matthew Henry's *Commentary on the Bible* and Wesley's *Notes on the New Testament*. The names discussed in our household were of those who, I was led to think, were the giants of their time – Thomas Champness, Peter Mackenzie, Spurgeon, and Hugh Price Hughes. It was a home where Billy Bray was mentioned with gratitude and reverence.[140] Later on I heard the new men discussed, like young preachers sent out with their first note. They were the striplings of that time – Samuel Chadwick, Dinsdale Young, Campbell Morgan, Scott Lidgett, Ferrier Hulme and F. L. Wiseman, who was always referred to as 'young Luke Wiseman'.[141]

Why have I dwelt upon these things? It is because I feel that the glory of Methodism is in its appeal to the common people. The grace of God gives the freest and fullest access of the man to his Maker, giving to every believer the full unlimited and illimitable freedom of the Son in the Father's House. No ordination, no Church prestige, no ecclesiastical orders can give to any member of our Church what cannot be possessed by the poorest and humblest believer living in utter poverty in a city tenement or country cottage. Those are some of the elementary and fundamental truths of Methodism, and, if anything is done to undermine those truths, the catholic sense of the Methodist people will be touched to the quick and they will be found as a people proudly and impenitently and irremovably Protestant. Methodism was cradled in the study of the Epistles of Paul to the Galatians and to the Romans. Those two epistles are the Gibraltar of Methodism, and when we lose our hold upon them, the institution may survive, but Methodism itself will be dead.[142]

---

140. Billy Bray (1794–1868), Cornish tin miner and evangelist.
141. These were the leading Methodist ministers and preachers of the day.
142. Isaac Foot papers.

John Wesley

ISAAC FOOT: Although I was brought up in a home where, in my childhood, 'Mr Wesley' was mentioned almost as if he were the fourth person in the Trinity, Wesley was not one of my special heroes. Those I found in Tyndale, Cromwell and Abraham Lincoln. My political sympathies were such that I was not attracted by Wesley's frigid Toryism and, when I was a youth, I would far rather have heard a speech of Dr John Clifford than have read a sermon of John Wesley. Two interests in later life brought me closer to Wesley. First was my growing interest in the apostle Paul. The other heroes were indeed of the Himalayan range but Paul was

John Wesley (1703–91).

the Everest. Wesley greatly helped me in his interpretation of the apostle. The other interest was the Greek New Testament. My knowledge of New Testament Greek is very slight. I only began to pick it up for myself after middle age and then mainly because I found the great commentaries were closed books to me. One of the standing regrets of my life is that, when I was a youth and had time to learn, I did not realise what was open to me in the interest and importance of New Testament Greek. Later on the Greek Testament captured my interest as a book, and, having succumbed to the temptations of a book collector, I have gradually obtained here and there, over many years, all the early copies on which I could lay my hands. As another one has come along, say, after long waiting, the first edition of Erasmus or at long last the 'Complutensian Polyglot'[143] I have been drawn more and more to think of John Wesley's Greek Testament and the way in which he gave that priceless treasure to his people.

In 1932 on Wesley Day, celebrated on 24 May, a mural tablet was unveiled on the New Building of the Methodist Book-Room in London, inscribed as in the illustration overleaf.

---

143. The name given to the first printed polyglot edition of the entire Bible, with Hebrew, Latin and Greek translations, completed in 1517. Only 600 copies were published.

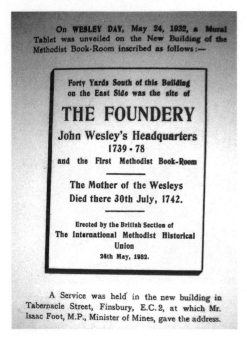

On WESLEY DAY, May 24, 1932, a Mural Tablet was unveiled on the New Building of the Methodist Book-Room inscribed as follows:—

Forty Yards South of this Building on the East Side was the site of

THE FOUNDERY

John Wesley's Headquarters
1739 - 78
and the First Methodist Book-Room

The Mother of the Wesleys
Died there 30th July, 1742.

Erected by the British Section of
The International Methodist Historical
Union
24th May, 1932.

A Service was held in the new building in Tabernacle Street, Finsbury, E.C.2, at which Mr. Isaac Foot, M.P., Minister of Mines, gave the address.

The mural tablet on John Wesley's Methodist Book-Room in London, unveiled with an address by Isaac Foot on Wesley Day, 24 May 1932.

On this occasion Isaac Foot gave this address:

One hundred and ninety years ago, that is on 11 November 1739, John Wesley preached for the first time in the building known as the Foundery. That building was afterwards acquired for the sum of £150, and, having been repaired, became the first Methodist chapel in London. For forty years it was the headquarters of the people called Methodists. Here John Wesley had his home; here his mother, Susanna Wesley, lived and died; here met the first Methodist Society class in London; here a few years later was held the first Methodist Conference. The building comprised not only the chapel, but the first Methodist Book-Room; and over all was the belfry, which, in a more strenuous generation than our own, called the people to worship at five o'clock every morning. Here 193 years later, within a few steps of this historic building, we are met to honour the memory of our great ancestors.

At the little meeting room in Aldersgate Street on 24 May 1738 John Wesley felt his heart 'strangely warmed'. That great event took place in a religious meeting. John Wesley, when he passed through that experience of the warmed heart, was hearing someone read Luther's 'Preface to the Epistle to the Romans'. Was there ever in history anything more wonderful than the way in which the apostle Paul, Martin Luther and John Wesley were brought together in rich and fruitful spiritual succession? We are today celebrating what happened in the year 1739. That was indeed a memorable year in Methodist history. On 2 April in that year, John Wesley preached at Bristol for the first time in the open air and from this day must be reckoned a new era in the religious history of England. On 4 April Wesley formed his first Methodist Society at Bristol and, again in that month, he established his first Methodist chapel at Bristol. On 14 June in the same year the first Methodist lay preacher began his work. On 11 November there was the first preaching at the Foundery, and in December there was established the United Society of Methodism...

We are met to rejoice in the work that he did, or rather the work which God accomplished through him. This work went far outside the world of Methodism. It brought new

The Foundery: John Wesley's headquarters and the first Methodist Book-Room.

life to the dissenting Churches and influenced the mother Church of England and inspired the Evangelical movement. Wesley's work had its results in the education of the people, the mitigation of our penal laws, the reform of our prisons and the abolition of the slave trade. That influence, indeed, went outside the Churches and had its effect upon history. This is Empire Day, and it is manifest that, were it not for the life and work of John Wesley, the history of this country and this empire would have taken a different course.[144]

There was another great event in the year 1739. In that year was published the book which I have in my hand. It bears upon its first page the words 'Hymns and Sacred Poems, by John Wesley, Master of Arts, Fellow of Lincoln College, Oxford; and Charles Wesley, Master of Arts, Student of Christ Church'. That book was the first of many. The mighty miracle of that time was that we had not only one man, but two. Here on this book the two names appear. Where the work of one left off and the work of the other began, no one can say. Methodism in its beginnings was marked by an outburst of song. When John Wesley had felt his heart strangely warmed in Aldersgate Street, he came at once to his brother, Charles, who, on the previous Sunday, had gone through the same experience. Charles says: ' We sang the hymn with great joy.' That hymn, we are told, is the first hymn in the second part of this book:

Where shall my wondering soul begin?
How shall I to all Heaven aspire?[145]

---

144. Since 1901 Empire Day was celebrated on May 24, the day of Queen Victoria's birthday.
145. Charles Wesley wrote this hymn on the day of his 'conversion', the day before his brother John had his heart 'strangely warmed'.

Prayer of Jas as a child-sitting on mothers — lap before bed

That hymn is one of the most famous in the history of song. The story of early Methodism is the story of salvation and lyricism. It was not a likely time for song. It was an age of materialism, of hard rationalism, of dim ideals and of expiring hopes. Yet, in the wilderness, waters broke out and songs in the desert. In thousands of homes mothers, in teaching their children, have commenced with Charles Wesley's hymn 'Gentle Jesus, Meek and Mild'. In times of the great Christian festivals men of all Churches find their natural expression in Charles Wesley's words. At Christmas time we have inevitably 'Hark the Herald Angels Sing', and the service on Easter morning needs for its consummation the glorious hymn 'Christ the Lord Is Risen Today, Alleluia!'. When we come to say farewell to our dead we turn almost naturally to the hymn 'Jesu, Lover of My Soul'.

The Methodists brought into our national life the contribution of joy. It was the joy of great discovery. They were like the man who finds the treasure hid in the field and for joy thereof goeth and selleth all he hath. Their experience was like that of Christian in *The Pilgrim's Progress* when the burden was taken from his shoulders and the three Shining Ones sent him on his way:

> The first said unto him: Thy sins are forgiven thee; the second stripped him of his rags and clothed him in a change of raiment; the third also set a mark on his forehead and gave him a roll with a seal upon it which he would have him look at as he ran ... Then Christian gave three leaps of joy and went on SINGING.

This is the best picture of the early Methodist – a song in his mouth and the roll in his hand. Our fathers sang because they had something to sing about. They sang their way around the world and they gave us our heritage, which is our special heritage, a hymnal saturated with Scripture. The sacerdotalist may tell us that the Bible is not safe in the hands of the individual believer. We are evangelical Protestants, and it is our assurance that the devout believer, when he turns to the Book, never reads it alone:

> Come, O thou Prophet of the Lord,
> Thou great Interpreter divine,
> Explain Thine own transmitted word
> To teach and inspire is Thine;
> Thou only canst Thyself reveal,
> Open the Book, and loose the seal.[146]

Wesley went all over the country and always had with him one Book.

There is today the danger of a famine of the Word. We are like Christian when he had lost his roll. Great stretches of the New Testament have become almost unintelligible to our generation. There is the need for the return of Pauline teaching. If Paul's teaching

---

146. Hymn by Charles Wesley.

passes out of Methodism the vitamins will have gone from our blood. The Bible is still our most priceless possession. We are today face to face with new problems and new difficulties, different from those the Wesleys faced. It is not necessary for us to bind ourselves to the methods and to fight with his weapons. He himself broke precedent. He himself challenged the methods of earlier generations. Had he not marked out this new course for himself he would have died the forgotten leader of an obscure sect. It is for us, not slavishly to follow his methods, but to catch his intensity, his intrepidity of spirit and his consecration and to draw our strength from the same unfailing source. In these days we have our special work to do and our own contribution to make. We need Wesley's conviction and intensity. In a world giving itself to the scramble after pleasure we need the quietness and serenity of joy.

We have our special contribution of fellowship. Fellowship is the supreme need in a generation of antagonism between class and class, suspicion between man and his neighbour, alienation between people and people, and of aggravated nationalism when the peoples of the world seek a vain refuge in an impossible isolation. In days like these we can gain our inspiration from the work and example of Wesley, who, beginning with intimate relationships – 'Ye neighbours and friends of Jesus draw near' – was led to reach out into all the world:

O Jesus ride on, till all are subdued,
Thy mercy make known and sprinkle Thy blood,
Display Thy salvation and teach the new song,
To every nation and people and tongue.[147]

Isaac Foot was proud of John and Charles Wesley's special associations with the Westcountry:

When John Wesley wrote in his *Journal* on Tuesday 17 May 1743, 'My brother set out for Cornwall,' he could not have known how wonderful a chapter had begun with that simple entry. Cornwall seemed to have for John Wesley an exceptional attraction, and the story of his association with the county has yet to be told. 'Behold, a sower went forth to sow',[148] and here Wesley's seed brought forth a hundredfold. No other single man has written his name so indelibly in the life and history of the Westcountry. Wesley was an amazing traveller, covering thousands of miles year after year, reading as he went and 'riding with a loose rein'. On Thursday 4 September 1746, Wesley preached at Plymouth at half-past four in the morning and then left for Cornwall. Crossing the Tamar at Cremyll, he rode, of course on horseback, through Millbrook to Looe, a distance of 16 miles. Having dined

---

147. Hymn 40 in Wesley's *Collection of Hymns*.
148. Matthew 13:3–9.

there, he then rode on over Tredinnick Ferry to Fowey and then through Grampound on to Gwennap.[149] That was a journey of over 60 miles, and, finding the congregation waiting, he began his second service for the day and, as he says, had 'no faintness or weariness'.

Recently there was a proposal to erect a monument commemorating the work of Wesley in Cornwall but the suggestion brought no result. It was felt that the monument of Wesley, even more than that of Christopher Wren, was to be seen by any observer who cared to look around him. In every town throughout the length of the peninsula, and in almost every village and hamlet, the Methodist people have, during the last century and a half, set up their spiritual home and habitation. These buildings, especially those erected in earlier years, have behind them a story of romance and sacrifice not less inspiring than that which tells of the cathedrals and the glorious parish churches. These places, often plain and severely simple, were erected mainly by the sacrifice of the peasantry and labouring folk. In the earliest days, certainly, they were built by the pence of the poor. Simple they had to be. In a certain sense they were the effort of homeless folk who felt they had somehow to get a roof over their heads. Here, it may be, is no tower or gleaming spire; here the traveller will not find

The high embowed roof,
With antique pillars massy proof,
And storied windows richly dight
Casting a dim religious light.[150]

The Cornish Methodist would be among the first to acknowledge that, without its parish churches, Cornwall would be unrecognisable. These are a common possession and part of the whole communal heritage. But the Methodist Church is also a part of Cornwall's story. Here, too, is the reminder of the things that are eternal. Let the traveller who seeks to understand the life and outlook of Westcountry folk pause and reflect, even when, to his surprise, he comes across the little church in some narrow lane, or alongside a moorland road or midway between some scattered farmsteads. A hundred years ago Thomas Carlyle, it will be remembered, went with Emerson for a walk over the long hills near Craigenputtock. They sat down and talked of the immortality of the soul. 'Christ died upon a tree,' said Carlyle, 'and that built Dunscore Kirk yonder.' Every one of these Methodist churches has the same foundation whatever may be the date carved upon its stones ... It may be that the reminder of the sacrifice and generosity of our forebears, which made possible for us these spiritual homes and hearths, will quicken the sense of responsibility which comes with our inheritance and that we may be fortified to meet the call of our own generation as we ask: 'What mean these stones?'[151]

---

149. Gwennap Pit, an open-air amphitheatre with good acoustics where John Wesley preached.
150. John Milton, 'Il Penseroso' (1633).
151. Isaac Foot, 'Foreword', in Lawrence Maker, *Cob and Moorstone* (Epworth Press, 1935).

Frogwell, the tiny Methodist chapel where Isaac Foot first preached when courting his wife Eva in nearby Callington.

MICHAEL: These were the words my father wrote on John Wesley. For my father the essential thing in Methodism was that the poorest member of society could enter into as rich a spiritual experience as the leader of the church. When he himself, later, wrote more fully on the subject of William Tyndale, he appreciated even more what was Tyndale's contribution to the whole development of and publication of the English Bible. For this he said later, 'the rejoicing should be abounding both in heaven and more still on earth'.

The Bible in personal life

The 400th anniversary of the martyrdom of William Tyndale, the first translator of the New Testament into English, was celebrated in 1936, followed by the 400th anniversary of the putting of the English Bible in the churches in 1938. Isaac Foot was one of several asked to make a broadcast on this occasion.

In a noble passage, Sir Arthur Quiller-Couch, writing some years ago of the Authorised Version of the Bible, said it was 'the most majestic thing in our literature and, by all odds, the most spiritually living thing we inherit'. 'It is', he said, 'in everything we see, hear, feel, because it is in our blood.' Indeed it is a very precious part of the experience of life. Here, in the New Testament, is a book that never grows stale. The more it is read the fresher it becomes. Often the page that is most familiar, and has been read a hundred times, is suddenly lit up with a new meaning, and this new interpretation often springs from one's own experience. That is one of the glories of the Bible – the illumination of experience. After all, is it not a thrilling thing to read the New Testament, with the knowledge that the lines on which you dwell have been studied and pondered by earnest men and women throughout all the generations ... The English Bible is a part of our inheritance. It remains the one continuing factor in our British life. Edmund Burke said of the state that it is a partnership not only between those who are living, but between those who are living, those who are dead and those who are yet to be born. Those great words are truer of the British Bible than they are of the British state. It is the enduring bond that links up the early days of the Venerable Bede and of Alfred the Great with our own generation. It is the closest tie of the English-speaking peoples in all parts of the world. It is one of those ties which, though light as air, are as strong as links of iron. It is the first mark of our blood relationship with our kith and kin throughout the Commonwealth. The Englishman without his Bible is deprived of one-half of his inheritance.

The importance of the New Testament is its message – not merely something written nineteen hundred years ago, but something as fresh as if it were written this morning. It has a timeless appeal and is relevant to every age. The Book is the gift of One who is not dead but who is alive – alive for evermore. It is His Book. Because it is His Book it is the Book of Hope. It is a Book of Hope because every line of it was written after Easter morning. Because it is His Book we can find assurance and confidence and quietness of mind. Disasters and wars may destroy much, but they can only bring down those things which can be shaken, but, after all the havoc and desolation brought by man's folly and wickedness, there will remain the things which cannot be shaken. What can never be shaken is the Word of God. All the beauty and significance of the written word comes from Him of whom it was said: 'In the beginning was the Word, and the Word was with God: and the Word was God.'[152]

As a leading Free Churchman in the 1930s Isaac Foot was invited to take up many offices – president of the National Brotherhood Movement 1936–7, vice-president of the Methodist Conference 1937–8, president of the Sunday School Union 1938–9 and president of the National Commercial Temperance League 1936–40. He spent these years travelling all over the country, addressing these different audiences. As president of the Sunday School Union in 1938, Isaac Foot spoke of his own debt to the Sunday school and its importance in teaching the Bible to future generations:

I have accepted the heavy responsibility of the national presidency of the National Sunday School Union mainly because this is Bible Year. My debt to the Sunday school goes back a very long time, in fact to the days of my father's youth. That was the day when my father,

---

152. Isaac Foot's broadcast, 1938.

with a number of other youths, had gone along to the Mission Hall in the Devonshire village which was his home, with the intention of mocking the preacher. He was so impressed by what the preacher said that, on the following Sunday, he went down to the Sunday school and offered his services. As a boy, I was taught by a rather illiterate farm labourer, but this village teacher left a deep impression on me, not by what he taught – but that he tried to teach at all – his object in taking the trouble, after hard manual labour, to instil his faith into a class of unruly boys.

It is not possible to estimate what this country owes the Sunday school. I gladly pay tribute to Sunday school workers up and down the land. I esteem them the salt of the earth and if I can give them any encouragement I shall count it a very high privilege. The Sunday school and the Bible stand together. If one goes, the other goes. I am convinced that a disappearing Sunday school means inevitably a disappearing Bible and a disappearing Bible means the weakening of everything that is precious ... In the conflict for the rightful claims of the New Testament many forces are engaged, but the Ironsides in this army are the Sunday school teachers and workers. I greet them in the Lord Jesus Christ, and I shall count it as a privilege if I can help them. If we relinquish the Sunday school for a single generation, everything most precious would disappear, the dykes against paganism would be broken down and the Bible would be virtually lost. The danger is that the vested interests are making desperate efforts to win the youth of the country. The public houses and the gambling interests are making great inroads on the youth of this country.

20 Isaac Foot the local preacher

From the age of nineteen in 1899, when he was accepted on Full Plan as a Methodist local preacher, Isaac Foot preached every Sunday in the Methodist chapels, at first in the local Methodist circuits around Plymouth and later in all parts of the country. He was following the example of his father, Isaac Senior, a Methodist local preacher for sixty years. When his son was first elected to Parliament, his father reminded him that his work as a Methodist preacher was of far greater importance than his work as an MP.

HUGH: My father's experience as a public speaker was gained in the court room and in the chapels around the Plymouth area. All his life he was a dedicated Methodist. I think he was the best preacher I ever heard. There wasn't much difference between his speaking and his preaching. He was an orator in the great tradition. He enjoyed the whole business and the development of a theme or an analogy, jest, something which had to be prepared for. Timing – he understood timing very well and the making of a speech was a work of art which so seldom you hear these days. Although he didn't rely on his notes when speaking,

The Methodist Church Long Service Certificate presented to Isaac Foot in 1959 for sixty years of service as a local preacher.

I know how he used to do his notes on the back of an envelope or something. He would very often take his commonplace books with him to quote from and then would turn back and he had a little trick of making people wait for the quotation. People would get a bit anxious, whether he was going to find it or not. I remember him looking up and saying 'No good us all worrying' or something like that. We used to say in the family that he overquoted.

JOHN: I think, in his time, my father preached in every Methodist chapel throughout Devon and Cornwall – many of them on many occasions. His sermons were very powerful. I think they were perhaps his finest accomplishment. He used to give a great deal of attention to writing them – his sermons were not just something thought up the evening before. He would work upon it for weeks at a time and the preparation of a new sermon was a considerable event in the family. We were all aware that a new sermon was emerging – in labour as it were. And then we would all go off to hear this and he would consult us all afterwards as to what we had thought of it. And invite our criticisms. Because of the trouble he went to and because he was a considerable theological student, he had a very big theological library and for perhaps fifteen years of his life when we were living in Plymouth this was his main line of reading.

Isaac Foot loved to preach in the small chapels of Devon and Cornwall, as his granddaughter, Sarah, remembers from when she was a child:

I was lucky enough to be born into a Methodist family. My grandfather walked all over Cornwall and Devon, preaching in small chapels in out-of-the-way places. He enjoyed it all immensely and did it with a real sense of joy ... I never heard him give a sermon without feeling enriched by the experience. His faith and the joy he derived from it was almost over-powering. But there was nothing sombre about his religious feeling. It lit up his life from within and he was able to impart this to others. The strength of his living faith came through with enormous power so that I can remember the sound of his voice and the great brilliance with which he could impart his religious experience ... He loved to go to the more remote chapels of Devon and Cornwall to preach and was still attending and participating in such services in the last ten years of his life. A couple who lived on the edge of Bodmin Moor say they can remember him in his younger days arriving bare-back on a horse to preach nearby. His way of imparting his religious feelings to us was not in dreary silent Bible readings on serious meditating Sundays, but he would recite great chunks of the Bible in his rich and energetic voice. On Sundays he would sit at his beloved piano and strum out the tunes of the hymns, half-shouting and half-singing the words, and it was impossible not to be infected by his enthusiasm.

The Rev. Henry Carter paid this tribute to Isaac Foot the Methodist preacher on his taking up the office of vice-president of the Methodist Conference:

A year ago the Methodist Conference designated Isaac Foot as its vice-president, the high-est office to which the conference can call a layman. Our fathers were friends and fellow-workers in the Ebenezer Wesleyan Circuit in Plymouth and Isaac and I have been friends since boyhood. I recall talks at a time when he was on a quest for certainty whether the Wesleyan ministry or business or public life was his true vocation. Professionally he became a solicitor, winning high repute in and beyond Plymouth. Notwithstanding his rich record of public service as MP, it is certain that the Methodist Conference called Isaac Foot to the vice-presidency because he is a Methodist – not in name merely, but in reality; Methodist by ancestry, Methodist by conviction, Methodist in active service. Quarterly meeting, synod and conference know him well, but I am confident that it is as a local preacher in Westcountry circuits that he really 'finds himself'. Understanding what the Evangelical Revival achieved in England, he is our representative lay exponent of its doc-trines and claims on the modern mind. He is always ready to expound the case for Free Churchmanship. Isaac Foot is Methodist in faith, in fervour and in testimony. Methodist audiences up and down the country in the coming year will listen to the ringing call of moral idealism. Church and Country! Methodist and Mankind! The vice-president sees the life of the spirit and the strife for the soul of the nation as one. 'Peace, liberty and social justice' were his watchwords as an MP and where are the deeper meanings of these social claims to be learned as surely as in the New Testament? He will admit no cleavage in thought or service between the message of the pulpit and the needs of the nation.[153]

MICHAEL: In his letters we have seen how my father developed and delivered his sermons as a Methodist. He believed with absolute assurance that God intervenes directly at the most critical moments in the lives of his heroes and heroines. He showed in his speeches, lectures and sermons how the greatest leaders revealed the special hour when God spoke to them. Some of the earliest occasions are derived from the Bible itself. But they also embraced all the other great figures my father admired. The reader can see in this sermon of my father's how these heroes were an especially significant group of people who had changed the world.

'The Word and the Man'

Luke, chapter 3, verses 1-2: 'In the fifteenth year of Tiberius Caesar ... *came the Word of God.*'

What made the fifteenth year in the reign of Tiberius Caesar a great date in the history of the world was the coming of the Word of God. The Word of God came, just as it had come in times past to Amos, to Isaiah, to Jeremiah and the rest. It came – it was not something arising from within the man, but something coming to them from without – not something born in the mind of man but something born in the mind of God. God had something to say; God wanted to speak to man and he was searching for a voice through whom he could speak. And the Word of God came unto John. 'And John came into all the country about Jordan, preaching.' It was not God's message to John but God's message through John. It was not the vision of God that came to John; that might have made him the visionary. It was not the revelation of God that came. That might have made him the anchorite, the recluse, the hermit. The vision or the revelation might have kept him in the wilderness. But the Word of God came to John. It was the Word that drove him forth. It was the Word that made him the herald, the prophet, the preacher. What God needed at that time was not the visionary. The visionary has his place in the spiritual economy of the world but God needed the missionary; not the mystic but the evangelist; not the hermit or the anchorite but the witness – the martyr. And the Word of God brings John out of the wilderness into the marketplace, out of the desert into the villages and cities, into the inevitable conflict with evil, into the clash with the wickedness of the King himself, and the word of God rings through the King's court – 'It is not lawful for thee to do this thing.' The Word of God takes him into the prison cell; the darkness of that cell is only to be lit

---

153. *Methodist Recorder*, July 1937.

CWENNAP PIT. 1926.

1926: Isaac Foot preaches at the annual Whit Monday service at Gwennap Pit, the open-air amphitheatre cut into the side of Carn Marth near Redruth, where John Wesley once preached to 20,000 people.

up with the flash of the executioner's sword; and John – so soon, not yet thirty years of age – has run his course. That is what the coming of the Word of God meant to John, the son of Zacharias – a very real business to him. He had no doubt when the word came. In the fifteenth year – not only in the fifteenth year – John knew the day and the hour in the wilderness but not only in the wilderness – John knew the place – he could have taken you to the very spot where this great thing happened to him: 'On that great day in my life and at this place the Word of God came – that is where this happened to me, and I John, the son of Zacharias, became the messenger of the Lord.' He knew the time; he knew the place.

That is how it happened to Isaiah: 'In the year that King Uzziah died I saw the Lord, high and lifted up and his train filled the Temple.' Isaiah knew the time; he knew the place. That is how it happened to Saul of Tarsus: 'It was on that day I was on my way to Damascus. At midday, O King Agrippa, I saw in the way a light – I heard a voice saying unto me: "Saul, Saul." And then Festus cries out, 'Paul, thou art beside thyself, thou art mad!' 'I am not mad, most noble Festus. I was not at that time caught up into some third heaven. It was on the main road to Damascus. I can take you to the spot where it happened. It was a very real thing that happened to me there just as real as those chains!' Paul knew the time; he knew the place. That is how it happened to Jacob. He knew the time: it was during that night – that long night, that terrible night – it was just towards the breaking of the day. That was the time and the place was just on the other side of the brook called

Jabbok: Leah and Rachel and the children were on the other side; he was on this. And if, in after days when he spoke of that, the greatest transaction of his life, his friend would say: 'Jacob, it was an hallucination – a dream,' Jacob had his answer: 'If it was, as you say, an hallucination, a dream, how comes it that there is a place which is still called Penuel; whence came this scar upon my body and why is it that to this day I still have it upon my thigh?' He knew the time; he knew the place.

The Lord does not always come in the same way. It is God speaking who has created man in His own image. There is the high mystery of grace and personality. And no two personalities are the same. To Moses in the desert, the Word comes in the bush which burns and is not consumed; and the Word comes to him in his full manhood. To Samuel, who is dedicated for his long life service, the word comes when he is yet a boy and the voice at night came clearly through the courts of the Temple: 'Samuel, Samuel!' To the youth Elisha, it comes one early morning when he is ploughing on the hillside and he felt something fall across his shoulder. It is a mantle and there passing away from him is a stranger. And Elisha runs after him and says: 'What is your name?' 'My name', says the stranger, 'is Elijah the Tishbite,' and Elisha says: 'I am ready.' And Elijah, looking at the ruddy face of the young man and recalling the heartbreak and the sorrow and the sacrifice of the prophets calling, says: 'Go back again, for what have I done to thee?' 'No,' says Elisha. 'It is your mantle but it is God's call. I am ready.' And, in after years, when he has become so much the leader and the champion of the people that they said he was the horseman and the chariots thereof, Elisha looked back to his youth and recalled the time and the place when the Word of the Lord came to him.

So, in these different ways, the same Word of God comes to different men. With Saul of Tarsus it was at midday at high noon, but with William Wordsworth it was at the sunrise. For Saul, the grown man in the towering plenitude of his intellectual power, it seemed fitting that the great event of his life should come when the mighty sun was at the height of his triumphant course, but for William Wordsworth, the youth, it was fitting that it should come at the break of day:

> Glorious as e'er I had beheld – in front,
> The sea lay laughing at a distance; near,
> The solid mountains shone, bright as the clouds,
> Grain-tinctured, drenched in empyrean light;
> And in the meadows and the lower grounds
> Was all the sweetness of a common dawn –
> Dews, vapours and the melody of birds,
> And labourers going forth to till the fields.
> ... I made no vows, but vows
> Were then made for me; bond unknown to me

Was given, that I should be, else sinning greatly,
A dedicated Spirit.[154]

A common dawn – but yet that common dawn marked the great day in the calendar of Wordsworth's life. Wordsworth, writing of it many years later, remembered the time and remembered the place.

So was it with another youth just about that time. It was in June 1785. Thomas Clarkson, the foremost champion in the abolition of the slave trade, is on his way from Cambridge to London on horseback. Yesterday he had read in the Senate, home of the University, his Latin essay, for which he had to be awarded the gold medal. The essay was on slavery and the slave trade. And on his way back next day the subject filled his mind and a voice said to him: 'If these things you wrote of are true ought they not to be stopped? And if they ought to be stopped who ought to do it?' At last he gets off his horse in sight of Wade's Mill in Hertfordshire and sits on the turf by the roadside, holding his horse by the reins. And the youth goes home and from that time his whole life is dedicated to that cause. No effort was spared, no labour was too heavy. Many years later Wordsworth dedicates his sonnet to him. His cause has been won and he is an old man but Wordsworth recalls that early call and dedication:

But thou, who starting in thy fervent prime,
Did first lead forth that enterprise sublime...[155]

It all went back to that time and place – that June morning in 1785, there in sight of Wade's Mill in Hertfordshire.

So it was with John Bunyan. It was, he tells us, on the twelfth day of November in the year 1660. The place was the village of Samsell, near Harlington in Bedfordshire. He had been asked to come and preach and when he arrived it was learned that a warrant has been issued by the magistrates and that, if he preached as he had undertaken to do, he would probably be taken to prison. And John Bunyan went into the close or little garden and walked up and down thinking it out:

Shall I preach or shall I not preach? Preach and take the chance of prison or shall I cut and run? At last this consideration fell with weight upon me – that it was for the word and way of God that I was in this condition, wherefore I was engaged not to flinch a hair's breadth from it.

Bunyan had to pass through much trouble and many vicissitudes, but he never forgot 12 November: and the little garden behind his friend's house at the village, Lower Samsell, in Bedfordshire. And was it not so with John Wesley? It was on 24 May 1738 that Wesley

---

154. 'Summer Vacation', *The Prelude*.
155. 'To Thomas Clarkson, on the Passing of the Bill for the Abolition of the Slave Trade' (1807).

wrote in his *Journal* the familiar words: 'In the evening I went very unwillingly to a Society in Aldersgate Street where one was reading Luther's 'Preface to the Epistle of the Romans'. About a quarter before nine, while he was describing the change which God works in the heart through Christ, I felt my blood strangely warmed.' He knew the time and he knew the place.

As President of the National Brotherhood Movement in 1937 Isaac Foot spoke on his great hero the apostle Paul and the theme of brotherhood:

I want to read you the concluding part of the most beautiful story in the world. The father had killed the fatted calf and was rejoicing because the Prodigal Son had come home, but when the elder brother heard about it, he was angry and would not go in; and therefore came his father out, and entreated him ... And he said unto him, 'Son, thou art ever with me and all that I have is thine. It was meet that we should make merry and be glad; for this thy brother was dead, and is alive again; was lost and is found.'

The words I want to speak about are 'this thy brother'. The father did not condone what the Prodigal Son had done ... He did not make light of his offence. But when the elder brother said: 'This thy son,' he said: 'No, this thy brother.' And what Jesus meant to teach, in telling that parable, was that the relationship counts for everything. Brothers – that is the charter of our movement – 'All ye are brethren'. The first experience of the early Church was expressed in brotherhood and, when those people came into the rich experience which changed their lives, they expressed it in brotherhood. Sometimes we hear of the brotherhood and the Church. In the New Testament sense there can be no Church unless it is a brotherhood fellowship...

Take St Paul and how much he spoke of the word 'brother' and what it meant to him. Paul argued every case in terms of brotherhood ... In Paul's Epistles to the Romans and the Corinthians, when he wrote those great soaring arguments like Milton, seeking to justify the ways of God to man, he always began or pressed home his points with the word 'brothers'. When he brought to an end that great passage in the fifteenth chapter of the 1st Corinthians upon the Resurrection, 'But this corruptible must put on incorruption, and this mortal must put on immortality' – those words that have brought comfort to countless thousands throughout all generations he concluded with the appeal: 'Therefore, my beloved brothers, be ye steadfast, unmoveable, always abounding in the work of the Lord, forasmuch as ye know that your labour is not in vain in the Lord.' He once wrote a Letter to the Galatians, lashing them for their defections and backslidings. When he had finished the letter of rebuke, perhaps he was a little afraid of his harshness and he added, at the end in his own handwriting, just the word 'brothers'...

Paul joined the Brotherhood movement and he became its first president. He was bound to be the leader in any movement to which he belonged. He hadn't any insignia or chain of office but he was an ambassador in chains and his insignia were the marks of the Lord Jesus. Paul judged all these questions in the light of the fatherhood of God. And how much that fatherhood meant to him! It is a very wonderful thing, the way the apostle speaks of the fatherhood of God. This lonely man, an exile from his father's house, driven out from his own society, without the love of woman or child, had a great love for home. He regarded the Church of God as being the great family hearth, the hearth of the family of God. But Paul's faith was always that the glory of the sonship carried with it the responsibility of brotherhood. Who is our brother? It is like the question, Who is my neighbour?

The answer is found whenever we say 'Our Father...'. He never taught us to say 'My Father'. He taught us to say 'Our Father'. And so any man who repeats the words 'Our Father' in sincerity adopts the responsibility for a very big family. And it was the same voice which said, 'When ye pray, say "Our Father"'... Then there was that sterner voice speaking in the very beginning of history, when God came to Cain and said: 'Where is Abel, thy brother?' The blood that had been shed was not only the blood of a murdered man – it was the blood of a brother! If you want an example of what brotherhood meant in the early Church, take Philemon. He had a slave who had run away and probably had stolen some of his master's money. This man came under the influence of Paul and became a Christian. And Paul sent him back to his master with a letter, and said, 'This man comes back to you, not as a slave but as a brother, a brother beloved.'[156] It was that principle of brotherhood that one day, please God, will kill war.

I will close with just one illustration. A ship was wrecked on a southern coast, and all the crew were swept away, except one, who was seen clinging to the mast. The men at the coastal village watched, waiting to put their boat out. One of the men ready to go was James, the only remaining son of his mother – because John had years before gone from his home and had not come back. When the boat was going out, she tried to stop him because she was afraid that, if he were lost, she would be left alone – but she was proud in her heart because he refused to be held back. Then the rescued man was brought back, and, as the boat neared the shore, James was standing up in the boat shouting to his mother. He cried: 'Mother, we've saved him – and it is John!' And the belief of the Brotherhood movement is that the joy of the mother is only a faint expression of the joy in the heart of God when His son, when His child, comes back. It is the purpose of our movement that every man and woman in this country shall be made to realise that there is for him a place in the great hearth of God, the hearth of the Father of our Lord Jesus Christ, of Whom every family in heaven and earth is made.[157]

---

156. The slave was Onesimus.
157. Broadcast, 28 February 1937.

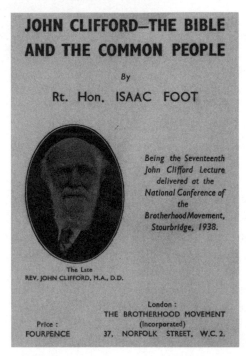

JOHN CLIFFORD—THE BIBLE AND THE COMMON PEOPLE

By

Rt. Hon. ISAAC FOOT

Being the Seventeenth John Clifford Lecture delivered at the National Conference of the Brotherhood Movement, Stourbridge, 1938.

The Late
REV. JOHN CLIFFORD, M.A., D.D.

London :
THE BROTHERHOOD MOVEMENT
(Incorporated)
37, NORFOLK STREET, W.C. 2.

Price :
FOURPENCE

Isaac Foot's John Clifford Lecture to the Brotherhood Movement in 1938.

John Clifford: The Bible and the common people

As we have seen in his letters, Isaac Foot, as a young man, had sought out and learned his preaching skills from some of the foremost Nonconformist preachers of the day. One of his earliest and special favourites had been the Baptist minister Dr John Clifford, whom he had first heard in London as a young man.

Amongst the many men I have met in all walks of life, religious and political, I have met none greater. From first to last Dr Clifford was the man with the Book. The son of a Chartist, a child worker in a factory earning his first weekly wage of half a crown, preacher, orator and prophet, it is difficult for this generation to realise something of his commanding authority in our Free Church life during the first quarter of this century. I had the great honour to know John Clifford – and I have the privilege of lecturing upon one who was the hero of my youth and earlier manhood ... I trust you will not think it out of place if I tell you how I came into personal touch with that great man. I was a boy of sixteen at the time I first saw him. I was living in London, and homesick for the Westcountry. The friends with whom I lodged at Bayswater attended the services at Westbourne Park, and their conversation was frequently of one whom they called 'the Doctor'. I got to learn that 'the Doctor' was Dr Clifford and, on Sunday evening, I went with my friends to hear him. I took my place in the long queue of waiting visitors and felt highly favoured in being allowed a seat at all. In due course the Doctor appeared. He did not look at all like a minister, nor did he talk like one. I wasn't quite sure that his address was a sermon. I had been brought up in the warm evangelical atmosphere of Westcountry Methodism, where, every Sunday evening, the sermon was expected to lead up to the direct appeal for personal decision, and the service was thought incomplete without the prayer meeting. Here was something different. The subject was, I think, 'Mr Balfour and Philosophic Doubt'. I was not sure that I could follow it, and on the whole I was doubtful if my folk at home would regard this sort of thing as the proper way of keeping the Sabbath.

But, all the same, there was something very appealing about the man. I went again and again. I liked to see him bring up his books under his arm and place them on the table by his side. I liked to hear him quote from Emerson and George Eliot, Carlyle and Ruskin, Wordsworth, Lowell, George Meredith, Browning and Mrs Browning. I liked to hear him when he prayed – all gentleness and tenderness. I remember hearing him when, on occasion, he was stirred with indignation. My opportunity lasted only a few months, but when I returned to the Westcountry, I took home with me such impressions that ever after the very name of 'Doctor Clifford' somehow evoked a warm response within me. Ten years later Dr Clifford came to Plymouth for a Free Church demonstration. He was my guest, and the honour of entertaining him almost overwhelmed me. I recall how he slept in preparation for the meeting at night, and I can still kindle at the remembrance of his eloquence. In the pulpit he was generally restrained and pre-eminently the teacher. On the platform he allowed himself greater freedom. That night something had roused his fire. Some proposal had been made for a compromise which he thought unworthy. He called on us to reject it and cried:

Shall we now
Contaminate our fingers with base bribes
And sell the mighty space of our large honours
For so much trash as might be grasped thus?
I had rather be a dog, and bay the moon
Than such a Roman.[158]

I can see him still shaking his fingers free from the threatened contamination. In his high moments one forgot his spare, wiry form, and the man seemed to dominate the assembly. His head looked massive and his eyes flashed fire.

He was pre-eminently a man of the common people. To what sources can we trace his life and character? The cottage in which he lived as a child, the little schools in which he was taught, the factory in which he worked as a boy, the social disabilities and injustices from which he suffered, the Chartist sympathies of his father, all helped to make him a man of the people. The one gentle influence of those early days was that of his mother. Like Thomas Carlyle, John Clifford could never refer to his mother without a softened voice and a tender regard. When, at the age of seventy, he was presented by his brother ministers with his portrait, in his reply he was moved to tears and said: 'I am as grateful to you, my dear friends, as I was when, as a lad, I ran home with my half-a-crown after a week's work to give it to my mother.'

Dr Clifford's dearest earthly possession was his Bible. He was an omnivorous reader and built up his own library, but the book that made him was the Bible. Clifford was like

158. William Shakespeare, *Julius Caesar.*

John Wesley, and in the same sense, a man of one book. Have we ever tried to think what the English Bible meant to John Knox, George Fox, Milton, Cromwell, Bunyan, John Bright, Shaftesbury and Spurgeon? If there had been no English Bible should we ever have heard of them? I am confident that were it not for the Bible we should never have heard of John Clifford. He started with the Book when he was a child, he studied it all his life, it was his theme throughout his abundant ministry, he was its champion through three generations, and in his old age he gloried in its possession. He learned from it his love of liberty, and the Chartist's son found here the Magna Charta of all enduring freedom.

To Clifford the Bible was the book of the common people. That phrase was constantly upon his lips. I heard him once take it as the text for his speech in the midst of a political campaign. The very words 'the common people' fired his imagination and the people in that little country town heard the Baptist, the Protestant, the Biblical scholar and the Chartist's son and 'feared he would make an end'. He hated privilege. He grasped, as few men have done since Luther, the mighty implications of the central Reformation doctrine of the priesthood of all believers. The arrogant claims of an ecclesiastical hierarchy always stirred him to protest, and he would have regarded the modern philosophy of political dictatorship as blasphemy against the Holy Ghost. One of his favourite texts was Matthew, chapter 23, verse 8: 'But be not ye called Rabbi; for one is your teacher and all ye are brethren. And call no man father on the earth; for one is your Father which is in heaven. Neither be ye called masters; for one is your master, even the Christ.'

Dr Clifford knew what the Bible had done for him and for others beset by poverty and social disability. He knew the meaning of Paul's injunction: 'But be ye transformed by the renewing of your mind, that ye may prove what is that good, and acceptable, and perfect will of God.'[159] He knew that those words were addressed, not to scholars and divines and theologians, but to the ordinary disciples of the early Church. Dr Clifford kept his commonplace book, and, if he had been living today, I think you would have found in it the sonnet of the American poet Anderson M. Scruggs:

Glory to them, the toilers of the earth,
Who wrought with knotted hands in wood and stone
Dreams their unlettered minds could not give birth,
And symmetries their souls had never known.
Glory to them, the artisans, who spread
Cathedrals like brown lace against the sun,
Who could not build a rhyme, but built instead
The Doric grandeur of the Parthenon.
I never cross a marble portico,

---

159. Romans 12:2.

Or lift my eyes where stained glass windows steal
From virgin sunlight moods of deeper glow,
Or walk dream-peopled streets, except to feel
A hush of reverence for that vast dead
Who gave us beauty for a crust of bread.[160]

I have hanging on my walls at home the well-known portrait of Dr Clifford, a copy of the painting made when he was seventy years old. I would like to have one of the old man sitting at his desk seventeen years later, and writing in his journal, only a few days before he died: 'My grandmother, a disciple of John Wesley.' What is the story of that woman? Did she herself hear John Wesley preach, and did the Lord open her heart, as He did Lydia's, so that she attended to the things which were spoken by Wesley?[161] How much a simple record like this adds to the significance of Aldersgate Street! The Word of God is preached by the man with the warmed heart; it is heard and welcomed by the woman and becomes the heritage passed on to her grandson, and he, at the end of his abundant life and glorious ministry, writes in his journal: 'My grandmother, a disciple of John Wesley.' A few days later he scribbled some notes on the compensations of old age and these his biographer found after his death, within the covers of the copy of Emerson's *Essays*,[162] given to him by his Sunday school teacher seventy-five years before. The scribbled notes concluded with these words: 'Life is a battle at every stage, but the conditions of the fight differ at different stages. Man is a soldier to the last, and, if he is a true soldier he dies, sword in hand, still fighting, and then at the last says, "I have fought the good fight: I have finished my course."'[163] These were probably his last written words; they were from his beloved Book, and fittingly they were a quotation from his great hero, the apostle Paul. In the race we run we will strive to remember that he is one of the witnesses by whom we are encompassed, and that the torch we carry was once borne by him.[164]

---

160. Isaac Foot had this poem, 'On Seeing a Marble Building Cleaned', in a commonplace book. He met the author in America in 1943 and got his signature.
161. Lydia, a Christian convert in the Bible, at whose house Paul stayed in Philippi.
162. Ralph Waldo Emerson (1803–82), American author, poet and philosopher. His *Essays* were published in 1841.
163. 2 Timothy 4:7.
164. The seventeenth John Clifford Lecture, 1938.

21 The temperance cause

Rev. Henry Carter: Isaac Foot is pre-eminently a warrior in the temperance cause. He serves as senior treasurer of the Methodist Connexional Temperance and Welfare Department; as chairman of executive of the Temperance Council of the Christian Churches; and as president of the National Commercial Temperance League. When the brewers launched their collective advertising campaign in 1933, it was Isaac Foot's incisive speech at a luncheon of the London division of our league which was hailed as the best answer, and published as 'Blood Money?'.[165]

Isaac Foot: I joined the temperance movement when I was a boy of eight or nine. I was brought up in a part of Plymouth where there were slums and crowded courtyards, and, often at night, there were dreadful scenes of violence and disorder, especially when the public houses were emptied. I saw many things when I was a child which others, apparently, took for granted but which seared themselves into my memory. Brawls and fighting were nightly occurrences and I had the sense of living alongside an abyss and I think something of my hatred of the ravages of strong drink were learned from those early experiences. One day I read in the window of a business firm in Old Town Street, Plymouth, that the pledge not to take strong drink could be signed within. I thought it over and went in. A book was produced, I put down my name, and went home the proud possessor of a pledge card with an illuminated border.

Some thirty-five years before that, and almost at the very same spot, my father had had an experience not quite so fortunate as mine. Having come in from the neighbouring countryside as a young journeyman carpenter, he found that, with strong drink, he was not so good a workman as he was without it. His special job, strangely enough, was making boxes for a company of wine merchants. He had to drive hundreds of nails every day, and he found that, after taking a glass or two of liquor, he could not drive the nails home quite as cleanly and truly as he could before, and, being proud of his workmanship, he thought he could best protect himself against frequent invitation to drink if he signed the pledge. One evening, putting on his better suit of clothes, he went out to find the place where he could sign the pledge. As he came along Whimple Street – now, with Old Town Street, disappeared – he found provision had been made for him. There, at the entrance to a long passage, was a wooden notice board, with the large capital letters PLEDGE OFFICE, and there was the friendly hand and outstretched finger telling him the direction he should follow. The significance of the three golden balls hanging above the board was lost on the young countryman, and, following the directions given, he explained to the astonished tradesman behind the counter that he had come to sign the pledge.

---

165. Tribute to the vice-president, 1937.

An Altered Individual

I learned the truth for myself, and, as I grew up, I saw many scores of cases of the 'altered individual'. In most instances the case was not one of drunkenness at all but I have known the reticent man become dangerously communicative. I have heard the reserved man become almost insolently self-exposing. I have seen the peaceful man become publicly quarrelsome. I have heard the man normally self-respecting become offensively libidinous, even in general company and I have known the keen businessman, with whom the secrets of his employers and colleagues are normally absolutely safe, become so loose tongued in his cups, that, as a result of one or two ill-guarded words, hundreds of pounds were lost in the middle of some negotiations.

As a member of Parliament Isaac Foot had played a leading part in fighting what he called 'sectional' interests in the House of Commons. Here he traces the development of the temperance movement.

As the inevitable clash has arisen between the sectional claim and the public interest, two movements have been formed, one the movement that can be called the Drink Party and the other the movement that can be called the Temperance Cause. Both movements are there, whether we recognise them or not. Both movements have their organisations, and in this regard, the liquor trade has the enormous advantage. Wealthy, united, undivided by any question of policy, the trade is concerned only to make and sell as much of its product as possible. What has actually happened is that the vast resources of the trade have been used to create a demand where it did not exist, and to stimulate the desire for strong drink and to provoke the appetite for it. It is here that we see private enterprise at its worst, and it is because this vested interest is selfish, unrestrained and unscrupulous, that the temperance movement has arisen.

The temperance movement stands for the public interest. That is our proud claim for it. The men and women who belong to that cause have no personal interests to serve, they have no money to make out of their activities, they get no titles or emoluments. They are largely poor people who find great difficulty in maintaining their organisation, and their persistence and fortitude from year to year is often a standing miracle. That is the temperance movement, the temperance cause, the temperance party. The public interest depends on the direction and vigilance of the individual, and, when he or she goes, the cause suffers and sometimes is sadly maimed. The greater the service of the one man, the greater the loss when he goes. That is why there is the need for the party, the association – that is why there is a Rechabite Society, the Order of Good Templars, the Band of Hope, the National Commercial Temperance League or the United Kingdom Alliance.[166]

---

166. All these were temperance organisations at that time.

I have seen the persistence and devotion and fortitude of those who, through youth and middle age and in older life, have sustained their cause. For the most part they are obscure folk, socially undistinguished, rarely holding public office, and often women mainly occupied with the manifold cares of the home. The glory of the temperance cause is the fidelity of the women. Most of them are not widely read or highly educated, but, like Cromwell's soldiers, they know what they fight for and love what they know. These people I have come to regard as the salt of the earth. I have learned to honour them and to value their friendship. Of all these people, I have never met any who regretted in later years their association with the temperance cause. The men and women of the temperance movement know the meaning of Wordsworth's phrase 'the homely beauty of the good old cause'.[167][168]

MICHAEL: As we have sought to trace in my father's story, he could translate religious ideas into action as well as and even more consistently than anyone else. Quite often, as I had the best opportunity of seeing for myself, it was my mother, at some of the supreme moments, who would call him back from the riverside to direct political action. She could see him there at his very best. His truest heroes then were the men who translated their religious beliefs into direct action, with Oliver Cromwell and Abraham Lincoln at their head. In all my father's sermons and speeches, the recurring theme is one of hope. 'Hope,' he would whisper, and the little Cornish chapel would be utterly still, 'the gospel of Hope'; he had the congregation in the hollow of his hand. Within a few sentences the language could become stirring and resonant. Outside, the world seemed sharply brighter than when we went in, and we would return to our Sunday dinner, the best of the week, bubbling with unaccountable optimism, touched no doubt by the beauty of the words, the Bible's, Wordsworth's or his own, all uttered in a voice as rich and memorable as Devonshire cream.

Isaac Foot's harvest service sermon

I am getting my text from the twenty-seventh chapter of the Acts of the Apostles, verses 35 and 36: 'And when he had thus spoken Paul took a loaf of bread and gave thanks to God in the presence of them all: and when he had broken it, he began to eat. Then were they all of good cheer, and they also took some meat.' My subject is a loaf of bread. I always look when I come to a harvest festival first of all for a loaf of bread. See if it is in a place of honour ... so often bread is taken for granted. There is such beauty in bread – beauty of sun and soil, beauty of patient toil. Wind and rain have pressed it and quite often blessed it. 'Be gentle when you touch bread.' These words from the twenty-seventh chapter of the Acts of the Apostles are one of the greatest passages in all literature. This is the story of the ship – a ship with 276 persons on it, or 275 with the apostle Paul, and the 275 panic stricken, fearing immediate death. The one man who sustained that

---

167. 'Written in London, September 1802'.
168. 'Is There Not a Cause?', 2nd Ernest Winterton Memorial Lecture, 1949.

company was the apostle Paul and we read that, when there was neither sun nor stars and all hope was taken away from them, Paul stood forth and said: 'Be of good cheer.' And in the midst of panic there was peace and in the midst of despair there was hope. And in the very heart of the storm there was comfort and courage. And the symbol of this was a loaf of bread. You will see what the text tells us that Paul did with the loaf. He took the loaf and he made it divide. He took the loaf and thanked God for it. He said this is bread but it is not bread. And he made the loaf divide. The secret of his strength on the ship was his belief in God. And he told these people: 'God the Father Almighty, who made the heaven and earth, made this loaf of bread. It is his loaf too.' And it was that that was his secret – not that he was braver than they were. They were brave men too – those soldiers were men who had faced death on so many fields. He wasn't a better mariner than the rest. It wasn't the fortitude of the strong man. It was the fate of the weak man. The story of this chapter is the story of a weak man and a frail ship and Almighty God.

He took the loaf and made it divide. He took the loaf and, when he gave thanks, he made it Eucharistic. A wonderful word, 'Eucharist' – a very beautiful word, standing for a very beautiful thing – thanksgiving. In the New Testament the Eucharist means only 'thanksgiving'. Of course, it reaches its highest height when the company of the leaders meet around the Lord's table to thank him for his supreme gifts, but, wherever the loaf is broken in thankfulness, there is the Eucharist. The shepherd, alone upon his hill, tending his sheep at the break of day, if he takes his food with thankfulness to God, that is the Eucharist – in the New Testament. John Bunyan spent ten years of his life in prison – not much of a prison fare but, when he broke his bread with thankfulness, he did it in the company of all the angels, the archangels in their company of Heaven.

The Eucharist can be everywhere. The Eucharist can be sung, it can be spoken and very often unspoken. So Paul took the loaf of bread and made it divine, he took the loaf of bread and made it Eucharistic. He took it and made it missionary because he took it in the presence of them all. He might have had his bread alone, he might have had it with Luke and his fellow-disciples, but he had it with them all, the 274 who were left – he had it with them all and the loaf of bread became God's missionary, it became evangelic.

In the last verse, 276 of them all came safely to land (not some fairy tale – actual fact – real history) and the fury of the Mediterranean Sea had broken up the ship and the 276 all got ashore. A very momentous journey and a very momentous escape because, if they had gone down, we would have lost half of our New Testament with them. We should never have had Paul's Epistles to the Corinthians or the Galatians or to the Philippians or to the Ephesians, or to Philemon. We should never have had the Acts of the Apostles. We should never have had these stories. But Luke was saved with the rest and Luke gave us the Acts of the Apostles and he gave us the Gospel of Luke, the most beautiful book in the world. If he had not been washed up with the rest on that Mediterranean Sea, we would never have known the story of the Good Samaritan and we should never have heard the story of the Prodigal Son.

PART VII

1935–9
Crisis

22 1935 Isaac Foot loses in Bodmin

In October 1935 Mussolini's invasion of Abyssinia provoked an international crisis and challenge to the authority of the League of Nations. Stanley Baldwin, the British Prime Minister, pledged that the National Government would back the collective action of the league to deal with this crisis.

MICHAEL: Before the dissolution of Parliament and general election in November 1935, in the debate on this international crisis, my father was addressing the Prime Minister, expecting that, as it had pledged, the British government would resist Mussolini's recent attacks on Abyssinia and support the League of Nations.

Isaac Foot: This war is a war between two Christian peoples, a war between a so-called civilised country and a so-called uncivilised country, a war between two members of the League of Nations, two signatories of the same covenant. But, most serious of all, it is a war between a white people and a coloured people. Our Empire is not a white Empire. Five out of six of the people of this Empire are coloured people. I wonder if Hon. Members saw the message that was sent by the Moslem Association of India, asking what would be the position of their co-religionists in Abyssinia? It is not merely Africa that is responding on this matter, but India is beginning to tingle with this question as well. I was surprised at the contempt shown by Signor Mussolini for these coloured people when he asked: 'Has the League of Nations become the tribunal before which all the Negroes and uncivilised peoples, all the world's savages, can bring the great nations which have revolutionised and transformed humanity?' I should not have very much regard for the League of Nations if I did not think that that was the tribunal to which they could go for the protection of their interests, and I would like to reply to Signor Mussolini: 'Hath not the Ethiopian eyes; hath he not ears; and, if you prick him, will he not bleed?'

The Secretary of State for Foreign Affairs never rose higher than when, in his speech at Geneva in September, he made that declaration on behalf of the small nations and the backward peoples of the world.[169] I am a great lover of *The Pilgrim's Progress* and I remember

---

169. The speech by Sir Samuel Hoare, the British Foreign Secretary, in support of collective action by the League of Nations.

that Great-Heart was not content to get to the Celestial City himself, but took along with him Mr Fearing and Mr Ready-to-Halt. The right hon. Gentleman, when he made that declaration, like Mr Great-Heart when he said, 'Let those who are most afraid come near to me,' was standing by the principle of which Wordsworth spoke over a century ago of this country being 'a bulwark for the cause of man'. It is inevitable that Europe and Africa have to live together in the same world, but I am sentimentalist enough to believe that the relation of Africa to Europe will depend very largely upon whether Africa conceives of Europe in the terms of Signor Mussolini or of David Livingstone.[170]

In the general election of 1935 the Conservatives won a total of 387 seats, 33 of which were held by the so-called National Liberals. Labour won 154 seats. This election was a disaster for the Independent Liberals, who won only 21 seats. Herbert Samuel was defeated as was Isaac Foot in Bodmin. Isaac Foot wrote a letter of thanks to his supporters: 'We went down in the fight but we are a proud people still because we sacrificed no conviction, bartered away no principle and kept the faith ... I prize very highly the many friendships that have been established during the last twenty-five years. There is no friendship like that which comes from fighting together for a good cause.'

MICHAEL: My father's defeat in the 1935 election was not expected and was a particularly bitter one. It had been caused by some of his closest friends deserting the Liberal cause at that moment. Everybody interested in Westcountry politics, my father included, could not have imagined that he would never win another parliamentary contest. His powers as a speaker, inside the House of Commons as well as outside, had now become plainly established. Three of the Liberal Nationals who had continued their support of the National Government, Sir John Simon, Walter Runciman and Leslie Hore-Belisha, had joined in an attack on him in his own Bodmin constituency. Each of these had chosen to send a message of support to my father's Conservative opponent in Bodmin at a critical moment and my father, after the election, thought that each of their constituencies should be told the truth about what had happened. Simon had been a close friend of his before the Simonite heresy; the other two he had suckled in their Westcountry constituencies. However, the ferocity of internal party disputes knows no limit, and my father repaid this scurvy treatment with one of the most selfless odysseys in British political history. After the election he hired halls in Spen Valley, St Ives and Plymouth Devonport, the respective constituencies of the three miscreants, and delivered to their electors elaborate, fully authenticated indictments of their political records, worthy of any trial in Westminster Hall. Never to be forgotten was the climax which I heard in Devonport Guildhall. With immaculate timing, he quoted the deadly curse drawn from one of my father's unexpected favourites, Lord Alfred Douglas, in 'The Traitor', the last lines of which were:

170. Hansard, 23 October 1935.

Rise as he may to his desired goal;
Ay and God speed him there, I grudge him not.
And when all men shall sing his praise to me
I'll not gainsay. But I shall know his soul
Lies in the bosom of Iscariot.'[171]

'Mr Foot in bitter mood in St Ives'

Just when the strain was heaviest in this election, when we were fighting with our backs to the wall in Bodmin, at that very moment came the letter that was put in the *Western Morning News* two days before the election in which your MP Mr Walter Runciman said he trusted all Liberals in the division would, under present circumstances, give my opponent Mr Rathbone their support. Who wrote that letter? It was my colleague in the representation of Cornwall. Who helped to put me out? You know the answer. That was the representation made by your member. I don't suppose the brewers will send a formal vote of thanks to Mr Runciman but he certainly will have earned their gratitude. Perhaps, in their own phraseology, they will look upon him now as being a 'mainstay of the public house'. But it is not merely that. Our numbers in the House are disproportionately small. This letter was written by a brother Methodist and, when I read that letter, I turned up the Psalms and read these words: 'But, if it had been an enemy that reproached, me I could have born it.'

Runciman and Sir John Simon and Mr Hore-Belisha and the rest have had to buy the favour of their new associates by selling their old friends. Think of the pitiful position of all those people who have had to eat all the words of a lifetime. An issue that is raised by what has happened is a choice between Mr Runciman and Liberalism and when that choice is raised, I am for Liberalism. I wonder what those people think they are going to get from it all? How long do you think Sir John Simon and Mr Runciman will be allowed to keep their positions? As long as they are of any use to the Tory Party. And when their purposes have been served, they will be kicked out at forty-eight hours' notice. They have done it before and they will do it again ... Our country led the world in the wrong direction when they brought about a complete permanent reversal of our fiscal system. There are two men in this country responsible beyond all others for that course being taken and they are Sir John Simon and Mr Walter Runciman.[172]

MICHAEL: After the Tories had won the election of 1935, the National Government betrayed its commitment to support the League of Nations when on 18 June 1936 it announced that sanctions against Italy would be abandoned. Mussolini had won and the League of Nations was finally discredited. It was a lesson that was not lost on Hitler. This

---

171. 'The Traitor', sonnet by Lord Alfred Douglas (1870–1945).
172. *Western Morning News*, 25 November 1935.

was the beginning of the policy of appeasement and helped to prepare the way for the subsequent war in 1939. If the government had followed what my father was saying then, there might not have been a war. My father showed absolute consistency and perception in his attitude to the events of these following years of crisis.

In 1937, two years after leaving the Commons, Isaac Foot was made a Privy Counsellor in the Coronation Honours, an honour which he valued very highly. Among the many letters of congratulation he received was one from his sister, Janie:

'Right Honourable I.F.' Doesn't it look lovely!! At 7 a.m. there was a ring on the phone – Stan to tell the news! 'At last they've acknowledged his worth' said he! Jim didn't tell him of your note – we two kept the secret – tho' on Sunday when David and Paul, and wives, were here to dinner I quietly asked what a 'Privy Counsellor' really meant and David just as seriously gave me a satisfactory reply. He will smile when he reads his paper and conclude I was somehow 'in the know'. Thank you for the enjoyment of anticipation! That was very kind. After receiving the news I opened the Book to read my Psalm 115 and the first words I saw were: 'Not unto us, O Lord, not unto us, but unto Thy name give glory, for Thy mercy and for Thy truth's sake.' Farther on it reads: 'The Lord hath been mindful of us, He will bless us, He will bless the house of Israel.' Do you remember how Father used to say, after anything about Israel in the Psalms, – 'And Isaac too'. I so often think of it – 'Truly the Lord is good to Israel – and Isaac too,' he would say. Redeem Israel out of all his troubles –and Isaac too! And He did! He could never forget he had a beloved brother called Israel[173] – nor could I who knew him and loved him as a girl; so I put in 'Isaac too' for you.

And so, dear Isaac, you lost a seat in the Cabinet and in the House of Commons but God has given you an 'honourable' name and of course I am delighted. I feel sure that the Lord has guided by the skilfulness of His hands in all the ups and downs of your life and He led by the right way and the consciousness of being in His will and doing it is the rest of soul that means strength of body too. We are living in strange times truly and the doings on the Continent and elsewhere cause one to think hard – the floods are lifting up their voice but the Lord on High is mightier than the noise of many waters. 'In this will I be confident.'

My dear love to Eva – and to yourself – Yours affectionately Janie.

From his old schoolfriend Henry Carter:
Warmest congratulations! A fitting, the fitting, and richly deserved recognition of invaluable public service. Few will be as appreciative, none more pleased than I who have known your

---

173. Isaac Senior's brother Israel had been killed in an accident in Horrabridge in 1882.

loyalty to principle and duty throughout the busy years. Today 'Our Isaac', as Devon and Cornwall know you, is the recognised leader of free Liberalism in the western shires, and equally the spokesman of the laity in Methodism in that home of the Evangelical Revival.

In 1937 Isaac Foot had been installed as Vice-President of the Methodist Conference. Here a Methodist colleague reminisces:

When the Honours List is published from time to time I always look with a suppressed excitement to see if any of my friends are there. Great was my delight to see that Mr Isaac Foot has been made a Privy Counsellor. I don't know at all what the rights and duties of a Privy Counsellor may be. I must look it up now but I do know that all such are described as 'The Right Honourable', and if there is a man or woman beneath the sun more worthy of the title than Mr Foot such a person is unknown to me. I am thinking now of the delight it will give to the Westcountry to know that 'Our Isaac' is now a Privy Counsellor. His political enemies – he has no other – thought, when they turned him out of the Bodmin division at the last election, that his sun had set while it was yet day. But it proved to be only a momentary and rather black cloud that shadowed our little world for a moment, and then passed away. A man of such quality is never without a call, and some of us wonder if it may not have been in the nature of a kindly providence which took him from the House of Commons for a time, to set him free for other tasks. I am glad that he will not be tethered to parliamentary committees and the House while he is vice-president. We want him for our very selves, and all the time. His large audiences will rejoice in his genius. They will laugh at his stories, glow with his allusions to Cromwell, marvel at his knowledge of Shakespeare and Burke, and wonder how one head can carry all he knows. The delightful Westcountry accent will be a tonic to Methodism. He will relate all the implications of Godly living to great principles. There will be no anecdotes for their own sake: even if he calls your attention to violets that grow in Alpine valleys, the mighty hills will be seen in majestic outline in the background. Only a superb intellect can relate such pointed ethics to the fundamental truths of the universe.

It is necessary that we should hear Mr Foot at an open-air meeting when he is fighting an election to see one side of him. He knows and loves the common people. He never panders to a poor taste or flatters a worthless heart. Imagine a crowd of fishermen at Looe. They are gathered, expecting every moment to see him arrive. They tolerate other speakers, who are regarded as just filling up the time. Presently the car swings round the corner, over that very narrow bridge and comes to a stop. By now the other poor speaker has yielded to the inevitable. His splendid passage is cut short. After a general scuffle and much cheering, Mr Foot is on the stand and with a broad smile says in his best Cornish accent: 'Hello, my hearties! Here we are again!' An old man whose hearing is poor asks his neighbour:

'What did 'ee say?' 'He zed: "Hello, my boys." Ah, he's a blade, is our Isaac.' The deaf man agrees and they laugh aloud, while Mr Foot is getting under way and will presently be expounding the merits of free trade, or the importance of coal, or the shortcomings of his political opponents. Before that audience breaks up and the fishermen amble off to their boats or their homes, they will have heard a speech lit up by splendid eloquence and carried home to the hearts of the hearers, because they know that here is a man who believes what he is saying and who is competent to stand before princes. He would not yield to the sacrifice of what he conceived to be the secret of the nation's well-being and greatness; and, in a mad moment, many of his friends forsook him. But he has lost nothing of the affection of the people. They still trust him, and some day will follow him again.

A year or two ago I visited one of the smallest chapels in Cornwall for a weekday service. The people were grateful to me, but they were enthusiastic about Mr Foot. A Sunday or two earlier, as he was on his way to chapel, it was made known to him that the preacher could not take his appointment at this little Bethel, and they would be without a service. He drove off at once and preached to the edification of the little handful of devout chapel-goers. He probably sees nothing in this worth recording, but how easy it would have been for some men to have expressed regret and to have hoped for the best! Mr Foot is a Methodist whose heart is given to the Church. He does not come to the Sunday morning service just occasionally and simper while other people sing. He leads the singing in his own neighbourhood, and especially if it is one of Charles Wesley's great hymns. He knows that no one has ever set in poetic form the fundamental truths of the Christian religion so adequately as Charles Wesley. Yes, I should be very happy now at Pencrebar, where bluebells throw the loveliest sheen on those Cornish hedges; where the blackbird sings for very joy, and the whole countryside proclaims the exquisite handiwork of God.[174]

23 Isaac Foot, Apostle of England

MICHAEL: What my father actually did on the political platform in the next few years was truly, I believe, and I saw it at close quarters, Isaac Foot at his bravest and best, using every gift of eloquence at his command to hold back the Tory flood which threatened to carry our country and many other countries besides to catastrophe. He used every resource at his command to restore decent leadership to our country. Out of office, out of Parliament, with no influence to exert, except by personal inspiration and with that so often unheeded voice, my father's genius came to its full blossom, or so it seemed to me, since they were the years I knew him best. He grew to be what one of his chief heroes, William Tyndale, was called, 'Apostle of England', seeking to rouse his countrymen to face and destroy the Nazi

---

174. Richard Pryke, *Methodist Recorder*, 20 May 1937.

horror. When appeasement was still a respectable word in 1937, he fought a by-election at St Ives against all it stood for in our age. He hung his head in shame at the news of Munich and promptly invited a fresh flood of execrations upon it from Westcountry Tories with a column-long letter to the press exposing the infamy done in our name. He went back to the villages, where he had once fought the brewers, to fight the Hoares and Halifaxes and Hitler and Mussolini. His own Plymouth, he said, could suffer the fate of Guernica. Devon and Cornwall – he would never choose between his loves – were threatened with the same desecration.

These notes in Isaac Foot's papers form the basis of many speeches he made at this time:

My journeyings in the past months have taken me into all parts of the country, including Scotland and Wales, and I have had the opportunity of conversation with all sorts of people. In the short interval between one meeting and the next I am trying to sum up the impression I have gained. One very distinct impression is that our people are suffering from disillusionment and are in danger of surrendering to that temptation which, for want of a better word, we call defeatism.

In the north of England I was told our League of Nations meeting was not likely to be the success of former years as people had lost their faith in the league. The spirit that enabled our people to mount up with wings as eagles at the time of the peace ballot has for the time gone from us and we are finding it very difficult to walk and not to faint. The hectic policy of armaments is eagerly welcomed in some parts of our public life but, amongst most people, it is deplored as a confession of failure and an indication of the bankruptcy of the statesmanship of the world. The ordinary talk of the people is more and more of war and the ghastly day-to-day story of the horrors and devilries in Spain is making life more and more abnormal. How are we to carry ourselves in the midst of this confusion and bewilderment when we feel that:

> We are here as on a darkling plain
> Swept into confused alarms of struggle and flight,
> Where ignorant armies clash by night.[175]

Well, although the world may be mad, it is the world in which we have to live and, although this generation may be given up to the worship of false gods, it is the generation that we have to serve. 'To serve the present age, My calling to fulfil.'[176] So wrote Charles Wesley in the hymn which he has called the 'Marseillaise' of the Methodist Revival. I am not going to venture upon any detailed prescription for this sick world but I am sure that we have

---

175. Matthew Arnold, 'Dover Beach' (1867).
176. Charles Wesley's hymn 'A Charge to Keep I Have'.

one line of duty and that is to defeat 'defeatism', to refuse to surrender to disillusionment and resist the contagion of despair. One of the beneficial legacies of our long war with Napoleon – perhaps the only one – is the series of sonnets by Wordsworth which he called 'Sonnets to Liberty'. When he brought those sonnets to an end he made one claim for himself. These are the lines:

> Here pause: the poet claims at least this praise,
> That virtuous Liberty hath been the scope
> Of his pure song, which did not shrink from hope
> In the worst moment of these evil days;
> From hope, the paramount *duty* that Heaven lays
> For its own honour, on man's suffering heart.

These words by Wordsworth were written out in one of Isaac Foot's commonplace books and were quoted by him very frequently over these years of crisis.

Hope is a pleasing sentiment and a happy possession arising perhaps from a genial optimism and a sanguine temperament. If a man has it all the better for him but, if he is without it, well, he can't be blamed because he looks at the darker side of things. Wordsworth, however, speaks of hope in another way. He calls hope a *duty* and puts the word in italics. I suggest that is worth thinking about. It is very certain that, if we are to give up hope, we are handing over the whole generation to those forces that thrive on man's despair. The man who ceases to hope, by his very surrender, encourages the epidemic of disillusionment. He abandons his place in the front line. Instead of encouraging his neighbour, he weakens him. The man who abandons hope helps by that very surrender to spread the panic and enlarge the territory of fear. One of the great tributes to Cromwell was that of a contemporary who saw, 'in the dark perils of the fire and in the big black of the war, Hope shine in him like a pillar of fire which it shed over all others'. The community will be saved by those who have learned from the New Testament the meaning of hope and the servants of Jesus Christ will best serve him in this time of discouragement and disillusion by spreading His radiant gospel of hope: and the word He spoke 2,000 years ago was meant for this generation too: 'Be of good cheer: I have overcome the world.'[177] That was the word of a conqueror and his is the only conquest that will endure.

---

177. John 16:33.

July 1937 The St Ives by-election

MICHAEL: At this same period the kind of Liberalism in which my father believed suffered some terrible set-backs. His own defeat in Bodmin in 1935 had been especially hard to bear, but, soon after, the defeats were happening on a world scale. He was especially outraged by the way in which the British government of the day abandoned its pledges to withstand the fascist assault and indeed invited by their betrayals even larger betrayals in Africa than they had in Europe. One particular place where he was the foremost exponent of the true international case was in the St Ives by-election. That constituency had never been an easy one for the Liberals to hold. Indeed, to Isaac Foot's special disgust, the Liberal member, Walter Runciman, whom he had personally introduced to the area, had deserted to the Tories in the most shameful manner. When in 1937, thanks to Runciman's departure to the Lords, a by-election was made inevitable there, Isaac Foot thought he had to take on the fight directly. Every kind of Conservative scare was mobilised against him. He was called a 'warmonger'. Even so he almost pulled it off. The majority against him was only 210. If that bitter struggle, or, as others believed, that brilliant contest, had gone the

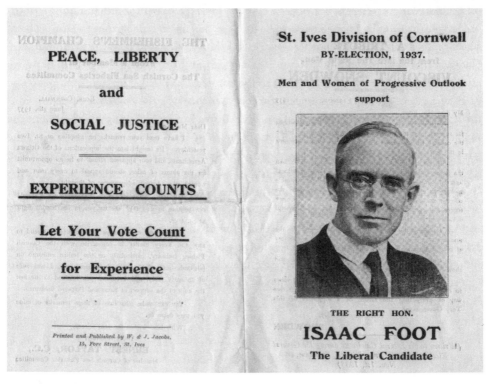

Isaac Foot's election address for the St Ives by-election in 1937.

other way, Isaac Foot would have taken his place in that new House of Commons as the champion of the real policies to save the peace. Several of his closest political friends were deeply saddened by the result. Sir Francis Acland, the Liberal member for North Cornwall, had been unable to come to speak for him during the campaign: 'Oh hell, how I kick myself. It's simply damnable. I've been cursing myself and our bad luck in these things ever since I heard the result. But, my word, what a fine fight you made of it.' Herbert Samuel, the leader of his party said:

> I heard the result with bitter disappointment. That so much effo rt on your part and on the part of all your helpers should have just missed success was most lamentable. I send all my sympathyto you and Mrs Foot. You did all that could possibly be done. To have been defeated was due to the political situation but to have come so close was due to your own personality and you may ta ke some consolation in that. Your commonplace book will have many passages inculcating fo rtitude when defeat is su ffered in a good cause and your memory will summon up the best ones!

Speaking of his defeat at St Ives, Isaac Foot said this:
I was thirty years of age when I fought my first election. Everything I have seen in those twenty years has simply gone to confirm my Liberalism. I have seen Liberalism crushed out in one country after another. I have seen it suffer in this country very largely because of its leaders. I have seen it suffer at the hands of charlatans, climbers and political adventurers. It has been kept going mainly by the rank and file, mainly by the loyalty of obscure men and women. I have a great respect and admiration for those who, even in derelict con-stituencies, have kept to their Liberalism, who have faced every election with good heart. There is something indomitable in their spirit. I admire the way the women of the party have kept together. I believe there are certain causes in this country which, if they are saved, will have been saved by the women. Two of those are the cause of Liberalism and the cause of peace.

I have seen what has happened to liberalism abroad. Take Russia, where there has gone over liberalism the steamroller of communism. When I was a youth, we used to study what the great radical philosophers of Russia had to say. We read novels written by Russian writ-ers with their fierce protest against tyranny and social wrong. You have in Russia a condi-tion today, a condition of things which is an affront to the spirit of man. Take Germany. Our radicalism has been very largely taught us by the liberal philosophers of Germany. Think of the contribution the liberal philosophers of the nineteenth century have made. Where are the liberals of Germany today? They are behind barbed wire and in encamp-ments. They are in exile – some of them have been driven to suicide. That is what has hap-pened in Germany. What about Italy and its liberalism? Where are the liberals of Italy today? You will find them in exile in the islands of the Adriatic and the Mediterranean. You

211

will find some of them in the International Brigade in Spain, defending Madrid, and they are driven there to fight for liberty because they are denied it in their own land. You have a condition of things where there is a triumph of darkness and it is a remarkable thing that, when liberalism is crushed out, you are not left with an arid field, for another harvest comes. But it is the harvest of tyranny, dictators and arbitrary power. As liberalism has been crushed out in one country after another, the world has been slithering down to ruin and disaster.

In a speech the other day, General Smuts said: 'Fear, the meanest of all human motives, is now the master of us all.' That was the commentary he made on a Europe that had crushed out liberalism. We have a condition of things now in which we are not living like free men and free women in God's world filled with his bounty, but, upon the authority of men like General Smuts, we are living as if we were rats in a trap or animals in a jungle. What is the mark of civilisation? It is the conquest of fear. We are living in a Europe that is governed by fear. Well, fear and liberalism are sworn foes, and the purpose of liberalism is to defeat fear and bring hope. The poet Wordsworth once gave the definition of a liberal. Wordsworth spoke of a 'man of hope and forward-looking mind'. That is a definition of a liberal and the triumph of liberalism means the conquest of fear.[178]

24 William Tyndale and the English Reformation

MICHAEL: William Tyndale was one of the special sources of my father's inspiration and he seemed to derive a particular strength from it at this time. He was a devotee of Tyndale before some of the modern scholars had unearthed him; he knew how much the Word of the Bible translated into English had unloosed all the other grand, revolutionary, world-wide commotions of which he so much approved. In the modern world, however defined, the right to read was the first right of all. Here was the beginning of democracy in the very best sense of that debased word. Here was the way in which every man and woman, every boy and girl, could be given equal access, or something very near it, to the glories of the universe. Here was a form of levelling which could never be dismissed or derided. Isaac Foot himself had called William Tyndale 'Apostle' for providing the first translation of the Bible into English. On 6 October 1536 William Tyndale had been put to death for this 'blasphemous crime'. In 1936 my father had played a leading part in the celebrations of the 400th anniversary of the martyrdom of William Tyndale. In 1538 Royal Injunctions were issued directing that the Bible in English should be set up in every parish church through-out the land. So in 1938 further celebrations were held to mark a 'momentous event leading to spiritual renewal in our religious life'. Again my father played a leading part in this.

---

178. Isaac Foot papers, 9 July 1937.

No other Englishman had done as much at this time as Isaac Foot to revive the name of William Tyndale. More than ever in those shameful years of the crisis, it was the appeal for fresh exertions in the language of Tyndale which could save us and this was the language in which my father preached his doctrine from Devonport to St Ives. He did not himself adopt the title of 'Apostle of England' but no one was more fitted for it.

In a letter to the editor of the Times *in 1936, Isaac Foot had suggested a project to celebrate Tyndale's achievement:*

Sir, The commemoration of Tyndale's martyrdom this year has called widespread attention to his work but, unfortunately, for the great majority of our people, his actual translation is not available. His New Testament of 1525, the first printed in our language, has been described as the most interesting book in English history. Unfortunately, that book is possessed by only a few readers and I am told that even our ministers of religion rarely have a copy on their shelves. Those who have the book would wish their treasure to be shared with others. A book even more important is Tyndale's revised New Testament of 1534. This work is, of course, the primary version upon which all subsequent revisions have been based. This revised Testament of 1534 is only generally available, I believe, in *The English Hexapla*, a heavy volume, long since out of print.[179] Could not the commemoration of Tyndale be marked by the publication of his Testament of 1525 and his Revised Testament of 1534 in parallel columns? If this were done, the ordinary reader would be able to appraise for himself something of our indebtedness to this great man, and in the two versions, he would have before him the evidence of Tyndale's care and patience and diligent scholarship. If this suggestion could be adopted by one of our learned societies or by one of our great publishing houses, I think that the book would not only be welcomed by a large body of readers and Bible students, but would itself constitute a worthy and permanent record of the 400th anniversary of Tyndale's martyrdom and some reparation to his glorious memory.

I am, Sir, your obedient servant, Isaac Foot.[180]

In 1939 The Royal Society of Literature published an edition of Tyndale's New Testament as 'an act of homage to Tyndale' with an introduction by Isaac Foot, Fellow of the Society.

The editor's preface: This edition has been undertaken at the request of the Council of the Royal Society of Literature, acting on a suggestion made in a letter by Mr Isaac Foot. It has

---

179. *The English Hexapla* (1841) gives all six of the English translations of the New Testament to compare in parallel columns.
180. *Times*, 5 October 1936.

213

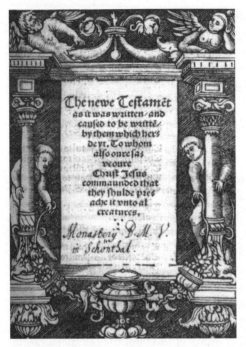

The title page of the first complete translation of the New Testament into English by William Tyndale, printed at Worms in 1526.

now been completed, but in a slightly different form to that proposed by Mr Foot. The editor thanks Mr Foot and the Bible Society for the loans of the volumes on which this edition is founded.

Isaac Foot's introduction: The 400th anniversary of the martyrdom of William Tyndale on the sixth of October 1536 gave an opportunity to the British people for acknowledging their indebtedness to the man whose service to the nation should be held in everlasting remembrance. In some thousands of churches and schools, passages were read from Tyndale's actual translation, and many people learned, for the first time, how close is the resemblance between the New Testament of today and Tyndale's rendering. When the revisers of the New Testament completed their work in 1880, they felt bound to begin their preface by placing on record their tribute to Tyndale. William Tyndale has come slowly into his fame. For many generations after his death he seems to have been almost forgotten. Sometimes our writers have allowed themselves to asperse his memory and disparage his achievement. Happily this tendency has changed in recent years. When Tyndale completed his New Testament in 1525 he wrote a postscript addressed 'To the Reader' apologising for the rudeness of the work and expressing the hope that he could revise it later.

This hope was in due course fulfilled and in 1534 the revision appeared. The English reader, therefore, now has made available for him, and for the first time in its entirety, the revised New Testament. Moreover, the reader has the advantage of seeing at a glance just what this work of revision meant for Tyndale, and, as he compares the changes made after the interval of years, he will find that, great as Tyndale was as a translator, he was even greater as a reviser. Here in the revised Testament we have revealed something of the patience and conscientiousness and unwearied diligence with which Tyndale did his life work. The changes generally show the desire for the truer translation and the simpler expression, but sometimes they are made only as a result of a more delicate sense in the choice of words. If Tyndale had not lived to revise some passages, we might never have had in our English speech some cadences which are dearest in our memory.

'Blessed are the *maynteyners of peace*' is correct translation, but 'Blessed are the *peace-makers*' is a phrase we should not like to have lost. In 1525 Tyndale wrote of the Prodigal Son 'Then he *remembred hym selfe* and sayde...'. In the 1534 edition the phrase appears 'Then he *came to him selfe* and sayde'. '*See that* youre light so shyne' in 1525 becomes '*Let* your light so shyne' in the revision; 'The *faveour* of oure lorde Jesus Christ' in the benediction closing the Second Letter to the Corinthians is changed to 'The grace of oure Lorde Jesus Christ'. 'And ye shall fynd ese unto your soules' becomes 'and ye shall fynde rest unto youre soules'. The passage in St Mark 'For *unto suche belongeth* the kyngdome of God' becomes most happily 'For *of suche is* the kyngdome of God'. '*Beholde* the lyles of the felde' is changed to '*Consider* the lilies of the felde'. Why Tyndale changed the word from 'Beholde' to 'Consider' we do not know, but what enrichment is given by the later choice!

Within a year after Tyndale's death his work was included in what was known as the Matthew Bible compiled by John Rogers, and this Bible became the basis of all successive revisions. We have this year been celebrating the 400th anniversary of the setting up of the Bible in the parish churches. The book then sanctioned was this same Matthew Bible, and in that compilation the whole of the New Testament and the larger part of the Old Testament were the work of William Tyndale. When in 1604 the revisers commenced their work for the Authorised Version, they had before them not only the work of Tyndale, but all the translations that had appeared during the seventy years following upon his death. A study of the *English Hexapla* will help to show that they took full advantage of these, but when the English Bible of 1611 left their hands the work of Tyndale remained largely undisturbed. In many instances (and some highly important) where King James's committee departed from Tyndale's translation the revisers of 1881 have restored his original words. The most notable instances of these restorations is '*love*' (instead of '*charity*') in St Paul's great hymn in the thirteenth chapter of the First Corinthian Letter. The recovery of the word '*flock*' (instead of '*fold*' in the 1611 version) in St John 10:16 making the passage read 'and there shall be one *flock* and one shepherd' is no less important. 'Except ye *be converted* and become as little children' has now been changed to Tyndale's first translation 'Except ye *turn*...'. 'For they all did cast in of their superfluity' was Tyndale's translation from the story of the poor widow and the rich men. For some reason the committee of 1611 changed the significant word 'superfluity' to 'abundance'. Tyndale's word has now been restored, and with it the main point of the parable.

In these cases and in scores of others the reader of the New Testament will find new light thrown upon the page by Tyndale's translation, and again and again, if he refers to his Greek Testament, he will find that Tyndale gets nearer to the meaning of the original word or phrase than either the revisers of 1611 or 1881 ... If every new translation is another commentary, how great should be the interest of this book, showing how Tyndale, with the text of Erasmus before him, read line after line of the Greek, and, pondering upon its

215

meaning, then sought to express both the meaning and the beauty in the synonyms and common speech of his native land. The persistence of Tyndale's work is in fact the outstanding miracle in the history of English letters. After four centuries of war and peace, of achievement and vicissitude, the faithful labour of this scholar and martyr remains vindicated ... His words are daily on our lips, his phrases have become part of our household speech, his cadences are treasured in every part of the world where the English language has gone. What other Englishman has touched so many lives?

July 1938, Isaac Foot.

25 1938 Munich

MICHAEL: If my father had been returned to the House of Commons in 1937, he would have been the foremost opponent of the policies of appeasement in Europe – the true Apostle of England and what England stood for. This defeat by the forces of Conservatism in his own Westcountry might have shaken his spirit but he continued his fight to warn of the dangers of the policy of appeasement. In the first few days after the Prime Minister, Neville Chamberlain, had returned from his meeting at Munich with Herr Hitler on 29 September 1938, where he had agreed to the cession of part of Czechoslovakia to Germany, claiming to have brought 'Peace in our time', most observers, even the most critical, thought they must acknowledge his sincerity. Among the first to voice his views clearly was my father when he presented his case in a letter to the editors of his local newspapers.

1 October 1938, letter to the editors of the Western Morning News *and the* Cornishman:

As a number of public engagements in other parts of the country will prevent me from speaking in the Westcountry for another fortnight I ask your leave to make a few observations. I hope to join in the public thanksgiving to Almighty God for deliverance of the past week. War, although not the worst of all evils, is a most dreadful extremity and the intense relief that we have been saved from this calamity will be felt in every home throughout the land. I join with other Englishmen in thanks to the Prime Minister for the unsparing and courageous efforts he has made to avert this disaster. I am, however, unable to share in the unrestrained enthusiasm of the past few days. I cannot forget that only ten days ago we were compelled by duress to present an ultimatum to a small and brave country to force them to consent within a few hours to a concession affecting vitally their economic and political independence. We had to do this, not because we believed the policy was right and just, but because a pistol was being held at our own heads. Yesterday we were forced to present another ultimatum and again the Czech people were compelled to yield to what their Prime Minister described last night as 'ruthlessness unexampled in history'. Last night, after learning of the natural rejoicings of the London crowds, I listened to the message from Prague when the description was given of the enforced evacuation of district after district. The names of the many towns were read out. The recital of these names must have sounded to the Czech people like clods falling upon the lid of a coffin. What would have been our feelings if the names had been English names and the surrendered zones English counties? I thought of the unhappy people and wretched peasants faced with the desperate choice: either to leave their homesteads, their holdings and precious soil or to stay and risk the blessings of the Nazi regime. Last night we learned that Prague had ordered a day of mourning. I hoped that somehow the sound of the hectic rejoicings of London would not break in upon their grief.

Mr Chamberlain told us yesterday that he had returned home bringing with him 'peace with honour'. On the same day the Czechoslovakians, side by side with whom we might have been fighting next week, spoke of a 'ruthlessness unexampled in history'. Mr Chamberlain is not a ruthless man, but he has been obliged to take part in forcing this policy upon a helpless people because he has himself been under the pressure of a ruthless man who, as Mr Chamberlain told the House on Wednesday, declared he was prepared to risk a world war rather than modify his plan or alter his date. As to Russia, I do not even yet understand how it is that, after our official announcement a few days ago that, in the event of the Czech frontier being violated, we should be fighting with Russian troops as our allies, we can now talk and act as if Russia had disappeared from the map of the world.

The Prime Minister announced yesterday that a new document had been signed by Herr Hitler. If this new promise means a change of heart, I am profoundly thankful. His career, however, hitherto, has been marked by broken covenants. Within the last few weeks we have seen our country torn with fear and emotion; a free people have been threatened into burrowing underground; our parks and open spaces have been turned into trenches and our children carted into the country. In addition heavy financial losses have been inflicted on private citizens and public institutions and colossal burdens placed on the Exchequer. Why? Because of the deliberate choice of this one man and because, forsooth, having announced his date, he could not wait. It is for these reasons that some of us read, with mixed feelings, of the banquet at Munich and were glad we had not to share in that hospitality. There would have been too many Banquos claiming the right to sit at Macbeth's table and we should have been left wondering as to the menu of the concentration camps, the whereabouts of Herr Schuschnigg[181] or the prison fare of Pastor Martin Niemoller.[182] For these reasons and many others there are some of us whose relief is mixed with a sense of shame, because of the action our country has been forced to take, and, whatever the example set by others, we shall decline to stick the swastika in our coats.

---

181. Chancellor of Austria at the time of Hitler's take-over.
182. A Lutheran pastor who was imprisoned for his resistance to the Nazis and Hitler.

On the whole, we would rather be damned with President Beñes than saved with Hitler. We hope, despite our new international affiliations, we may be still allowed to read Wordsworth's sonnets to Liberty:

Never may from our souls one truth depart,
That an accursed thing it is to gaze
On prosperous tyrants with a dazzled eye.

Isaac Foot, Pencrebar, Callington.[183]

Moral responsibilities: Methodism's contribution to future peace
Isaac Foot gave this interview on the 'peace' and the issues confronting the Churches:

You say I may be absolutely frank and I propose to be so. Anything I have to say must be prefaced by a tribute to the Prime Minister for the unsparing and most courageous efforts he made at the eleventh hour to avert the unspeakable disaster of war ... That, however, does not discharge the Prime Minister from his responsibility for the policy anterior to the harum-scarum diplomacy which marred his interviews with Hitler at Berchtesgaden and Godesberg. For some months the Prime Minister, setting aside the warnings, has chosen to drive against the red lights. His policy has alienated a great body of opinion throughout this country. Today there are insistent demands for national unity in the face of the impending dangers but I am afraid that unity will not be forthcoming until our people have a fuller confidence in those who are managing the affairs of the nation. It is very certain that the Prime Minister will have to make his objective very much clearer before he will be able to enlist the ungrudging confidence of the organised workers of this land.

What has stuck in our throats is the claim that we have now secured 'Peace with honour'. The 'peace', apparently, is so precarious that the energies and resources of the next five, or maybe ten years have to be spent on rearmament on a vast scale, threatening the economic security of our whole social structure and a piling up of burdens for our children and grandchildren. The armaments may be necessary but to call such a condition of things 'peace' is a degradation of a noble word. As to the 'honour', whatever was thought in the hectic elation of a fortnight ago, no one with any moral sensitiveness would think of using that word today. It is now clear that Germany will secure even more than Herr Hitler demanded at Godesberg. It looks as if there will soon be no Czech state at all – 'where the carcass is, there will be the vultures be gathered together'.[184]

Czechoslovakia has ever been the democratic thorn in the totalitarian flesh. Herr Hitler has now accomplished his purpose, for, within a few months, Czechoslovakia will either have dis-

---

183. Published in the *Cornishman* 6 October 1938.
184. Matthew 24:28.

appeared or will remain only as a satellite state. In the meantime, we are seeing the dreadful results inflicted on this unhappy people, upon whom the blow has fallen. The Lord Mayor of London tells us that what he has seen in Prague is enough to break anyone's heart. It is bad enough to be refugees, but apparently the refugees are now forbidden even a refuge. Leaving aside the Jews, who, under the threats of Hitler and the edicts of Mussolini, seem to be destined to be vagabonds on the face of the earth, there are scores of thousands who refuse to bow the knee to the Nazi doctrine and they are to be driven back to endure the sufferings threatened by Henlein,[185] who has learnt only too well in the school of persecution of Hitler and Goering. The tragedy is that, if we had not intervened in this miserable business and had told the Czechs that we could do nothing for them, they would have been far better off than they are now.

As it is, we cannot wash our hands of our responsibilities towards these peoples. Apart from all political considerations, there is a serious moral responsibility towards these people and, if we refuse to recognise this and ta ke refuge in Cain's question 'Am I my brother's keeper?', we shall inevitably suffer if there is any justice in the working out of history ... The issue is whether European affairs are to be determined by the statesman or the gunman and whether the world is to live under law or under arbitrary powe r. Because arbitrary power has been the determining factor, we have the attempt to solve long-standing problems by ultimatums. Putting a pistol at our heads, Herr Hitler has compelled us to join with France in putting a pistol to the head of Dr Beneš and his colleague. Ancient frontiers are being wiped out and new divisions made, not even with the surgeon's knife but rather with the butcher's chopper. Territories are being sliced away after a few hours' discussion with less than a hundredth part of the consideration which would be given to the question of the extension of a city or the amalgamation of two Methodist circuits. What permanence, I ask you, can be expected from these arrangements, determined not by right or reason but simply by the power of the swo rd? What a legacy we are bequeathing to the next generation!

We are slowly realising that dictatorship and democracy cannot live side by side. Last week Hitler rebuked and rated us for expressing our opinion about things that were happening in Germany. If Herr Schuschnigg is kept without trial in what was formerly Austria, I suppose we must make no comment. If the independent Germans in the annexed territories of Czechoslovakia are driven into concentration camps and flogged with Henlein's whips, we must accept that as in the ordinary course of things. And if Pastor Martin Niemoller, acquitted after public trial, is kept in solitary confinement and slowly done to death, we must keep our indignation inarticulate. Apparently Herr Hitler has never heard of the Communion of Saints. With the elimination of the teaching of St Paul from the Nazi Bible, there has disappeared the conception of that Christian fellowship which ignores all political frontiers whether devised by either Jew or Greek.

---

185. Konrad Henlein (1898–1945), Sudeten-German politician who agitated for the German annexation of the Sudeten-German lands.

December 1938: Privy Counsellor and sons' reunion at Pencrebar. Isaac with Michael, recently adopted as the Labour candidate in Devonport; John, the candidate for Bodmin; and Dingle, the Liberal MP for Dundee.

Turning to the moral issues confronting us all and especially confronting our own church, the greatest danger I foresee is that, in our disillusionment, following the breakdown of the League of Nations and the loss of whatever moral gain arose from the last war, we may surrender to the spirit of hopelessness and put our trust only in what Kipling called 'reeking tube and iron shard'.[186] The contribution of the Christian Church must be to resist the spread of this contagion. I know that the Methodist community comprises men and women of all political parties and it is a good thing that it is so. But we have our special responsibility. Fellowship is the life-blood of Methodism and we ought to be able to make a contribution that is needed by the stricken world. Methodism must be independent of this government and of any government. We have higher standards to observe than those of any Cabinet or any Parliament. Our worldwide membership forbids us from becoming subservient to any dictator or nationalism. And when we say 'Our Father' we ought not to make any prayer which forgets that, side by side with us, is the victim of tyranny in other lands – the refugees in Czechoslovakia, the suffering women and children of war-stricken China and the Ethiopian deprived of his rights and stripped of the possessions of his native soil.[187]

---

186. 'Recessional' (1897).
187. *Methodist Recorder*, 20 October 1938.

MICHAEL: I recall that time quite well, when some of us participated in the last by-election conducted in Britain before the actual outbreak of war. It took place in North Cornwall in 1939 and the Conservative candidate plastered the hoardings with the poster: 'You are reading this in peace because you live under a National Government.' It was all part of the campaign against the Liberal or socialist warmongers who had wanted to send aid to Spain and the posters were still there, slightly tattered, when war came to Britain on 3 September 1939.[188]

A Foot family gathering in the late 1930s. The three eldest brothers were now married: Dingle to Dorothy, Mac to Sylvia and John to Anne. Clockwise from top left Christopher, Michael, Mac, Dingle, John, Dorothy, Sally, Eva, Isaac, Anne and Sylvia. Only Jennifer is absent in France.

188. Michael Foot, *Loyalists and Loners* (Collins, 1986).

PART VIII

The Second World War

26 'Drake's drum beats again: an omen of our coming victory'

MICHAEL: Now that the war had come, Plymouth, my father's Plymouth, our Plymouth, was the one most badly hit, more concentratedly even, than Coventry or London by Goering's air force. It was no compensation that this was what my father had prophesied would happen if the German raiders were allowed to destroy Guernica. Plymouth's defiance had to be expressed in historic terms and my father understood. This was his answer when Plymouth was still reeling from the assault of 1940. His sermon now was 'England Arise'; and England did. As a child, my father had stood on Plymouth Hoe when the statue of Sir Francis Drake was erected and, like Drake, had looked out across Plymouth Sound a thousand times. Now, when the little ships went to Dunkirk or when the Luftwaffe raided Plymouth, he claimed to hear Drake's drum and, less credibly, that all other Westcountrymen heard it too. Hitler, threatening invasion, standing for nothing but 'brute violence and proud tyrannic power', would have to meet much beyond his understanding: 'the land of William Tyndale and John Hampden and Oliver Cromwell and John Milton – the Britain of Marlborough – another famous Devonshire man – and John Wesley, of Chatham and Burke and Thomas Paine and Charles James Fox'. That was my father in 1940.

In 1940 the BBC invited Isaac Foot to make a broadcast in this critical year of the war. He chose as his title 'Drake's Drum Beats Again'. This was the broadcast he made to the British Empire and to America on 16 August 1940:

On the sixteenth of August 352 years ago, Sir Francis Drake and his fellow-seamen were returning from the North Sea after putting the finishing touches to the defeat of the Spanish Armada. A few days ago, I walked along Plymouth Hoe and looked again – I suppose for the thousandth time – at the statue of Sir Francis Drake. Mainly because of the sharp impressions of early boyhood, that memorial has, I suppose, meant more to me than all the other statues in the world. There he stands – the compass in his hand, the globe by his side, looking out upon Plymouth Sound, and across those shining waters that were the theatre of his mighty exploits. We Westcountry folk like to think that he stands there always on guard.

DRAKE'S DRUM
Beats Again

AN OMEN OF OUR COMING VICTORY

By

The Right Hon. ISAAC FOOT

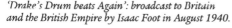

'Drake's Drum beats Again': broadcast to Britain and the British Empire by Isaac Foot in August 1940.

The statue of Sir Francis Drake placed on Plymouth Hoe in 1884.

A few miles away from Plymouth is Buckland Abbey, near his birthplace, the home of his later years and there, in the heart of the country that he loved, is his drum, the drum which he took with him round the world, the drum emblazoned with the coat of arms he took after Queen Elizabeth knighted him with the touch of her golden sword. A suggestion has been made that the BBC time intervals should be filled with the beating of Drake's drum, and some have said that the drum might be taken to be one of our great national institutions. It is more fitting that the drum should rest at his home, near his birthplace, and in the very heart of the country that he loved.

We in the Westcountry do not need to have the sound of the drum brought to us over the air. We can hear it without that help. Some of you will recall that, in November 1918, when the German fleet surrendered and the British fleet, after four years of constant action and ceaseless vigil, closed in around the enemy vessels, men on board the admiral's flagship heard the long roll of a drum. When, after careful search and enquiry, neither drum nor drummer could be found, they realised the truth and by common consent one man said to another: 'Drake's drum!'

Drake he was a Devon man an' ruled the Devon seas
    (Capten, art tha' sleepin' there below?)
Rovin' tho' his death fell, he went wi' heart at ease,
    An' dreamin' arl the time o' Plymouth Hoe.
'Take my drum to England, hang et by the shore,
    Strike et when your powder's runnin' low.
If the Dons sight Devon, I'll quit the port o' Heaven
    An' drum them up the Channel as we drummed them long ago.'[189]

Of course there are some matter-of-fact people who tell us that this Drake's drum business is only a legend, and that, in these hard days, we need something more than ghosts and legends to rely upon. Well, supposing that we got rid of all these ghosts and legends – what then? Supposing we wiped out from our memory all the great names of the past and all that we know of Drake and Raleigh and Grenville and Blake and Nelson – what sort of a fleet should we have left? Surely it means something that we give to every one of the ships of His Majesty's Navy a name. When, a few months ago, the sailors who had fought the German battleship the Graf Spee marched through Plymouth, the names on their caps – Ajax and Exeter – were borne through the streets of the city like an oriflamme.

At that time many blue jackets marched with them who bore on their caps the name of H.M.S. *Drake*. Now, there is no ship in our fleet that is called by that name, but all men belonging to the Royal Naval Barracks in our city are reckoned to be serving on H.M.S. Drake. So, whatever happens at sea, there are always a number of our sailors who go about 'armed with [that] crested and prevailing name'.[190] The name of Drake means a great deal to us now. In his own day, his very name became a terror to his enemies. His name meant to them the Dragon, and in their terrified imagination he became almost like the Dragon of the Apocalypse. The cry of '*El Draque! El Draque!*' brought confusion and panic like the descent of a fireship.

Here in the Westcountry, we are never surprised to hear the beating of Drake's drum. Our fathers heard it beat when the *Mayflower* made its way out of the Sound. When Drake from his place upon the Hoe watched it sail, that ship was to him like another *Golden Hind*. Our fathers heard it beat when Fairfax and Cromwell came down to thank the people of Plymouth for the defence of the town during the long siege of the Civil War. Admiral Blake heard it, when, sick unto death, he was just able to reach the entrance to Plymouth Harbour, and he died with his great heart lifted by the sight of the hills of his beloved Westcountry and the sound of Drake's welcoming drum. Nelson heard the roll of the drum when he came to be made a freeman of the borough, and Wellington heard it, too,

189.'Drake's Drum' was one of a collection of poems published as *Admirals All* by Sir Henry Newbolt (1862–1938) in 1897.
190. Francis Thompson, 'Dedication to Coventry Patmore', *New Poems* (1897).

when he set out with his troops from Plymouth to defeat the menace of an earlier tyranny. The drum was heard to beat again when Napoleon, a prisoner after Waterloo, was brought into Plymouth Harbour upon the Bellerophon. Again and again, it has sounded during this war, especially when the troopships have come, bringing the men of the Empire who have travelled over those waters into which Drake was the first to take an English keel. The drum was heard to beat when we had the miracle of the deliverance of Dunkirk. Drake's heart went out to those men who manned the little ships that saved the British Army. Those ships were very much like his own – many of them were about the same size – and they went to and fro upon the waters that were made famous by the battle of Gravelines, when the Invincible Armada was driven into confusion.[191] The drum beats now, day after day, as Drake watches the sky over the English Channel, and as he rejoices at the heroism and courage of the young mariners of the sky, who seem to have taken the old ships – the *Golden Hind*, the *Revenge*, the *Victory* – high into the firmament, and who are vindicating hour after hour their spiritual descent from those who fought at Crécy and Agincourt, at Blenheim and Trafalgar and Waterloo. When we hear the drum it tells us many things. It tells first of the confidence Drake and his fellows had in the presence of the enemy. He and his seamen had to fight against an immense power – a power that seemed overwhelming – but when they challenged that power they found it was not so strong after all, and they had a saying that Philip of Spain was a Colossus, but a Colossus stuffed with clouts. Drake's seamen were like 'Ironsides' of a later generation. 'It was ever the fashion for Cromwell's pikemen to rejoice greatly when they beheld the enemy.'

The supreme contribution of Drake was that, in a time of grave national peril, he breathed into the people of England his own intrepid spirit and assurance, and took away the terror of the enemy:

Drake nor devil nor Spaniard feared,
Their cities he put to the sack,
He singed his Catholic Majesty's beard,
And harried his ships to wrack.
He was playing at Plymouth a rubber of bowls
When the Great Armada came;
But he said, 'They must wait their turn, good souls,'
And he stooped and finished his game.[192]

The beating of the drum also tells us of Drake's trust in the common people. He gave dignity to the common seaman and loved to say that any boy who sailed with him would be reckoned a gentleman. He insisted that on his ship – that wonderful ship the *Golden Hind*,

191.Naval battle of 1588 in which the English defeated the Spanish Armada.
192. Sir Henry Newbolt, 'Admirals All', *Admirals All*.

the first English ship to plough a furrow around the world – there should only be the fellowship of common service and the brotherhood of common sacrifice. 'I must have', he said, 'the gentleman to haul and draw with the mariner, and the mariner to haul and draw with the gentleman.'

It was on the same voyage – perhaps the most momentous voyage in our history as a sea-faring people – that Drake cashiered all his officers so that for a time everyone on board his ship held the same rank as an ordinary seaman. He did this to demonstrate that on his ship all distinctions between one man and another were for order and convenience and not of nature and necessity. The common sailor who sailed with Drake was raised in stature and, when the Prime Minister the other day said that this war was a war of the unknown warriors, Drake beat his drum again. Drake had confidence in his country and confidence in the common people, but his supreme confidence was in God. 'Never was a fleet so strong as this,' he said, as the Armada approached, 'but the Lord of strength is stronger.' Listen to his letter written to Walsingham at that time of national danger:

> There must be a beginning of every matter, but the continuing unto the end yields the true glory. If we can thoroughly believe that this which we do is in defence of our religion and country no doubt our merciful God for His Christ our Saviour's sake is able and will give us the victory, though our sins be red.

This is what Drake's drum tells us in the Westcountry, but, of course, I don't suggest that it is only in the Westcountry that the sound is heard. Drake took his drum with him all round the world. That is why its beat can be heard all round the world today. If you listen you can hear it – everywhere, in every land where Briton joins Briton to defeat this present menace of darkness and evil; in every distant station where the two or three are gathered together in common danger and common hope. The young airman, high in the firmament, keeping guard over the Motherland, or striking day after day and night after night at the heart of the enemy's power – he can hear it; the sailor in whose veins Drake's blood still flows; the merchant seaman, who, even whilst I am speaking, is risking his life, to carry to and fro food and precious cargo. Everywhere throughout the whole Commonwealth, the drum can be heard. In the Far East and in the islands of the South; over the great stretches of Australia; from the north to the south of Africa, in India, in Kenya, in Singapore; on the heights of Abraham, in Haifa and Amman and upon the walls of Jerusalem; in the Red Sea and in the Mediterranean and upon every ocean.

Nor is it only throughout the British Empire that the drum is heard. This mighty conflict has become a war in which national boundaries and state frontiers have become irrelevant. The frontier today is the frontier of the human spirit. What we have now to defend is the land slowly recovered by the long achievement of human freedom. Drake's drum can be heard everywhere where freedom is counted the precious thing, just as the shot fired by the embattled farmers at Lexington Bridge was heard all round the world. That is why Gettysburg can never be only American soil.[193] That is why we English people can pass from Drake's statue at Plymouth to the statue of Abraham Lincoln standing outside the doors of Westminster Abbey, and remember that he fought, not for American interest alone or for any material advantage, but that certain precious things should not perish from the earth.

Hitler, threatening invasion, reckons his forces and tries to calculate ours. He will have to meet a good deal that is altogether beyond his reckoning and beyond his understanding. If and when he does come, he will be attempting the invasion of Shakespeare's England, the land of Sir Walter Raleigh and Queen Elizabeth. They will come at the sound of Drake's drum, and others, too, like William Wallace and Robert Bruce, Owen Glendower and John Knox and Montrose. Destitute himself of any moral greatness or spiritual resource, this mean, cruel man, standing for nothing but 'brute violence and proud tyrannic power',[194] seeks to crush the land of William Tyndale and John Hampden and Oliver Cromwell and John Milton – the Britain of Marlborough, another famous Devonshire man, and John Wesley, of Chatham, and Burke and Tom Paine and Charles James Fox.

We like to think in these days that it is not only their England which is being defended; it is the land also of the great adventurers, who dreamed of a wider England, and who found our shores too narrow for their ranging spirits, and who wrote the large Imperial legend of our race. They were all of Drake's great company; John Davis and Martin Frobisher, Sir John Hawkins, Sir Humphrey Gilbert, Sir Richard Grenville, Sir Walter Raleigh, Sir Henry Vane, Edward Winslow, John Winthrop, and William Penn. These were the men who, as they travelled to and fro, thought of the sea not so much as 'a moat defensive to the house' but as a glorious highway, and who, taking their little ships across distant and often uncharted waters, or founding their settlements on far-off shores, formed those ties which count so much today, ties which though light as air are as strong as links of iron. It is their land that we are now called upon to defend. 'Goodbye, dear England!' said John Winthrop,[195] as his ship left our shores.

For the defence of this land of such dear souls, this dear, dear land, all these will rally at the sound of Drake's drum, with Wordsworth and Burns and Shelley and Scott and Cobbett and David Livingstone, and Florence Nightingale and Edith Cavell and countless others – an exceeding great army. All the old admirals will come led by Nelson. The invader will have to meet, not only the British Navy of today, but what Evelyn Underhill has called 'The Naval Reserve'.

---

193. The battle of Gettysburg fought in 1863 in the American Civil War.

194. John Milton, *Paradise Regained* (1671).

195. John Winthrop (1588–1649) was one of the leaders of the *Mayflower* expedition.

Rank on rank the admirals
Rally to their old commands:
Where the crash of battle falls
There the one-armed hero stands.
Loud upon his phantom mast
Speak the signals of the past.

Where upon the friendly wave
Stand our squadrons as of old,
Where the lonely deed and brave
Shall the ancient torch uphold,
Strive for England side by side,
Those who live and those who died.[196]

In this hour of grave peril and high privilege we are indeed compassed about with a great cloud of witnesses.

27 The Foot family in the war

MICHAEL: When the war had finally sta rted in September 1939 our own family was scattered all over the world, although we all looked back with love to Pencrebar, Callington, which my mother and father had especially made their own. My brother Dingle was in London, soon to be appointed as the Minister of Economic Wa rfare in Churchill's wartime government. Mac and his wife Sylvia were, for a short space, in London, soon to be despatched back to the Near East war zone. My next brother, John, joined the army. My sister Sal was still teaching children to ride horses and later became a land girl. My younger sister, Jennifer, was caught in Grenoble, where she was learning French. She soon found herself fully occupied in wartime Jerusalem. Christopher was keeping the family business going in Plymouth but soon joined John in the army. I was left in London with, however, a special chance of renewing my relationship with my mother in Callington, which is the excuse for all this recital of the family rigmarole. My asthma ke pt me out of any military service but she often suspected I might be inviting greater perils. Her opposition to all kinds of alcoholic consumption was even stronger, if conceivable, than my father's. Whatever I was up to, I tried to report properly, especially on political questions, where I was discovering that she might be more sympathetic to my peculiar deviations than the rest of them, even than my father. When, some years before, I had made the decision to leave the Liberal Party and join the Labour Party, I thought secretly

196. Evelyn Underhill (1875–1941), 'The Naval Reserve' (1914).

Christmas 1938: The Foot family together for the last time before they were separated by war.

that she had understood my action better than the others. When, a little later, I had settled in London, I was able to report to her that I had heard Donald Soper in Hyde Park. She, naturally, hoped that he would help to return me to the family's Methodist faith, whatever the appeal of Soper's Socialism.[197] In 1938 I had been adopted as the Labour candidate for Devonport. That was a constituency held by a huge majority by one of my father's old friends and enemies, Leslie Hore-Belisha. No one ever thought I had a chance of displacing him but I was making friends with the leaders of the Labour Party in the dockyard.

This was the time when the Mother of Seven came into her own. She was proud of what her brood were doing across the world. All through those years, my mother stayed at our home in Callington. My father was travelling back and forth to London, with one major propaganda trip to the United States in 1943.

In 1940 Winston Churchill appointed Isaac Foot the Liberal Party's representative on the Security Executive Committee, one of three permanent members whose job it was to coordinate the work of all the security services during the war. In 1944 Isaac Foot described his family's wartime experiences in this letter to a former Parliamentary colleague:

197. Donald Soper (1903–98), a socialist Methodist preacher, frequently preached in the open air at Speaker's Corner in Hyde Park.

229

I have now been working for about three years on the Security Executive, generally known as the Swinton committee. We deal with the coordination of national security. There are three of us and we call in representatives of all the government departments as occasion arises. I took on the work at the request of the Prime Minister. It is an unpaid job – takes most of my time – and is very interesting. It shuts me out from practically all other activities. I get home for the short weekend and generally I take a service on the Sunday in one of the village chapels near to my home.

My wife is carrying on most nobly – no domestic help, soldiers' canteen, magistrate's meetings, Sunday school and Society Class[198] and much else. Dingle is doing quite well I think but I shouldn't like his job. Whenever he appears at the family table he is generally greeted as the 'baby starver'! Mac has just been transferred to Cyprus as Colonial Secretary. He finds his work fascinating. His wife and children were evacuated to South Africa from Amman, Transjordan, but they are now joining him again. John, my third boy, is a captain in the Army, just now nursing a broken leg sustained in battle practice. His wife, an American girl, and children have just returned from America, to which they had returned in 1940. My elder daughter, Sally, is a land girl and my daughter, Jennifer, is working in Haifa, Palestine. Christopher, my youngest boy, is a lieutenant now in Persia. Michael – rejected for the Army – has just relinquished the editorship of the *Evening Standard* and intends to devote himself to politics and writing. He wrote the anonymous *Trial of Mussolini*, of which about 150,000 copies were sold. He represents the outside left of the Foot team! He is a fine boy and when it comes to all social questions he has a fire in his belly.

I keep up my reading and find my main interest in my library. I am always intending to write something but I never do. I had a grand time in America but it was pretty strenuous – about 100 public engagements in about 100 days – in 15 states and about 25,000 miles of travel. I am wholly in agreement with you about the problems arising after the war. When we think of these things there is comfort as you say in the knowledge that God has his purposes too, unknown to us. There is a lesson in God's rebuke to Elijah – 1 Kings chapter 18. Elijah thought everything would appear with himself and then learned that God had his purposes and Elijah's successor already designed.

The Plymouth Blitz
In a letter to his wife, Anne, in America in 1941 John Foot described two nights of the worst raids on Plymouth on 20 and 21 March, when the offices of Isaac's firm of solicitors, Foot and Bowden, at 21 Lockyer Street were destroyed:

---

198. Society Class is the Methodist term for weekly class meetings such as the women's or young men's. Eva took a weekly women's class.

There was a two-day blitz on Plymouth. They came over about 9.30 p.m. on two successive evenings and bombed the place for three hours, dropping high explosive, then showers of fire bombs and then high explosive again. Pop wrote to say that the office was burned out so I got five days' compassionate leave. The sight of Plymouth is rather shocking. There had been no attempt to go for military objectives. The whole attack was concentrated on the centre of the city. Our office was bombed on the second night. I don't think an incendiary hit it – it caught alight from some neighbouring building. Mr Bowden was in the town during the raid and went home at 1 a.m. when the raiders had gone, thanking God that anyway the office had survived. He came down the next morning and was told on the way that it was burned down after all. I'm afraid it was a bit of a shock to him but he's getting over it now. The front and back walls are standing but the inside is all gone. I saw my poor Dictaphone lying on top of the rubble – a few pieces of twisted metal. That cut me more than anything. By one good chance the strong room survived. This is a great mercy and fortunately, after the first night, Uncle Stanley has had the good sense to crowd all the deed boxes he could inside it. If that had gone I don't know how the office could get going again. Even so, the loss of papers is appalling and will make things extremely difficult.

The offices of Foot and Bowden at 21 Lockyer Street (centre), *destroyed in the blitz.*

We've opened a new office in Houndiscombe Road, off Mutley Plain. I was able to give some moral support and get a few things arranged but there wasn't really much I could do to help. Pop has stood up to it very well and is in high spirits. It's a big loss to him of course, but he is taking it magnificently, though every penny he's got must have been in the business. Someone rang him at his home at 4 a.m. to tell him his property was burning. He said: 'Is there anything I can do?' When he was told that there wasn't he simply said: 'Then I might as well go back to bed again' – which he did and slept soundly till 9 a.m.

All this gives you a strange feeling of insubstantiality of material possessions. We are all alive – so what does the rest matter so much. Mother is cheerful and going off to her class at the chapel with the usual regularity. An economy campaign is on foot to try and mitigate the financial disaster. Pop is hard up for cash but I gather that Michael is seeing him through, till things are straightened out a little! Michael is disgustingly rich. The *Daily Herald* asked him to come over to them. He turned it down. The manager of the *Express* got to hear of this and told Beaverbrook. Beaverbrook asked what terms the *Herald* had offered and was told that Michael had turned the invitation down without asking terms. So B. said: 'What would they have offered him?' The manager thought they'd have offered at least £1,500, so B. says: 'Then pay him that.' So Mike's salary is raised from £20 to £30 a week. When Pop told him of the losses in Plymouth Michael said: 'Don't you worry. I'll make you and Mother an allowance of £10 a week.' But I guess it won't come to that! Michael is now generally recognised as the best writer in Fleet Street, so I guess he's worth his £30 a week. Chris, who is now a corporal, on hearing of what had happened, wrote offering £1 per week out of his pay! It's all very strange and rather funny in many ways. Pop is very buoyant and learning where to put the oil in the car now Gregory's gone. Such are the depths we have fallen to. Mother is finding out how to run the petrol engine which pumps up the water and how to manage the lawn mower.

I think everybody's been made a bit light-headed by the enormity of the blow at Plymouth. You walk down the street and see old gentlemen surveying the wreckage of their businesses and cracking jokes with the rest who're in the same plight. There's a War Damage Bill to compensate people who are bombed out but nothing's to be paid till after the war, I believe. So what good will that be, I'm not sure. It's funny to walk down Mutley Plain and see a diminutive shop which was probably a newsagent's a fortnight ago, with 'Pophams'[199] over the top. About 17 firms of solicitors have been bombed out I believe. Solicitors' offices are popping up in all kinds of curious places. There is a tremendous opportunity to rebuild the town, as it should be built – with a great space in front of St Andrews, as I always thought there ought to be. I hope to God the City will show some common sense and not try to put it all back again as it was.

---

199. Pophams was a large department store in Plymouth before the war.

Eva described the family's experiences in one of her regular letters to her daughter-in-law Anne.

12 April 1941

John was home a fortnight ago on special leave; he came down very kindly to see if he could help us all in the Plymouth disaster; you will have heard from him about the demolition of the office and all the worry and trouble and loss that it is causing, and also other valuable property of Dad's was destroyed. As we hardly know where we are with regard to financial matters, we are trying drastically to reduce expenses and have dismissed our two men who are a big expense and luxury and expect to rely on jobbing help some days a week, cutting the lawns and pumping the water ourselves. Of course there is a great deal to do and I don't yet quite know how we shall get on. We are not starving or bankrupt or anything of that kind and we hope to be able to stay at Pencrebar so don't worry about us at all. The whole Foot family has turned up trumps.

Spooner's Corner, Old Town Street in the centre of Plymouth, devastated in the blitz in 1941.

233

The worst blitzed city: the centre of Plymouth seen from the Guildhall tower after the blitz in 1941.

It would make you sad to see Plymouth – all the shopping centre gone – Popham's, Spooner's, Dingle's etc and St Andrew's Church and the Guildhall; I haven't been in yet but may go with Dorothy on Monday. Dad and Mr Bowden have of course been terribly distressed but are now feeling rather better; other people's business of course is in a hopeless muddle, owing to the loss of manuscripts and papers but it will get sorted out in time. Fortunately the strong room with a good many documents was safe.

MICHAEL: My mother followed closely as anybody in the world what was happening in the war and to us in London. I have her copy of *Guilty Men*, written by me in 1940, in which she inscribed her own name 'Eva Foot'. I think she was a good deal prouder of the sequels – *The Trial of Mussolini* in 1943 and *Brendan and Beverley* in 1944, both of which I wrote at Pencrebar. The whole Foot family had a pretty good record of fighting fascism along the lines which our father thought should have started earlier. No one spread his ideas more faithfully than the 'Mother of Seven', whose letters became more frequent as the war proceeded.

In November 1941 Eva wrote to Michael in London, thanking him for his birthday gift:
I hope you yourself are keeping well and are getting a room for yourself where you can sleep and work. I hear you have set the Thames on fire with your leaders: I do wish we

could see them. Congratulations! I am basking in reflected glory with you and Dingle. We should like to see you.

Love and many thanks, Mother

20 June 1942

Many thanks for your letter and magnificent cheque; I feel like a pauper in accepting cheques from my sons – son, I should say, as you are the only one who has ever been in the position to lend so much money; it amuses me to think that the one who is nearest to a Communist is the only real capitalist. I can imagine it will take time to get the office of the *Standard* into wo rking orde r, you really ought to get some sort of break or change. I am really delighted to hear your health is so much better. Are you still having treatment? I think the money will go on till the end of July thank you. Where are you living now, if anywhere? John tells me you are looking 'shaggy'; please rectify this before I come! I hear rumours of ladies of various European nationalities but presume they are entirely legendary.

Very much love, Mother

5 November 1942

I have been meaning to write to you for some time, but the days go by filled with small trivial matters and you are concerned with world-stirring events ... Sometimes I wonder if you are as free as you ought to be and if you are not paying too big a price for fame. Professor Joad[200] – with whom we lunched at our friends the Abdys on Monday – was saying some very flattering things about you; I expect Dad has told you. He expects you to be one of the leaders of the future and I hope you will be spared to play a great part; sometimes I think of what a power you would be with all your gifts of speech and leadership if you could take a decided Christian line and what tragedy it will be, with all you may achieve, if you miss the one thing that really matters and put your faith on material solutions and political schemes only. Forgive this preaching; we are so proud of you that we wish the best for you. I haven't the same interest in the *Standard* now you don't write the leaders; I am sure the paper will suffer. They seem so pedestrian after your colourful style. It is getting late and I must go to bed.

Very much love Mother. My bank account is low!

21 July 1943

Many Happy Returns of the day! For once I haven't forgotten. May the future bring you all happiness in your work, your health and in your whole life. I don't somehow feel you are

---

200. Professor C. E. W. Joad (1891–1953) was a contributor to the BBC wartime programme *The Brains Trust*.

quite in the job best suited to you: I hope something better is before you, suited to your special genius and traditional idealism. I pray and trust that your health may be restored; I wish I could look forward to special happiness for you in other ways. Would that you had a settled home and had not to spend so much time in restaurants and elsewhere! I have had two more letters from Dad (in America); he is ke pt very busy and thinks he is doing good wo rk.

Michael was named after the Irish Nationalist patriot Michael Davitt (1846–1906), one of the founders of the Irish National Land League. His mother's letter refers to this.

28 July 1943
Congratulations on your fine article on the League and also your Mussolini article of Monday. I thought, as I read the latter article, of another 'thunderclap orator' and 'flaming' journalist whose gentleness and kindness made him beloved in the journalist world and also among his own staff and whose father and mother gave him the name and, it was hoped, the enthusiasms and ideals of another patriot; their hopes have been justified.

With love Mother

In one letter written in reply to his mother's concerns about his lifestyle, Michael wrote:

You must believe me that the picture that you draw of a prodigal son dependent on whisky is totally false. I have no craving for drink and can refrain from it for weeks and often do. I am quite aware of its dangers. I am happy in the world because I am violently interested in all that goes on around me. My chief abiding passion is to discover fresh things about the world. I long for every hour that I can spend with books that thrill me. Those hours are cut monstrously short by many occupations but if you think that I would throw any of them heedlessly away on a stupid habit you are wrong. I do drink occasionally but the chief reason is that it is the easiest way of talking to people I want to meet. You will no doubt say this is weak but I honestly think I am not a better or worse person for it. Whisky is no cure for asthma. It is a cure for tiredness but bed is a better one and I will always prefer it. Therefore, dear Mother, please do not worry about me. If you have more to say about this, please say it. Who has a better right to do so than you. And if you were feeling things which you were afraid to say to me I should be very sorry. As you say I must lead my own life. At the moment it is one of great interest. Don't work too hard and look after yourself.

Eva signed her letters to the newspapers 'Mother of Seven'.

24 April 1942 Pencrebar, Callington, Cornwall. To the editor of the *Evening Standard:*
Sir, I have read with considerable interest and appreciation the leading article of the 22nd inst.

of your paper.[201] Your – I may say – brilliant leader writer views with discernment and a grim irony what is happening in these days of tragedy to the political party system and the House of Commons. It certainly gives to some of your humble readers grave trepidation that the affairs of this country in this unparalleled crisis should be in the hands of such unknown nonentities as those who are almost automatically being added to the House at eve ry by-election. What I cannot understand is that your writer alludes more than once to 'two parties.' Does he ignore intentionally, or through ignorance, the once great Liberal Party, the only party that has always fought for freedom for the individual and for the press and that now perhaps is small numerically because it has not been willing to shed principles but has always fought against bureaucratic and state control and has even given up office at the call of conscience. Liberal principles in action would have saved the world from the abyss into which she has fallen; but the people, in their ignorance and their sloth and their indifference, preferred politics made easy and listened to the catch-cries of To ryism and Labour, both largely reactionary. Please forgive taking your valuable time in this way, but your writer would, I am sure, wish to reply.

Mother of Seven

In 1944 Eva wrote this to the editor of the Daily Herald:

Sir, I always read with considerable interest Michael Foot's column in your paper. Although not a socialist, I admire his fiery sense of justice and his hatred of all hypocrisy. Pe rhaps, as he gets older, he may become a little more merciful to human frailty, while retaining his hatred of abuses. I was somewhat disappointed by the title of his article of Friday 2 February. Who, I wondered, are the miserable, misguided people whose politics are their only hope? On reading further, I found they were the miners of a village of Glamorgan, south Wales; they had built themselves a town hall, library and cinema all in one. An admirable effort surely! Would that there was such a hall in every village! 'It was a monument', says Michael Fo ot, 'to endless sacrifice and political faith; it had transformed the village; it had given health and education to the children and higher wages to the men; in a wo rd, their politics gave them the hope of a release from bondage and triumph over sorrow and despair.'

I would like to remind Michael Foot that there were Methodist chapels in this and every other Welsh village long before the hall was thought of, chapels supported through the despairing years of unemployment by the men and women for whom they, and what they stood for, were as bulwarks of faith and hope; chapels where they had first learnt the ideals of their politics. In something of the same atmosphere I suspect Michael Foot's glowing idealism had rise. Politics and religion are inseparable.

Mother of Seven

---

201. Written by Michael.

28 1943 '100 speeches in 100 days'

Isaac Foot himself believed that his most useful contribution to the war effort was the trip he made to America in 1943 at the request of the British government. Eva gave news of this trip in a letter to Anne.

1 April 1943 Pencrebar

I have a great piece of news; Dad is going to America on a speaking tour – with special attention to the Methodists; he has been asked by Brendan Bracken for the Ministry of Information. It is what I have wanted ever since the war started, as I did not consider his present job adequate. He only had the letter yesterday so I do not know when he will be coming or where he will be going but he will see you all anyhow. Dingle told me a week or two ago that Bracken had spoken to him about it. Dad has been studying American history exclusively for many months and has his subject all taped – 'Our Common Heritage etc.'. He is excited and very pleased; I wondered if he would go, but there is no doubt about that. We will let you know more particulars as soon as we know ourselves.

Nancy Astor wrote Isaac Foot a letter of congratulation:

We are delighted to hear that you are going to America; just a dream come true! And if you aren't the greatest success, I shall get the blame. I have been trying to get you over there for the last two years; not that I did in the end, but the Lord does answer prayers.

Eva wrote a letter to Isaac in London on the eve of his departure for America, which he subsequently copied into his commonplace book:

Dear Dad

I have come home today feeling sad. I don't like the idea of your being away so long and all the risks you run; it would have been so much easier for me if I could have gone with you; but that of course was impossible. I shouldn't feel like this when I have been wanting you to have the opportunity to go for so long; I feel it is your job. You know my special gift for saying the wrong thing at the wrong time in the wrong way but I have heart and it all goes with you; the children only come a close second.

All love and good wishes Eva

Isaac replied:

Thank you for your letter. It is almost worth going away to get a letter like that. I think you know that I have grown fonder and fonder of you as the years go on and there is no one whose company I long for more. You are not less but more my sweetheart than when I first had the incredibly good fo rtune to meet you. I know my weaknesses and unwo rthinesses and I know that if it had not been for your care and discipline I should have made a pretty poor show.

Isaac Foot arrived in America on 21 May 1943. In the next three months he travelled thousands of miles by train and delivered over a hundred speeches and sermons. His letters to Eva, written almost daily, give details of his travels and experiences. The first stage of his tour was in the area around the Midwest and the Great Lakes, where American Methodism had its greatest support. During this time he was addressing various Methodist conferences held in the different American states.

```
                                        May 21, 1943
            METHODIST CONFERENCE ITINERARY

            THE RT. HON. ISAAC FOOT

                    ***

TUE.                                                        11:30 p.m.
WED., MAY 25  -  Leave New York, Grand Central Station - 3:05 p.m.
Wed.                                                 3:57 a.m.
THU., " 27  -  Arrive Muncie, Indiana - 6:18 a.m.

Thu. " 27  -  Speak at North Indiana Conference

                Presiding Bishop - Bishop Titus Lowe
                                   305 Underwriters Bldg.
                                   Indianapolis, Ind.

SAT.,   " 29  -  Leave Muncie, Indiana - 10:37 a.m.
                 Arrive Indianapolis, Indiana - 11:50 a.m.
                 Leave        "           "   - 1:25 p.m.
                 Arrive Chicago, Ill., Central Station - 6:00 p.m.
                 Leave     "      "  , Union      "    - 9:00 p.m.

SUN.,   " 30  -  Arrive Minneapolis, Minnesota - 8:00 a.m.

WED., JUN 2  -  Speak at Northern Minnesota Conference

                Presiding Bishop - Bishop Ralph S. Cushman
                                   1987 Summit Avenue
                                   St. Paul, Minn.

THU.,   " 3  -  Leave Minneapolis, Minn. - 8:00 a.m.
                Arrive Chicago, Ill., Union Station - 2:55 p.m.
                Leave      "     "  , LaSalle St. " - 11:30 p.m.

FRI.,   " 4  -  Arrive Rochester, N.Y. - 12:27 p.m.

SAT.,   " 5  -  Speak at Genesee Conference

                Presiding Bishop - Bishop Charles W. Flint
                                   Hotel Statler
                                   Buffalo, N.Y.

                Leave Rochester, N.Y. - 7:30 p.m.
                Arrive Auburn, N.Y. - 10:20 p.m.
                            Central
SUN.,   " 6  -  Speak at/New York. Conference

                Presiding Bishop - Bishop James H. Straughn
                                   Methodist Center
                                   Seventh Ave. at Smithfield
                                   Pittsburgh, Pa.
```

Isaac Foot's Methodist Conference itinerary on the first stage of his speaking tour of the USA in 1943.

Map of the USA showing the places visited by Isaac Foot in 1943.

Isaac wrote his first letter home to Eva on 22 May 1943. She did not receive it until 30 June.

22 May 1943 Roosevelt Hotel, Madison Avenue, New York
Dearest

I reached this hotel last night. It is a good hotel but a bit expensive. Eve rything is expensive here, and, were it not for the entertainment I shall be receiving I should not be able to manage on the allowance of 12 dollars a day. I went along to the headqu a rters here and found that the first engagement was at Worc e s t e r,Massachusetts, where I am expected to preach, if you please, at the Conference Session tomorrow morning. I have spent the afternoon getting up my sermon notes. I go by sleeper. Apparently there are a series of Methodist confe r-ences for the several states and I am appointed to speak in Indiana, Minneapolis, New Yo rk.

23 May 1943 Hotel Bancroft, Worcester, Massachusetts
Dearest

I got here through the night and this morning, Sunday, I preached the Conference Sermon at Wesley Church – attendance 1,668 people, bishops, ministers, choir of 100, 40 collections. After a long struggle, I succeeded in resisting wearing a gown. For the first time in its history a gown-less preacher took the pulpit. I think I shall go to the Church of Rome to get a simpler form of service! My sermon on 'Hope' seemed to please them all. For the first time in history the Conference Sermon was preached by someone other than the President! I was introduced this morning with solemn ceremony, the church crowded to the roof and a really magnificent building. I go back to New York tomorrow and then start on my travels to places I never heard of before. Will you please keep these letters as a record of my journeyings.

28 May 1943 Hotel Roberts, Muncie, Indiana
Dearest

This is a remarkable little city with a magnificent Methodist chapel where the conference is meeting. I gave my address to the conference yesterday morning and spoke for about 40 minutes to about 1,300 people, the church being crowded. The conference meetings are crowded from day to day and I should regard Methodism here as being about as strong as Methodism was with us forty years ago. The devotion was led this morning by a Negro pastor who sang 'Were You There When They Crucified My Lord?' – just as well as Paul Robeson. I do not get very much time for reading or preparation. Probably my best work is talking with the people at lunch, dinner etc. There seems the friendliest feeling towards England. I think my visit is fully justifying itself.

31 May 1943 Curtis Hotel, Minneapolis

Dearest

I left Muncie, in Indiana, on Saturday morning. The bishop called on me after Devotion at the church on Saturday morning and I had about six minutes in bidding the conference farewell. The whole conference stood up while I departed – most embarrassing. The travelling on Saturday was pretty bad. I got into the train from Indianapolis to Chicago on my way here. The carriage was like Jericho in the last war. Hell with the lid on. I arrived here yesterday, Sunday morning. I preached both morning and evening at two different semi-suburban churches. I have adapted my 'Philemon' sermon and it went quite well both times! The conference does not start here until Wednesday, when I address the opening session. My engagements on this first part of my tour are mostly in the north-west – at the head of the Mississippi River – on the other side of the Allegheny Mountains – a very important part of the U.S. – both historically and geographically – and very different from New England and New York etc.

5 June 1943 Hotel Rochester, Rochester, New York

I addressed the conference here this morning and got on alright – and tomorrow I preach the Conference Sermon, which is usually taken by the bishop. The service is to be broadcast – so I shall have a potential audience of about a million or so. Those who do not turn off their tape will probably hear about Philemon and Onesimus [202] – slightly altered and adapted. My programme for July is now being worked out and I am then to go to Virginia, Kentucky, Georgia, South Carolina and so on. I have done about 3,000 miles of travel so far in America and have been here 16 days. By the time I have finished the tour I shall have seen far more of America than most Americans have done.

'Britain Says U.S. Casual about the War' – interview with Isaac Foot

Somewhere in the soft voice and delayed-action humour of the Rt Hon. Isaac Foot one bumps into blue British steel that turned back the Luftwaffe in the Battle of Britain. Foot is in America on various missions for the British government and will speak before the Genesee Annual Conference at West Avenue Methodist Church. But today, in the privacy of his hotel room, he was unofficial, informal and delightfully blunt. 'You Americans', he insisted, ' do not yet realize the urgency of the war. You are too far from the battle lines. I scanned New York papers for details on the war and what do I find? Jack Dempsey's divorce action. American publishers have ten times more newsprint than Britons and they devote only one-tenth of it to the war news. England devotes

---

202. Philemon was the owner of the slave Onesimus, who ran away and sought refuge with Paul, who converted him. Paul's Epistle to Philemon was an appeal, begging him to be merciful to his runaway slave.

four-fifths of her space to war news. There is little interest in a prize fighter's domestic squabbles in a country where any day a bomb is likely to wipe out a man, his family and his home between tea and toast at the breakfast table. Your coal strike is a luxury which wouldn't have happened in England because England couldn't afford it. A strike of any kind in England just now is simply outside the realm of possibility.' Foot then drove his point home: 'There were no strikes in America on the morning after Pearl Harbor!' The Briton is flabbergasted by the casualness of American wartime routine, by the wealth here of food and other supplies, by American high prices. 'I can live much more cheaply in England. In England people are discouraged from buying.' Typically British, he condemned American tea brewers: 'You have not learned that the pot must be warm before you put in the tea, which must be just covered with boiling water and allowed to soak for one minute. Then add remaining amount of water – be sure it's boiling – and let it steep.'

Foot is no parlour observer. He was in Parliament, a member of the King's Privy Council and the India Committee. One son edits a London newspaper, a second holds office in the Churchill government, a third was at Dunkirk and came out alive, a fourth is in the army and a fifth in North Africa. He has two daughters. One runs a farm in England. The other works for the government in Palestine. 'There will be a family reunion after the war,' he pledges.[203]

15 June 1943 Hotel La Salle, South Bend, Indiana

On my arrival here, after my night journey, I had to go at once to be introduced by Bishop Lowe to the conference. It is the conference for north-west Indiana. Methodism is very strong in Indiana and they have three conferences to cover different parts of the state and I am taking part in all three. My address seemed to give much pleasure, especially to the bishop. On the Sunday morning I preached at Mishawaka, about 6 miles away. The singing was perfect, a nice large roomy church – full to the door – about 800 people. The young minister seemed overjoyed to have me there and the reception of people who wanted to shake hands – about 100 – lasted about half an hour. Then, in the evening I spoke about an hour, at the final meeting of the North-West Indiana Conference here. Again sweltering heat, most men sitting with their coats off, everybody fanning themselves with the service paper but it was a big meeting and my address as half a speech and half a sermon. The Englishman – other than the businessman on business – is a rare thing in a place like this. They want to know what is really happening in England and how the people have stood up to things. So far there has been nothing but praise for England and an apparent strong desire for good relations etc.

203. *Rochester Times*, 5 June 1943.

17 June 1943 Hotel Blackhawk, Davenport, Iowa
Dearest

Michigan is crowded with Cornish people. Out of the eight ministers in the bishop's cabinet, with whom I had breakfast yesterday morning, six were born in Cornwall. Yesterday I
spoke to any number of Cornish people from St Neot, St Ives, Penzance, St Austell. The
superintendent of the district has been at Callington. There is one Methodist church at
Detroit, St Paul's, made up nearly entirely of Cornish people. These Methodist conferences
provide me with big meetings wherever I go and I don't suppose any other Englishman has
ever had the opportunity of speaking in the Middle West and the Mississippi valley as I
have done. It is this district that turned isolationist and against Woodrow Wilson. It is
therefore a good thing that I am speaking here and the Methodists are so strong here that
they could do anything if they had a proper strategy. I have developed my speech pretty
well by this time. The difficulty generally is to get what I have to say in the allotted time.
The bishop, after I had spoken today, asked all those present of English birth to stand up.
About 1 in 5 stood up. I said the bishop's request was quite unnecessary as I had been able
to pick them out while I was speaking by the special radiance on their faces! All my meetings start with 'All hail the power of Jesus' name'! This gives me my introduction on the
hymn 'Diadem' sung at the Bradford Station – at Kansas City – and every state I now enter.
This leads up to the Mayflower Compact of 1621 on to the first words, 'In the Name of
God Amen'. Also the Plymouth motto 'Turris Fortissima Est Nomen Jehova'.[204] This links
up the new Plymouth and the old.

24 June 1943 La Salle Hotel, Chicago
Dearest

I am, as you will see, at Chicago. I got to Lakeside, Ohio, on Tuesday. It is a wonderful place
on the Lake Erie – a vast holiday property belonging to the Methodists. I spoke for an hour
in the auditorium yesterday. We had about 2,000 people present! One of the ministers was
formerly at Wesley when I was a youth and he was overjoyed to see me. On the whole, yesterday was my best meeting I think. I speak tonight as the only speaker at the Temple, a
huge Methodist building at the centre of the city. I have worn my new clothes today for the
first time. I now wear a belt! – assisted by braces, suspenders in this country, and a soft
shirt. I shall soon be a cowboy. My meetings on the first part of my tour have been most
remarkable. I have been welcomed as if I were the President of the Conference. My addresses have, I think, improved in quality and sometimes the audiences insist upon my standing up to acknowledge their applause. My head hasn't swollen and in fact I am much thin-
ner than when I arrived in America and I have lost pounds in weight. I am now appearing

---

204. 'The Name of Jehova is the Strongest Tower' (Proverbs 18:10).

in my American clothes, no waistcoat and stiff collar. Everywhere I go there is a long row of people with English associations who want to shake hands. Yesterday a minister came up who was a local preacher with my father. He was born in Plymouth. Another was a Hoe Grammar School boy who was there with me.

I don't know what the next month will be like but my engagements will not be with the Methodist conferences. Probably I shall be having a much quieter time, certainly not such crowds. Anyhow, the first 36 days have been a remarkable experience. Probably no one else – if they had come as a stranger – could have been given the same reception and could have reached such large companies. Beside that, the preaching has given me a much larger constituency than I should have had only with the meetings. The conditions have been difficult – about one night in four in the train and this heat which soaks my shirts. I am glad to have got through the past five weeks and to have completed the programme, but I shouldn't like to have to do it again. Anyhow, I feel the effort of getting away has been amply justified even if I do nothing more and the sacrifice has been worthwhile. You know how irritable and miserable I am just before speaking and preaching. Well I have been constantly preparing, fearing to let an occasion down. So far I have not had any bad flop.

In the second stage of Isaac Foot's tour, begun on 4 July 1943, he travelled further south and to the far west.

4 July 1943 Cosmos Club, Washington, D.C.

I wrote you on Saturday afternoon just before my big day here. Well, it's over thank God. Yesterday morning I preached at the Temple Methodist Chapel. About 1,500 present, including about 100 standing and some hundreds turned away. For the second time I resisted the urgent invitation of the minister to wear a gown. My sermon went off alright and my salutation to the Stars and Stripes went down really well. I drew the picture of the Swastika being put up over one capital after another – every capital city so outraged being recited in slow succession, then the point that the bloody rag was to be set up over London, the Abbey, St Paul's etc. but, instead of the Swastika, the Skull and Crossbones of the Gestapo – another flag over Westminster Abbey. Today is a public holiday – Independence Day. On Tuesday I had an hour with Halifax.[205] A very interesting talk. I had the chance of telling him something about Methodism. I think I have made the position clearer and better between the embassy and American Methodism. He said he would like to meet the Methodist Board of Bishops later on. I am going to lay the wreath on Lothian's grave before I leave here.[206] The press interview me practically everywhere and I have been pho-

---

205. Lord Halifax (1881-1959), British ambassador to Washington 1941-6.
206. Lord Lothian, the former British ambassador to Washington, had been a friend and Liberal colleague of Isaac's. He died suddenly in 1940. Isaac Foot took a twig from a fir tree Lothian had planted at Pencrebar to put on his grave at Arlington.

tographed to death. The success of my visit is far beyond anything I had anticipated. If I have any form, I think I am speaking at the top of it. The people love to hear about England and they lap up any literary quotation like new milk. All I can now do is to concentrate on this job – on the whole I suppose the best single piece of work I have ever done for my country.

24 July 1943 Henry Grady Hotel, Atlanta
Dearest

A most interesting thing has happened at Chicago. In some of my meetings I have quoted 'London Bridge Is Falling Down, My Fair Lady'. A minister heard me quote it in New York and, when he heard me say it was written by a Chicago lady, he said he would find out the lady and would arrange for her to attend the Chicago conference and to receive a gift of flowers from me. Sure enough he rooted her out after much difficulty. She accepted the invitation to attend the Fellowship Luncheon of the Lay Leaders. I made a most gracious and felicitous speech – really one of my tip-top efforts and presented a gorgeous bouquet of roses to the lady – about 55 years old – very charming. She made an excellent speech in reply. I said I had noticed the poem quoted in a letter to the *Times* in December 1940 and had passed it on to Michael for the *Evening Standard* after writing it in my commonplace book. Apparently the little poem has had a great vogue in Canada – it has been printed and reprinted and set to music. I took some poems to make my luncheon speech of thanks equal to the occasion and for 10 minutes or so I soared into the empyrean. 'The little piece of wood so little significant but when the wood is sharpened into the shaft of an arrow and feathered with poesy, then how swift its course and how far its flight!' Anyhow the folk were very pleased, the press took notice of the event and we were photographed. Another literary excitement! You remember my constant quotation of the poem of Anderson M. Scruggs: 'Glory to them the toilers of the earth'. I noticed he was from Georgia. Today I thought he might be living in Atlanta. I looked up the name 'Scruggs' in the telephone book and, lo and behold, there was the name – 'Anderson M. Scruggs'. I rang him up and told him of my long interest in his poem and asked if I might call to see him. He seemed overjoyed at my request and I am going to his place on Tuesday. He says he will try to come to hear me preach tomorrow.

26 July 1943 Henry Grady Hotel, Atlanta
Dearest

The Atlanta engagements have gone off like a house on fire! I preached in a large church here in the city in the morning and intended to speak at the open-air service at the Emory University in the evening. I found at the last moment that they preferred a sermon so I took

N-742   THE CROSS AT LAKE JUNALUSKA, N. C.

E-4489

The cross at Junaluska erected by the Wesley Bible Class Federation of the Western North Carolina Methodist Conference, where Isaac Foot spoke to the Methodist Conference in 1943.

'On Seeing a Marble Building Cleaned': Anderson Scruggs's poem, one of Isaac Foot's favourites for quotation, written out in his American commonplace book and signed by the author in Atlanta on 27 July 1943.

the same subject – 'Hope' – with considerable adaptations. The Methodists have about 50 churches here in this one city of about 300,000 people. It was only at the close of the meetings that I heard of Mussolini! I flung my hat in the air. What a deliverance!![207] This morning I spoke at the Methodist ministers' meeting and answered questions. Then I spoke at the Rota ry Lunch – a crowded house with leaders of business, newspapers, churches etc. – a really big occasion. I altered my address to deal with Mussolini and served a great hit with the qu otation of 1 Kings, chapter 21, verses 17–19 and also with the *Star* leading article on the fall of Addis Ababa. Look this passage up. There is something about these South people that is very attractive. I wired to Brendan Bracken last week saying my expectations of service here have been exceeded a hundredfold. On the whole the best job in my life.

6 August 1943 The Terrace Hotel, Lake Junaluska, North Carolina

On Monday I leave for the Far West and my program includes Los Angeles, San Francisco, Denver and I finish my speaking tour at Detroit, where I preach on August 30 at the church run entirely

207. The Allied invasion of Italy and Mussolini's overthrow.

by Cornish people. The bulk of my work has been done! I have put all I have into this job. Sometimes I have done better than at others and, at the first, I had to get into my stride, but my speeches have, I think, improved as I have gone on. The response of the people has been quite humbling to me. The affection of the people for England and the sympathy for the suffering is most touching. I have had to devote all my mind to this work and have concentrated everything upon the successive engagements and on the whole it is the best job I have done in my life and it has been in a good cause. The visit in 1939 seems to be remembered by everybody who was there.[208] That gave me an introduction to the Methodist people that 20 years' effort would not have secured otherwise. The travelling at times has been a trial of physical endurance. The excessive heat and the effort of lugging about my bags when no porters were available has exhausted every ounce of my strength, but I did not expect a picnic when I came over and the rough has been small compared with the smooth. I have never for one moment regretted my decision to come and I don't want to be thanked for this effort for my country during the war. I hope to get back alright but, even if I don't, this was the thing it was right to do.

11 August 1943 On the train over the Rockies

I am in the train now. I get to Los Angeles tomorrow morning. The railway is the single longest journey in America – 2,300 miles. The train, called the Super Chief, is the last word in convenience. The train with 2 massive engines has to cross the Rockies and has to make an ascent of over 7,000 feet. It is made up of about 18 immense coaches and has a restaurant car, barber's shop and everything. I get to Los Angeles tomorrow morning and leave there for San Francisco on Sunday evening. I then go to Denver in Colorado and I then go to Detroit where my program ends. I am rather nervous about the Far West engagements. I don't know how the people there will compare with the others. This railway journey is an experience one will never forget. We are now travelling over an immense tableland about 5,000 feet above sea level. The making of this railway to the Pacific coast was one of America's greatest achievements. I sometimes think this journey of mine is just a dream. By the time I get back I shall have been in about 30 states and spoken in 18 of them!

17 August 1943 San Francisco

I reached Los Angeles last Thursday and my programme there was most interesting. On Sunday morning I preached to about 1,800 people and the service was broadcast. I also broadcast on the Saturday afternoon – a sort of Brains Trust on the Forces Freedoms. Previously I addressed a large assembly at the University of California – about a thousand people – mostly young servicemen. Then I came to San Francisco. I addressed a Club Luncheon yesterday, broadcast today and spoke at a public meeting tonight. California is beautiful beyond all

---

208. Isaac and Eva Foot had visited Kansas City in 1939 to attend the Methodist Conference.

description. No wo rds can picture it. Sir Francis Drake touched the coast here and I have made the most of the fact. I went out to see Drake's Bay – the place where Sir Francis Drake is supposed to have landed in 1577. The tour is still ve ry successful – amazingly so. I have now passed through 31 out of the 48 states. I have taken 81 speaking engagements, small and large, including the sermons. I cannot be accused of idleness anyway.

25 August 1943 Brown Palace Hotel, Denver, Colorado

On Saturday last I received from Bishop Oxnam a letter of thanks on behalf of the Board of Bishops. The letter is couched in most generous terms. I have sent a copy to Dingle and have asked him to let you have a copy. It contains a message to the British Methodist Church and to the world in general. Bishop Oxnam says that, with the exception of Winston Churchill, no single person has done more than I to strengthen good relations between the two peoples etc. I suppose, as far as Methodism is concerned, this may be true. No one has had anything like the same opportunity. I expect it is impossible for you to realise how far I have travelled and the area I have covered. Even Americans seem amazed at my program and my itinerary. I should think the British government has spent about £500 on my travelling! Still I think they have had their money's worth. I have not spared myself and have accepted every request made to me.

Colorado has been a new experience. Pacifism and isolationism are rife there particularly among some Methodist ministers and the Church leadership there is not very friendly to England. Generally I have been working with ministers of British parentage or ancestry, but some of the ministers here are of German ancestry. Naturally they regard the war from a completely different point of view. Of course, I am very pleased to get such a letter but you need not think I am getting swollen headed. Because of the pacifist atmosphere at Denver I took special care with my speeches and tried to be at the top of my form.

Bishop Oxnam's letter from the Council of Methodist Bishops in America
Within a few days you will complete the all-too-heavy schedule we arranged for you and will be en route to England. On behalf of the Council of Bishops of the Methodist Church, may I express our deepest appreciation of your extraordinary contribution to us. In a little more than a hundred days you have delivered nearly 100 addresses, visiting 15 of our states, east, north, west and south. I am writing with care when I use the word 'extraordinary' in connection with your service. I know of no single visitor, save only the Prime Minister, who has had a greater influence in deepening the friendship of the English and the American people. Throughout your addresses you have stressed the necessity of translating our ethical ideals into realities. But the ethical ideals you have proclaimed are those that lie at the heart of the religion of Jesus. The result is your message has come with the authority of our faith and at the same time has reached the minds and hearts of the

American people whose real spirit is democratic. We have come to know England better because of you. The ideals for which this war is waged stood out in bold relief. You have steeled our resolve to see the conflict through to the bitter end. But you have done much more than that. You have held before us the vision of an ordered world, grounded in justice and brotherhood. I sincerely trust that you will convey to our Methodist people in Britain and to all others whom you may meet the love of our people and assure them that the ties of a common language, a common objective and a common faith are of such a nature as to insure our unity in the hours when we shall face problems at once baffling and highly complex, problems that we intend to solve in the interests of an organised world. We are deeply indebted to you, Sir, and shall long remember your messages phrased in such charming English and bearing such penetrating insight.

In real respect, believe me, ever sincerely yours, G. Bromley Oxnam, Secretary, the Council of Bishops of the Methodist Church, Boston Area.

Isaac Foot's interview in Old Colony Memorial, a weekly newspaper in Plymouth, Massachusetts
Mr Foot was eulogized as a personality of unforgettable stimulation, inspiration and sincerity with an inexhaustible knowledge of British and American history, the Bible and current affairs. In a reply to a query as to the fate of his home town, Mr Foot said that all the historic part of Plymouth had been destroyed, including his own property, and hoped that some day some person of wealth and funds, raised through contributions, would enable a replica of the statue of Sir Francis Drake which stands on Plymouth Hoe to be erected in Plymouth, Mass., a perpetual reminder of the friendship between the two countries: 'How fitting it would be that there across the ocean the statue of this man whose defeat of the Spanish Armada determined that America would be an English country, should look from one Plymouth to the other.'

Questioned as to what was the principal need in the post-war period to ensure peace among mankind Mr Foot said: 'Moral leadership. The world is learning that material possessions are not the first thing in life. The war will be the greatest test for the Christian community everywhere as to the leadership they can give to the politician. The United States must lead in the post-war period.'

Asked as to his impressions of America, Mr Foot said that he was impressed by the apparent super-abundance of food, the unscarred countryside, the undevastated cities, and the few signs of war. He said he had to keep reminding himself that there was a war, whereas in England the people could not forget the war.[209]

---

209. 25 September 1943.

Eva's letters to Anne tell of Isaac's return home
19 October 1943

It was wonderful to have Dad safely home and full of news of you; I have to keep on asking him for more details of you all; he enjoyed the children immensely and his stays with you. However he travelled round America by himself with all his junk will always remain a mystery! I would love to have gone, but I couldn't have stood the heat or the railway travelling. He was thrilled with the whole experience and wouldn't have missed it for worlds, though it was very strenuous; I would not have believed he could have done it.

Cromwell and Lincoln: a comparison

MICHAEL: In 1944 my father gave a lecture to the Royal Society of Literature in which he compared his two great heroes, Abraham Lincoln and Oliver Cromwell, and it was one of his great prides that, all during the period of the Second World War from 1939 to 1945, when the statues of some lesser people were moved into safe underground cellars for protection, that the statues of Oliver Cromwell and Abraham Lincoln still stood in Parliament Square. My father used to say that he thought they often had conversations between one another, what he describes as 'high colloquy'. In 1943, right across America, he had been sending a message about the need for cooperation and understanding between liberal America and Britain in the war. Now in 1944 he was seeking to interpret the events of the past in a way which would lead the whole world to a more liberal future. We publish here excerpts from this lecture.

Statue of Abraham Lincoln near the Houses of Parliament, with American servicemen looking on.

Statue of Oliver Cromwell in Parliament Square.

In close proximity, in the heart of the greatest city in the world, stand the statues of Oliver Cromwell and Abraham Lincoln; the one on guard outside the Houses of Parliament, the other overlooking the threshold of the Abbey. The one, of the Englishman, only erected after keen and bitter controversy; the other, of the American, given his place of central honour amid general approval and acclaim. Both statues have stood there during all the years of war, and, whilst we have found places of temporary shelter for the statues of Charles I and George III, Oliver, the Lord Protector, and Lincoln, the sixteenth President of the United States, have kept their place, and, whilst much around them has suffered, they themselves have looked on, so far, unscathed. Cromwell stands there, holding the Bible and his sword. Had a Bible and sword been placed likewise in the hands of Lincoln the symbols would have been equally fitting. I like to think that when night falls upon the great city, these two men join in high colloquy. Born in different centuries and in different lands, they would have no difficulty in understanding each other, holding in common their language, their inspiration, and their purpose.

This paper deals with two great men. If Cromwell or Lincoln had been born ten years earlier, or ten years later, the likelihood is we should never have heard of either of them. Some would say it was the mere chance of history that, when the Civil War, with all its immense consequences to England and the world, broke out in 1642, Oliver Cromwell was there, aged forty-three, in the plenitude of his capacity, and that when Stephen Douglas, in 1854, proposed the repeal of the Missouri Compromise, Abraham Lincoln was there, at the age of forty-five, at the precise moment when he was best fitted to challenge Douglas and all the implications of his policy.[210] These circumstances, which we might dismiss as mere chance, were, in fact, accepted by both men as the mark of a high vocation, and, rightly or wrongly, they regarded themselves as instruments prepared and fitted to meet the challenge which they could only ignore at the peril of their souls.

The noblest tribute to Cromwell in this generation has been made not in this country, but in America, where Professor Wilbur C. Abbott has published *The Writings and Speeches of Oliver Cromwell*. Harvard University is in New England, and New England and Oliver Cromwell have a close association. From the first, Oliver took an immense interest in the colonies. New England lay very close to his heart. Many of his nearest friends had been driven out of England and had gone to America. Oliver knew why they had gone. Again and again he speaks of the enterprise of these kindred spirits who had set out to find a home where they could enjoy a freedom of conscience and of religious practice denied to them in their own country. He was indeed once on the point of emigrating there himself. 'So near,' comments Clarendon[211] mournfully, 'So near was the poor Kingdom at that time

---

210. The Missouri Compromise of 1820 had limited the spread of slavery in certain states. Lincoln led the opposition to its repeal by the leading Illinois Senator, Stephen Douglas.
211. Edward Hyde, first Earl of Clarendon (1609–1674), a historian and statesman who supported the Royalist cause in the English Civil War.

to its deliverance.'

Had it not been for Cromwell the history of New England would have been very different. The Civil War resulted as it did because of Cromwell's leadership. On that all the authorities are agreed. And if, as Professor Trevelyan contends,[212] the result of the Civil War decided the whole future of England, then, in a sense, Cromwell enabled New England with her free institutions to survive, and, in sustaining New England, he made possible that son of Massachusetts, Abraham Lincoln. However that may be, Cromwell's interest in New England was repaid a thousandfold. Defamed here, he was honoured there. When the Commonwealth crashed in England its ideals were preserved in America. There even the regicides found asylum. The epilogue to *Samson Agonistes* is the history of the United States of America. The fact that Cromwell and Milton were Englishmen, says Bryce,[213] could never be forgotten even when the ties between the two countries were strained to breaking point. The place Cromwell takes in America and that Lincoln takes in Britain is something more than an academic question and a great deal more than a mere literary theme. It is an American historian who has told us that the influence of a common inheritance in literature has counted most heavily just at those times when political differences might have led to war. The Atlantic is a wide ocean. Between the two countries we need to build and maintain all the bridges we can. Two of these bridges today are the American admiration for Oliver Cromwell and the British admiration for Abraham Lincoln.

At about the same stage in their lives each of them came to public eminence and national fame. It was at the age of forty-five that Cromwell first became famous at Marston Moor, and it was at the age of forty-nine that Lincoln first gained national attention as the result of the debates with Stephen Douglas in the senatorial contest in Illinois. Cromwell was fifty-two years old when, after the battle of Worcester, he became the first man in England, and Lincoln was fifty-one when he was elected President. At the age of fifty-four Oliver became Protector, and at fifty-five Lincoln was re-elected for the Presidency. Cromwell died in his fifty-ninth year, Lincoln in his fifty-seventh. Both men had about five years of power and supreme eminence. Both died in such a manner and at such a time that their death was regarded by many of their contemporaries as a deep national loss. These two men, so alike in the development of their lives, so alike in the seeming untimeliness of their death, were alike too in this – they were both the man of a crisis. But for the outbreak of the Civil War in this country it is most unlikely that we should ever have read of Oliver Cromwell. Again, if there had been no repeal of the Missouri Compromise, there would have been, as far as history is concerned, no Abraham Lincoln. The crisis was, for both men, in the true sense of the word, a judgement. Each man responded in his own fashion to the special challenge of his time, and, in the hour of his

212. G. M. Trevelyan (1876–1962), English historian, Master of Trinity College, Cambridge 1940–51.
213. James Bryce (1838–1922), historian and politician.

nation's emergency, each man became the incarnation of the movement of the people.

Both men had a deep reverence for the law, and regarded the honest administration of justice as an inescapable obligation. It is remarkable how the desire for the reform of the law was expressed in almost identical language. Both men knew the value of public opinion and always relied upon it. Early in his recorded speeches Cromwell reveals his concern to keep in touch with public sentiment: 'For in the government of nations that which is to be looked after is the affections of the people.' Lincoln, as far as we know, never read Cromwell's words, but he was of the same mind. His opponents, as well as his admirers, paid constant tribute to his understanding of the mind and temper of the people, and his patient effort to make crystal clear to them what were his purposes and policy: 'Public opinion settles every question here; any policy to be permanent must have public opinion at the bottom – something in accordance with the human mind as it is.' That is what Lincoln said at Hartford, Connecticut, on his way from Springfield to the White House.

Both men, in their desire to gain the support of public sentiment, looked to the common people. 'The common man' is the most frequently used term in international politics today, but the words are not the invention of our century. Cromwell knew something about the phrase. There is the famous apology for the troops he loved to lead: 'I had rather have a plain russet-coated Captain that knows what he fights for, and loves what he knows, than that which you call a gentleman and is nothing else. I honour a gentleman that is so indeed.' Plain men; the plain people – Lincoln knew the meaning of those words if ever man did. Shortly after the outbreak of the war he summons the special session of Congress and in his message he says:

> I am most happy to believe that the plain people understand and appreciate this. It is worthy of note that, while in this the government's hour of trial, large numbers of those in the army and navy who have been favoured with offices have resigned and proved false to the hand that pampered them, not one common soldier or common sailor is known to have deserted his flag. The greatest honour and the most important fact of all is the unanimous firmness of the common soldiers and the common sailors ... This is the patriotic instinct of the plain people.

I suppose it is a commonplace to say that both Cromwell and Lincoln were great patriots and devoted lovers of their country. Yet the vision of both men stretched far beyond their own frontiers. They were conscious of the vocation of their nation in the world. During the debate in the Council of State in 1654 Cromwell pleaded: 'God has not brought us hither where we are but to consider the work we have to do in the world as well as at home.' He begins his speech at the opening of his first Protectorate Parliament on September 4, 1654, with the proud words: 'You are met here on the greatest occasion that I believe England ever saw, having upon your shoulders the interest of three great nations, with the territories belonging to them. And truly, I believe I may say it without an hyperbole, you have upon your shoulders the interest of all Christian people in the world.' The eyes of the Protestant world turned towards him as, before, men had looked for protection to Gustavus Adolphus.[214] The Jews began to think of the possibility of Oliver being the long-promised Messiah, the Huguenots gathered behind his 'crested and prevailing name' as the pilgrims in the Allegory gathered behind Mr Greatheart, and the persecuted flock in the Vaudois valleys found their only shelter in the championship of Oliver Cromwell, the only Englishman of that time, probably, of whom they had ever heard. And just as Cromwell would have had little sympathy with the war cry 'England for the English', Abraham Lincoln could never have become the patron saint of those who love to call themselves 100 per cent Americans. Whilst on his way to Washington after his election Lincoln broke his journey to speak at Philadelphia, and he asked his audience to remember the world-wide significance of the Declaration of Independence: 'It was not the mere matter of separation of the colonies from the motherland, but that sentiment in the Declaration of Independence which gave liberty not only to the people of this country, but hope to all the world for all future time.' 'This issue', he said in his message to Congress in July 1861, 'embraces more than the fate of the United States.' It was an issue affecting what he called 'the whole family of man'. In what many regard as his supreme utterance, that of the Gettysburg Cemetery in 1863, he spoke of certain precious things which must not be allowed to 'perish from the earth'.

In the tragic irony of events these two men, both profound lovers of peace, were called by hard circumstance to control and sustain a long and dreadful war. It was the destiny of each man to be called upon to carry on a war which, as it developed, seemed ultimately to depend upon his single will and resolution. If Cromwell had failed the Civil War would almost certainly have ended with the armed return of the Stuarts, sustained in part by forces from Scotland and Ireland as well as foreign powers. At times the whole conflict seemed to depend upon the single resolution of Oliver. 'He was a strong man,' so runs one tribute, 'in the dark perils of war, in the high places of the field, hope shone on him like a pillar of fire when it had gone out from all others.' That tribute can with equal force be given to Lincoln. Nothing is more manifest than that if this one man's hope had failed – to use a phrase of George Washington's in the hour of his extremity – 'the bottom would have fallen out of the whole business'. The resolution of Lincoln seemed to be strengthened under the blows of successive defeat. When things looked at their worst he wrote down these words with great deliberation: 'I expect to maintain this contest until successful, or till I die, or am conquered, or my term expires, or Congress or the country forsake me.'

What sustained both men was their belief in their cause. 'This Cause, this Business' – these words were constantly on Cromwell's lips. Each man came to believe that he was the

214. Gustavus Adolphus (1594–1632), King of Sweden from 1611 until his death in battle, famous as a military commander.

trustee, and, in the circumstances, almost the sole trustee of the 'cause'. There developed most clearly in both these men a deep sense of personal obligation. Each man spoke frequently of the oath that he had taken, the one as Protector, the other as President. Once Lincoln was challenged on his action in enlisting Negroes as soldiers, and when he replied at Baltimore in April 1864, he set out the grounds of his obligation: 'Upon a clear conviction of duty I resolved to turn that element of strength to account; and I am responsible for it to the American people, to the Christian world, to history, and in my final account to God.' Both men made their appeal to what they called principle. Speaking at the opening of the Little Parliament, Cromwell said:

> And as I have said elsewhere, if I were to choose the meanest officer in the Army or Commonwealth I would choose a godly man that hath principles, especially where a trust is to be committed, because I know where to have a man that hath principles. I believe if any man of you should choose a servant you would do so, and I would all our Magistrates were so chosen.

Both men were lovers of liberty and haters of arbitrary power. Their belief in democracy rested not on any political theory, but on their belief in the supreme value of human personality. To Cromwell every man was an immortal soul, created by God in his own image. His argument for toleration was never in the language of the mass or the class, but always in the terms of the individual: 'If the poorest Christian, the most mistaken Christian, should desire to live peaceably and quietly under you, soberly and humbly desire to lead a life in goodness and honesty, let him be protected.' So he pleaded with the Little Parliament in 1653. And again in one of his moods of religious eloquence: 'The mind is the man.' So, too, with Lincoln. With him the slavery issue came down to rest ultimately on the one question – the question he put again and again to the people of America and to his own conscience. That question was 'whether the Negro is not or is a man'.

Cromwell and Lincoln both found the basis for all their political beliefs in their religion. Their love of liberty, their toleration, their conception of the sovereignty of the individual conscience, all ultimately rested on that foundation. Cromwell was, of course, primarily and finally a religious man. There are many who, whilst they recognise the religion of Cromwell, have their doubts of Lincoln in this regard. If, however, Lincoln was not a man of deep and sincere religious belief there is no explanation of the greater part of his public life. Upon the walls of the superb memorial at Washington are inscribed the Gettysburg speech on Lincoln's right hand, and the Second Inaugural on the left. If he was not a religious man those majestic words would seem to be mockery and blasphemy. Both men avowed themselves to be the instrument of the Almighty. They use the word 'instrument' again and again. They spoke frequently of their own prayers to God, and constantly besought for themselves the prayers of others.

Both men believed in what Cromwell called 'providences'. Both desired most earnestly to know what was the will of God and, when they learned what that will was, they sought to do it. They relied for their guidance on the teaching of events and on their interpretation of history. This was with Oliver his constant theme, and side by side with his utterances we can set Lincoln's reply to the deputation from Chicago, 'Whatever shall appear to be God's will, I will do', and his statement to his cabinet that he accepted the result of the battle of Antietam as the sign given by God for the proclamation of emancipation. Both looked to events for direction and guidance. Cromwell found the will of God revealed to him in the unbroken series of successive victories from Winceby Fight to Worcester, 'God's crowning mercy', as he called it. Lincoln had the more difficult task of trying to learn God's will from the lesson of the many defeats of a prolonged and bitter war.

It is, I suppose, a commonplace to say that both Cromwell and Lincoln were men of the Bible. More than any other great political leader in the world's history Oliver was a man of one book. Lincoln, too, has been called a man of one book, but the description in his case is not wholly true. Other elements contributed to his style. Shakespeare, Euclid, Bunyan, and Blackstone all had some share in the miracle of his literary achievement, but, whenever he came to make his supreme appeal, it was from the Bible that he took his chosen word. The most important speech of his life – in the sense that it determined his career more than any other – was built up and around the declaration 'a house divided against itself cannot stand'. If any one phrase had to be chosen to be inscribed on the base of every statue erected to his memory, surely those would be the words, so important were they in his own political career, so expressive are they of his life work in maintaining the unity of the nation. Lincoln, without doubt, knew his Bible, but with Oliver the book had become somehow part of himself. It was in his blood. Apart altogether from the frequent textual quotation, the language of the Scriptures is in the texture of his ordinary phrase and speech. The Biblical references and allusions throughout his written and spoken word run into many hundreds. Sometimes a paragraph of Cromwell is an exposition of the Biblical passage showing a penetrating understanding of the scriptural text. His special study seems to have been the Psalms, the Prophecies and, above all, the Pauline Epistles. Cromwell was far more than a constant reader of the Bible; he sought earnestly for the meaning, and his letters and speeches contain some of the most searching sermons in our theological and exegetical literature.

I have used the word 'literature' advisedly. Both Cromwell and Lincoln were men of letters. I assume the claim would at once be conceded in respect of Lincoln. The twelve volumes of his published works are a precious part of the literature not only of America, but of the world. But what of Cromwell's speeches? Can they in any sense be compared with those of Lincoln? It must be remembered that Lincoln, in this regard, had many advantages over Cromwell. He spoke the language and used the vocabulary of the nineteenth century, whilst Oliver's thoughts were clothed in words and phrases which have often become archaic and distant. As compared with Lincoln, he had cruder material and rougher tools. Again, Lincoln's speeches were generally written with extreme care, sometimes committed to memory, and delivered after long deliberation. In many instances they were virtually state documents, public manifestos and formal vindications of the administration. When they were delivered they were carefully and fully reported, and we have on the printed page just what Lincoln said, no more and no less.

Cromwell's speeches, on the other hand, were not written. He seems generally to have spoken without manuscript, and a day or two later was unable to recall the words he had used. Reporting in those days was in its infancy, and we can only guess how much Cromwell's speeches have suffered in transmission, both in error and omission. Even as they have come down to us, with all the imperfections of faulty transmission, Oliver's speeches constitute a priceless part of our literature. It is the fashion for some modern writers to sneer at Cromwell's oratory, and yet the discovery of the full report of one of his lost speeches would arouse more interest than the like event with any other in the long roll of our national orators.

Cromwell's letters were different. Some were meant for all to read, but most of them were only intended for the person to whom he actually wrote. The letters to members of his own family circle and his intimate friends are the most precious part of the whole collection. Unfortunately there are very few of Lincoln's letters of this intimate and family interest. Whilst Lincoln's letters were written from his home, or his lawyer's office, or the White House, those of Cromwell were often written from the field of battle, on his journeys, or in the midst of actual military operations. In these circumstances, it may be claimed that Oliver's letters constitute a body of literature unsurpassed for historical interest. Read side by side with the events which they describe, these letters, numbering over four hundred, extending over about thirty of the most eventful years in our history, and written by the man who himself took a leading part in the actions which he describes, must surely give to Cromwell an enduring place as one of the master-writers in English literature.

Tuesday 3 September was the day of Dunbar. On Wednesday 4 September Oliver writes several letters from the field of battle. But one of the seven is written to his wife in London. Here it is; this was the communication she received from the victor of Dunbar:

For my beloved wife, Elizabeth Cromwell, at the Cockpit. Dunbar, 4 September 1650.

My Dearest,

I have not leisure to write much. But I could chide thee that in many of thy letters thou writest to me that I should not be unmindful of thee and thy little ones. Truly if I love you not too well, I think I err not on the other hand much. Thou are dearer to me than any creature; let that suffice. The Lord hath showed us an exceeding mercy; who can tell how great it is. My weak faith hath been upheld. I have been in my inward man marvellously supported; though I assure thee, I grow an old man, and feel infirmities of age marvellously stealing upon me. Would my corruptions did as fast decrease. Pray on my behalf in the latter respect. The particulars of our late success Harry Vane or Gil. Pickering will impart to thee. My love to all dear friends. I rest thine, Oliver Cromwell.

That is how the news of Dunbar reached Elizabeth Cromwell in London. In time it reached all England, and then later it reached New England. It reached, among other places, a little town called Hingham in Massachusetts, where there lived a man who, some ten or fifteen years earlier, had come over from the west of England. His name was Samuel Lincoln. I wonder how the news of Dunbar reached him, and what he thought of it, and whether in the tradition of the family it was passed on to a boy who was given the name of Abraham? Dunbar was fought on 3 September 1650; on the same day, 3 September, 1651, there came the crowning mercy of Worcester, and then seven years later came another 3 September, when the victor of Dunbar and the victor of Worcester knew he was to die. Those who watched by his bedside during those last few days heard him pray. The words never intended for mortal ears have yet been preserved to us:

Lord, though I am a miserable and wretched creature, I am in covenant with Thee through grace. And I may, I will, come to Thee for Thy people. Thou hast made me, though very unworthy, a mean instrument to do them some good, and Thee service; and many of them have set too high a value upon me, though others would wish and be glad for my death. Lord, however Thou do dispose of me, continue and go on to do good to them. Give them consistency of judgment, one heart, and mutual love; and go on to deliver them and with the work of reformation; and make the name of Christ glorious in the world. Teach those who look too much on Thy instruments to depend more upon Thyself. Pardon such as desire to trample upon the dust of a poor worm, for they are Thy people too and pardon the folly of this short prayer: even for Jesus Christ's sake. And give us a good night, if it be Thy pleasure, Amen.

Abraham Lincoln, as far as we know, in the circumstances of his death had no such opportunity for spoken prayer, but we may be sure that had his last petition come down to us, it would still have been a prayer like Oliver's, in the humility of his spirit, in the forgiveness of his enemies, and in the request not for himself, but for his people and his beloved land.

This lecture was published as a pamphlet in 1945 with the addition of quotations and notes, and copies were sent by Isaac Foot to many of his friends.

MICHAEL: Looking back at this lecture now, it is clear that my father was already raising the greatest issues facing the world leaders after the war. Some of his contemporaries showed their appreciation of this and of Isaac Foot's contribution to improving Anglo-American friendship.

30 January 1945, Lord Astor:

Thank you for your most interesting booklet. I am delighted to have it and have read it with great interest. Its publication just now should make a substantial contribution towards a better understanding between the English-speaking peoples. This is important in view of the fact that when the military menace presented by the aggressors is out of the way there is a serious risk that competition between commercial and other interests in America and in the British Commonwealth will lead to jealousies and misunderstanding.

All best wishes, Yours, Astor

A tribute from Lord Rochester

It would be difficult to exaggerate the value of the service rendered by Mr Isaac Foot to the cause of Anglo-American cooperation by his recent mission to the United States. And now we are placed still farther in his debt by the publication of his lecture entitled 'Oliver Cromwell and Abraham Lincoln: A Comparison', just published by the Royal Society of Literature. This is a further invaluable contribution to the cause of Anglo-American good will. Long may Mr Foot be spared to devote his constructive abilities to the service of Great Britain and the United States of America. His unselfish devotion to public duties, and the high standard of service he sets, not only enrich British and American public life, but also render the greatest service to the world at large. Mr Foot's lecture is the result of patient, exhaustive, and enthusiastic research and is dramatically vigorous. The parallel Mr Foot has drawn and the congruency he has shown in the lives of the great American and the no less great Englishman are provocative of thought, and his many apt and striking quotations make the reading of his little book a sheer delight.[215]

'Let Us Keep the Two Flags Flying Side by Side – Britain and America after the War'
Isaac Foot wrote this article on the need for continuing the close relations between America and Britain at the end of the war.

I was travelling through the United States in 1943 at the time when the Allied forces first broke their way into what had come to be called Hitler's European fortress. The first of the gates to be forced open was Sicily. I recall the excitement and exhilaration when it was

---

215. *Methodist Recorder*, 15 February 1945.

made known that the invasion of Europe had actually begun. Day by day the news was eagerly caught up. It was important that, in this first assault upon Hitler's prison, the two flags were flying side by side. When I was given the privilege of the American radio, I spoke of the lesson of the two flags and suggested that, when the prison-house of Europe was at last opened and all the captives set free, those two flags would be more torn and tattered than they were then and would have been so stained by the blood of their people and of mine that, when the last Bastille had fallen, we should hardly be able to distinguish the one flag from the other.

That was two years ago and now the prison doors are opened and the work of liberation has been completed. The two flags have indeed been side by side. Let us rejoice that the work has been done and that, in the providence of God, it has been done together, and that, humanly speaking, the victory could not have been won by the one nation fighting alone. The friendship and cooperation of Roosevelt and Churchill have been a primary factor in the common achievement. Eisenhower and Montgomery have, while rightly praising their own men, always generously acknowledged the prowess and capacity of those of other nations who fought side by side with them. In the hour of victory it would be well if on both sides of the Atlantic, in all our spoken and written words, we remembered the injunction of the Apostle – 'in honour preferring one another'.[216]

Now what of the future? Having won our victory what are we to do with it? That, I suppose, is the question uppermost in our minds today. I recall a passage of Joseph Conrad occurring in *Lord Jim* – a book which should be reckoned one of the most powerful sermons preached to our generation: 'But the fact remains that you must touch your reward with clean hands, lest it turn to dead leaves, to thorns in your grasp.' That too was the constant theme of John Milton. We are all familiar with the lines in his 'Sonnet to Cromwell' when, after recording his victories in the field, he wrote:

Yet much remains
To conquer still; Peace hath her victories
No less renowned than war: new foes arise,
Threatening to bind our souls with secular chains...

Milton, in those few lines of poetry, sought to gather up what was the constant lesson of his prose writings. Addressing his fellow-countrymen he wrote: 'God has gloriously delivered you the first of all nations' and 'You ought to do nothing that is mean and little or anything but what is great and sublime.' And then he uttered his solemn warning which is surely relevant also to our own day:

---

216. Romans 12:10.

But if it should fall out otherwise – which God forbid – if, as you have been valiant in war you should grow debauched in peace, you that have had such visible demonstrations of the goodness of God to yourselves, and his wrath against your enemies ... you will find in a little time, that God's displeasure against you will be greater than it has been against your adversaries, greater than his grace and favour has been to yourselves, which you have had larger experience of than any other nation under heaven.[217]

These prophetic words might well have been pondered on both sides of the Atlantic today. Milton is one of the kings of literature whose writ runs to the uttermost confines of the English-speaking peoples. Remembering Milton's warning, how should the two nations face the future? There may be some who think the mere fact of our comradeship in arms will suffice, and that, after the common sorrows and joys of the two peoples, their alliance in arms is bound to lead to fellowship in the achievements of peace. We well may pray that this shall happen; but we must give some heed to the solemn warnings of history. One of the most melancholy chapters in the records of the human race is that of the aftermath of military alliances. In 1918 the war in Europe came to an end when Germany was defeated by the allied arms of Britain, France, America and Italy. The grievances of Italy, arising from the division of the spoils, were the theme of Mussolini when he sought to marshal his people against the alleged arrogance of Britain in the threat of the enforcement of sanctions. France and Britain, within a few years of the defeat of Germany, were alienated in sentiment and policy. America and Britain, held together by the exigencies of war, drifted apart under the influence of a precarious peace. The allies of the Great War, standing apart, left the road open for Hitler's march to the Rhine and Mussolini's invasion of Albania and Abyssinia.

In the gracious providence of God, we are now given a second opportunity. There are many signs that we have learned the lessons taught us by the history of the uneasy twenty years between the two great wars. I was deeply impressed, when in America, by the evidence of the close study which was being given, particularly by the churches, to the problems of international responsibility. The Methodist Church of America undertook a nationwide campaign to educate their people upon the questions relating to a durable peace. Underlying all the proposals was the assumption of a close and sincere and friendly relationship between the peoples of America and Britain. That relationship, if it is to be enduring and fruitful, must have something more than a political significance and an economic advantage. Ultimately it must be the expression of the deep truth the Apostle had in mind when he wrote of 'the fellowship of the Holy Spirit'.[218][219]

---

217. Milton's 'Defence of the People of England In Answer to Salmasius's Defence of the King' (1692).
218. 2 Corinthians 13:14.
219. *Methodist Recorder*, 10 May 1945.

PART IX

After the war

July 1945 Four Foots stand in the election

In the general election held in July 1945 at the end of the war, Isaac Foot was invited to stand as the Liberal candidate in Tavistock. His son John had been adopted before the war as the Liberal candidate in his father's former constituency of Bodmin. Dingle, who had remained in the government throughout the war, was standing for re-election in Dundee. Michael had been adopted in 1938 as the Labour candidate in Plymouth Devonport.

The Foot family reunited at Pencrebar in 1945, with the four grandchildren (left to right Paul, Sarah, Kate and Winslow) at the front.

Three of the four Foot candidates in the general election of 1945: Isaac, the Liberal candidate in Tavistock; John, the Liberal candidate in Bodmin; and Michael, the Labour candidate in Devonport.

Hugh remembers that night of the 1945 election, which was a disaster for the Liberal Party, winning only twelve seats:

Michael was the only member of the family to win in the election of 1945. My father was beaten at Tavistock; Dingle, who had been member for Dundee for fourteen years, was beaten too; John was beaten in Bodmin. As the news of the defeats came in our home, one after another late that night, there was only Michael's win in Devonport to lighten the general gloom. My father used to say proudly that our family had lost more parliamentary elections than any family in England.

29 1945–6 Lord Mayor of Plymouth

MICHAEL: The most startling political events which took place at the end of the war in Plymouth were the sweeping victories of the Labour Party. I was one of the three Labour candidates who won in their Plymouth constituencies. Devonport had never before even registered a decent Labour vote. My truest friend and agent, Harry Wright, knew the place best of all and thought we hadn't got a chance. One of the newly elected Labour council's first actions was a generous gesture to my father when he was unanimously elected the new Lord Mayor of Plymouth. Even though he was a Liberal, they had a special respect for his Methodist connections. Westcountry Methodists, as my father had often proved, swept across all frontiers and could play a most healing part in the future.

On hearing that her brother was to be Lord Mayor, Isaac Foot's elder sister, Janie Nash, rejoiced that a member of the Foot family should be chosen for this role:

My dear Isaac, You will have been surfeited with 'Congrats' by now but here is one more from your 'eldest fond sister'! It was a real surprise to open Saturday's Morning News! Now we know why you didn't get in at Tavistock. How proud your father would have been! He certainly would have been a few inches taller! Perhaps he knows! It's one of my fancies that good news travels round in the Celestial City. Did not Our Lord say that the bells of Heaven rang over the good news of a prodigal's return! I feel sure you are going to have a very enjoyable twelve months, you must make up your mind to enjoy it. I will say what Mr Gentle said when Father was made circuit steward – 'He will add lustre to the position'. Just what I think. The word that came to me was 'Them that honour me I will honour'. You have got a great opportunity so I will say like the mother of President Truman: 'Now Harry, mind you behave yourself.' With much love, Janie

Isaac and Eva Foot: the Lord Mayor and Lady Mayoress of Plymouth.

The new Lord Mayor of Plymouth, November 1945.

MICHAEL: Plymouth, my father told me, had played a bigger part in the modern story of freedom than anywhere else. Plymouth had played the foremost part in the protection of Parliament in its just war against the Stuart Kings. Just across the road from Lipson Terrace, where we were born, stood Freedom Fields, where the victory against the royal odds was celebrated. We passed it every day on our way to school. Then in the years of the war Plymouth led the rest of the nation in its endurance and triumph. In 1945 when he became Lord Mayor, my father went to every school within the city wearing the robes and chains of his office and told the children how Francis Drake and the citizens of Plymouth had helped save England and freedom again as in 1588.

In a broadcast Isaac Foot recalled how when he was a boy the then Lord Mayor of Plymouth had visited his own Jago's School.

The day at Jago's School I remember best was the one when the mayor came to Jago's, clad in his red robes. He told us he was an old boy of that school. I was eleven at the time and I thought I might one day wear those robes myself. My interest in the history of my native town began, not with any formal lesson, but with a chance visit to the Plymouth Guildhall. We were taken there upon some public occasion. The storied windows, richly bright, were lit up by the

morning. They were storied windows indeed –
every window had some story to tell of some
great event in the history of Plymouth, and in
the spaces below there were names inscribed –
the names of those who had been associated
with the town – Gilbert, Hawkins, Frobisher,
Raleigh, Drake and the rest.

Nothing was said to my knowledge. If so,
I have forgotten the homily but the time I
spent there taught me for the first time that I
belonged to a famous town and I must have
walked home swelling with pride. From that
time I got into the Guildhall as often as I
could. If the door was open I would slip in,
and soon I had those names by heart. One
window interested me above all the rest. That
window depicted the Siege of Plymouth.
What was the siege? What was the Sabbath
Day Fight? What was the fighting about, anyway? Why were there so many names upon
that one window? There was nobody, at that

*Window at Plymouth Club in Lockyer Street
depicting the siege of Plymouth from 1643–6, and
showing King Charles I summoning the town to
surrender.*

time, who could answer these questions for me. It was only years later that the memorial
stone was set up in Freedom Fields, with the inscription telling of a battle fought on the
Sabbath Day about 300 years ago. That battle, we now know, decided not only the fate of
Plymouth, but in some measure the future destiny of England. That memorial should have
been put up long before. Under enemy action the old distinctive historic Plymouth has disappeared. The Guildhall, which taught me so much, will never be there for Plymouth boys
in the future. The window, the historic streets are so much dust and rubble. If, as the old
Greeks used to say, 'the city teaches the man', is it not our business to lose no time in
rebuilding our city so that not more than one generation of our children shall be condemned to grow up in a shell and a ruin?

'Mother Plymouth sitting by the sea.' That familiar phrase we owe, strangely enough,
not to a Plymouth man but to a traveller from another country.[220] 'Mother Plymouth!'
Somehow the association is natural. Exiles from Plymouth, wherever they meet, greet each
other as members of the same family. Plymouth folk all over the world have a common
dialect, and, wherever they dwell, their windows are open towards Jerusalem. Pericles
besought the youth of Athens to feed their eyes upon the city from day to day till love of

---

220. A phrase used by an American writer, Elihu Burritt, in *A Walk from London to Land's End and Back*, published in 1868.

Athens filled their hearts. That is what many of the sons and daughters of Plymouth have done. When Ernest Radford wrote his song about Plymouth Harbour, it was at dawn in the Bay of Naples.[221] I, too, have been in Naples Harbour at the break of day, and that was a memorable sunrise. But the exiles sang, not of Naples, but of Plymouth:

> Oh what know they of harbours who toss not on the sea!
> They tell of fairer havens, but none so fair there be
> As Plymouth town outstretching her quiet arms to me,
> Her Breast's broad welcome spreading from Mewstone to Penlee.

That was one exiled lover of Plymouth and here was another – Captain Tobias Furneaux was a boy born in 1735 at Swilly, Devonport. On the second voyage of Captain James Cook to the southern seas, young Furneaux was given second command. The two ships lost touch with each other, and the young seaman had to find his way alone for some fourteen hundred miles. He wrote the narrative of that illustrious voyage, and made a chart of the coast of Tasmania, then first explored by an Englishman, and, wherever he went, he somehow saw resemblances to Plymouth and to his homeland. 'That Cape', he wrote, 'was much like Rame Head of Plymouth. One of those rocks', he observed, 'rose from the sea just like the Mewstone', and in his chart he marked these places with the names familiar in his home town. That little island was the Mewstone; that solitary rock he named the Eddystone, and that row of islands he named after his birthplace, the Swilly Islands. He died at Swilly at the age of forty-six. Like so many others, this intrepid seaman, happy as a lover, took the name of Plymouth with him right round the world.

From the story of their own city the children of Plymouth can learn more than most of the history of their own country and the world beyond. As a boy it was of the world beyond that I used to dream. What I liked most of all was to see the ships go out to sea; the anchor hauled up, the great ropes loosened, then the ship would pass out slowly to the world beyond. Since then I have seen many ships go out of Plymouth Harbour. I had to represent the town when, with civic honour, we bade farewell and Godspeed to Sir Ernest Shackleton setting out on his voyage to the Antarctic. His ship, I remember, was called the Quest, and from the voyage he was never to return.

The world beyond! If that is what the Plymouth boy dreams about he can go up to Mount Wise and see the statue that was not there when I was at school. It is the statue of Captain Scott of the Antarctic. He was a Devonport schoolboy; he must have dreamed much of the world beyond, and, indeed, he went to its utmost limit.

Then, if they will, the sons and daughters of the city can go up to Freedom Park, what I still like to call Freedom Fields, and read the inscription on the monument which commemorates the Sabbath Day Fight, when, on 3 December in the year 1643, the hard-

---

221. Ernest Radford (1857–1919), British poet, critic and socialist – his poem 'Plymouth' was written in 1900.

The Scott Memorial in Mount Wise, Plymouth, commemorating Captain Robert Scott's expedition to Antarctica.

The Mayflower Stone, put in on the Barbican in 1891, and the memorial, built in 1934, to mark the point where the Pilgrim Fathers set sail for America on 6 September 1620.

pressed Plymouth garrison and the townsmen resisted and defeated the attack of the King's Army, led by Prince Maurice. It was about the time of that critical battle, and that deliverance, that the townsmen adopted as their motto, the words declaring that the name of the Lord is a very strong tower: 'Turris fortissima est nomen Jehovah'.

Then, from Freedom Fields, the boys and girls of Plymouth can go down to the Barbican where, if they will, they can learn much of a world beyond from the Mayflower Stone. It was on 6 September 1620 that an 'un-noted sail put out to sea from Plymouth to the England of a dream'. Happily for the future of the world the Pilgrims took with them, as their last memory of England, the courtesy and kindness of their friends in Plymouth. The association of the Mayflower with Plymouth would appear to be one of the miracles of history. It was only after their voyage had actually begun that adversity drove the Mayflower into Plymouth Harbour, and then, on their voyage to America, adverse circumstances again took them many hundreds of miles from their purposed destination, and at last they found shelter inside the protecting arm of Cape Cod, and they landed actually at a spot which had already been named Plymouth by an English traveller some years before.[222] Chance, some

222. Isaac Foot wrote to the *Times* pointing out that it was given the name 'New Plimouth' by Captain John Smith six years earlier and that this name was also the choice of King Charles II.

will say. Well, Plymouth folk know of no better – they believe in an overruling providence. Twice it has been my high privilege to represent our Plymouth when visiting the Plymouth of New England, once during the war, and once when I was deputed to represent the Mother Town at the Mayflower celebrations of 1921. That was a great day for me: when I had to give my message to the thousands of people gathered there, they rose to greet me and they sang. And what they sang was 'Home, Sweet Home'. I could hardly tell whether I was at Plymouth Rock or Plymouth Hoe.

Then again, these children of ours can go up to the Hoe and stand below the statue of Sir Francis Drake. There he is with the globe by his side, and the mariner's compass in his hand, and looking out to the world beyond. He indeed went right round the world and was the first Englishman who ever did it. When I was a boy, that was the only statue on the Hoe. It was quite enough for me. I saw it nearly every day, and often Francis Drake and I were there alone. I didn't know much about him then – somehow he and I became friendly. Well, the sea is in our blood and most of our history can be told in the story of the ships.

Hitherto, I have spoken of Plymouth in history with very little picture of the city herself. Here we are, about 200,000 of us at the head of two rivers, the Tamar and the Plym, and the town lies at the base of the Tamar tableland, and its foreshore is washed by the intermingled waters that come from the distant Cornish hills as well as from the Devon moor. Plymouth is the metropolitan city of the whole wide-stretching Tamar valley. It belongs as much to Cornwall as to Devon. In my early days the Plym meant more to me than the Tamar. Wordsworth would have called the Plym a 'sylvan wanderer through the woods'. The Plym is also the gateway to Dartmoor. Somehow I came to think of Dartmoor as the mighty rampart of my native town, and to me the several tors stood like sentinels keeping constant watch in war. Once every year my father took the whole family on a pilgrimage to the nearest of the Dartmoor hills. It was the Dewerstone.

We all climbed the hill, and from the topmost height we could see stretched before us pastoral Devon, and the winding river, and then Plymouth, and beyond Plymouth the gleaming sea. Ours was a singing family, and, once the nine of us had gathered at the top, we always sang a hymn. And the hymn was about Beulah Land, and in this way I came to think of Plymouth as Beulah Land. I should hardly know where to draw the boundaries of my Plymouth, but, as lovers use secret names to one another, so my name for my Plymouth is Beulah Land. The hymn we sang had a chorus, and it ran like this:

Oh Beulah Land, sweet Beulah Land,
As on thy highest mount I stand,
I look away across the sea,

Where mansions are prepared for me,
And view the shining Glory shore,
My heaven, my home, for evermore.[223][224]

It was this historic and cultural heritage of his native city that Isaac Foot wanted to celebrate when, in November 1945, he and Eva were installed as the Lord Mayor and Lady Mayoress of Plymouth. This was the message he sent out to the children of Plymouth:

Dear Boys and Girls

For over five hundred years the citizens of Plymouth have met every year to choose their mayor, or their Lord Mayor, as he is now called. This year I have been chosen to fill this ancient and honourable office. A small number of your fellow-scholars have been invited to the Mayor-choosing ceremony, and I am sorry there is not room for you all. This is why I am sending you this message. You, too, are to be reckoned amongst the citizens of Plymouth. We have just come through the greatest war in the history of mankind. We have had a wonderful deliverance. Indeed, there was a time in 1940 when it seemed we might be overwhelmed. The enemy had overrun the Continent of Europe and only the narrow seas divided us from what at that time seemed irresistible might. In that dark hour, August 1940, I was invited to broadcast a message to this country, and a few days afterwards, to the Empire and the outside world. I thought then I could best gather what I had to say under the story of 'Drake's Drum'. That story enabled me to say something about my native city, and about Sir Francis Drake, who was himself once the mayor of Plymouth. I am sending to each one of you a copy of that address. I would like you to read it for yourselves, and perhaps you can get your people in your home to read it as well. I hope you will learn all you can about this city of ours, which stands second only to London in English fame. Plymouth has been scarred and broken by war, and we have to rebuild our city in a shattered world. That will be a long business if it is to be done well. I want you to be ready to take your full share in that great enterprise. I send to you all, and to all those in your homes, my best wishes.

Yours sincerely, Isaac Foot

---

223. Words written in 1876 by Edgar P. Stites, music by John R. Sweeney – in the Sankey Methodist hymn book. Taken from Isaiah 62:4.
224. Isaac Foot broadcasts, 1946 and 1950.

'City face to face with colossal problem'

My main ground for apprehension in taking office is the year upon which we are about to enter. It is the first year of peace. We are already realising the problems of peace are tenfold more difficult than the problems of war. We are caught up in the dreadful aftermath. Ours is a scarred city but we can thank God that they are honourable scars. The heart of our city is no more than a ruin. I learnt much from the city as a boy. The boys of today can learn something of the price that has to be paid for liberty from these scars. Plymouth paid a high price for freedom. So many landmarks disappeared. I suppose it is true no city in Britain suffered as this city ... It seems to me the thing about which we must concern ourselves now is the foundation we are going to lay. On the financial position we are undoubtedly face to face with colossal problems in this city – burdens to carry which, if not nationally borne, will crush us to powder. It is well we should face them. Our claim is that it is not our responsibility and we expect our representatives to urge upon the country that the immediate need is for expediency, urgency and a quickening of the machinery for making it possible to meet our present needs.[225]

'The picking-up-the-pieces Lord Mayor'

Miss Lois Deacon, secretary to ten of Plymouth's Lord Mayors, remembered him for his 'eloquence, his Devonshireness, his love of Plymouth history and tradition, qualities which were relieved occasionally by his absentmindedness, as when he left the parlour one day for one of his tours of Plymouth schools arrayed in his scarlet robes and gold chain, but with a trilby hat crammed on his head. A sprint by Sergeant-at-Mace Saunders down the garden path drew the Lord Mayor's attention to this solecism.' She recounts the occasion when Mr Foot entertained a party of delighted French schoolchildren by singing 'Widecombe Fair' right through with a strong Devonshire accent. Of all the Mayor-choosings she attended she was most impressed by that of Isaac Foot at the Central Hall in 1945. His speech at the ceremony was an inspiration to a city which had suffered so much in the war. 'He set us all glowing again ... the memory of a scintillating year ... Oh the wit that sparkled about! And how I loved it all!'[226]

In a broadcast to the people of Plymouth in January 1946 Isaac Foot spoke of his pride in the revival of Plymouth after the terrible suffering of the war 'The Next Step?'

Some eight years ago in 1937 I heard early one Monday morning that Wesley Chapel in my native town, Plymouth, had been destroyed by fire during the night. Wesley Chapel meant more to me than any single church in the world. Wesley was the church my father and his

---

225. *Western Morning News*, 10 November 1945.
226. *Western Morning News*, 6 November 1969.

contemporaries had built seventy years before. It was the place in which I had been first taught to worship, the place in which I had been christened and my children christened after me, the pulpit in which I had first learned to preach and the sanctuary in which my mother had worshipped Sunday after Sunday for fifty years or so – and it was all gone. No material loss has ever seemed quite so dreadful to me. What we learned from that calamity was that, with the building destroyed, there remained the fellowship – the fellowship which was there before the building was erected, and which remained after the building had gone. The building had gone, the church endured.

Some four years later in 1941 there came upon the same city the blow which struck down not one church but many. That Friday night, early in 1941, from my home some twelve miles away in Cornwall I saw my native town go up in flames. The fire shot up into the sky making the night heavens lurid and almost apocalyptic. I thought that, after that holocaust, nothing could be left, but, immediately after, I went into the city and looked around. And then it was that I knew I loved Plymouth. At first it seemed as if everything had gone, all the familiar sights had disappeared. The streets of my boyhood, full of warmth and colour, the streets along which I had walked four times a day when a boy at school – they were gone, gone as if they had never been there at all. I should never see these things again. Night after night, fire and death rained down from the skies and, before the fury had spent itself, most of the churches of Plymouth, great and small, had disappeared. The most treasured material possession of Plymouth was St Andrew's Church and that went as well. And then there came something of the same reaction that had marked the loss of Wesley Chapel five years before. Sherwell Chapel, the cathedral of Westcountry Nonconformity, had been gutted by fire and then, as the sorrowing people passed the familiar place, they saw the words that had been written over the porch of the remaining walls.[227] The words were 'Sursum Corda'. The citizens read the words 'Lift up your hearts' and as they passed one could almost see the response in their eyes: 'We lift them up unto the Lord.' I passed Sherwell this morning. The words are still there.

Then, as I have said, there was St Andrew's Church. St Andrew's is at the very heart of the city. Plymouth and St Andrew's have, in a sense, grown up together and the church is regarded as the common inheritance of the people irrespective of their religious persuasion. It was our chief link with antiquity. It was the church where the Elizabethan seamen had worshipped and where they assembled in gratitude after their historic voyages that founded the British Commonwealth; there was the stone marking the place where the heart of Frobisher and the heart of Admiral Blake had been buried; there our forebears had met to take the Solemn League and Covenant; there they had gathered to take the Oath of Allegiance when the town, standing as it believed for the liberty of the subject and the privilege of Parliament, closed its gates even against its own King. It was almost as if the

---

227. Sherwell Chapel was then a Congregational chapel.

The burnt-out shell of St Andrew's Church in the centre of Plymouth after the blitz in 1941.

foundations of the city had been shaken when, after a night of death and terror, we learned that St Andrew's was gone. And then again came the inevitable word, almost before the enemy planes had disappeared from the sky, the word had been written and appeared above the north porch on one of the remaining walls – the word was 'Resurgam'. That word brought hope to the stricken city and gave us the measure of the tyrant's power. I saw the word again this morning: 'I shall rise again'. By a merciful deliverance the tower of St Andrew's had been spared. There it stood like God's sentinel on guard over the City and the people recalled the proud motto which had been theirs for over three hundred years – 'Turris Fortissima Est Nomen Jehovah'. The words seemed like a challenge to the many. 'The name of the Lord is a very strong tower.'

The dead of the city were buried in a communal grave and the people returned to their homes sustained by the words 'Be not afraid of them that kill the body and after, have no more that they can do'. In the same disaster houses and shops and administrative buildings disappeared under the attack – many indeed disappeared so completely that the occupiers could hardly tell next day where their several places had been. Still, even for those outside the churches, 'Sursum Corda' and 'Resurgam' had set the high example. In every instance it was the case of the 'Next Step'. After the burning of Wesley Chapel and the loss of Sherwell Chapel and the destruction of St Andrew's there came, first of all and as the Next Step, the affirmation of faith. It is Joseph Conrad who has defined faith in God as the 'refusal to acquiesce in the insignificance of events'. In every case the Next Step was the affirmation of faith in God. The enemy fury had destroyed much but a great deal remained. The enemy might indeed have destroyed every material possession and not one stone might have been left standing upon another throughout the city. What then? What then? Without putting their thoughts into words, the people realised that the community remained and that there was a Plymouth which was something independent of bricks and mortar and streets and sewers. The very destruction of the churches led the worshippers to feel that something remained independently of towers and spires and buildings and classrooms. What remained was the fellowship. They realised, perhaps more than ever before, the significance of that master word of the New Testament, fellowship. And there came to them the fuller meaning of the Apostle's prayer with which he concluded his letter to the Corinthian disciples: 'The Fellowship of the Holy Spirit be with you all.' And, when the disciples in Plymouth looked upon their ruined properties, they came to realise that they had only lost the things that could be shaken and that the things that could not be shaken remained. They learned that there were territories where the power of evil could not invade and spiritual realms where the writ of the tyrant and dictator could not run. In the years following those nights of destruction, the fellowship has been held together. The stricken churches have come to each other's assistance. The common material loss has quickened the sense of underlying spiritual unity.

As with the fellowship in the church, so it has been with the civic spirit of the community. Within two years of the disaster there was published in our city a book entitled *A Plan for Plymouth*.[228] That book was indeed one of the most remarkable documents of the war. It was in the very midst of the abomination and desolation that the book appeared. It was as if the people had said: 'You see around you Plymouth as it is. Here in this book you can see the Plymouth as one day, please God, it shall be.' That was the triumph of the civic spirit of the community. When, just over two years ago I was in Plymouth, Massachusetts I was told how the people of that daughter town immediately the news of the disaster had crossed the Atlantic, met almost spontaneously to arrange for relief to be sent to 'Old Mother Plymouth'.

May it not be that the experience of Plymouth can be taken as a symbol for Europe and the world? What saved us was the spirit of our people. They were sustained in their hours of trial by their ideal of a reconstructed city arising one day out of the ruins around them. Indeed, had it not been for that vision, the people might well have perished. What saved our churches was the knowledge that, with the material loss, the fellowship endured. With

---

228. This was drawn up in 1943 by the city engineer, James Paton Watson, and Sir Patrick Abercrombie, the town planning consultant. It was published by Plymouth City Council in 1944.

both people and churches there was the act of faith. 'Sursum Corda' can be written not only above Sherwell Chapel in Plymouth but above a broken Europe and a disrupted world. 'Resurgam' is the word which should be written not only above the porch of St Andrew's but over every ruined church in every desolated country.[229]

During his year as Lord Mayor Isaac Foot determined that Plymouth should celebrate the historic anniversaries which occurred in an appropriate way.

1920–1 The celebration of the tercentenary of the voyage of the Mayflower

In 1920 Plymouth had held its own celebrations of the tercentenary of the pilgrims' voyage. In 1921, as deputy mayor, Isaac Foot had represented his own Plymouth at the tercentenary celebrations of the landing of the Pilgrim Fathers in Plymouth, Massachusetts. Isaac described these ceremonies in letters home to Eva:

Boston, 30 July 1921

This morning I went to Plymouth. It feels rather funny to steam into a station marked 'Plymouth' especially when the station you pass through before is named 'Plympton'. Plymouth is a delightful little town. It is decorated most lavishly: the main street is over-arched with banners, each marked with the name of a Pilgrim. The pageant is a big business in the open – huge stands having been erected. It includes a real *Mayflower* – which comes in from the sea. The purpose of my coming seems to have been served – they seem very glad to see me. The *Boston Transcript*, which is the paper here, puts my name at the head of the other guests.

Mayflower Inn, Plymouth, 2 August 1921

The President's Day yesterday was immense. I was introduced to him and Mrs Harding. He was mighty genial and she was nice as could be.[230] I met all the other dignitaries. The excitement is a bit whirling but the holiday is immense in as much as business matters are absolutely forgotten!

On the train to Washington, 9 August 1921

In the evening I addressed a large assembly in the open air, numbers assessed at 10,000. The speech was a success – although I say it – every word was heard by the furthest listener and the crowd, although to the extent of about 50 per cent it was non-English, was responsive and approving. I did not get to bed until nearly one. I am glad last night's 'do' went off so well. All the Boston papers report the speech. The kindness of the Plymouth

---

229. Broadcast, 20 January 1946.
230. Warren Harding (1865–1923) was elected President of the USA in 1920.

people has been wonderful and I shall have a famous story to tell on my return. My visit
has hold on the popular imagination and the editor of the Boston Transcript told me
today at lunch my visit has been commented on a great deal.

Report on Isaac Foot's part in this celebration

Two fine concerts were given on Sunday evening with the additional feature of an address
on the part of Deputy Mayor Isaac Foot of Plymouth, England. While 'Auld Lang Syne'
was being played an automobile, with Deputy Mayor Isaac Foot and Chairman William T.
Eldridge of the Selectmen of this town, rolled up. The official representative of the over-
seas Plymouth was attired in his robes of office, and, as he stepped forward and greeted the
audience by lifting his black satin official chapeau, a large portion of the audience rose to
its feet in acknowledgement and as a mark of respect, while hands were clapped with
vigour. Bowing in acknowledgement of his reception Mr Foot spoke as follows:

'I welcome this opportunity of bringing to the Plymouth of New England the greetings of
Plymouth of Old England. There is no town in England which has closer associations with
the New World than my native town of Plymouth – the town, described in happy phrase

*'Isaac Foot, the Deputy Mayor of Plymouth, England is greeted by Chairman Eldredge of the Plymouth
Massachusetts Selectmen in August 1921 on the occasion of the celebration of the Tercentenary of the Pilgrim
Father's landing here. Mr Foot was attired in his official regalia consisting of a gorgeous purple, fur-trimmed
robe, black satin cocked hat and heavy silver chains with the coat of arms bearing the motto "Turris Fortissima
est Nomen Jehova". He is here to deliver a message from his town.'*

by one of your own poets as 'Old Mother Plymouth sitting by the sea'. Out from the waters under Plymouth great seamen have gone on their adventurous quest. She has been the home or birthplace of daring mariners whose names shine like stars in the history of my country – Drake, Hawkins, Raleigh, Frobisher, Gilbert, Captain Cook, Lord Nelson and Captain Scott. Among these we are proud to reckon that company of intrepid men and women who in the providence of God sailed from Plymouth there and found their way to Plymouth here. It is one of the most famous coincidences in history that unexpectedly and undesignedly they found their home in the Plymouth of England and were brought by what they thought were adverse winds and circumstances into the Plymouth of America. Out of the thousands of miles of this coast they were led to choose this spot which had been named Plymouth years before they started on their momentous voyage. Was there not in this the guidance of a hand, stronger and kinder than man's hand and a directing wisdom higher than the wisdom of us?

'Now, after the passing of three hundred years, I come to wish you well and to tell you how great is our pride in your mighty progress and our joy in your success. Like you, we honoured the memory of the Pilgrims and no less do we honour the memory of their descendants who one hundred and fifty years ago later asserted their liberties against her tyrannical power. Today I am at Plymouth Rock but tomorrow I hope to stand with no less reverence upon that spot

Where the embattled farmer stood
And fired the shot heard round the world.[231]

'Every intelligent Englishman will recognise that the men who fought under Washington won our freedom as well as their own. Between your town and mine there is nothing but the sea. The sea of which Shakespeare wrote:

This precious stone set in a silver sea,
Which serves it in the office of a wall
Or as a moat defensive to a house
Against the envy of less happier lands.[232]

'But you have taught us to think of the sea not as a moat defensive to our house but as the great highway of friendship, along which your troopships came to bring timely succour in the hour of our bitter need. The bonds, which were strong before, were made indissoluble by sacrifice in a common cause. May the friendship between your town and mine be but a symbol of the enduring friendship between our two countries. Without the friendship of

231. Ralph Waldo Emerson wrote this 'Concord Hymn' in 1837 to commemorate the battle of Lexington in 1775, the first battle of the American Revolution.
232. *Richard II.*

England and America the peace of the nations is impossible. Given that friendship there is some hope and guarantee of the healing of the stricken world. May your town and mine flourish together. May the ties which unite us never be severed. Mine is a pilgrimage of sentiment, an embassy of good will. As the fathers of my town greeted yours 300 years ago, so I greet you again and wish you Godspeed.'[233]

In 1946, on the anniversary of the sailing of the Pilgrim Fathers, Isaac Foot as Lord Mayor laid a wreath at the Mayflower Stone in the Barbican and cabled this message to the chairman of the Selectmen of Plymouth, Massachusetts:

Being assembled at the Mayflower Stone I send you, on this anniversary of the sailing of the Pilgrims, who founded the greatest republic the world has ever known, affectionate greetings of the people of Plymouth to the townsfolk of Plymouth, Mass. I thank your people who helped our stricken city by sending clothes and food during the blitz.[234]

1643–6 Plymouth in the Civil War – the siege of Plymouth

In March 1946 Plymouth held a week of celebrations to mark the tercentenary of the raising of the siege of Plymouth and of Cromwell's visit on 25 March 1646. This was an anniversary Isaac Foot wanted to celebrate above all others. He was immensely proud that his native city had played such a key part in the opposition to the King in the Civil War. To mark the Sabbath Day Victory which saved the city from the Royalists in 1643, he reintroduced the custom of holding a service at the Freedom Fields Memorial in Plymouth Freedom Park on 3 December every year. The inscription on this monument reads:

Upon this spot on Sunday 3 December 1643, after hard fighting for several hours, the Roundhead garrison of Plymouth made their final rally and routed the Cavalier army which had crossed the outworks and well nigh taken the town. For many years it was the custom to celebrate the anniversary of this victory, long known as the 'Sabbath Day Fight' and recorded as the 'Great Deliverance' of the protracted siege, successfully sustained by troops and townsfolk on behalf of the Parliament against the King under great hardships for more than three years.

Isaac Foot recalled this siege:
Below the ruins of our Guildhall, beside the shell of our municipal buildings, the shattered law courts and the walls of St Andrew's, we can remind ourselves of the sacrifices and sufferings of our forebears who, three hundred years ago, stripped themselves of their

---

233. Taken from Frederick W. Bittinger, *The Story of the Pilgrim Tercentenary Celebration at Plymouth in the Year 1921* (Memorial Press, 1923).
234. *Western Evening Herald*, 6 September 1946.

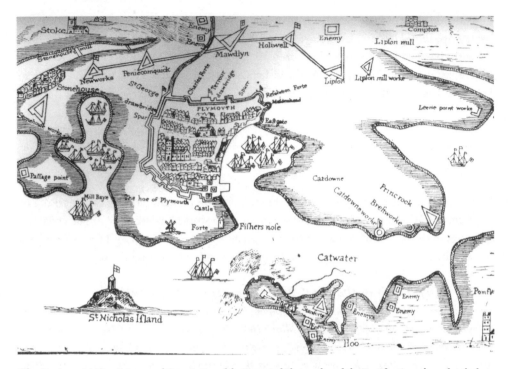

The siege map: 'A True Mapp and Description of the Towne of Plymouth and the Fortifications thereof at the last Siege 1643'.

material possessions and in great numbers even gave their lives, contending, as they believed, in the defence of liberty. Five years ago, almost to this very day, this city suffered the onslaught of a ruthless enemy. The people endured and survived because they knew that this war was for the preservation of something dearer than their property and more precious than their lives. Three hundred years ago the people of Plymouth endured like sufferings in what they believed to be the same cause. Five years ago it was to preserve our national existence and freedom. Three hundred years ago the battle was for civil liberty. Both then and now the struggle was maintained by the ordinary citizens and the common people. In the Civil War, which decided very largely the future of England, Plymouth was called on to play a foremost part in the struggle for internal liberty. Siding, as she herself declared, for King and Parliament, she sustained a siege, which, with slight intermission, lasted from December 1642 to the beginning of 1646. No other town in England had a like ordeal. Other cities were besieged for shorter periods or, being besieged, fell and capitulated. Not so Plymouth. The whole Civil War can be studied within the narrow circle surrounding Plymouth. The siege was marked by two crises – the Sabbath Day Fight of December 3 1643 and the summons from King Charles, September 1644. The histories have not brought out the imminence of the peril and how near the danger came. How sacred Freedom Fields should be, not only to the people of Plymouth, but to people of all nations. It is right for visitors to go on Plymouth Hoe and see the Mayflower Stone, but they should also see Freedom Fields. Whoever changed the name of 'Freedom Fields' to 'Freedom Park' should suffer six months' imprisonment for malicious damage!

Isaac Foot continued to ensure that Plymouth remembered this event by laying a wreath each year at the Monument in Freedom Park.

*

In July 1946 Plymouth enjoyed two weeks of celebrations of the 400th anniversary of the birth of Sir Francis Drake. A souvenir programme for this was sent to all schoolchildren with this message to the children of Plymouth.

About this time 400 years ago Sir Francis Drake was born near Tavistock. The exact date of his birth we do not know. Early in life he became a Plymouth man, and the names of Drake and Plymouth will be associated as long as there is a history of England. There is an old record that, when he was a small child, the young Francis was brought by his parents in a time of civil tumult into Plymouth for protection, actually finding shelter, it is said, on St Nicholas Island, which afterwards, in his honour, became known as Drake's Island. It was from Plymouth Harbour that Drake sailed on all his famous voyages. He was the first Englishman to plough his furrow right round the world. That famous furrow began and ended with Plymouth Sound. Ours is a stricken city and a large part of our material wealth has been taken from us as a result of the onslaught of the enemy. We are, however, still rich in our fame and no enemy action could rob us of our proud memories. One of the proudest of these memories we intend to recall, please God, next July in the commemoration of the birth of our foremost citizen in history.

30 1946 'Look for me in the Nurseries of Heaven' – the death of Eva Foot

Eva Foot died on 17 May 1946.

Eva Mackintosh Foot 1878–1946

SARAH: It was during my grandfather's year as Lord Mayor that my grandmother, Eva Foot, died. She had had an operation in hospital in East Grinstead and my grandfather went with her. After the operation and being told that all was well, he caught a train back to Plymouth where he was to attend an official function, but a message was delivered to him when the train stopped at Reading. My grandmother was failing. By the time he got back to the hospital she was gone. Somehow his duties as Lord Mayor seemed to help him through the terrible time of grief.

MICHAEL: I last saw my mother when she came to visit me in the House of Commons before her operation. No one was expecting her to die. My father chose the quotation above from the poet Francis Thompson for her funeral service – they both had complete faith in the afterlife and that he would find her there.

The many tributes to her show in what esteem she was held, both in her own right as leader of the Sunday school and women's classes in her local Methodist church, as J.P. and school governor, and as Isaac's partner in his political career and at the centre of her family.

Mrs Isaac Foot

Mrs Isaac Foot was a fine representative of a type of woman that has helped to build up Britain's greatness. Quiet, unassuming, scorning the vanities of personal adornment, Mrs Foot exercised a wide and lasting influence. With inflexible principles and deeply religious, she inspired with her convictions and by her example thousands of children of the Methodist faith. A staunch Liberal, she helped her husband in many contests. During the last months of her life she gave him wise counsel and unfailing aid as Lady Mayoress of Plymouth. She was the centre and inspiration of a devoted family, four of whom became President of the Union at Oxford and Cambridge, before making their mark in politics, journalism, the law and colonial administration.[235]

The Foot children all had special memories of their mother.

HUGH: My father was a person wrapped up in his public life and his thinking and his read-ing and she was the very practical runner of us all and the household and the real centre of the whole family. My mother was the inspiration of our lives, working and planning for us all the time, uncompromising in her strict adherence to Methodist and Liberal principles, always long suffering and compassionate. Never complaining, never short tempered, she made us all laugh at ourselves and at each other. My picture of her is as she sang in a high, clear voice, sel-dom quite in tune, in our family pew at the chapel in Callington or slipped away to take her Sunday school class or her place at our crowded dining table with tears in her eyes as she help-lessly laughed at the nonsense we talked. And at night, when she at last abandoned her efforts to get us to go to bed, she would give us all a brisk nod at the door of the library with a final comprehensive loving rebuke. She set us all an example of devotion and gaiety.

DINGLE: Although our mother was half Scottish – her family came from Glen Fincastle in Perthshire – we were brought up as Westcountry Methodists. This was of great importance. Every Sunday we went not to church, but to chapel. The sermon was generally

---

235. Lord Astor, *Times*, 25 May 1946.

delivered by a lay preacher – possibly by my grandfather or by my father. The household was ruled by my mother. Everything was done according to her standards. Although we were in no way impoverished, we never had baker's bread. Every loaf was cooked in the family oven. Every Saturday morning, as a child, I was sent to the market to buy two pennyworth of yeast. In particular, my mother's Cornish pasties had to be eaten to be believed. One of them became famous. In the 1945 election Michael was Labour candidate for Devonport. My mother had not wholly approved the defection from the Liberal party. But family ties prevailed. In the middle of the election she cooked him a pasty and wrapped it in the Labour Party's colour. One of my sisters carried it. It was delivered to Michael as he was addressing a great public meeting. He unwrapped it. In accordance with the shouts of the crowd he ate it then and there. He won the election.

MICHAEL: What my mother meant, especially to those who knew her best in Callington, was splendidly recaptured in her granddaughter Sarah Foot's book.

SARAH: Over and over again all through my life people have told me how wonderful my grandmother Eva Foot was. It was from her side of the family I inherited my Cornish blood of which I am so proud and my name. My grandfather was a Devon man, who later lost his heart to Cornwall. 'Quietly she was a great help to so many people around Callington,' Olive Venning, an old friend of the family, told me. 'She never made a fuss about it and not many people knew of the things she did for so many.' Mrs Venning had known my grandmother from her youth when she had been in her Sunday school class ... She was the perfect partner in life for my grandfather. Equalling him in intelligence, she had a more practical outlook and a very strong character and devoted herself to his welfare and that of the children, though continuing with her own interests and work. She was the one to discipline the children and obedience to her wishes was absolute. She was the one also to make sure my grandfather appeared in time for functions and properly dressed, as he was famously absentminded. She accompanied him during all his campaigns and spoke for him in his constituency, joining in the canvassing with enthusiasm and determination.

Nancy Astor wrote this to Isaac Foot from America:

Dear dearest Friend, My heart aches for you and yours. Especially you. I know what this will mean. I wish I had stopped on and I might have helped. It's a bitter blow. But she's alright – 'Trials are proof of God's care.' Well, this parting grief makes us realize that life must be eternal. She can't die and, oh, how her children will thank God always for her and you. She was so good to me. I valued her good will and love so much. Love to you all, Nancy Astor

Nancy's son, David Astor, wrote this to Isaac Foot:

I only met Mrs Foot a few times in my life but her distinction of mind and hearing made an impression on me that I shall long remember. It was easy to see at Callington the quality of the home life presided over by her gentle and fine spirit. The time I once came there to tea gave me a picture of family life that one could not help feeling tremendously drawn to. One felt that your wife's spirit diffused an atmosphere that was gay and witty with an underlying peace and calm which gave the discussion of great ideas and causes its proper setting of integrity and depth of sentiment. My mother always regarded her as being in every sense one of her best friends and I am sure will feel her loss deeply.

Isaac Foot's close friend Norman Birkett wrote this:

To lose the companion of forty-two years of happy married life is a blow of the heaviest kind and no words of mine can do anything to assuage the grief which such a loss brings. But you have sources of consolation which are the secret strength of your own life and of that I will say nothing, save this – that you will find in them your strength and stay in this grievous hour. There came back into my mind at this moment the lovely sonnet you once gave me in the House of Commons:

> To know thine eyes are tearless though mine weep:
> And when this cup's last bitterness I drain,
> One thought shall still its primal sweetness keep–
> Thou had'st the peace and I the undying pain.[236]

Isaac Foot described Eva's funeral in a letter to his son Mac, who was abroad at the time:
I went in to see your mother an hour after she died. I was alone. Mac, it was most wonderful to see how, within that hour, your mother had recovered in her beautiful face all the serenity and naturalness. The day before I had seen her weak and faint; now it was all gone. Just the touch of laughing irony on her lips as if she was making one of those comments that used to put us in our place. There was peace, assurance, happiness as if she had seen a vision. You would have felt the glory of it.

The event put the whole countryside into sorrow. The letters came in by the hundreds – over 900 altogether I think. Mac, there never has been and there never can be again such letters. I was overwhelmed by the tributes in which everyone joined, rich and poor, high and low. Your mother had captured the heart of Plymouth. She met ever so many people

---

236. Philip Bourke Marston (1850–87), 'Not Thou, but I', taken from David McPhail (ed.), *The Book of Sorrow* (Oxford University Press, 1916).

during the six or seven months of office and they fell in love with her. I am told that no death has ever given such a sense of personal loss in the history of the city. And, of course, you will know what it has meant to Callington ... For the two services I decided to have no mourning, no flowers, no funeral trappings of any kind whatever. It was made a service of thanksgiving, the first at the Methodist Central Hall in Plymouth and then at Callington. Both services were the most wonderful I have ever seen. There was no address whatever but the singing was the most impressive I have ever heard. All her favourite hymns and the climax came with the singing of the Te Deum (Jackson's setting). The hall was filled in every inch of space and could have been filled twice over. There were no funeral marches but the favourite Sunday school hymn tunes played when we had all taken our places. Then her coffin was brought in whilst we sang her hymn 'My Jesus I Love Thee, I Know Thou Are Mine'. Mac, it was wonderful to hear these 1,500 people singing but I only heard her voice – 'If ever I loved Thee, my Jesus, 'tis now' – I have never thought of her as being in any coffin or grave ...Then came the Callington service. The chapel filled as never before. I was standing very near the spot where I put the ring on her finger forty-two years ago. The weather was beautiful. The congregation walked in their hundreds to the little cemetery, where we sang 'Tell Me the Old, Old Story' – an amazing setting on that afternoon with Kit Hill overlooking everything and the Cornish hills in the distance – her hills, Caradon, Cheesewring, Hawkes Tor. The loss seemed incredible and bewildering. It was like looking in the familiar mirror and seeing no reflection on one's face. I have found comfort in the rallying of the children. Your mother was very proud of you. Every scrap you sent to her is in her desk. She treasured every word of praise you received. How she would have rejoiced in your honour. I think she knows all about it. Hers was a very happy life and you helped to make it happy and so did Sylvia, bless her. God bless you Mac, Dad

After Eva's death, Isaac Foot returned to continue with his engagements as Lord Mayor until November 1946.

The suggestion that her life and standards were adapted to mine is wholly wrong. Hers were the standards in the family we all kept to. There was only one throne in the home – that was hers. The decision to accept the Lord Mayoralty was mainly hers. She herself shrank from it. It was not her line of country at all. Titles, honours, prestige, precedents were terms that had no meaning for her. She regarded with much apprehension her capacity to deal with state occasions. It was remarkable that within a week that had all changed. I know Plymouth better than she did. The Plymouth people took her to their hearts. The stories of individual sufferings and distress that reached her; as far as time allowed she tried to search these people out. Some things made her weep over the city. I must continue with my public engagements. 'You owe it to Plymouth,' she would say.

31 The Cromwell Association

DINGLE: In our home we had twenty or thirty busts or portraits of Oliver Cromwell look-ing down upon us. Whatever other interest my father was pursuing at any one time, he was always loyal to the seventeenth century of the days of Eliot and Pym and Hampden and Cromwell. For the last few years he has had a wonderful time. It has been a sort of orgy of tercentenaries.[237]

In 1937 Isaac Foot was one of three founder members of the Cromwell Association. As its first Chairman, he explained that it was to be:

'A non-political and non-sectarian body to perpetuate the memory of the Lord Protector and mark the authentic sites of his battlefields and the buildings connected with his life, to put right an historical injustice, to research work into contemporary records and for commemorating his great day on 3 September.'

Isaac Foot with a bust of Cromwell on the stairs of Pencrebar.

237. 1951 broadcast.

Isaac Foot and Arthur Russell-Smith, the first honorary secretary and treasurer, led the way in carrying out these declared aims. The association's first achievement, in 1938, was to place memorial tablets on Cromwell's house at Ely and the Old Grammar School at Huntingdon 'so that all that pass that way shall realise their fame'. The plaque on the school reads 'Oliver Cromwell Lord Protector of the Commonwealth attended this school about 1610'.

Isaac Foot, speaking outside the former Huntingdon Grammar School: It is fitting that the first effort of the association to commemorate Cromwell and his great work should be made in Huntingdon, where he was born on 25 April 1599 and where he spent his early years. He was born in a house not far from this school. Cromwell lived in Huntingdon as a boy, grew up in the town as a young man, remained here until he was turned thirty years of age and then went to live at St Ives close by. It was in this old grammar school that he imbibed from Dr Beard, his schoolmaster, some of those truths that he put into practice in later years. He represented Huntingdon in Parliament and gave a fame to the town of which they had every reason to be proud. We think it fitting that there should be a memorial here at this grammar school, to which he walked daily from his home, not so much for the sake of his reputation as for our sakes and for the sake of the children, the boys and girls, living in this town. We want more of these memorials put up so that in the days to come the children

The Old Grammar School in Huntingdon, sketched in 1845. Oliver Cromwell was taught in the building on the left, which now houses the Cromwell Museum. (Huntingdon Local Record Office)

would be told what it means. Every boy and girl in this town of Huntingdon should be proud of this town where Cromwell was born and so live that the town will be proud of him or her. We rejoice in the fact that Cromwell is now honoured in his home town and we thank God for his work and his life and the contribution to English life and freedom.

In the next few years the Cromwell Association carried out its stated purpose to erect memorials on the 'authentic sites' of the major battlefields of the Civil War – these were the battles of Edgehill (1642), Marston Moor (1644), Naseby (1645), Preston (1648), Dunbar (1650) and Worcester (1651).

1644 The battle of Marston Moor

In 1939 Isaac Foot had unveiled a monument erected by The Cromwell Association to commemorate the battle of Marston Moor.

In 1944 he wrote this letter to the editor of the Times*:*

Sunday, 2 July, will be the 300th anniversary of the battle of Marston Moor. When the memorial on the site of the battle was unveiled on 2 July 1939, your leading article stated that 'the ceremony should serve to commemorate not only great men and noble deeds, but perhaps even to remind a preoccupied world of the spirit in which Englishmen have always fought for the things which they believe really matter'. Believing that these reminders are more than ever necessary today, the Cromwell Association, in cooperation with local representative bodies, will hold a service of commemoration at the memorial on the afternoon of 2 July. Similar services will also be held on that day in the village of Tockwith and the City of York.
I am Sir, your obedient servant Isaac Foot

MARSTON MOOR MEMORIAL
July 2nd, 1644

Programme of Unveiling
July 1st, 1939

Marston Moor Memorial unveiled July 1st, 1939 on the eve of the 295th Anniversary of the Battle—fought July 2nd, 1644

Singing by the Choirs and Children of Long Marston and Tockwith, under the conductorship of Miss Wilson, Organist, of Long Marston

ADMISSION TO ENCLOSURE BY PROGRAMME

The programme for unveiling the monument erected by the Cromwell Association on the site of the battle of Marston Moor, 1 July 1939.

'There are more English soldiers buried here than in any other English field.' Speaking at the scene of the battle-field near the village of Tockwith, Isaac Foot described Marston Moor as 'the decisive battle of the Civil War':

On the 300th anniversary of the battle, we are gathered not to extol the victors or to glorify the achievements of Cromwell, but to salute victor and vanquished, paying tribute to those who fought for the King and those who fought for the King and Parliament and above all to remember the common soldiers who, Cavalier and Roundhead alike, were buried together by the York peasants on that field in a common grave. Within the narrow space of the Ouse, the Nidd and the Wharfe lies some of the most historic soil of England. There is 'on that rich earth a richer dust concealed'.[238] On the second of July every year English men and women might well make their pilgrimage to honour these brave men who, gaining nothing for themselves, gave so much for us.

The Civil War itself was the decisive event in English history. Had the King's army won, England would have taken her place alongside the absolutist monarchies of Europe and parliamentary institutions would have disappeared. So argues Trevelyan. For better or for worse Marston Moor would have been lost, Charles would have been back at Whitehall, many heads would have fallen on Tower Hill and the history of England and with England the history of Europe and America would have taken another course.

In memory of Pym: the 300th anniversary of the death of John Pym

One aim of the Cromwell Association was to 'put right an historical injustice' by drawing attention to and celebrating the many anniversaries and great names of this period of seventeenth-century Britain.

In 1943 Isaac Foot wrote this letter to the editor of the Times:
December 8 1943 is the 300th anniversary of the death of John Pym. On behalf of the Cromwell Association I shall, on that day, be placing a wreath in St Margaret's Churchyard, Westminster, at or near the spot where Pym's remains were buried in 1661 when they were removed, with those of others, from the Abbey. Any who share with us the desire to do honour to the memory of this great man are invited to attend this ceremony. A similar service will take place on 6 December at Tavistock, the constituency which Pym represented in Parliament. I am your obedient servant Isaac Foot

On this occasion Isaac Foot was invited to make a broadcast on Pym's importance in history:

John Pym was a man who was greatly loved and fiercely hated. How did it come about that John Pym should be so loved and so hated during his lifetime? To answer that question we

---

238. Rupert Brooke, 'The Soldier' (1914).

have to go back to the year 1629 when, after dismissing his third parliament in anger, Charles decided to govern the country without parliaments. The very word 'parliament' was to be banished from our English speech. For eleven years our Parliament house remained untenanted. Then, early in 1640, Charles, in desperate straits for money, was forced to call his 'Short' Parliament. That 'Short' Parliament revealed that, in John Pym, the nation had found a spokesman who could voice their grievances, and a leader who could unite all those who were determined upon reform and the restoration of our ancient liberties.

Again Charles, in his anger, dismissed Parliament, but thereupon, his difficulties multiplied, his need for money became yet more desperate and Pym, seeing the opportunity, got the people to press for the recalling of Parliament. Pym prepared the petition that was presented to the King, and, when the summoning of another parliament was at last announced, he, with his friend John Hampden, rode throughout the length and breadth of the country on what must have been our first general election campaign. The result was that when the Long Parliament – the most famous parliament in our history – met at Westminster, Pym was already the recognised leader of those members who had made up their minds that this time Parliament and not the King should be the real ruler of England. Gradually the leadership of Pym asserted itself. He grew with the opportunity. He had, as we have seen, largely made this Long Parliament, and the Long Parliament, in a sense, made him.

Pym insisted on three things. First, the supremacy of the law: the King of England, he contended – whatever Kings were elsewhere – was not an absolute monarch, but one limited by the law. Second, Parliament was to control the Crown instead of the Crown controlling Parliament, and the King was to appoint only those advisers who commanded the confidence of Parliament. Thirdly, within Parliament itself, the Commons were to have the deciding voice in imposing taxation and granting supply, and, in the event of differences between the two Houses, the Commons were to have the last word. Now, these three principles of Pym's policy are today the accepted axioms of our constitution, but in Pym's day, they were almost revolutionary.

When the fierce controversies of Parliament gave place to the more desperate argument of Civil War, the leadership of this man became recognised more than ever. He had only sixteen months to live when war broke out, but these were given over to ceaseless activity in the House, in the City and in the conference of war. Regardless of all personal conditions, he spent his fortune, his health and all the resources of his capacious mind in the service of the Commonwealth. The son of Charles I had his revenge when, twelve years after the execution of his father, by his express wish and command the body of John Pym was disinterred from Henry VII's Chapel in the Abbey, and thrown, with the remains of others, into a common pit in Saint Margaret's Churchyard. Some of the most precious dust in England lies not within the Abbey, but without. And we can say of him what was said of his friend Sir John Eliot: 'No stone marks the spot where he lies, but as long as freedom continues in England he will not be without a monument.'

also William Shade

293

1944 The tercentenary of the death of Admiral Robert Blake, General-at-Sea

In 1944 Isaac Foot was a leading member of the Robert Blake Memorial Committee, formed to raise funds to pay tribute to Admiral Blake by placing a memorial tablet in Westminster Abbey, in memory of one whom he called 'one of our greatest sea captains in our naval history'. Blake had fought with the Roundheads in the Civil War and in 1649 was given command of the British fleet by Cromwell. In 1657 he died on board his ship on the way into Plymouth Sound. His heart was buried in St Andrew's Church, Plymouth. In 1957 Isaac Foot spoke in memory of Blake, to mark the 300th anniversary of his death:

At the break of day on the seventh of August three hundred years ago, the ship *George* entered Plymouth Sound. It was laden with precious cargo – the body of Robert Blake, General-at-Sea. He had sailed his last voyage. As his fleet of eleven ships came into English waters it was known that he was about to die. He had hoped to see his beloved Westcountry once again. As they came towards Plymouth, the other ships were sent on up the Channel, but the *George*, with two other ships, was turned into Plymouth Sound in the hope that the great seaman might yet reach his native soil. But it was not to be. Within sight of home his great heart broke. The body was brought ashore. The people of Plymouth, who had gathered to greet their great hero, stood in silence as a grief-stricken community represented a grief-stricken nation. The body of Blake was taken to London to be buried later in Westminster Abbey, in solemn state, but his heart was buried in St Andrew's Church here in Plymouth. That was most fitting. Plymouth became his second home. If Blake had to die, it was fitting that this great sailor should die at sea, and Plymouth was the rightful place for the burial of his heart. Of the letters of Robert Blake that have come down to us many were written at sea, and many at Plymouth, some from Plymouth Sound.

The words chosen for the memorial tablet were as follows: 'In Memory of Robert Blake Admiral and General of the Fleet, who, trusting in God and in the valour of his countrymen, wrought great victories for England at sea and worthily maintained the honour of the nation. He was born in 1598 at Bridgwater and died during his last voyage home on August 7 1657. One who desired no greater worldly happiness than to be accounted honest and faithful in his employment.'

3 September: Cromwell Day

The main purpose of the Cromwell Association was to 'perpetuate the memory of the Lord Protector' and to restore his reputation as 'one of the greatest Englishmen'. One way in which it planned to do this was by restoring the practice of commemorating Cromwell Day, on 3 September, by holding a service in front of Cromwell's statue in Parliament Square outside the Houses of Parliament. It was not until 1949 that the Cromwell Association was able to hold this service. Isaac Foot was the speaker at this first service, which became an annual event.

It may be asked why is the ceremony taking place here and why on this day. Well, this year is the 350th anniversary of his birth and 3 September was Cromwell's day. It was the day of his death. Our commemoration is timed for 3 o'clock. It was at 3 o'clock that he died. To him death was deliverance and the beginning of his fuller service elsewhere. It was the day of the victory of Dunbar and it was the day of the victory at Worcester – 'the crowning mercy' as he himself called it. When, on 6 September, the news of Worcester was brought to the Parliament of that time, it was enacted that there would be an annual commemoration of the natural deliverance for all future time. We have, therefore, express parliamentary sanction. This is the first time this commemoration has taken place but it is intended to mark the day in like fashion for future years. We might not have so considerable a ceremony but it is our hope that no 3 September shall pass in future years without some wreath being laid or some open and public tribute being made.

Isaac Foot giving the address at the Cromwell Association's celebration of the tercentenary of Cromwell's death by Cromwell's statue in Parliament Square on 3 September 1958

It is asked why the commemoration should take place here – the answer is a statue was placed here fifty years ago and this is the most fitting place. The Cromwell Association has already marked the burial place of John Pym. That we did in 1943. In the year of 1954 we intend to mark the burial of Elizabeth Cromwell and in 1958 the 300th anniversary of Cromwell's death will be marked throughout the civilised world. I venture to prophesy that, at that time, whilst a service will most fittingly be held here, there will be nowhere where there will not be some token of gratitude paid.

Dr Maurice Ashley, who took over as chairman of the Cromwell Association in 1951, later paid this tribute to Isaac Foot's role in restoring the reputation of Cromwell:

His home in Cornwall held a wonderful collection of books and of Cromwelliana, Civil War pamphlets and portraits. They could picture him amongst all this. In these days people could be rarely found who read and thought so deeply on the history and greatness of their country. There was a pugnacity about him too, especially typified during his days in the House of Commons, a fighting spirit that called to mind a figure of the Cromwellian period.

32 'Liberty and the Liberal heritage'

In 1947 Isaac Foot was elected president of the Liberal Party Organisation. He toured the country in a campaign to make the Liberal Party an effective force in British politics once more. He was determined that the party should maintain its independence and not succumb to any overtures to form a 'common political front' with the Conservatives in order to fight the next election.

The following is a short excerpt from the Ramsay Muir Memorial Lecture which Isaac Foot was invited to give in 1947 on the theme of 'Liberty and the Liberal Heritage'. After looking at the different interpretations of the word 'liberty' he continues:

I have been quoting today in particular three names – those of Milton, Burke and Wordsworth, and the conjunction of these three names leads me to the other aspect of my lecture today. In my title I have spoken of liberty as a heritage. I want you to think of freedom as an inheritance. Many people have been asking me about Burke and what to read about him. I can only say I had my political education largely through Burke. I was living at my home in Plymouth when we had there a Liberal candidate many years ago; his name was Charles Mallet, afterwards Sir Charles Mallet. He came down for the election campaign of 1906 and for the first time in my life I began to hear about a man named Burke. Mr Mallet constantly quoted him. I remember then getting a little book in the Temple Classics edition.

The lesson of both Burke and Wordsworth was that liberty is an inheritance, and that 'Freedom's battle once begun is bequeathed from bleeding sire to son'. Between them Milton, Burke and Wordsworth cover a period of over two centuries in our history. Milton was born in 1608 and died in 1674. Burke, born in 1729, died in 1797. Wordsworth, born in 1770, was twenty-four years of age when Burke died, and he himself lived until 1850. The first distinction of these three men was their zeal for freedom. Burke learned to love liberty mainly from the example of Milton, and that love he transmitted to the youth Wordsworth.

Edmund Burke was in so many ways different from Milton, but their blood kinship was in their love of liberty. Every writer upon Burke seems constrained to couple his name with Milton. 'Burke at his best is England at her best' – that was Acton's tribute, and Burke was at his best when he wrote in vindication of English liberty. His speeches on America and his Letter to the Sheriffs of Bristol are worthy to take their place beside Milton's 'Areopagitica' and his sonnets and Samson Agonistes. 'These speeches', says John Morley, 'are almost the one monument of the struggle (with the American colonies) on which a lover of English greatness can look back with pride and a sense of worthiness.'[239]

---

239. John Morley (1838–1923), Liberal politician and writer.

Freedom is, of course, the common concern of all our fellow-citizens, but it is a plain fact of history that the achievement of free government has been mainly associated with what we call Liberalism. It was the cause of freedom which called Liberalism into existence. Were it not for the struggle for liberty, there never would have been any Liberal Party at all. If you asked me when Liberalism began, I should find it difficult to answer. I think probably the Liberal Party began somewhere about the time of the Reformation. The Liberal Party as a party began when Hampden and Pym made their preparation before the summoning of the Long Parliament in 1640. It was the men who sustained the cause of King and Parliament against that of the King and Divine Right, and fought the Civil War which determined the constitutional future of the country, and saved us from being swept into the vortex of Continental monarchism. From Pym's day there has always been a company of men and women called by all sorts of names – Roundheads, the Country Party, Whigs and then Liberals – but representing under all these different names one definite tradition in our British life. Those names include Sir John Eliot, John Pym, John Hampden, Oliver Cromwell, John Selden, Milton, Vane and Sidney, John Locke and Adam Smith, Charles James Fox, Burke and the younger Wordsworth, Grey of the Reform Act, Erskine, Macaulay, Lord John Russell, John Stuart Mill, Gladstone, John Morley, Campbell-Bannerman, Asquith, Edward Grey, Lloyd George and, shall we not add, Donald Maclean, Lothian, Ramsay Muir and so many others.

Liberty is never something achieved; it is always something that is being achieved. It is a war in which there is no discharge. But, although the fight for liberty never ceases, the battleground changes in every generation. In our generation, as I see it, the men and women of Liberal mind would make a declaration along these lines:

We stand for representative institutions as the expression of democratic government. We desire the rehabilitation of Parliament, and the restoration of the proper authority of the House of Commons. The authority of the House of Commons is weakening as it becomes less and less the representative of the people and all the people, and more and more the engine of the executive. We believe that the executive has to be watched with jealous vigilance and that Parliament will only recover its rightful authority as it is made more truly representative of all the citizens. Accepting the principle of majority government, we demand for minorities, however small, their rightful share in choosing our governors who administer their affairs, and who make the laws under which they live. We are against any extension of the power of the state which denies to the individual his inalienable rights. We are against any power being given to any section of the community which is denied to the ordinary citizens, even if they are unorganised and few. Next in importance to the individual citizens we place the family. The home, in our belief, is a nobler institution than any organisation framed by the ingenuity of man. Whatever strikes at the family life cuts the ligaments of the Commonwealth...

Isaac Foot speaking at a Liberal Garden Party at Pencrebar with Jeremy Thorpe, the future Liberal leader, to his left.

We desire something more than free government. The worst tyrannies may be those independent of the laws, and can be exercised in the home, the factory and the workshops and in the daily social life. Our ideal is not only free government, but social liberty. About 300 years ago John Milton wrote of a free Commonwealth. He spoke of 'a free Parliament; which then only will indeed be free, and deserve the true honour of that supreme title, if they preserve us a Free People'. And, again, he said: 'As men by nature free; born and created with a better title to their freedom than any King hath to his crown.' In his last speech as leader of our party, Mr Asquith, as he then was, spoke of 'passing on the torch'. Civilization, indeed, has been saved by the passing of the torch. In this generation the torch is in our hands. The light we carry was handed on to us by the great runners of whom I have been speaking. It is their light as much as ours. If Liberalism were to die that light would go out. If, in our generation, the Liberal Party should fail, then, even whilst we are running in the race, the torch would flicker and die. By God's grace that shall not happen. We may not be great men and women, but we carry a great light. This is what gives distinction and honour to the humblest Liberals in the obscurest part of the land. They for a time carry the light, a light which is not only for this country but for the whole world. There is something common to every country and to every colour and every speech may confuse, but light is understood everywhere. In a dark world the light bearers form a shining company. It was of a liberated slave and of a man of another colour and race, a victim struck down by a tyrant, that Wordsworth wrote:

Thou has left behind
Powers that will work for thee; air, earth and skies;
There's not a breathing of the common wind
That will forget thee; thou hast great allies;
Thy friends are exultations, agonies
And love, and man's unconquerable mind.'[240]

Isaac Foot continued to campaign on behalf of his party. Following the general election of 1950 he wrote this letter to the editor of the Times:

Sir, In these days when apparently we are all being urged to vote against something, may I draw attention to what has happened in this end of the country? In Somerset the Conservatives were in a minority of 20,109 votes. They have taken all the six seats. In Dorset the Conservatives were in a minority of 8,000 votes. They have taken all four seats. In Devon the Conservatives had a majority of 2,402 votes out of nearly half a million. They have taken eight seats out of ten. In Cornwall the Conservatives were in a minority of 23,335 votes. They have taken four seats out of five. And all this, sir, took place under what is called the Representation of the People Act. I am, Sir, your obedient servant Isaac Foot

---

240. Wordsworth's 'Sonnet to Toussaint L'Ouverture'. L'Ouverture (1734–1803), a freed slave, was a leader of the Haitian revolution.

33 'Pit and Rock'

Sarah remembers life at Pencrebar after the war:

Pencrebar was the house that was to mean home to me all through my childhood, as my parents were always on the move abroad. It was a magic house with all the ingredients, it seemed to me, essential for a happy home. It was always full of uncles and aunts who adored children. There were endless games on the wide terraced lawn looking down on the wooded slopes of the Lynher valley. I can remember Uncle Michael, who enthusiastically joined in, throwing himself down on the garden steps trying to recover his breath and wheezing frightfully from his asthma as he laughed helplessly at us all. There was Uncle Chris, who always came with brown paper parcels of sweets and fruit, who saw us off on trains always with a comic and an apple, who fetched and carried for one and all, surely the most unselfish man I have ever known. Uncle Johnnie was often there with his wife, Anne, and children, Kate and Winslow. A special treat was his puppet show in the little theatre he built himself. He was the only one of the uncles who inherited his grandfather's gift of being clever with his hands. For some time when I used to stay at Pencrebar, after my grandmother's death, both my aunts were in residence. Aunt Jennifer ran the domestic side of life, having returned from India with her two eldest children. With her hair twisted on top of her head, with her warm smile, gentle ways and fine features; with her sturdy frame and her deep chuckle of a laugh; with her obvious concern and compassion for all the family's problems, she eventually took the place of my grandmother in the family. She bore everyone's woes and complaints as if they were her own. She was as intelligent and well read as her five brothers. Aunt Jen reigned supreme in the kitchen. Through the wide-sashed windows of the kitchen I could look across the courtyard to the stables and for some years my Aunt Sally filled this lovely building with her ponies and horses and ran a small private riding school. My cousin Kate and I worshipped this aunt. She too was steeped in literature and particularly poetry, which she would often recite to us as we rode through the country lanes. Through the aunts' and uncles' attentions and just their presence the strong family ties were made, never to be broken. At the head of it all was my grandfather. His affection to us was all-embracing, glorying in our triumphs or virtues and finding them when others might have missed them.[241]

In 1951 Isaac Foot married Catherine Elizabeth Taylor, known as Kitty to the family.

---

241. Sarah Foot, *My Grandfather Isaac Foot* (1980).

Isaac Foot with his second wife, Kitty, whom he married in 1951.

MICHAEL: Nothing could compare with the love and companionship which my mother gave to my father. Her sudden, quite unexpected death in May 1946 during my father's year as Lord Mayor of Plymouth was, as it can be imagined, a terrible blow. He continued the rest of his public life in the same way as she would have wished, but no one or nothing could repair the loss. Maybe his best comfort was the new commonplace book he compiled containing many of her favourite passages of poetry or writings which they had read together. Jill Craigie, when she was starting to make her film about Plymouth,[242] had been noted by my mother – 'She's the one for you,' she is supposed to have said. After our marriage it was Jill who built a special relationship with my father. They both had plenty of interests in common such as a love of music and a respect for strange heroes such as Oscar Wilde. My father, on his frequent trips to London, was provided with a bed in our house in London. It was to Jill that my father first broached the idea of a new addition to his family. The proposal was for his marriage to Kitty Taylor, née Dawe, one of my mother's oldest friends. No one honoured my mother more than Kitty and, after their marriage in 1951, she certainly eased the last few years of his life at Pencrebar. Whatever happened, he would not move from there with his books.

---

242. *The Way We Live* (1946).

SARAH: I think my grandfather was the happiest man I have ever known. He certainly suffered great disappointments – the death of his wife and his defeats in elections are just some examples. But I never remember seeing him other than full of enthusiasm. Rages he vented, certainly, over an unjust world and the consequences on others but he obviously considered himself a most fortunate man and the happiness he felt he passed so easily to others. There are those who have not been part of the Methodist faith who believe it is full of killjoys who are determined that all pleasurable things in life are sinful. As far as my grandfather was concerned, this could not have been further from the truth. In my grandfather's house there was constant laughter, a great eagerness for learning, an encour-agement to listen to all kinds of music and a great love of the theatre – he took us to the pantomime every year. Although he loved classical and particularly choral music he would also take the whole family to a Gilbert and Sullivan operetta and show his pleasure with great enthusiasm throughout. My grandfather's passion for music was given birth in his earliest years when he learned to sing loud and clear the Methodist hymns he loved all his life. In his last years Johann Sebastian Bach was his great love and often, when staying at Pencrebar, we would wake on a Sunday morning to hear some of this great composer's music throbbing through the floorboards of the house. He was also a brilliant raconteur of funny stories. His love of football and cricket was legendary in the family and his

Isaac with his sons John, Mac and Michael, watching Plymouth Argyle in 1958.

Isaac with his five sons, Dingle, Mac, John, Michael and Christopher, at Pencrebar in the late 1940s.

loyalty to the Callington cricket team and Plymouth Argyle were two of the most important things in his life. One of the things the family liked to do together was to attend Plymouth Argyle football matches and all the family remained loyal to the team ever afterwards. My grandfather enjoyed every minute of these occasions and would shout and cheer louder than anyone. When Plymouth Argyle was defeated there was a general air of gloom around the house and just as much rejoicing when they won.

There was a sort of tribal feeling in the family: everyone always ready to ridicule and criticise each other but heaven help anyone outside the family trying to do the same. My grandfather would say, 'If anyone bites the Foot family they bite granite.'

Isaac Foot: I think of all the main issues that have been some satisfaction to me over the last twenty years or so is that my family, whatever may be their differences of expression, all stand pretty much for the same principles and are on the same road. I'm sometimes reminded of the drummer at Horrabridge in the band – a very small man with a very big drum. Performing his drum one day and beating it with great vigour, he lost sight of the fact that the band in front had gone on a road to the right and he continued 100 yards of his own. A little boy overtook him and said, 'Look here, mister, band's gone that way.' 'That's alright, son. Don't you trouble about that, we're playing the same tune alright.'

303

Well, I think that the same tune is being played by the family alright and I am rather gratified at the tune. On the whole I sometimes make reflections, looking back on the children coming one after another, that before I was married I had seven theories as to the way to bring up children and now I have seven children and no theories at all.[243]

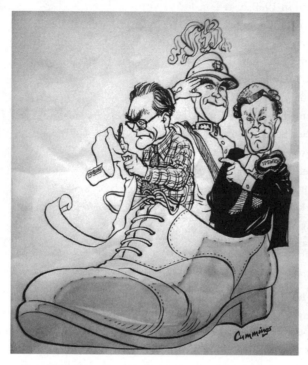

'The Old Boot': Cummings portrays three of Isaac's sons – Dingle the lawyer and Labour MP, Mac the colonial Governor and Michael the journalist and MP.

Isaac Foot greatly appreciated the letters he received about his family. On 19 May 1940 Norman Birkett wrote to congratulate him on Dingle's appointment as parliamentary secretary to the Ministry of Economic Warfare in Churchill's wartime government:

My dear Isaac, I have been thinking of your pride in Dingle and his achievement by sheer merit and no disavowal of principle! I am glad for you and proud of him! 'The rock from which...!' But he has always had politics in him and he has already done notable work. How did Michael's book go? I hope it was a great success. Dingle must make you feel very proud and Michael and John and the family. And how are you in these grim days? One of the most dreadful things of this war for me is that I am not educated or trained for a world at war. All the things that are needed most are really foreign to my world. But I do what I can ... What the future brings is all unknown: but it is good at this time to think of old friends with affection and to rejoice in the pride which they can feel. Yours always Norman

---

243. 1953 broadcast.

HUGH: Our father took a tremendous interest and unreasonable pride in the activities of his offspring. When Michael wrote *The Pen and the Sword* he was overjoyed that one of his sons should have ventured into literature and history. When I was governor in Cyprus he followed every development with the keenest anxiety and it was a special satisfaction to him that, shortly before he died in 1960, a settlement in Cyprus was achieved. We, on our side, would go to him for guidance and for encouragement. Once when I finally returned from Cyprus I was offered a commercial job at any salary I liked to state. I was not attracted by the prospect but I went to see him to tell him of the offer. He said he would think about it and next day at breakfast he said: 'I have thought about that offer. If you accepted it your enemies would know what to say, but your friends wouldn't.' And one day when the situation in Cyprus was at its worst and seemed to be in hopeless bloody deadlock, I received a telegram from my father which said: 'See Second Corinthians 4:8–9.' I turned from my anxieties to look it up and found this text to encourage me in my adversity: 'We are troubled on every side, yet not distressed; we are perplexed but not in despair; persecuted but not forsaken; cast down but not destroyed.' I sent back this telegram: 'See Romans 5:3–4: 'And not only so, but we glory in tribulations also; knowing that tribulation worketh patience; and patience experience and experience hope.' My father's opinion of my biblical knowledge was rightly low. The fact that I had been able to cap his text made him shake his head in wonder for long afterwards.

On 20 February 1959 Herbert Samuel wrote:
My dear Isaac, You have a right to feel happy and proud over the outcome about Cyprus, after so much perturbation and anxiety. I feel impelled to send you a word of affectionate congratulation.

MICHAEL: In 1948 my father wrote me this letter on my election to the National Executive of the Labour Party:

> My dear Michael, The whole family – as far as I can judge – swells with pride and apprehension. We don't think much of your party, but this is their best manifesta-tion of intelligence and discernment. If they go on like this then there is some hope for this old Country! The election synchronised with the second anniversary of your Mother's leaving us. She will be very pleased about it. Love Dad

When I was defeated in Devonport in the general election of 1955 my father sent me a first edition of Jonathan Swift. Written on the flyleaf was: 'This book from my library at Pencrebar is given, with my love and some reluctance, to my son Michael, as a token of con-solation on his defeat at Devonport in the general election, 26 May 1955. I recall defeats at Totnes, Plymouth, Bodmin, St Ives and Tavistock in the years 1910, 1918, 1924, 1935, 1937 and 1945. On the whole these defeats were more honourable than my five victories.'

It was now with his father's encouragement and the loan of many of his rare books on the subject that Michael decided to write a book on Swift and Marlborough, published as The Pen and the Sword *in 1957. Isaac Foot described his pleasure with the publication of this book:*

He consulted 200 of my books on the subject, some of them not easily procurable and spent some time here working on it in the attic at Pencrebar ... I told Mac on the telephone today that anyone can be an member of Parliament or governor of Cyprus. But this is the summit of the Foot family's achievement – a historical work that will be read in fifty years' time.

In 1957 Eden Phillpotts wrote to thank Isaac for sending him a copy of Michael's book:
Thank you for this fine book – I look forward to enjoying it. Your son has chosen a remarkably interesting page of literary and political history and he will illuminate it for he is a gifted writer of the Queen's English and handles our grand mother tongue with a distinction and respect for style largely lacking in this generation of younger writers today. Always your old friend.

In the same year Norman Birkett also wrote to thank Isaac for sending him a copy of Michael's book:
Thank you for the copy of Michael's book, which I am reading with great interest and pleasure. I saw with pleasure too that you had encouraged him to write the book. Hugh's advancement is a great joy to us and the Foot family has made a very great contribution to our national life, not the least of the contributions being made by one ISAAC ... Life goes past too quickly for me and I was interested to notice in reading Faber's Jowett that he was depressed continually on this account. But of course he was not 'marching through Emmanuel's grounds' as I remember you singing when I stayed with you. Much love to you all and especially to those who are still of the household of faith! Yours ever Norman

On 20 November 1959 Birkett wrote this letter to Isaac:
Dingle has been arguing a case in the Privy Council where I was sitting ... and I thought I would drop you a line to say how often you have been in my thoughts. You have good reason to be proud of your sons and family and Dingle's future is I think quite assured. Had Labour won I should have expected him to be one of the Law Officers of the Crown. I have accepted the invitation to preside at the dinner to celebrate your 80th birthday when it is held. Whenever I pass Cromwell on my way to the Lords I think of you and the Cromwell Society honoured me greatly in asking me to preside at what will be a great function. I hope all your family will be there to support you on what promises to be a great occasion. Will you come to lunch with me in the Lords and we will raise an Ebenezer – 'Hither by thine help I'm come!' I think one of life's good gifts is the love of reading for it goes on with me when other things like walking begin to be troublesome! Sometime let me know how life treats you. Your book on Milton is always at my right hand.

He wrote again on 29 January 1960:
What a lovely thought it was to send the snowdrops! My wife will be writing to you, but I could not forbear to send a word of warmest thanks for the glow it gave my day ... I often think of the days when you sat down at the piano and played the great hymns and how you sang 'And let our songs abound', which had been sung at your father's funeral. Indeed my mind is full of grateful memories of you to which I will now add the SNOWDROPS. Michael seems to be getting a national figure and I love to see his wonderful belligerence on the television and I always say when it is over – people wouldn't believe that he is really a wonderfully kind man. Yours ever Norman

Sarah expressed the family's pride in their father and grandfather:
Isaac Foot's sons, who all inherited many of his fine qualities, have perhaps gained far wider recognition than he ever did. Yet they all agreed that none of them could hold a candle to him either in his self-taught knowledge, his gift for oratory, his wit, his most endearing personality or in the way he held most closely all through his life to his original beliefs and ideals, never considering any compromise. To know him was to be enriched for life. It was not his knowledge or his gift of speaking 'with the tongues of men or angels' or his understanding or even his faith which had endeared him to us all. It was, without a doubt, his great love for people and for life itself that was easily his most outstanding feature.

MICHAEL: For my father the river Lynher below Pencrebar was 'the guardian of his tranquillity'.

Isaac with his dog Roddy by the river Lynher below Pencrebar.

307

Isaac Foot with his second wife, Kitty, and his granddaughter Alison at a Liberal garden party at Pencrebar in 1951.

In his later years Isaac delighted in his ten grandchildren and they in him. In May 1950 Isaac wrote to his grandson David Cadson Highet, then living with his parents in India:

My Dear Dai

This is a letter from your Grandpa.

Please tell your mother than we want you to come home to Pencrebar as soon as possible. There are five dogs and about a dozen ponies all waiting to see you.

There is your Cadsonbury waiting for David Cadson Highet. There is your river, and your great big stones, waiting for you to throw in with such a *splash, splash*.

Please tell your mummy that your grandpa is getting on alright. That the Jefferies are looking after him very well, and that he gets his tea about 5 o'clock every morning, and that he is always intending to put his books in proper order, but hasn't done so yet, and perhaps never will, and that Dingle and Dorothy come down every now and then, and Michael and Jill come along sometimes, and John and Anne, and Chris at the week-end.

You can give your mother all this news.

Give my love to your mother and father.

Love to you from Grandpa

A postcard of Cadsonbury, near Callington below Pencrebar above the river Lynher, which Isaac Foot sent to his grandson David.

On 23 February 1960 Isaac Foot and his family celebrated his eightieth birthday. His eldest grandson, Paul, wrote to his grandfather:

Dear Grandpa

> Today is called the feast of Isaac Foot
> And future February's shall ne'er go by,
> But he in it shall be remembered.'

Many happy returns of your birthday! 80 years of great achievement and learning are crowned today and I hope the population of Callington (and I'll throw in Newbridge) will rise to the occasion with great rejoicing. I am very excited at the moment as I go to America this weekend to debate for the Columbia Broadcasting Corporation! Quite something eh? I leave on Friday and return on Monday. I think the motion will be for the abolition of capital punishment with reference to Chessman.[244] I am very busy and very happy and look forward to seeing you and Kitty in March. A saffron cake arrived yesterday and was devoured almost at once! Thank you. Pit and Rock. Many happy returns Paul Mackintosh Foot

---

244. Caryl Chessman was executed in California in 1960, having become a *cause célèbre* for the movement to ban capital punishment.

The whole family gathered to celebrate – apart from Mac, who was then Governor of Cyprus and nearing the end of his term with the independence of Cyprus. Mac sent his father this telegram:

So sorry we can't be with you tomorrow. We are confident we shall finish our job here soon and then we shall come to report to you. Pit and Rock – love Mac.

Hugh's last memories of his father
He was the finest speaker and preacher I have ever heard. When I arrived back in London one evening on my many returns from Cyprus for consultation, I learnt that he was to speak at the National Liberal Club in an hour's time with his friend Lord Birkett. I changed quickly and hurried to the dinner. It was the last time I heard him speak in public. He was then eighty years of age. He had slowed up a little; his speaking mannerisms were more pronounced; he could not resist overloading his speaking with innumerable quotations. But what a delight it was to hear the magic of his oratory once more. What humour, especially when he was telling a story in Westcountry dialect, what timing, what elegance and music in his speech.

Isaac planting a tree in the grounds of Pencrebar on his eightieth birthday.

Isaac Foot at the age of seventy-eight in 1958.

PART X

Isaac Foot the lawyer

After his admission as a solicitor in 1902 and going into partnership with Edgar Bowden as Foot and Bowden, Isaac Foot had built up a large solicitor's practice in Plymouth. His sons John and Christopher later joined him as partners in this practice. Foot and Bowden became a large and well-known firm in Plymouth. Isaac Foot also served as a Justice of the Peace and in 1945 was appointed vice-chairman of Cornwall Quarter Sessions, serving as its chairman from 1953 to 1955.

Norman Birkett to Isaac Foot:
I was at the dinner of the Oxford University Law Society last night and when I got home today I found the Law Society's journal there with your fine and most interesting address ... it appears to have been the greatest joy and delight to all ... I read it with avidity and could hear your very tones as you told of the juryman who had left his 'verdick'![245]

34 'The lawyer outside his profession'

In 1956 Isaac Foot gave this address to the Law Society's annual conference in Newquay:
We have heard that this is the first time you have met in Cornwall. I wonder why. You will know, of course, that this is the land of the saints – Saint Austell and so many other names; in fact, half the parishes of Cornwall seem to be called after the saints. I am wondering whether some of my professional brethren that I have met elsewhere feel quite at home in this saintly atmosphere. I suppose that they consented to this short discipline because they saw that it was only to last a week. I remember the advertisement that was put up in the north of England which said: 'Visit Holy Island. Tread where the saints have trod. There and back, half a crown.' There has not always been a welcome for lawyers in Cornwall. It was Wordsworth, you remember, who, in a very wonderful poem, expressed little welcome to lawyers:

> A Lawyer art thou? Draw not nigh!
> Go, carry to some fitter place
> The keenness of that practised eye,
> The hardness of that sallow face![246]

---

245. Isaac Foot papers, 1956.
246. 'A Poet's Epitaph' (1800).

312

I had a talk on last Tuesday afternoon with a very eminent Cornishman, one of the great historians of our generation, Mr A. L. Rowse,[247] and he told me that, in Tudor times, they could not get any of the people of Cornwall to meet the judges. When they first sent down the Justices-in-Eyre, as they were called, they met none of the people of Cornwall, because, when the people of Cornwall heard that the justices were coming, the whole population took to the woods! There was the later example of the judge who at that time – it was the year 1549 – was called the provost marshal. There had been some disturbances in Cornwall shortly before – there have been many disturbances from time to time – and the judge, whose name was Sir Anthony Kingston, came down to investigate. He was entertained at a great civic feast by Mr Nicholas Boyer, the mayor of Bodmin, and whilst the feast was in progress the sound of hammering was heard in the yard outside, and when the feast was over the mayor asked the judge what was the meaning of the scaffold and who it was for. 'Oh,' said the Judge, 'it's for you first of all, Mr Mayor' – and Mr Mayor was the one who had to be put up and hanged. Since that time there has been a certain reluctance on the part of civic authorities in Cornwall to meet the judges of the High Court. But none of the records show whether the cost of that civic feast was borne out of the local rates or out of the national Exchequer.

I have the advantage of the personal friendship of some of Her Majesty's judges; they have been colleagues of mine in the House and long personal friends and I have often challenged them upon their reluctance to come on the Western Circuit. I reminded my friend Norman Birkett that he could face any part of the country, but that he never came on this circuit because he was afraid to face a Cornish jury. It is a very wonderful thing, a Cornish jury, and the first time I addressed a Cornish jury I was far more nervous than they were. It was during the war and there were seven of them. The foreman, I think to assure me that he was a friend of mine, addressed me every time as Mr Isaac, and, when he was asked about the verdict, he said that the man was guilty. The question was then put by the clerk, 'Is that the verdict of you all?' and he replied: 'Yes, Mr Isaac, five of us guilty and two not guilty.' I will leave it to the lawyers present to decide how I found upon that verdict. Then there was the famous case of the judge who came down here for the first time, and was very fearful about how he would manage his jury. The case had lasted five days and it was then six o'clock: were they to go on or to adjourn until the next day? It was a case with a lot of law and fact in it and he had heard about the difficulties of dealing with a Cornish jury, so he said: 'It would be better if we met in the morning.' He spent the night in the study of the evidence and came to court next day rather tired but still conscious that he had done his duty. When he got into the court there were, to his amazement, only eleven men in the jury box, so he asked: 'Where is the other man?' and the foreman got up and said: 'That's alright, sir, it's Ebenezer Tregarkis up to Altarnun. 'E's got a cow bad and I told 'im 'e could go 'ome – but it's alright, sir, 'e's left 'is verdick with us.'

---

247. A. L. Rowse (1903–97), Cornish historian and writer.

I want to deal with the lawyer in Parliament as I have seen him. I hope that you will forgive any personal reminiscences, but I saw a good many lawyers in Parliament during the years I was myself a member under five different Prime Ministers. The lawyers I particularly remember are Sir Robert Horne, Sir Thomas Inskip, Sir Douglas Hogg, Sir Kingsley Wood, Sir John Simon, Sir Rufus Isaacs in his later years – I did not know him when he was Attorney-General – Sir Stafford Cripps, Sir Patrick Hastings and Sir William Jowitt. I also knew a very great lawyer, Lloyd George, who was by far the greatest orator of my generation, except, perhaps, James Maxton. I only knew him, of course, in Parliament in his later days, but I remember, once when I was with him at Churt, spending the week-end there, discussing some public question, he told me about his earlier days and he mentioned an article he had been asked to write for which he had been offered a pound a word. He said, 'Isaac, a pound a word; think of it, my boy. How different from fourpence a folio!'

I would like to speak now about the lawyers of the Crown. They have played a great part in history, but, on the whole, a small part in comparison with others. It is strange that these men at the very head of their profession, with very high attainments, with great forensic gifts, sometimes the masters of the assembly in a court of law, have played so small a part in the House of Commons. Quite remarkable. There have, of course, been great officers of the Crown. There was one called Sir James Mackintosh,[248] a great name a hundred years ago, a name that is now almost forgotten. He it was who wrote the reply to Edmund Burke which was considered the best answer to certain of Burke's statements in his *Reflections on the French Revolution* – a work that had wonderful results and was said by, I think, Trevelyan to be the angel's trumpet which roused the fiends. Mackintosh made his reply to Burke in a book that received great commendation, but later on, when the excesses in the French Revolution became known, Mackintosh retired from his earlier position and there were some people who looked upon him as having betrayed his earlier radical ideals. Under the Pitt Sedition Bill a young Irish priest was hanged and there was a discussion on the matter in a London club. Mackintosh went out of his way to speak slightingly of this young Irish priest, and Dr Parr, a literary man of that time, turned upon him and said: 'Yes, Jamie, bad enough, wasn't it, but it might have been worse, you know. He was an Irishman and he might have been a Scotchman; he was a priest and he might have been a lawyer; he was a rebel and he might have been a renegade.'

Then there was Sir Samuel Romilly, of whom Augustine Birrell said that he was his ideal as a lawyer, a member of Parliament and a gentleman. He was one of the descendants of the Huguenot refugees. I do not suppose we shall ever be able to reckon what the world owes to the Huguenot refugees. When Louis XIV signed the Revocation of the Edict of Nantes he signed the death warrant of his own country and into every land there went these refugees, with their high standards, and their character, and perhaps it was due to

---

248. Sir James Mackintosh (1765–1832) wrote *Vindiciae Gallicae* in 1791 in reply to Burke's *Reflections* of 1790.

them that, in North America today, English and not French or Spanish is the language spoken. One of these refugees had for his grandson Sir Samuel Romilly, who was a great fighter against the slave trade to which I shall refer directly, a great orator and a great lawyer. There were many who thought that he ought to have been the Leader of the House of Commons, and Creevey went to the Prime Minister, Wellington, and suggested that Sir Samuel Romilly was the man to lead the House of Commons, but Wellington said: 'No. The House of Commons never liked a lawyer for a leader,' and that was the reason why he never became the Leader of the House.

I, of course, being a lawyer, sympathised a bit with the Law Officers of the Crown, but I recognised that they were fair game and once I myself tried to make game of one of the Law Officers. Whether it was to his advantage or mine in the end I do not know. The Law Officer concerned was my personal friend Sir William Jowitt. He was bringing in the Pensions Bill in the year 1929, the Widows' Pension Bill. When he had introduced the Bill I got up and drew attention to one of its clauses and asked him if he would give a fuller explanation of the clause which he was asking the House to accept. I read the clause, which went as follows:

Unless in any case the context otherwise requires any reference in this Act to the Principal Act or to any other enactment contained in that Act shall be construed as a reference to that Act or to that enactment as amended by this Act and any refer-ence in this Act to the Insurance Act or to any enactment contained in that Act shall be construed as a reference to that Act or to that enactment as amended by any other Act, including this Act.

I read it out and everyone in the House sympathised with me, but I said I knew very well that if Sir William Jowitt, who had the most beautiful voice in the House and the most handsome presence, repeated it, what was strange and uncouth to me would be so changed by his manner and bearing that it would sound like an ode of John Keats or a sonnet of Wordsworth. And the next day, 19 November 1929, the *Evening Standard* adopted my suggestion and published this sonnet:

Two voices are there. One is of the Law,
One of the people. Each a mighty voice.
The former doth apparently rejoice
In words that tax the brain and crack the jaw.
'Unless the context otherwise require'
(So limpidly the legal accents flow),
Should this new Act refer, we'd have you know,
To any other Act, then it transpired
That each enactment in the aforesaid Act

(Or may be in the other, never mind),
Shall constitute, when signed and countersigned,
A reference to something which in fact
May or may not mean something inasmuch
As legal talk is largely double dutch.

I had great pleasure in going into the office of the Law Officers of the Crown and handing to Sir William a copy of that issue of the Evening Standard.

There was another great lawyer to whom I will now make reference, Sir William Blackstone, who in the year 1765 published the first volume of his *Commentaries upon the Laws of England*.[249] It was about that date that the case of Wilkes was being debated in the House of Commons,[250] and Blackstone, being a supporter of the government of that day, spoke in favour of the exclusion of Wilkes. But thereupon a layman, whose name was Grenville, rose and produced Blackstone's own book showing that, upon Blackstone's own arguments, Wilkes should not have been excluded. They waited for Blackstone to make his reply, but it was some time before he could recollect what he ought to say. Blackstone came in for a good deal of criticism and a Mr Junius,[251] a nice friendly writer of the time, began to take an interest in Dr Blackstone and to call public attention to him. One thing about Junius was that he could generally in one sentence deal very effectively with a man. He once said of someone that 'he became a minister by accident and an apostate by design', and when he came to deal with Dr Blackstone he wrote:

> Dr. Blackstone recollected that he had a place to preserve though he forgot he had a reputation to lose. We now have the good fortune to understand the doctor's principles as well as his writings. For the defence of the rule of law and of reason the doctor's book may be safely consulted, but whoever wishes to cheat a neighbour of his estate or to rob a country of its rights need make no scruple of consulting the doctor himself.

The mention of Blackstone brings me to what I want particularly to speak of, the struggle against slavery. I mentioned just now that it was in the year 1765 that Blackstone published the first volume of his *Commentaries*. But something else happened in that year. At that time there was a man living in Mincing Lane, London, named William Sharp, a surgeon, who was known for his kindness and his hospitality to the poor. Among those who came under his care was a Negro named Jonathan Strong who had been brought as a slave to this country; he had been maltreated by his master and abandoned, and, knowing that William Sharp

---

249. Sir William Blackstone (1723–80) wrote his *Commentaries* between 1765 and 1769.

250. John Wilkes (1725–97) was seen as a champion for freedom when, as an MP, he led opposition to George III's government – he was acquitted of seditious libel.

251. The real identity of Junius was unknown – a pseudonym of a writer who wrote letters to the papers attacking George III and his ministers.

received everybody, he came to his hospital, where he was cared for. One day a man named Granville Sharp,[252] brother of William Sharp, saw the Negro, Jonathan Strong, asked about him and, when he learned his story, cared for him; like the man in the Bible, 'when he saw him, he had compassion upon him'.[253] One day, about two years later, the owner of Jonathan Strong, who was a lawyer from Barbados, saw his slave, recognised his property, and proceeded to sell him for thirty pounds. The Negro, in his distress, got in touch with Granville Sharp, who protested that such a thing could not happen in this country. 'This man', he said, 'is a man – not a horse, nor a chattel, nor a piece of furniture.' But he was told that, according to the law of the land, Jonathan Strong was a chattel and could be sold just like a horse. Granville Sharp was not a lawyer and had never read a law book in his life, but he set himself to study the law of the country for the sake of Jonathan Strong and he became the greatest lawyer of his generation though his name was never on the roll.

Granville Sharp's link with Blackstone came when he tried to engage Blackstone because he had been sued for damages by Jonathan Strong's owner for taking his slave. Every lawyer was against him and those he instructed told him that it was no good his going on with the struggle. They reminded him that, back in the year 1729, the Attorney-General and the Solicitor-General of that day had given an opinion that a man coming from the colonies could bring his slave with him as his servant, and that he could do what he liked with the slave. That was the opinion upon which the slave owners relied, so much so that something like 12,000 slaves had been brought into this country at that time. In 1772, not very many years after Granville Sharp's first meeting with Jonathan Strong, was fought the case of James Somerset. It was not entered as the case of James Somerset in the law reports; it was called the case of the Negro. Granville found himself opposed by everybody, including Mansfield, the Lord Chief Justice of that day, who tried by every means in his power to avoid giving the decision he was in the end compelled to give – that, as soon as a man landed upon the soil of England, he was free. As I said, Granville Sharp was not a lawyer, but he had to get the help of lawyers. He had no money to speak of – he began life as a draper's apprentice; but his brothers helped him and every penny he had was spent for other people in fighting all the vested interests of his time. He had against him every lawyer in the land, the Solicitor-General, the Attorney-General, and in the end the High Court judges and the Lord Chief Justice of England. In the end he won his case, and at last the Lord Chief Justice in Westminster Hall had to say: 'The black must be discharged.' Still no name was mentioned.

Of course, Granville Sharp had to get the help of counsel. One of the younger counsel was to make a reputation as a very great lawyer – Francis Hargrave[254], whose name ought to be written in gold in all the records of the laws of England. Sharp had four counsel

---

252. Granville Sharp (1735–1813) was a leading anti-slavery campaigner who founded the Society for the Abolition of the Slave Trade in 1787.
253. Luke 10:33 – the story of the Good Samaritan.
254. Francis Hargrave (1741–1821), antislavery campaigner.

already, but this young man wrote to him only a month or two before the case sta rted and said that, though he had never pleaded in court before, he was very interested in this mat-ter and would like to plead. So, if you turn to the reports I have here before me of the case of the Negro, you will find column after column of the erudition and learning of this young man, Francis Hargr ave, who afterwards became editor of *State Trials* and of whom Lord Lyndhurst said that there was no man in England who understood the law better than he.

I have here the original of a letter which is in my view one of the great letters of English history. It runs to eight pages and is written in Granville Sharp's hand. I do not know what its price is in the market, but no price could be enough for it as a document of liberty. It is worthwhile, particularly for lawyers, to read it because in one way Granville Sharp was the greatest lawyer of his day. He stood for the man. Previously Granville Sharp had written a memorandum which was circulated to all the judges and, in the end, convinced even Mansfield, the Lord Chief Justice, that he had been wrong and that every man in England was free to sue for and defend his rights and that force should not be used without a legal process. In the course of that memorandum he argued that 'everything depends upon whether the man is a man'. Was the African a man? Was it right that the African was a man when in the law reports they had written 'the case of a Negro'? In later days others, like Thomas Clarkson, said that they fought against the slave trade, but Granville Sharp fought for the slave. For him the real issue was that the slave was a man.

Many years later, in the village of New Salem in America, there was a tall, lanky youth who had scarcely any education, but had learned to read and was fond of books. And one day there came a stranger from a far distant part who asked him if he would buy a trunk full of household stuff which had some books at the bottom; the youth bought it but did not open it for some time, and then later on when he looked at the books he found that one of them was Blackstone's Commentaries. The name of the young man was Abraham Lincoln and it was the reading of that book which caused him to become a lawyer. And he, too, always asked the same question – whether the Negro slave is or is not a man. When he fought Stephen Douglas for the Senatorship of Illinois, Lincoln was an unknown lawyer and his opponent was famous as a man of affairs and a very good man, too. In their argu-ments, Lincoln always brought Douglas back to the one question about the Negro – 'Is he or is he not a man?' and never allowed Douglas to escape from that question. I will read you just a few words of what Lincoln had to say in the course of that debate: 'The doctrine of self-government is right, absolutely and eternally right, but it has no just application as here attempted, or perhaps I should rather say that whether it has any application here depends upon whether the Negro is or is not a man. If he is not a man, in that case he who is a man may, as a matter of self-government, do just what he pleases with him; but if the Negro is a man, is it not to that extent a total destruction of self-government to say that he, too, shall not govern himself? When the right man governs himself, that is self-government, but when he governs himself and also governs another man, that is more than self-government, that is despotism. If the Negro is a man then my ancient faith teaches me that all men are created equal' – those are, of course, the words of the Declaration of Independence, 'all men are created equal' – 'and that there can be no more right in connection with one man making a slave of the other.' Lincoln had read his Blackstone to some purpose. It is a tragedy that Blackstone fell so low in the Granville Sharp controversy, but he regained his glory through the words of Abraham Lincoln.

I want to conclude by laying emphasis upon three things. The lawyer outside his profession stands for three things – liberty, justice and the law. You cannot separate them, they are a threefold reality. You cannot have one without the other. The law is important and, as I hope to show directly, also, there is the love of justice. One of my friends, A. G. Gardiner, once told me that he was writing a book in which Mr Justice Hawkins was being dealt with and he thought he would ask Asquith what he thought of Hawkins. Asquith was a man of very little speech and all he said was: 'Hawkins loved injustice.' Sometimes you strike the name of somebody off the roll; Asquith struck the name of Hawkins off the roll. The man who loves injustice should never be a lawyer. Do you remember how Thomas Hardy finishes his book about Tess? I never pass through Dorchester without looking at that gaol where the black flag went up when Tess was hanged. Remember how Hardy ended that last paragraph: '"Justice" was done; "Justice" was done, and the President of the Immortals speaking in Aeschylean phrase had finished his sport with Tess.' You will notice that Hardy puts the word 'Justice' in inverted commas, for he knew it was not justice. When I was a young man and finished that book I threw it down in my anger. If you are to get justice done, and you cannot get it done by lawyers, can you trust it to anybody else? Can you trust the law itself to anybody else?

My son Mac, who is just back for a week from Jamaica, rang me up yesterday and wanted to know where I was and what I was doing. When I told him he said: 'Alright, Dad; not too many quotations, mark you.' However, I would like to quote something he once told me – something that impressed me very greatly, that when the Vichy government fell there was a town in Syria, where he was at the time, where, for two or three days, there was no government, no police and nobody who knew whether there was any law at all. He told me it was most wonderful how, in the course of three days when there was no government and no man could say to the other: 'So far goest thou and no further,' how the underworld took possession of the place, and the man who had a grudge against another found him with a dagger, and the ruler of the place was the man who had the gun. That is why Cromwell once said he would rather have bad government than no government at all.

So much for the law. Then there is liberty. You have seen Cornwall, and I wonder, if when you go back, you will think not only of the beautiful parts of Cornwall, its north coasts and the rest, but something also of its glory. Every bridge that you cross as you go back, if it is an old bridge, was once piled with dead. Every stream that you see in Cornwall once ran with the blood of men who fought out a very great struggle. The struggle was over the law. There were good men on both sides, but the question which divided them was which law was to prevail. And thousands of men gave their lives in that cause. There were those who believed in the law of Parliament and those who believed in Divine Right and their conflict was fought out by good men on both sides.

We had, among others, a man named John Hampden, who, although he was a Buckinghamshire squire, first went to Parliament as member for the Cornish town of Grampound. He stood by the law. They had then a forced loan sanctioned by Parliament, and they called him before the Council and said that he was a man well able to pay the loan and asked why he had not done so. And Hampden replied: 'I should be content to lend as well as others, but I fear to bring upon myself the cause of Magna Charta which should be twice a year against those that infringe it.' And when Edmund Burke wrote about the incident later on he said: 'Would twenty shillings have ruined Mr. Hampden's fortune? No! But the payment of half twenty shillings on the principle by which it was demanded would have made him a slave.' That was what the struggle for the law meant. Rightly or wrongly they fought for the law, the law of Parliament, and that is why we have got constitutional government today. They fought that issue out here to the point of Civil War, but with little cruelty because there were great gentlemen on both sides, and this county was almost equally divided upon it. They fought for the law, for justice and for liberty, but who is going to defend them now if you do not?

We have heard here about other professions. Other professions also have their prerogatives, but if the law is to be valued, who knows about it except those of us who have spent our lives in the study of it? We have an obligation to the law. We are educated people; we have lived by the law, and we have a great obligation to it. If the lawyers of the country fail, then liberty will fail; that is why all our struggles in the end have depended upon the law. We go back then to earning our livings. There will not perhaps seem to be a very intimate association between the details of our daily office routine and the principles of justice, but we can love justice and seek to serve it, can we not? Remember that, in standing by the law and upholding its greatness, our influence will spread throughout the country. What the world needs today is law. The tragedy of Europe is that there is no law. The tragedy in so many places is that the traffic goes where it will, and there is no red light; and if there is a red light, there are many who delight in driving against it in international affairs. I once talked to Willie Graham, a great friend of mine, who was President of the Board of Trade in the Labour government. He had been in Geneva and came back rather depressed. I asked him how he had got on and he said: 'Well, Isaac, I had the impression over there in Europe that the sewers were getting the upper hand of the main streets.' If that is not to happen in the country, all depends upon us, and I doubt if there is any company of people of similar number with greater power than those represented here. That is why our profession is a noble profession. That is why it is worth all that we can devote to it in the cause of those three things, liberty, the love of justice and the maintenance of the law.

PART XI

Isaac Foot, the greatest book collector

MICHAEL: My brother John's drawing of our father reading in his library at Lipson Terrace became his bookplate which he put at the front of all his books. No. 1 Lipson Terrace, where we first lived in Plymouth, was getting fuller and fuller of books and I'm sure that's one of the reasons why my father moved out to Pencrebar near Callington, a larger house where he could see the great potentialities for bookshelves. Forever afterwards, at an enormous rate, month by month, more and more books poured into the house. He didn't collect books just from an acquisitive instinct – he read them, and the staggering thing about his library was to see how many of these books he had read. You could always know when he had read a book because he marked books more extensively than anybody I've ever seen. He could not merely put his hand at once on almost any book, but he could also put his hand on the page in the book where he recalled something had been written and there it was marked. I suppose he must have read, on average, something like four or five hours almost every day of his life and he read everything. He would collect books on one subject for a period when he was at work on a particular era or subject. It was only in the last twenty years or so that he increasingly concentrated on first editions and the books became more valuable. He would often tell me that he had gone and bought a book that morning which he obviously shouldn't have done and he felt very guilty about it and he would explain how he was going to smuggle it into the home. Sometimes he would go and buy whole sections of people's libraries where he wanted particular things and then all the other books would arrive at Pencrebar too and my mother wanted to put some restriction on these unrestricted imports.

My father was reluctant to part with any of his books. He confirmed this with the inscription in a first edition of Swift he gave me: 'Given with some reluctance'. Once my father had discovered Jill's interest in Oscar Wilde too he produced two volumes, each of them with his lovely bookplates and a loving message to us, both which of course we treasured and keep in my own Oscar Wilde collection. In 1959 my father's lifelong love of literature was recognised when he received an honorary degree in Literature from Exeter University.

DINGLE: A book sale for my father is an almost irresistible temptation. At all events he very rarely resists it. When my mother was alive there was some outward check on the new additions to the library and books purchased at an auction in London would be smuggled into the house in twos and threes. Now there is no check whatsoever. We have very spacious

Isaac Foot in his library at Pencrebar.

attics which used to serve my brothers and myself as bedrooms. No one could use them for that purpose now. They are filled with enormous and ever-growing piles of volumes. It is not, however, a random collection. What happens is this. Every two or three years he suddenly develops a new enthusiasm. It may be anything from the journey of St Paul to the works of Guy de Maupassant. I remember, at different times, the Greek New Testament, the days of Burke and Fox, the American Civil War, the novels of Conrad and Hardy, the career of Sir Francis Drake and even the modern detective novel being the prevailing, one might almost say, the exclusive theme. On each occasion, of course, he has to acquire every book that has ever been written on the subject. Over a long period of years this process inevitably results in a formidable tonnage of books.[255]

SARAH: Pencrebar bulged with books. The library, the most popular room in the house, where a fire was always lit from morning to night, was lined with books from ceiling to floor. He knew where every book was and would often break off in the middle of a conversation to reach for one or climb his little ladder to find the volume he needed, never for a moment hesitating in finding the exact one he wanted. In this room he did all his

255. 1951 broadcast.

322

reading, heedless of the confusion that went on around him. Under his Anglepoise lamp he sat, puffing at his pipe, rising every now and then with a grunt to knock it out on the granite fireplace, returning unabashed to his reading, throwing only a glance or some quip in our direction. Books were to him the loveliest things in the world but he was very generous with them, giving them as presents on special occasions to mark the importance of the event, although he often wrote in the inscription that he gave the book with regret. My Uncle Michael once said that he thought his father would have been happy to spend the whole of his life reading. It was my grandmother who said to him: 'Come along now, the world is waiting to be saved.'

In 1959 Isaac paid three of his grandsons, David, Christopher and Jasper – his daughter Jennifer's children – two shillings and sixpence each to count all the books in all the rooms at Pencrebar.

Library:	6,000
G.T.:	1,300
E.B.:	1,256
Passage: Back stairs to G.T.:	3,007
Your Bedroom:	600
Dark room:	4,080
Sal's room:	800
Chris's room:	722
Dark rooms neighbours:	760
Dark room passage:	825
Drawing room:	600
Dining room:	2,450
Hall:	115
Porch:	1,444
Bodlein:	7,685
Rhodes House:	3,000
R.H. passage:	1,600
O. kitchen:	1,000
Main Stairs:	100
Attick stairs:	210
Attick:	25,379
Middle bedroom:	800
Total	59,909

This was their list, written out by David in one of his grandfather's commonplace books. (EB and GT are two of the front bedrooms, known as the English Bible Room and the Greek Testament Room).

35 Sixty years of book collecting

Sixty years – these are the operative words. The only excuse I have for talking on book collecting is that I have been at it now for quite a long time. It takes longer than sixty years to build a library, but in that time you can collect quite a lot of books, if the money holds out, and there is house room enough. A library is a different matter with its balance and catholicity, its space and order. That needs more than sixty years – a generation or two. Sometimes one of our great English families has done immense service to the nation in the collection and preservation of books through generation after generation, and even through the centuries. Wherever I hear of such a library being broken up, or see it being dispersed and scattered in an auction room, it seems to me almost like the destruction of an ancient monument, the pulling down of an abbey, or the dilapidating of a cathedral. Fortunately, there are the great public libraries, which, being immune from taxation and unconcerned by the increase in the death duties, can continue as the reminders of that enduring partnership of which Burke spoke – 'the partnership not only between those who are living, but between those who are living, those who are dead, and those who are yet to be born'. Mine is the humbler theme of the work of one man's life. Thomas Hobbes spoke of man's life as being 'solitary, poor, nasty, brutish, and short'. Rejecting most of his epithets, I agree that life is short when it comes to the collection of books.

I don't want anyone to think that there was anything heroic about the early book enterprises of mine. Books meant sacrifice, of course. They were always bought at the beginning of the month, never at the end, and sometimes I had to choose between a book and a meal, but I felt no grievance because of these limitations of mine. I have often been hard up but I have never known poverty. Probably it was a good thing for me that I learned by self-denial the value of a book when I got it. Having paid so much for it, I felt I ought to read it. An inherited library could not have meant so much to me. Both in collecting books and in learning about them, I had to start from scratch. At that time I knew very little about books. I did not know their relative worth, and could not estimate the place of the different writers in the hierarchy of literature. This I had to pick up as I went along. Sir John Lubbock's list of the hundred best books appeared about that time, and I took that list as being as final and authoritative as the Ten Commandments.

I can understand someone saying, whilst I am telling this story, this is all very well, but why all this fuss and bother? Why this hesitation between book and meal, between a Stead's Penny Poet and a bus ride? Weren't there public libraries in those days of your boyhood? Yes, there were public libraries, and I was glad of them. I used them and used them to the full, especially for the fiction that I read. But a library book has never meant much to me. If a book is of any interest, I want it for my very own. I want it for the second reading, perhaps the third, or the fourth. I want it with my name in it, with my own mark and symbols and underlinings and references. I still get books from the library but they are not citizens like the rest. They form a class apart, like the aliens in our midst who move about with a passport, limiting the time of their visit. The wise advice given me by my elders was: use your libraries by all means but get your own books. Unless the book is your own it will never become what it ought to be, your friend.

The struggle is always pretty much the same. In the auction room, when you have already gone far beyond the limit you set for yourself, there is the same inward contention. The one voice reminding you of the needs of your household, the income tax demand note, the puckered brow of your bank manager, and the other voice – 'Well, you wanted the book, didn't you? You have come up all the way to buy it, haven't you – it's your line of country, isn't it? If it is worth that to anybody else surely it is worth that to you – and you might never have the chance to get it again.' Of course, these voices have to be pretty quick about it, because all this argument takes place whilst the auctioneer's hammer is finally poised in the air – Going, going, gone. In a split second the hammer may fall and the book you had set your heart on may have gone – irrecoverably gone.

Of recent years I have never counted my books but I suppose there is no great writer who is not represented somewhere amongst them. Wherever there is a great book that has made history, like Gibbon's six volumes, or Adam Smith's *Wealth of Nations* or Darwin's *Origin of Species*, I have a desire for the first edition of it. Mere rarity or oddities do not appeal to me. I am not troubled if my first volume of Thomas Hardy's *Dynasts* is dated 1904 instead of 1903. I would rather have a ragged first edition of *Under the Greenwood Tree* than none at all. I am not excited to learn that my first edition of Charles Reade's *Cloister and the Hearth* is the more valuable because on page 372 of Volume 2 there is the uncorrected sentence: 'Catherine threw her face over her apron and sobbed'. Because of these admissions, the real bibliophile will probably reckon me amongst the Philistines, but there it is. I am no authority on current prices, and, as I do not sell any books, I have made no study of their market value. When I am interested in a man, I like to have his books. If possible, I want the first edition. I want a portrait of him if there is one to be had, and then something of his handwriting, preferably a letter. After that I get, if I can, the books that have been written about him, but, generally speaking, I would rather have a man's letters than all the biography. Of course, being a personal collection and not a library, my books reflect my likings and preferences. For that reason I have a great deal more of William Tyndale than of Sir Thomas More, and, if I can get all I want on John Wesley, I will leave to someone else all he wants on Horace Walpole.

Any man's collection of books is like a river with many tributaries. The interest of a river is in the little spring or stream with which it began. There is Robert Louis Stevenson. I think I have all his books, and from time to time I have acquired all the first editions. I think I have read everything of any importance written about him. A short time ago I took the chance to find some of his manuscripts and paid for them more than I could reasonably afford. Sentiment and a boy's memories turned the scales and I was glad to have them. But valuable as these manuscripts were, I wish I had kept those old copies of *Chums* in which I first read his *Treasure Island* and, if the volume containing that serial should come into the market, I shall probably be found among the bidders.

I have been reading Hardy – his poetry and prose – most of my life, and when I can't read him I still like to look at his books, even at their titles as they stand there, side by side. Some of his early editions take a bit of getting, and for a clean copy you may have to wait a long time. I remember many years ago going into a shop in a back street in Plymouth where they sold all sorts of things with a few books as a side-line, and I picked up three of them. They formed a set. The price was marked in pencil – 'three volumes, one shilling'. That pencilling of about forty years ago I have allowed to remain. I didn't know anything about first editions at that time. Later I was to learn that I had the first edition of 1891, with the honeysuckle design, and I also learned that the price paid for a like copy was about seventy pounds.

It was later in life that another small stream began to arise. That became a mighty tributary too. Somewhere about 1914 I began to read a book by an author whose name was new to me. I got this book from Plymouth library. Its title was Nostromo. The book irritated me because it demanded more attention than I liked to give a book I had borrowed for diversion. As I read on, I found I was farther ahead with the story at the end of the early chapters than I was when I got three parts through. I thought I would take the book back and have done with it and yet it seemed too good to leave unread. I began it again, read every line with care and found it began to fascinate me. Who was the writer of that book? Joseph Conrad. From this time I began to read Conrad. I have read every line he wrote and all his books are there in splendid array. It took me some time to get *Almayer's Folly*. That cost me ten pounds and was in Lord Rosebery's library. I suppose I shall never have the time to read all Conrad's books again, but there are half-a dozen of them I should like to read once a year.

I remember that there was a second-hand bookshop in Plymouth and in the long shelf outside the main window bargains were often to be found. One day I picked up a little book – a Temple Classic in the cloth binding. The title was *Speeches on America* by Edmund Burke. It was a fairly new book, dated 1906, and the price was one shilling, but it was worth to me a thousand pounds. It had an introduction and contained, besides the two speeches on America,[256] the 'Letter to the Sheriffs of Bristol'. That little book I read and reread until I almost know the 234 pages by heart. That little Temple Classic I still have, and I sometimes think of it as the little wicket gate through which I passed to the splendours of Burke and all that he has taught me of political philosophy and civil wisdom.

---

256. 'American Taxation' (1774) and 'Conciliation with America' (1775).

There are other main streams but I dare not stay to speak of them – Wordsworth, Thomas Carlyle, Browning and John Wesley. The ideal house, of course, would be the one where there would be enough room for one to be set apart for each of the main personalities around which the collection is gathered. In a house such as mine that is not possible but nonetheless these heroes of mine have their special place here and there as space allows and as I pass from this part of my house to another I am conscious of a difference of atmosphere which to others would be unnoticeable. Those shelves are for Devon and Cornwall; these are for Greece and Rome; that far attic is given up to Napoleon and the French Revolution; that is Joseph Conrad's corner; and that Robert Louis Stevenson's. There are my Shakespeares and my Wordsworths.

Beyond these, there are for me a few dominating themes and towering personalities. First, the history of the United States, with the books on Abraham Lincoln and the Civil War. I would like to have a room for them. Then John Milton – his books need a room of their own; then there is John Wesley and his brother Charles – their shelves are full to overflowing. Then Oliver Cromwell – his would be quite a large room. Then the apostle Paul – he would have a room to himself. And then the biggest room of all for the Bible – in manuscript, in Latin, and in English, and then the Greek New Testament, which I regard as the greatest book in the world – with the many editions I have from Erasmus in 1516 to Westcott and Hort in 1881. In making that last collection, I have had infinite pleasure and have taken some pride. Perhaps it is a foolish pride. But I add to that collection from month to month as opportunity affords. A complete collection of all the editions of the Greek New Testament would I suppose be beyond the scope of any one individual or public institution, as their number, we are told, is nearly a thousand, but if time allows and I could get together the 300 or so of most importance then I should begin to think that my collection of books had, in that particular at least, become a library.

'But why do you want to collect these books?' someone will ask. 'Isn't it just vanity? Aren't you yielding to the temptation of mere acquisition? And isn't there something vulgar about mere acquisition?' Well, to me, that collection of the Greek Testament would not be mere acquisition. It would tell from first to last one of the noblest stories in the history of the world – a story lit up with great names like those of Erasmus, Tyndale, Luther, the great printers of Venice, of Basle, of Paris and elsewhere who were not only printers but scholars and publishers and artists and missionaries of culture – of John Hill, and Bengel, Wetstein, Tischendorf, Samuel Prideaux Tregelles[257] and ever so many more down to Westcott and Hort of the last century. Every one of those books would be a star shining in that glorious firmament. Everyone would tell someone's life story and often would represent the labour of a lifetime. Every single book is a living thing. Every single book is a reminder of the great utterance of John Milton in his *Areopagitica* and his plea for the lib-

---

257. Tregelles (1813–75) was a Westcountryman and a theologian.

erty of unlicensed printing to the Parliament of England. Certain words of his should not only be inscribed on the walls of every library in the land, but without presumption above every collection large or small:

> For books are not absolutely dead things but doe contain a potencie of life in them to be as active as that soule was whose progeny they are; nay they do preserve as in a violl the purest efficacie and extraction of that living intellect that bred them ... Unless warinesse be us'd, as good almost kill a man as kill a good book ... Many a man lives a burden to the earth but a good booke is the precious life-blood of a master spirit, imbalm'd and treasur'd up on purpose to a life beyond life.[258]

36 Some adventures in book collecting

Although I have bought many books, I don't sell any, and I have kept no record of the prices I have given. Mere rarity does not appeal to me, and I am not constantly on the look-out for bargains. Sometimes, however, these prizes come along without my searching for them, and, when that happens, of course, I am pleased at my good fortune. It was about two years ago that I had great good fortune. I collect Greek New Testaments and know something about their history. I thought I had all the editions of interest and importance, and I was therefore surprised when a Testament was offered me which I had never heard of. The price asked for these two little volumes was, I think, forty shillings. After making the purchase I learned that this book, printed in Italy early in the sixteenth century, was only to be found in seven of the great public libraries of the world, and that there was no known copy in private hands.

The collector is very much like the man we read of in the Gospels, who comes with sudden surprise upon the treasure hid in the field. More often, however, he has to search like the merchantmen seeking goodly pearls. Some books I have been searching for for a long time and I may, one day, come across them. I have my own special sense of values. Sentiment counts a good deal with me. The books I covet might not stand high in the list of the bookseller's catalogue, but in my list they have first place. I have never longed over-much for a first folio of Shakespeare, but I would greatly desire to have the pocket Greek Testament that John Wesley used – the little Mirifico Testament of 1546 – with his name written in it. For a long time I was looking for the Greek Testament published by the great German scholar of the early eighteenth century John Albert Bengel. I wanted it because John Wesley's greatest book, his *Notes on the New Testament*, which once I had to study from end to end, was almost entirely based on the work of his mighty contemporary. There on

---

258. broadcast. September 1949.

my shelves was the first edition of Wesley's *Notes*, but where was Bengel to be found? Every time I looked at the *Notes*, with Wesley's famous portrait as its frontispiece, he seemed to say: 'Have you got your Bengel yet?' I got it at last after many years. It was at Edinburgh. There it was unmistakably – Bengel, Tubingen 1734. With some trepidation I opened the cover to see the price marked. Whatever the price was I know that the book had to be taken home. I should hardly be able to face John Wesley without it. The price was fifteen shillings. That pencilling also remains.

I suppose I should be put outside the pale as a proper collector by the mere fact that I do not object to the name of an earlier owner being written in the books that have passed for the time into my keeping. Indeed I prefer to know who were my predecessors in title. Of course, it depends a good deal on the name. There is, for instance, my copy of Thomas Carlyle's *Cromwell*. It is the first edition of 1845. I have many books from Carlyle's library. They all bear his bookplate, but he seems never to have written his name. I wish he had. But one book was an exception. It was his Cromwell. And in this copy Carlyle had written these words on the title page: 'Jane Welsh Carlyle Her Own T.C.' The making of that book had been a long desperate business, and poor Jane Welsh Carlyle had fully shared in the agony. It was two years or so earlier, while sitting darning stockings, that she had been amazed to see her beloved and distracted husband come into the sitting room at Cheyne Row and throw into the fire armsful of the manuscript he had so far written in his projected biography of the Lord Protector. She told her friends that the book never would get written. But it did get written after all. And I like to think that mine was the very first copy that came from the publisher, the very first fruits of that delayed harvest in which Carlyle wrote: 'Jane Welsh Carlyle Her Own T.C.'

I am very fond of an old book. I might not be able to read it. If it is in Latin I need a translation. I am not a classical scholar. But to me the story of the part played by the great scholar-publishers in making known to the people of western Europe the works of the classical writers of Greece and Rome is of amazing interest. What a lead these mighty printers gave in the revival of learning, and what pride they took in their craftsmanship! Of all these famous men, the greatest, perhaps, was Aldus Manutius, of Venice.[259] Behind every Aldine volume, with its proud design of the anchor and dolphin, there is such a romance that, if I lived long enough, and had money enough, I would acquire a copy of every book published by this noble scholar and craftsman. I have a good many of his books, but not long ago I secured a special one. Its possession set my heart aglow. It was the second edition of the works of Pontanus, but with that name we need not here be concerned.[260] Printed by Aldus Manutius in Venice, it was brought to England, and there, this beautiful book – a small octavo volume of 256 pages – was made more beautiful still,

259. 1449–1515, founder of the Aldine Press in Venice in 1494.
260. Jovianus Pontanus (1426–1503), Italian humanist and poet.

because it was given an English binding, and this work was done by John Reynes, the fore-most English binder of that generation. Through what hands had that book passed before it came down to me – nearly four and a half centuries later? I wish these earlier possessors had all written their names in it – generation after generation. Fortunately one man did write his name. He was Robert Ridley, a prebendary of St Paul's, and a rector of St Budolph. He happily for me not only wrote his name, but he told how this book had come into his possession. It was only after I had bought this book that I saw four lines written on the front page – in small Latin characters almost indecipherable. What the four lines said was this: 'This book was given to me, Robert Ridley at St. Paul's Cathedral London on the 24th day of January 1527 at four o'clock in the afternoon by Richard Pace.' Who was Richard Pace? Richard Pace, I found, was the Dean of St. Paul's, succeeding in that office the great John Colet. He was an ambassador to Rome, and to other foreign courts, a fore-most scholar, a leader in the revival of learning and a friend of Sir Thomas More. But he had even a greater title to fame. He was also the friend of Erasmus. Erasmus said of this Englishman that his learning and scholarship gave lustre to his native land. For me the inscription added a tenfold value to the book and it speaks to me – not so much of the works of Pontanus but of Aldus Manutius, of the friendship of Richard Pace and Erasmus and of that day, 423 years ago, when Richard Pace gave to his friend this book which doubtless he himself had brought across the sea as the symbol of the new learning which stirred Italy from end to end.

I collect Bibles. I have a great many, in many languages, some written before printing was known. I can only tell you tonight of one of these Bibles of mine. It is the *Pictorial Bible* of John Kitto, published at Edinburgh over a century ago. Who was John Kitto? John Kitto was born in Plymouth in 1804. He was born in Stillman Street, which is little more than a stone's throw from the street in which I was born. When he was thirteen years old, work-ing for his father, a stonemason, this boy John Kitto fell with a load from the top of a very high ladder. Almost miraculously his life was saved, but from that time until the day of his death he was stone deaf. He became a workhouse boy. He had, however, a hunger for books, and tried to satisfy his craving for reading by studying the books or papers dis-played in the widows of the booksellers' shops. To buy a few books he earned pennies by salvaging scraps of rope and pieces of old iron dropped by ships unloading in the harbour. Some Plymouth citizens, to their great honour, learning of the boy's plight, helped him in his studies, and in course of time this afflicted workhouse boy became a distinguished scholar, a worldwide traveller, a renowned author and the foremost popular educator of his generation. His main literary interest was the Bible and the crowning achievement of his life was the *Pictorial Bible*, which became widely popular throughout the three king-doms. Now John Kitto's Bible was especially popular in Scotland and shortly after his death it was reproduced by a firm of Edinburgh publishers in four quarto volumes. At that time there were living in Edinburgh a Scotsman and his wife, to whom a son was born 100 years ago. He was the only child and on his eleventh birthday they made him the gift of Kitto's *Pictorial Bible,* and on the first page of the first of the four handsome volumes they wrote this inscription: 'Robert Lewis Stevenson From his father and mother With their best wishes and prayers Edinburgh, November 13th 1861.'

The name is spelt 'Lewis', but on the next page is the boy's own signature 'Robert Louis Stevenson'. Why the spelling of the name was changed is well known. Probably no boy of eleven in the whole world knew his Bible better than that boy did. So, upon his eleventh birthday, and in this wonderful way, the book of the Plymouth workhouse boy passed into the treasured keeping of the boy in Edinburgh. I said 'in this wonderful way'. Others may not think it wonderful at all. Well, it is so to me and that is why I have tonight singled out this Kitto-Stevenson Bible of mine in preference to all the rest.

I would like to tell you of one further adventure in my collecting – a miracle this time. Some ten years ago I bought at an auction a lot which included, by sheer accident, an exercise book. It was an ordinary school exercise book of forty pages, filled with writing which seemed quite unimportant. I glanced at the book once or twice to see if it had in it anything worth keeping. Fortunately, the book was not discarded, as I noticed on the very first page a reference to Cornwall, and then I found it was the description of a tour made through the county, and beginning with 3 October 1832. There was nothing to indicate who the writer was. But whoever he was he had left his story unfinished, for the last line of the last page had an unfinished sentence. Then, after a long process of enquiry which I cannot stay to describe, I became assured that the writer was John Stuart Mill. Mill, at that time, was twenty-six years old. In a little book I wrote in 1946, I made some reference to this manuscript.[261] This reference, again by sheer accident, was brought to the notice of Professor Hayek of the London University. That university possesses many of the Mill manuscripts, and Professor Hayek informed me that, amongst their highly treasured documents, they had an exercise book giving the account of the conclusion of a tour in Cornwall. This exercise book of theirs of sixteen pages began with a broken sentence. How did their sentence correspond with mine? It did correspond and corresponded precisely. Written more than a hundred years ago, the two exercise books had somehow and at some time fallen into different hands, and, now after an indefinite lapse of years, and as the result of a long series of chances, they had come together again. And thus was restored to completeness the broken story told by a young Englishman, then unknown, but whose name before long was to become famous throughout the world.

Not many of my possessions are as miraculous as that one, but every book that comes into my home has some story to tell and every good book among them contains, as Milton tells us, 'the precious life blood of a master spirit'. For the time I have the honour of the

---

261. *Michael Verran of Callington and Thomas Carlyle* (Epworth Press, 1946).

company of these guests of mine. For a time – and only for a time – there is entrusted to my keeping this part of the greatest heritage of the spirit of man. These books are in Tennyson's phrase 'the noble letters of the dead', and yet, it is in the library that the thought of death seems almost irrelevant. Indeed was it not Tennyson himself who suggested that books, 'if read a'right, speak to us, not of death but of an enduring and living companionship'?[262]

37 The Isaac Foot library

MICHAEL: My father was still adding to his book collection in the last years of his life. In one of his commonplace books written out in 1950, he stated that 'for the last twenty years I have spent not less than £1,000 per annum on books'. My brother John said later that our father had mortgaged his properties up to the hilt to buy his beloved books. Right up to the time of his death my father kept up a correspondence with various booksellers all over the country. One of these was Maggs, one of the leading booksellers in London with whom he had always had good relations. Mr Clifford Maggs, indeed, accepted an invitation from my father to visit Pencrebar. He was always alert for books he knew would interest my father. My father could not resist a chance to acquire another edition of any of his favourite authors. In 1956 his correspondence with Maggs shows that he was still seeking to buy Greek New Testaments, English translations of Erasmus and anything of the Etienne Press. One of his latest acquisitions in 1957 was a copy of John Milton's Doves Press *Areopagitica* for which he paid £12 10s. Every true student of the story of English freedom knows of this book and the important part it played in sustaining the treasure of English freedom even through the darkest days of tyranny practised by the Stuart kings. It so happens that my father had sent me a much less valuable but still notable reproduction of this famous book when he had approved some political action in which I was engaged.

Before my father's death in 1960 there had been no talk or decision by him about what should happen to his library. Obviously my father would have wanted, first of all, that the whole library should be kept together. The family sought advice from one of the principal booksellers with whom Isaac Foot had dealt, but it was a request from the University of California to buy the whole library that settled the matter. My father had himself visited and spoken in this area in 1943. He had noted then that it was a part of the world which Sir Francis Drake had visited on his travels. So I am sure that the decision that the whole library should go there would have been approved by my father. This final decision and the details of the transaction rested with my brother John, who was in charge of my father's office.

---

262. BBC broadcast, January 1950.

THE ISAAC FOOT LIBRARY

A Report to the University by
Theodore G. Grieder

UNIVERSITY OF CALIFORNIA · 1964

In 1964 the University of California gave a detailed description of their purchase of the Isaac Foot Library, which is reproduced here.

Negotiations for purchase

Lawrence Clark Powell, now dean of the UCLA Library School, met Isaac Foot on the Santa Fe Super Chief in 1943. After Isaac Foot's death in 1960, an agent contacted the university about possible purchase of the Foot library; a note in Foot's effects suggested approaching Dean Powell. The matter was turned over to the Library Council of the university; and Edwin T. Coman Jr., librarian at Riverside and secretary of the council that year, handled negotiations. A final survey, to be discussed below, of the library at Foot's country house in Cornwall concluded negotiations; and the library was purchased for £50,000.

The survey

In the fall of 1961, Coman arrived in England to survey the library at Foot's house at Pencrebar, Callington, Cornwall. He was joined by Donald Fitch of the library at Santa Barbara, who prepared a sketch map of the Foot house and a detailed report on how the different collections were organised, no slight task considering that the books were placed

333

in all twenty-four rooms and four corridors of the enormous three-floor country home. The importance of this sketch was great; it helped the Library Council make preliminary decisions about distribution and enabled Theodore Grieder, the librarian in charge of the distribution of the collections, to know the scope and general nature of the library before it arrived in Santa Barbara. Also by agreement, the cartons containing the books were labelled by room or corridor location; when these 500 cartons arrived in fourteen 2-ton packing cases at Santa Barbara, they could, thus, be assigned to library areas designated to receive titular author, period and subject collections. To be able to preserve Foot's arrangement saved much time in basic organisation.

Theodore Grieder's report on the library, 1964

As a scholar-bookman, Isaac Foot built his library around his many interests. Law, politics, history, religion were all represented. Foot's collection of Richard Cobden's letters, a very large one, reflected his respect for the great free trader of the nineteenth century; there was a shelf of temperance works. The mark of the man is in these collections, as it is in the manifold activities of his life, in his political convictions, in his form of Methodism. It is in his wit, for which his rebuttals to parliamentary salvos were noted.

History

As a historian, Foot ranks as an authority on Cromwell and the Commonwealth period; one has only to read his review of Hilaire Belloc's biography of Cromwell to realise the depth of his learning in this field. He exchanged letters about seventeenth-century history with men such W. C. Abbott, the noted Harvard Cromwellian authority, and appeared to know the work of Firth and Gardiner by heart. A grasp of political, social, and religious thought is evident in his 'Oliver Cromwell and Abraham Lincoln', delivered before the Royal Society of Literature, of which he was a fellow. Scholarship, both historical and religious, is shown as well in his 'Cromwell: An Open Letter to the Lord Bishop of London from Isaac Foot' (Observer, Cambridge University Press 1938). That this history was alive for him is most evident in his 'Drake's Drum Beats Again,' a BBC broadcast in August, 1940, which contains what is certainly an outstanding affirmation of Protestant independency in the twentieth century. The bibliography of his writings, available at Riverside, is not compendious, but is substantial for a man engaged in so many diverse activities.

One of Foot's chief studies was English history, and his holdings in this subject were large. In post-1700 imprints, he collected some 4,000 volumes, exclusive of commentaries on the Civil War. Of the various periods into which these historical works fall, the eighteenth century was most fully represented, although his period collections from 500 AD to 1714 and from 1837 to 1903 were not inconsequential. His great interest in the Civil War and Commonwealth period was reflected in over 750 volumes about Charles I,

Cromwell and parliamentary history. Early imprints falling within 1640–60 were also grouped with this collection, so that in total it represented an impressive historical group.

The 3,000 Civil War tracts formed a separate collection, for which the Clark Library got priority. When one recalls that the Thomason pamphlets in the British Museum number 22,000, collected as they were being issued, Foot's acquisitions in this particular type of publication represent what may be an unparalleled achievement for a modern historian. In his own copy of Fortescue's catalogue of the Thomason tracts, Foot underlined the author's statement that few, if any, collectors have accomplished so remarkable an achievement; he was clearly aware of the historical distinction of his own collection. The collection of French history comprised over 2,000 volumes, of which 1,600 dealt with the years 1789–1815. Of some 1,600 titles, nearly 800 were about Napoleon and his family. The remainder was composed of general historical studies of the period, relations of campaigns, and biographies and memoirs of a considerable number of revolutionary and Empire figures. Present also were original issues of the *Journal de Paris* and a reprinted series of the *Moniteur*, and there was an extensive collection of assignats.

The American history in Foot's library had its chief strength in the Civil War, where there were a number of volumes about military campaigns and Lincoln. World history books, although amounting to over 1,000 volumes, were not of special interest; the classical period was, however, solid, and there were a number of works relating to the Renaissance in Italy.

Literature

Collections of English literature formed a significant number of the total volumes in the Foot library. There were 2,600 titles in the collection of English literature to 1800. Of these, 1,400 were eighteenth-century works, authors of the earlier periods of English literature, with the exception of Milton, not being very well represented. Doubtless drawn to Milton as the great voice of seventeenth-century dissent, Foot collected his writings intensively, and eventually acquired over 300 volumes by and about the poet and defender of the Commonwealth. Of these, more than forty were seventeenth-century imprints, including a number of particularly important editions. For example, there were both first and second editions of *Paradise Lost* and a first of *Areopagitica*. Most important reprints after 1700 were also present – Baskerville's, Bulmer's, and Cobden-Sanderson's Doves Press edition being a few of these, to say nothing of the many critical and biographical studies of Milton's life and writings. Whether textual critic or historian of ideas, the specialist will find many volumes of interest.

Nineteenth-century literary items numbered more than 6,500. Here Foot collected in depth. Specifically, Foot's collections of major authors in this period usually included biographies, collected works, and a number of various editions of individual works. There

335

were bibliographical titles as well, and a great many first editions. To name only a few, his collections of Hardy, Tennyson, Wordsworth, Dickens, Thackeray, Trollope and Swinburne are impressive. A checklist of some of Santa Barbara's most interesting nineteenth-century acquisitions shows, for example, eighty Swinburne titles, of which many are scarce, privately printed pamphlets.

There were over 4,500 twentieth-century volumes, with a great number of the private publications, autograph editions, and limited editions essential to full collections of modern authors. W. H. Davies, Beerbohm, Wells, Bennett, Conrad, the Sitwells and Laurence Housman were a few of those collected in depth, but a great many more first- and second-line authors were well represented. Riverside saw, wanted and secured this twentieth-century collection.

The literature of the 1890s appears to have had special interest for Foot; and the listings for the nineteenth and twentieth centuries show most of the authors, both major and minor, indexed in Holbrook Jackson's definitive *The Eighteen Nineties*.[263] In a way, the depth here is more surprising than Foot's scope of acquisition in well-known authors, and undoubtedly will provide much material for research.

The collection of English literary criticism eventually amounted to some 600, many of which would be very difficult to acquire today. Literary periodicals were also an interest, and the 1890s were again well represented by a number of somewhat short-lived, but important, belletristic publications, such as *Dome, Butterfly, Savoy*, and *Yellow Book*. Foot also had all issues of *The Germ*, Rossetti's scarce pre-Raphaelite manifesto.

Titles in French, American and world literature were chiefly valuable in allowing the three smaller libraries to increase basic holdings in these subjects. There were, of course, individual volumes of interest, such as early editions of Melville, Bierce, Stowe, Irving and Lowell. A notable author collection was that of Montaigne; the first edition of John Florio's rare and valuable translation of the *Essays* was the most impressive item in this group of some 130 volumes, largely composed of French and English reprints of the *Essays*.

Religion

Foot's Methodism was an integral part of his life, and it is not surprising to find that this Protestantism led him to collect widely in a host of areas related to the Reformation and the development of Protestantism on the Continent as well as in England. His chief interest was the development of English independency in the sixteenth and, particularly, the seventeenth century, as his holdings demonstrated; but his range of acquisition extended back in time from those periods as well as forward in time to the twentieth century, as his 4,000 volumes in post-1800 religious imprints made clear. Bible commentaries, biographies of English divines, the apostles (especially Paul and the Pauline Gospel),

---

263. Holbrook Jackson, *The Eighteen Nineties* (Grant Richards, 1913).

the Oxford Movement, and practical and theoretical expositions of nineteenth- and twentieth-century theological questions were numerous. For example, the category of expositions contained over 1,000 volumes. There were as well many reference volumes, and linguistic and grammatical studies of the Greek Testament. The whole collection will provide both primary and secondary source material for research yet undone. As one illustration, there was a whole series of throwaway pamphlets on the open-air evangelical movement in mid-nineteenth-century England, ephemeral works importantly related to British religious thought.

There were fewer titles in the Luther collection than had been anticipated. Nevertheless, the fifty volumes in this collection contained eleven sixteenth-century Continental editions of Luther's writings, eight imprinted at Wittenberg, and two sixteenth-century and three seventeenth-century English editions. In contrast, the Melancthon collection was larger than expected, containing thirty sixteenth-century titles, some of which are exceedingly rare. Foot also owned two autograph letters by Melancthon, certainly uncommon items.

The works by and about Calvin formed a small but noteworthy collection; it contained eleven English editions of various titles printed before 1640. The Tyndale collection was likewise small quantitatively, numbering only forty-one volumes, of which most were nineteenth- and twentieth-century critical works and biographies. But there were also octavo and quarto copies of the 1536 New Testament (which appear as the first two English Bibles in the listing of Foot's Bible collection) and sixteenth-century editions of *The Obedyence of a Christian Man, Wicked Mammon* and *A Briefe Declaration.* There was also a Francis Fry facsimile of Tyndale's New Testament, one of three illuminated copies on vellum.

Foot's Erasmus holdings were among his most interesting acquisitions, and must have been gathered over a period of many years. Among these, 164 volumes were modern editions and commentaries, augmented by contemporary editions of Erasmus's writings. There were about 100 contemporary Erasmus Continental imprints of the sixteenth century, not to mention sixteenth- and seventeenth-century English editions. Editions of the New Testament, paraphrases, adagia, and epistolae were numerous.

Whereas the library shows that Foot's sympathies lay with the independents of seventeenth-century England in the religious and political controversies of that period, his collection of Richard Baxter's Presbyterian expositions and disputations reveal his breadth of scholarly interest in the subject of dissent. As with works about or by Erasmus, Foot appears to have gathered these volumes over a long period, eventually acquiring more than fifty contemporary titles in many varied editions. There were also, consistently, some modem commentaries and reprints.

The Quaker collection, with its more than 200 volumes, was larger than any of the other author or subject collections in seventeenth- and eighteenth-century independency. The checklist of this collection shows over 170 titles printed between 1600 and 1800, accompanied by a smaller number of more recent historical and bibliographical studies. On this checklist, Barclay, Fox, Penn, and Penington are all represented. Some titles are rare; most are of interest, all have academic value. Noteworthy as a combination of these qualities are the seventeenth- and eighteenth-century editions of the works of Muggleton and Reeve, comprising thirteen titles in a number of editions. In collecting such antagonists as the Muggletonians, Quakers and the Quaker foe Baxter, Foot clearly demonstrated comprehensiveness in his learning; still other religious viewpoints, such as the Familist, the Baptist, the Anglican, appear in the Wing list of Foot's holdings.

The largest author and subject collection in religion was the Wesleyan. The titles here were chiefly related to John Wesley, but there were four early titles by Samuel and two early editions of Charles's hymns as well. There was even a small group of letters from or to John and other members of the Wesley circle. The checklist of John Wesley's writings shows some thirty-five eighteenth-century titles, exclusive of the original printings of seventeen parts of his Journal. There was also a wealth of more recent material among the 375 titles in this collection.

Since the history of the Reformation and Protestant dissent is inseparable from the history of the Bible, that Foot should have collected both Bibles and Greek testaments was to be expected. But the intensity and breadth of his collecting were beyond expectations. Few in number, the quality of manuscript Bibles is impressive. Particularly unique and valuable were his Greek New Testament (about 1200 AD, with illuminated portraits of the four evangelists); an elaborately illuminated Latin Bible (about 1300), belonging to James II of Aragon; and an English New Testament (about 1380), a beautifully written Wycliffite manuscript. The polyglot Bibles were also few, but represented well-preserved landmark editions of considerable academic and monetary worth: the Alcala, six volumes, 1515; the Plantin, eight volumes bound in nine, 1569–72; the Vitré, seven volumes bound in eight, 1645; and the Roycroft, six volumes, 1657.

Of other Continental and English Bibles, Foot possessed 240, representing a great many important editions from the inception of printing in the West to the twentieth century. Among the printers of the twenty incunabula Bibles were such great names as Eggestine, Ruppel, Koberger, Scot, Zainer and Bevilacqua. Among the fifty-six Continental Bibles of the sixteenth century appeared those by such famous printers and publishers as Regnault, Froschauer, Gryphius, Oporinus, Simon de Colines, Plantin and Senhanus. Imprints by Stephanus were also frequent in Foot's large collection of Continental imprints exclusive of Bibles. In addition there were twenty-two seventeenth-century editions by such printers as Blaeu, Elzevir, Maire, and Vitré. Elzevir imprints, like those of Stephanus, were numerous.

English editions of the Bible were also a special interest; and of the ones which it was still possible to obtain, Foot collected the great majority, the most notable omission being the lack of a 1535 Coverdale. Among the Foot volumes were both the octavo and one of the three quarto editions of Tyndale's 1536 New Testament. In addition, Foot owned the Great Bible of 1540, the Breeches Bible, several editions of Cranmer's Bible of 1540-1, the Bug Bible of 1549, Froschauer's Coverdale of 1550, both the 'He' and 'She' Bibles of 1611, and a great many others. Representing almost the entire history of Bible printing in England up to the Doves Press Bible of 1903-5, Foot's holdings totalled 125 volumes. The time and learning that went into the creation of this collection were great indeed.

An even more specialised interest was represented by the collection of some 450 Greek Testaments, which range from the Strassburg imprint by Wolfius in 1524. Foot also possessed the 1518 Aldine of the entire Bible in Greek – to nineteenth-century scholarly editions by Alforrd, Scrivener, Tischendorff and others. The Greek Testaments together with the scholarly studies related to them testify to the vitality and meaning Foot found in this area.

Imprints, manuscripts, letters
Exclusive of Bibles, the Foot Library contained only twelve incunabula, not a large number of pre-1500 imprints. Generally, however, these have historical as well as monetary value. Two theological commentaries by Robert Holcot, the noted English Dominican, are interesting examples. The 1488 Homer, printed by Bernardus Nerlius in Florence, is a most important work in fine condition; it is described in detail in the *UCLA Librarian*, xvi, no. 14 (May 176, 1963).

Of later Continental imprints, 1500-1700, Foot possessed so many that it was decided to organise them as a separate collection, listed by title individually, for voting and choice among the five campuses. Most of these titles are sixteenth-century, although Foot also collected a good many Elzevirs and other noteworthy seventeenth-century imprints. As with his Continental Bibles, Foot seems to have chosen these volumes both with an eye to their place in the history of printing and to their importance in themselves as early contributions to knowledge in a variety of subjects. Classics, both Greek and Latin, form the majority of these Continental works; and some authors, such as Cicero, Euripides, Virgil, Herodian, Juvenal, Ovid, Sallust and Terence, to mention a few, are represented by a considerable number of titles. There is scholarly wealth here, both in rare titles and in author collections with a variety of editions and critical commentaries. Non classical authors abound also. The first page of the working list reveals Ambrose (Chevallon, 1529), two editions of Casaubon, the Stephimus Dictionarium (1536), Dolet's *Commentarii Linguae Latinae* (Gryphius, 1536) and others. John Barclay, another random sample, is represented by two of his works from the Elzevir publishing plant, the *Argenis* and the *Eurphormionis Lusinini*, the latter a somewhat scarce volume; Descartes is represented by three titles, all Elzevir imprints, of which two are the valuable 1644 and 1656 expeditions of the *Principia Philosophiae*. Printers of Continental titles in fact form a kind of who's who in printing history: Aldus Manutius, Elzevir, Stephanus, Cartander, Blaeu, Froben, Simon de Colines, Quentell, Plantin and Regnault.

The pocket geographies, actually a special group of Continental imprints, were kept separate and ultimately amounted to sixty volumes. These were largely Elzevirs, but Maire, Hondius and Janson also printed these small testimonials to the seventeenth century's desire to know the world.

Foot's holdings in books printed in English before 1640, known to specialists as the Short Title Catalogue period – exclusive of works placed with other special collections, such as the Erasmus or Montaigne – totalled some 400 volumes. These were chiefly concerned with religious matters, but dealt with historical and classical subjects as well. In religion, such authors as Latimer, Cranmer, Hooker, Ussher and Whately were represented by a number of titles, as were a good many other divines whose contributions to ecclesiastical, and political, thought were important in the development of ideas leading to the English Civil War. Such literary names as Daniel, Drayton and Wither were also in evidence. In addition to other historical works, the working list for this collection shows a number of entries under James I and the East India Company. Both difficult to acquire in quantity and expensive, these volumes were, happily, distributed among all participating libraries.

The next period, that of the Wing bibliography (English, 1640–1700), covers the most crucial years in the history of dissent in England. Since such history was the heart of Foot's scholarly pursuits, it is logical that his holdings here should be large. In addition to the many Wing titles shelved in other collections – such as English history 1640–1660, Civil War tracts and the Richard Baxter group – the working list for this particular collection contains more than 1,900 titles, a large number indeed when the time and expense, not to say the scholarship, required to accumulate such a collection are considered. Many authors are represented by a number of different titles, very often with multiple editions of individual works. The emphasis is primarily religious, although historical, literary and classical titles are also in evidence. Relatively obscure divines are present in abundance: Hendrik Niclas (Henry Nicholas), three titles; Matthew Killiray, ten, of which the British Museum appears to have two; and Thomas Beverly, twenty-four, most of which are exceedingly rare. Such examples could be multiplied at length. Major divines are, of course, represented still more fully: Bossuet, 11 titles; Bishop Burnet, 55; Thomas Fuller, 12; Symon Patgrick, 15; and Edward Stillingfleet, 38.

Other important writers – Sprat, Glanvill, Roger L'Estrange, Dryden, Walton, George Herbert, Thomas Brown, to name a few – also appear. There are unique volumes, too, such as General Fairfax's copy of *Leycester's Common-Wealth*; a presentation copy, with some manuscript corrections, of Izaak Walton's *Lives*; and *A Collection of Ingenious Poems*, once owned by Elizabeth Farnese, Queen of Spain. Other unusual volumes will certainly turn up as participating libraries catalogue their acquisitions of Foot items printed 1641–1700, which promise to contribute much to scholarship in the University of California.

Letters, documents, and historical and literary manuscripts were only a subsidiary interest with Foot; but since the fact that he collected these at all was largely unknown, some unexpected holdings turned up. Among these were a number of letters from William and Dorothy Wordsworth; some Carlyle letters and the materials concerning the Squire controversy, which developed around Carlyle's edition of Cromwell's letters and speeches; some manuscripts by Arthur Symons; a series of letters between Mrs Hughes and Caroline Southey, Robert Southey's second wife; a beautifully bound series of Stevenson manuscripts and letters; and a large number of Richard Cobden's letters. It was known that Foot had some Cromwellian letters and other letters and documents related to the Civil War and Commonwealth, and the size of this group was gratifying.

Conclusion

In review, the Foot Library may be described as possessing three chief qualities: size, aesthetic appeal and academic value. Each of these is in turn related to the nature of the man who put such a library together; and Foot can be viewed as collector, man of aesthetic sensibilities and scholar. A collector may, of course, possess taste and learning but he can also be defined as a man who has a wider streak of the acquisitive than most other men. Certainly one sees this streak in Foot, and the story about his smuggling books into an overcrowded house against family objection is probably not apocryphal. He was certainly surrounded by parcels of recently purchased books when Dean Powell first met him. As a collector who controlled his own purchasing – unlike some noted men who have supplied money and very little else to the building of their libraries – Foot had constantly to be on the alert for sales, to browse personally in an untold number of bookshops in many different places, and to search for desired items with the aid of agents and dealers. Procured by all of these means, Foot's library reveals the bookplates and autographs of a good many other well-known collectors and libraries. He had, for example, a number of books from the Holland House library, and in that way came to possess volumes once the property of the Fox family. He also bought a great many books once owned by Charles Whibley, the fine Tory essayist and critic; Augustine Birrell, essayist and litterateur; John Drinkwater, the poet; and Harold Monro, poet and pioneer in a number of twentieth-century poetic movements. Foot's collection of Drinkwater's works was that once owned by the poet himself; and a good many of the rare titles which made Foot's holdings in early twentieth-century poetry impressive seem to have been collected by Monro as they appeared, some indeed having been printed by Monro's own Poetry Bookshop.

Foot's aesthetic sensibility was most clearly revealed in his Bible collection, his manuscripts, his sixteenth-century Continental imprints and his very numerous private press titles in nineteenth- and, particularly, twentieth-century English literature. His art collection was not of major importance in his library, but showed a substantial interest in that discipline; he appeared to be particularly interested in prints and caricatures, Leach, Cruikshank and Beardsley being among the satirists and illustrators whose work he owned. Thomas Bewick, the great engraver of birds and animals, was represented by several works of interest, among them two collections of proofs from his original woodblocks. All of Foot's works with more than usual aesthetic appeal were, however, related to his various author, period, and subject collections. A man of taste himself, he apparently bought books first for their content, only secondarily for the beauty of design or binding.

Foot's scholarship in religion, English history and English literature accounts for much of the research value of his library. But where he collected more generally as an educated layman, his books nicely supplemented the more basic research material. For instance, biography, that somewhat frowned-upon art, interested Foot greatly; in Victorian history and the large collection on the French Revolution, this biographical penchant was particularly noticeable. The Isaac Foot library possessed, thus, as the end result of a lifetime of scholarly collecting and educated buying, a wealth of resources for both specialist and general reader.

Tributes to Isaac Foot

Isaac Foot photographed by his daughter Jennifer.

Isaac Foot died on 13 December 1960, aged eighty years.

SARAH: In the end my grandfather seemed to die with the same grace that he lived. He quietly faded away. My step-grandmother said she was woken in the night by the silence. She was so used to the sound of his breathing that when it stopped she woke with a start. So on 13 December 1960 he died at his beloved Pencrebar in his own room looking out over the Lynher valley below, which he loved so much.

Lady Astor, 'beloved friend'

I am deeply distressed. He and I had been friends for so long. We had fought in opposite camps but it never really affected our friendship. He was a really remarkable man and he had splendid sons. I have lost a beloved friend and the Westcountry has too. It is a remarkable fact that most politicians are soon forgotten. In Isaac Foot the Westcountry had someone of whom it should always be proud.[264]

Mr Isaac Foot

One day – as I have heard Isaac Foot himself relate – he found himself the sole passenger in an early morning bus. The conductor was humming a tune, as conductors will. 'What's that tune?' said Isaac. 'Isn't it "Dare to Be a Daniel?"' 'Yes sir, it's my favourite hymn.' 'Mine too,' cried Isaac. 'Let's sing it together!' And they sang it lustily from first verse to last, while the bus rolled on. Isaac ever dared to be a Daniel. He would have enjoyed the lions' den and the opportunity of subduing beasts of prey, as he undoubtedly would have done, by the fire of his eloquence. One has seldom known a man from whom one differed so profoundly and so respectfully or who possessed so much evangelistic fervour with so little sanctimoniousness. His epitaph was written long ago: 'Integer vitae scelerisque purus'.[265][266]

Isaac Foot: a Westcountry man

There was no one quite like him. Each of us has distinctive memories. I remember Isaac Foot coming down to breakfast at the National Liberal Club, cheerfully informing some younger friends, not yet fully awake, that he had been reading his Greek Testament since 4.30 a.m. I remember Isaac, presiding over the Liberal Party Assembly at Bournemouth in 1947, lowering the temperature at one of its more restive and noisy moments with the assurance that he was capable of conducting its business 'without any gratuitous assistance from Mr Dingle Foot'. Then there was Isaac invoking a famous parliamentary occasion of long ago when a somewhat raw Labour minister had pleaded 'the law's delays' to the accompaniment of Isaac's quip 'and the insolence of office'. And Isaac on the telephone, advising a younger candidate: 'Tell them it is a lie. Tell them it is a damned lie. Tell them it is no less a lie because it is uttered by a Tory gentleman of title.' Isaac, advancing towards peroration, chuckling merrily over one of his favourite anecdotes almost as if it were new to him: 'There was an ancient countryman who in extreme illness turned his thoughts for the first time to religion. In came the minister and he wanted to make quite sure that his penitence was real. He said: "My friend, do you renounce the devil and all his work?" And the man said: "I should be very pleased to, Sir, but situated as I am I do not think I am in a position to make an enemy of anybody."' Isaac, arriving at St

---

264. *Western Evening Herald*, 14 December 1960.
265. 'Upright in life and free from sin'.
266. Sir Carleton Allen, *Times*, 19 December 1960.

Albans town hall, tired and a little strained after meetings in thirty counties, asking for fifteen minutes' solitude before he orated, but suddenly warming to a reminder of a speech of his in the old Queen's Hall in London on 12 October 1932, a fortnight after he had resigned his office as Minister of Mines in protest against the Ottawa Agreements. That speech is a striking example of his platform style. Isaac Foot believed in oratory as oratory. He disdained the contemporary practice of treating a speech as no more than an occasion for projecting chatty conversation into a public hall. He cannot, however, be termed a rhetorician of the old school, for he was his own school, happily quite unclassifiable. His were almost all great speeches. For the parliaments of 1922 and 1923, 1929 and 1931 Hansard will yield a noble crop.

Isaac Foot was, as they say, all of a piece and the key to his life and works is that he was a very great practising Christian. His religion and his political philosophy mingled and merged to form a whole that, in all circumstances, enriched his life and yielded unto it a new dimension. Methodism, Liberalism, the Authorised Version, Bunyan and Milton, Wesley and Watts and Wordsworth were his loves.

For Isaac Foot the Great Civil War was with us yet. The public issues which made the seventeenth century what it was had their counterpart in the twentieth. Good men had fought on both sides for Parliament and law and liberty, for the divine right of the Stuart kings. In every age and generation, the cause of civic and personal freedom needed such men as John Pym, John Hampden, John Selden and John Eliot – perhaps even harsher Cromwellian medicine. And who can say that Isaac Foot was wrong? In his own time he fought the good fight against the squirearchy of the Westcountry – and against the harbingers of the Servile State.[267]

MICHAEL: Of all the tributes to him the one which my father would have appreciated most was that of Norman Birkett in the *Times*. They were true bosom friends with more in common than any of the others. Each was as proud as the other of their Nonconformist ancestry. Each might enlighten the other with a beautiful exchange of letters at a time of crisis. In his letters to my father, Birkett often made kindly references to the rest of the Foot family, especially the eldest, Dingle, who was following in his father's political footsteps. Part of their common legal experience derived from the time when Norman Birkett had stayed at our house at the time of the trial of Mrs Hearne, who had been accused of multiple poisonings in a classic trial heard nearby. That trial, said Birkett, cut years from my life. 'But think of the number of years it put on the life of Mrs Hearne,' said Dingle, who was acting as his junior at this time. It was, indeed, Birkett's brilliant advocacy which had shaped the result of the trial, as of so many others in the period before capital punishment was abolished.[268]

---

267. Deryck Able, vice-president of the Liberal Party, *Contemporary Review*, February 1961.
268. In 1931 Birkett had stayed at Pencrebar whilst defending Mrs Hearne at Bodmin assizes. She was accused of murdering her husband by arsenic poisoning. She was acquitted.

Norman Birkett in the Times: I should be grateful if you would allow me to add a personal word to the tribute you paid to Isaac Foot. I had known him for more than forty years, not only as a great public figure so widely known and so universally admired, but I am glad to think as my close personal friend. I will not attempt to review his many activities in so many different fields but this at least ought to be said: that in everything he did he set standards of conduct and behaviour that are not the least of the great contributions he made to the enrichment of our public life. It was our association in the House of Commons long ago that first revealed to me his integrity of mind and character. When he spoke in the House he displayed the power of making himself believed that Clarendon thought was the only justifiable design of eloquence. And, if at times, some of his themes were not quite to the liking of the House, and if they were presented in the language of the zealot, he never for a moment lost the respect and indeed the affection of the most critical assembly in the world. It was, in truth, the triumph of character, for there was no mistaking his sincerity, his courage, and his passionate devotion to the great causes he so eloquently expounded.

In some quarters, because of his devotion to Methodism, and because the names of Bunyan and Cromwell and Milton were so often on his lips, he was thought of as a stern-visaged puritan, inclined to intolerance and severity of outlook. Nothing could be further from the truth. He was the kindliest, the friendliest and the most approachable of men and his passionate beliefs were never allowed to obscure his wonderful sense of humour, his gaiety of mind, and his wide human sympathies and understanding. So far from being stern visaged, his friendly disarming smile and his most attractive Westcountry speech have conquered many a heckler during the dust and heat of a contested election.

But perhaps the most important thing about Isaac Foot was that he was a great Christian. He was one of those fortunate men whose religious beliefs sustained him at all times and added an enchantment to life. If he was at home in the House of Commons, he was equally at home in the Cornish Methodist chapel at Callington. He delighted in the hymns of Charles Wesley and Isaac Watts and had much of the Authorised Version of the Bible by heart. When he became the vice-president of the Methodist Conference he visited almost every part of the country and I remember to this day a meeting in Buckinghamshire over which I presided when he spoke on Tyndale's New Testament. I recall the scholarship, the wit and humour, the humanity and the tenderness, the great love of English prose and the beauty of that address as one of the occasions when I heard a truly memorable speech by a great master. In these things in some small degree I was privileged to share, but the greatest privilege of all was to be allowed to share something of his life in his Cornish home at Callington. In your obituary notice you spoke of the remarkable family of which he was the head, but Isaac Foot among his sons and daughters was still the most remarkable of them all. His pride in his family was naturally very great, but the pride of the family for him was even greater. He had made himself a man of great culture and learning. His house was filled to overflowing with books and their virtue had somehow gone into him. He it was who set the pattern of public life and was the guide, counsellor and beloved leader of his notable family. Differences of view and outlook were bound to arise but the wise, understanding, tolerant attitude of the father and the affectionate admiration of the family never allowed the family relationships to be affected. The atmosphere of the home was very dear to the father and was, I am certain, the best possible training ground for public life.

He was the master of the felicitous quotation and the possessor of a remarkably choice vocabulary and whether he was quoting from some book on Cornish humour or whether he was reading a sonnet from his own anthology of poetry, or whether he was talking on the politics and personalities of the day, to be present was to feel the power of Isaac Foot's most gracious and stimulating personality. A very notable figure has gone from our public life, one of the great men, and left us all with a great sense of public loss; but his friends are filled with a great thankfulness for the example of a noble life so nobly lived.

Index

All numbers in *italics* refer to illustrations